Studies in Art, Heritage, Law and the Market

Volume 6

The book series *Studies in Art, Heritage, Law and the Market* provides an international and interdisciplinary forum for volumes that

- investigate legal, economic, and policy developments related to arts, heritage, and intellectual property;
- critically assess how and for whom art and heritage values come about;
- promote novel forms of user engagement, participatory presentations, and digitalization of arts and heritage;
- examine the processes that transform cultural objects and practices into arts and heritage; and
- highlight new approaches in preservation and conservation science.

The series addresses a need for research and practice in the fields of art, culture, conservation, and heritage including a focus on legal and economic aspects. It deals with complex issues such as questions of authenticity and provenance; forgery and falsification; the illicit trade, restitution, and return of cultural objects; the changing roles of museums; the roles of experts and expertise; and the ethics of the art market.

Naomi Oosterman • Donna Yates
Editors

Art Crime in Context

Springer

Editors
Naomi Oosterman
Department of Arts & Culture Studies
Erasmus University Rotterdam
Rotterdam, The Netherlands

Donna Yates
Criminal Law and Criminology
Maastricht University
Maastricht, The Netherlands

ISSN 2524-7425 ISSN 2524-7433 (electronic)
Studies in Art, Heritage, Law and the Market
ISBN 978-3-031-14083-9 ISBN 978-3-031-14084-6 (eBook)
https://doi.org/10.1007/978-3-031-14084-6

This Springer imprint is published by the registered company Springer Nature Switzerland AG
The registered company address is: Gewerbestrasse 11, 6330 Cham, Switzerland

Contents

Introduction 1
Naomi Oosterman and Donna Yates

Assay-ssination 5
Maria MacLennan and Kelly Ross

Design Crime in Context 25
Petra Seitz, Nia Thandapani, and Gregor Wittrick

The Evolution of the Belgian Art and Antiques Unit 45
Richard Van Herzeele

Fossil Trafficking, Fraud, and Fakery 61
Nussaïbah B. Raja and Emma M. Dunne

Illicit Excavations and Trade in Antiquities 81
Ziad al-Saad and Stefan Simon

New Security Challenges at Museums and Historic Sites: The Case of Spain 103
Estrella Sanz Domínguez, Francisco José Rufián Fernández, and Isber Sabrine

Revisiting the Looting of Site Q Through Lidar 121
Kirsty E. Escalante, Tomás Barrientos Q., and Marcello A. Canuto

Securing Borders and Restraining the Illegal Movement of Cultural Property to, from, and within, the Island of Ireland 145
Ted Oakes

Stealing Heritage in Canada 159
Cara Grace Tremain

The Theft of Your Soulmate 177
Summer R. Austin

UNESCO Emergency Response "First-Aid" Heritage Interventions in Syria During Armed Conflict 197
Joanne Dingwall McCafferty

Yellow Journalism 215
Gretchen Allen

Correction to: Illicit Excavations and Trade in Antiquities C1
Ziad al-Saad and Stefan Simon

Introduction

Naomi Oosterman and Donna Yates

This volume exists due to the particularly strong response we received for the call for our first volume in the book series *Studies in Art, Law, Heritage and the Market* entitled *Crime and Art: Sociological and Criminological Perspectives on Crimes in the Art World.*

While a number of the proposals we received fell outside of the edges of our attempt to integrate art crime research into sociological and criminological method and theory, they were, to be blunt, too interesting to turn down. As we discussed these submissions, we began to see them as providing wider context for the field of art crime research, and as expanding the very concept of art crime to spaces that both we, and we believe readers, had not considered. Embracing the expansion, we further invited contribution by scholars who we knew were pushing boundaries in this field. The resulting volume is eclectic to say the least, but it is from this diversity, we challenge any sort of restrictive definition of art crime, and thus art crime research.

In the sitcom *30 Rock*, Alec Baldwin's network executive character appears to solve the age-old debate by stating "We know what art is! It's paintings of horses!". We concur. We also concur with Justice Stewart's much over-used statement in the 1964 United States Supreme Court Case *Jabobellis v. Ohio* regarding pornography and, by extension, art: "[We] know it when we see it". However, we see it everywhere. In this volume, we see 'art' in its usual forms for art crime scholarship: in paintings and antiquities. However, we also see art in fossils and in violins, chairs

N. Oosterman (✉)
Department of Arts and Culture Studies, Erasmus University Rotterdam, Rotterdam, The Netherlands
e-mail: oosterman@eshcc.eur.nl

D. Yates
Department of Criminal Law and Criminology, University of Maastricht, Maastricht, The Netherlands
e-mail: d.yates@maastrichtuniversity.nl

N. Oosterman, D. Yates (eds.), *Art Crime in Context*, Studies in Art, Heritage, Law and the Market 6, https://doi.org/10.1007/978-3-031-14084-6_1

and jewellery, holes in the ground and even in the institutions meant to protect any, or all, of the above. Chapters in this volume, alternatively, zoom in on specific objects, on specific locations, and on specific institutions, considering how each interact with the various conceptions of crime that exist in those contexts. And as we scholars of art crime know, context matters.

One organisational drawback to pushing boundaries is that *new* boundaries are subsequently difficult to create and are potentially meaningless. While both of us co-editors like tidy subdivisions in our books (see our previous volume), none of the subdivisions for this volume that we tried out made much sense. Breaking these chapters up in an arbitrary way never seemed to add much to the meaning of the individual contributions or the resulting groups. Further we worried that such a division would prevent the reader from making their own meaningful connections.

Thus, we have shirked our curatorial duties and opted to present the chapters in alphabetical order by title. Further, we are stopping short of providing a bigger picture in this introduction, mostly because we believe there is not one, or rather we do not believe that the bigger picture is one that we can paint. The diversity of these contributions, once again, shows us that both art, and criminality related to art, is creative and unpredictable. Also, while we are delighted to provide a bit of commentary on each chapter as a preview for the reader, the authors represented in this volume are creative and unpredictable as well. Our summaries are poor substitutes for reading their contributions and we, the editors, have had our own horizons expanded by having the pleasure of editing the following.

In Chap. 2 "Assay-ssination: Reflections on the Cost of Jewellery and Gem Crime" , Maria Maclennan and Kelly Ross draw upon their deep academic and in-practice experience to discuss the role jewellery plays in crime. Through this lens, we see jewellery as not simply a target of theft, but an extension of the body and thus human identity: worn close, symbolic, meaningful. In that sense jewellery then becomes a means to crime, a weapon itself, or a pathway to solving crime.

In Chap. 3 "Design Crime in Context: Mass-Manufactured Design, Design-as-Art, and Chandigarh's Modernist Furniture", Petra Seitz, Nia Thandapani, and Gregor Wittrick use the ongoing appropriation and marketisation of modernist furniture developed for practical use in India to challenge how mass-manufactured items can, or should, fit into existing conceptions of authenticity, authorship, and more broadly art crime. Perhaps crime, in this case, is not a legally defined category, but is rather the denial of local creativity, the movement of objects that were meant for use into foreign art spaces, and the recategorisation of these objects as artworks?

In Chap. 4 "The Evolution of the Belgian Art and Antiques Unit", Richard van Herzeele takes on the seemingly familiar topic of art crime policing by focusing on Belgium's Art and Antiquities Unit. However, that familiarity falls away quickly when it becomes clear that the chapter does not only present the "evolution" of the Unit, but its apparent extinction. Stemming from interviews conducted with parties involved in and near the unit, the author presents a situation where institutional priorities do not appear to match the realities of art crime, and a much-needed specialist unit closes in a context that, by all accounts, is rife with art crime.

In Chap. 5 "Fossil Trafficking, Fraud, and Fakery", Nussaïbah B. Raja and Emma M. Dunne extend the boundary of art crime to include crime related to palaeontological remains: namely, fossils. Often regulated by the same laws that protect archaeological remains (which are, of course, very familiar to art crime specialist readers), fossils have been strangely absent from wider discussion of art crime. Yet within fossil crime we see so many familiar issues: transnational crime, forgery, (post)colonial domination and control, and at times academics who are unable to contextualise their own actions and needs within the broader societal landscape.

In Chap. 6 "Illicit Excavations and Trade in Antiquities: The Unsettled Challenge for Jordan", Ziad Al Saad and Stefan Simon return to another familiar topic for art crime researchers, that of illicit looting and excavations, illustrated with a case-study on Jordan. Relying on primary and secondary data, as well as professional expertise, the authors paint a daunting picture of Jordan's struggle with looting and subsequent trafficking of cultural objects. They subsequently provide recommendations for different stakeholders on how to deal, and counteract, the illicit trade in antiquities.

In Chap. 7 "New Security Challenges at Museums and Historic Sites: The Case of Spain", moving to Spain, Estrella Sanz Domínguez, Francisco José Rufián Fernández, and Isber Sabrine provide clear recommendations for the protection of cultural heritage sites, museums, and ecclesiastical buildings. Building on their extensive practical experience in Spain (and beyond), they unpack the complexity of both existing and novel risks to cultural heritage, providing a contemplation of the effects of the COVID-19 pandemic.

In Chap. 8 "Revisiting the Looting of Site Q Through Lidar", we return to the topic of looting, in this chapter focusing on the physicality of this issue at Maya sites in Guatemala. Kirsty E. Escalante, Tomás Barrientos Q., and Marcello A. Canuto present an effective method for documenting past acts of looting by combining geospatial analyses with site survey and archaeological excavation records. They show that the use of lidar not only provides insight into the methods of focus of looters, it also may provide the key towards matching looted and trafficked Maya objects to sites.

In Chap. 9 "Securing Borders and Restraining the Illegal Movement of Cultural Property to, from, and Within, the Island of Ireland", we are confronted with the ever-so-urgent and ever-current issue of the 'post'-Brexit negotiations concerning the island of Ireland. Not only does Ted Oakes provide a meticulous overview of the history of, predominantly, national and international heritage law and protection, he also clearly shows the effects that Brexit can have on increasing the smuggling activities between the borders of Ireland and Northern Ireland.

In Chap. 10 "Stealing Heritage in Canada", Cara Grace Tremain, comes back to the topic of policing, this time zooming in on Canada. Using interview and observation data, as well as secondary data from specialised art crime databases, Tremain shows us that, just like Van Herzeele's chapter, there is a lack of dedicated specialists in Canada, despite the evident existence of art and heritage crime.

In Chap. 11 "The Theft of Your Soulmate: Motivations for the Theft of Rare Violins", we continue to test the boundaries of what seems 'logical' in art crime research. Summer R. Austin argues that the theft of rare violins is more than just the theft of an object of immense cultural and economic value. It is, in her words, the theft of a soul mate. However, rather than focusing on the desirability of these objects, Austin turns the perspective and focuses on the intimate, and often complex, relationship that musicians have with these instruments as a pull for deviant behaviour.

In Chap. 12 "UNESCO Emergency Response "First-Aid" Heritage Interventions in Syria During Armed Conflict", Joanne Dingwall McCafferty writes a thought-provoking piece on UNESCO's Interventions in Syria during recent conflict. McCafferty argues that damage assessment and the development of recovery strategies should have been present in all areas of Syrian heritage, rather than the excessive and unbalanced focus on the Palmyra region. According to her analysis, it is evident that many of UNESCO's reactive intervention in Syria were not to be labelled as "preventative" or "early", despite UNESCO's own statutes and guidelines.

In Chap. 13 "Yellow Journalism: Neutralisation Techniques, Media Validation, and the Rothko Vandal", the final chapter of this volume, we conclude with a content analysis of the 2012 attack on Mark Rothko's painting *Black on Maroon* (1958) at the Tate Modern in London. Using the theoretical perspectives concerning techniques of neutralisation and embodied and cultural capital, Gretchen Allen meticulously describes the ways in which the media struggled with the vandal's justification of his actions, the movement called "Yellowism", and therefore subsequently legitimised 'artistic' art vandals.

From here, we simply invite the reader to explore these contexts, challenge them, and be challenged by them. With this expanded context we hope the ongoing picture that we are collectively developing of art crime is suitably, and intriguingly, more complex.

Acknowledgements Donna Yates' research towards this volume was funded by the European Research Council (ERC) under the European Union's Horizon 2020 research and innovation programme (grant agreement No. 804851).

Naomi Oosterman is an Assistant Professor of Cultural Heritage at the Department of Arts and Culture Studies of the Erasmus University Rotterdam, and an affiliated researcher of the Heritage under Threat research group of the Centre for Global Heritage and Development. In late 2019, she finished her doctoral dissertation on the criminal dynamics of art crime in the European Union. In her research, she focuses on the criminogenic aspects of the art world, the policing of art and heritage crime, and trafficking of antiquities.

Donna Yates is an Associate Professor in the Department of Criminal Law and Criminology at Maastricht University. Her research is focused on the looting, trafficking, and illicit sale of cultural objects and she has published extensively on this topic. She is a founding member of the Trafficking Culture research consortium (traffickingculture.org) and the principal investigator of the ERC-funded project Trafficking Transformations: Objects as Agents in Criminal Networks.

Assay-ssination

Reflections on the Cost of Jewellery and Gem Crime

Maria MacLennan and Kelly Ross

Abstract Jewellery is a provocative object which has a particular criminal allure due to several inherent qualities. As a commodity, the high value, portable, and concealable nature of jewellery makes it an attractive target for opportunistic thieves, organised crime gangs, and other criminal magpies. The 'value' of jewellery, however, is inherently polysemic, and thus the impact of jewellery-related crime is not limited solely to economic loss. Beyond the more obvious financial reasons that jewellery is increasingly a criminal target, lies a sinister betrayal of the centuries-old human preoccupation with precious metals and gemstones. With many items of jewellery operating as treasured family heirlooms, signifiers of meaningful relationships, or memorials for deep personal loss; the true cost of jewellery and gem-related crime is often painfully human—even the loss of life itself. Drawing upon the authors combined 35 years of research and professional experience across both law enforcement and the jewellery industry respectively; this chapter will discuss the spectrum of criminal activity related to jewellery and gemstones internationally. It will consider jewellery's ability to both provoke crime and simultaneously solve it; exploring the criminal attraction to jewellery and the motivations that lie behind jewellery crime, through to the inherent nature and forensic properties of jewellery and gemstones themselves as useful investigative tools in instances of crime, death, and disaster. The authors will conclude by highlighting the lack of awareness amongst the law enforcement community and the challenges faced by police in tracing, identifying, and recovering jewellery items. They will culminate by promoting the need for more proactive collaboration between law enforcement professionals and jewellery industry personnel, in order to prevent and deter individuals from utilising jewellery and gemstones as enablers of criminal activity.

M. MacLennan
Edinburgh College of Art, School of Design, The University of Edinburgh, Edinburgh, Scotland
e-mail: maria.maclennan@ed.ac.uk

K. Ross (✉)
Former Police Officer of the Royal Canadian Mounted Police (RCMP), Ottawa, ON, Canada

N. Oosterman, D. Yates (eds.), *Art Crime in Context*, Studies in Art, Heritage, Law and the Market 6, https://doi.org/10.1007/978-3-031-14084-6_2

1 Introduction

For hundreds of thousands of millennia, human beings have harboured an extraordinary fascination with precious metals and gemstones. Historically and materially, jewellery is a form of bodily adornment that is traditionally made from both, although it may often incorporate other diverse materials such as plastic, glass, or other found objects. As such, jewellery is very often a symbolic object of polysemic value; financial, personal, religious, cultural, sentimental, and social. Contextualised within the fields of art, design, and archaeology alike; jewellery has enjoyed extensive historical relationships with identity, death, and the human body, with art historians, designers, and archaeologists having explored jewellery's role and characterisation by human-centred experiences. Many jewellery pieces have a unique place in the human psyche, having been presented as a gift or passed down through familial generations as a treasured heirloom and as such, jewellery can often signify a meaningful relationship, event, or life stage between individuals living or deceased.

Although the definitions of jewellery and gemstones are many, for the purpose of this chapter's discussion, 'jewellery' may be categorised as a type of personal effects; a classification which collectively describes the inanimate belongings of an individual located on, or near to their person (Thompson & Puxley, 2007). A common feature of jewellery, 'gems' will similarly refer to all organic, inorganic, and synthetic gemstone materials, primarily intended for personal adornment and/or for personal investment.

Whilst jewellery itself is often shiny and new in appearance, the notion of jewellery *crime* is far from new. Like many longstanding attractions, the human preoccupation with jewellery has often manifested itself in more sinister ways, with jewellery artefacts increasingly implicated in a variety of criminal contexts. Collectively, jewellery and gem crime, or 'JAG', can be broadly categorised in the following three ways, each of which will guide and shape this chapter's discussion:

- *Targeted Objects*. The intrinsic qualities of jewellery and gemstones as luxury products or status symbols—often with additional cultural and/or economic value—mean that they are objects frequently and purposefully targeted by criminals, as a result of both ego and desire. Jewellery and gemstones may be further targeted in order to finance a greater spectrum of criminal activity; ranging from street level thieves who steal jewellery in residential break-and-entry crimes, through to more serious and complex cases of organised crime such as money laundering, drug trafficking, and in cases whereby criminal enterprises conduct transactions using diamonds as currency.
- *Killer Objects*. In addition to being a deliberate criminal target, jewellery and gemstones may be simultaneously implicated as the *subject* of crime itself. The nature of jewellery crime and the industrial context within which it often occurs, means it is often committed with weapons, possessing a tendency towards physical violence and resulting in injury or even loss of life. This includes the ability for jewellery and gemstones themselves to be weaponised by the

perpetrators of attacks, either accidentally (e.g., in the case of a swinging fist, fatally reinforced by a ring or knuckleduster) or deliberately (e.g., in the case of intentional asphyxiation by neck chain). As such, jewellery may even come to adopt the status of *killer* object—the very cause of death itself—and as a result, may physically harbour trace evidence such as DNA-encoded skin cells. As physical evidence, jewellery may act as a tangible representation or proxy for a person, crime, or event; assisting in instances of assault, homicide, long-term unsolved or 'cold' cases, and in the identification of human remains in a variety of contexts.
- *Forensic Objects*. From hallmarks, to serial numbers, to user personalisation; the inherent forensic qualities and physical properties of jewellery and gemstones mean that the very target or subject of crime may simultaneously come to be its solution. Owing to the highly identifiable and traceable nature of many jewellery items, jewellery and gemstones are often capable of playing both protagonist and antagonist in a variety of criminal contexts. The tools and techniques of the jewellery trade can help to forensically dissect and reconstruct the circumstances which surround crime, possibly even the individuals involved.

Throughout its discussion, this chapter will draw heavily upon the joint professional experiences of the authors, who collectively possess more than 35 years of expertise across both law enforcement and the jewellery industry respectively. Empirical evidence will be supplemented by references across academic literature, newspaper articles, internet-based resources, annual reports, and policy documents; situating different JAG crime types within the authors' broader argument that jewellery and gemstones remain undervalued and under-examined by law enforcement due to a lack of awareness and understanding as to their role and potential contribution within the aforementioned areas.

2 Targeted Objects: The Criminal Attraction to Jewellery

The criminal attraction to jewellery is multiplicitous, as are the motivations that lie behind jewellery crime. The vast majority of jewellery is small, portable, widely available, highly enjoyable, easily removable, relatively concealable, and quick to dispose of (Clarke, 1999, p. 26). As a commodity, jewellery is also very much unchangeable, with little loss in value over time, especially where materials such as gold or diamonds are concerned. It is therefore unsurprising that JAG crime is one of the fastest growing areas of criminal activity in the modern world (Jewelers' Security Alliance, 2021a, b).

Many criminals know all too well that valuable jewellery is gathered almost exclusively in the master bedroom of nearly every household; packaged up in a proverbial—perhaps even literal 'gift' box, ripe for the taking (Ross, 2008). Indeed, jewellery itself is amongst one of the most commonly stolen items in residential break-and-entry crimes across higher income countries of the world, with more than

$100,000,000 USD lost from the jewellery industry in the United States alone each year (Federal Bureau of Investigation, 2021). Whilst the data is elusive, the total financial cost of jewellery taken in residential thefts is thought to be significantly higher than the financial loss from the jewellery industry itself. Extrapolation of break-and-entry statistics and average jewellery loss suggests that approximately $2–3 million USD is lost per one million of the population in the United States and Canada (Ross, 2021). This suggests a total annual jewellery loss in the region of $1,000,000,000 USD as the result of residential theft.

In addition to being targeted by criminals as objects of desire, jewellery and gemstones themselves can be utilised *for* crime. In the greater picture, the organised criminal use of jewellery is an increasingly commonplace crime (Federal Bureau of Investigation, 2021). In the United States, border restrictions on currency have seen an increase in illicit money being transported through other commodities, with gold, jewellery, and gemstones offering the perfect vehicle through which to inconspicuously transport wealth. The incorporation of jewellery is well known to occur within drug trafficking rings and criminal organisations, with jewellery's role and function within these settings varying significantly based on both organisational hierarchy and the nature of the criminal activity (Ross, 2010). Recognising how jewellery is utilised within a criminal organisation can help law enforcement to understand not only the criminal activity itself, but the broader value of jewellery to the organisation; as a power or status symbol, as an accumulation or storage of wealth, as an alternate form of currency, and/or as a means of generating criminal profits. Each of these four avenues—status, wealth, alternate currency, and profit (SWAP)—are known methods of jewellery used within the criminal context (Ross, 2010). Whilst often used singularly, SWAP avenues are often used in conjunction with one another to facilitate crime in organisations of greater criminal complexity.

The connection of jewellery to drug trafficking, for example, is an established route through which criminals may trade stolen jewellery for the purchase of drugs (Stevenson & Forsythe, 1998). Approximately 70 percent of thieves are known to use this method, with a further 27 percent adopting the approach as a means to deliberately dispose of stolen goods (Stevenson & Forsythe, 1998). Accumulated jewellery is often further exchanged with higher-ranking dealers for more drugs and/or as payment in lieu of debt (Nelson et al., 2002). As a storage of wealth, jewellery is often accumulated by criminals before being sold back into the legitimate jewellery market at a substantially greater profit. In exchanging drugs for jewellery, the return on jewellery sales (to either the jewellery market or to other drug dealers) is often significantly more profitable than selling drugs for cash alone (Ross, 2010).

In one investigation involving a cocaine trafficker, the criminal had acquired a significant quantity of jewellery through cocaine trade deals, before selling it back into the legitimate jewellery market through jewellery stores and auctions (Ross, 2008). Criminal profits were used to purchase a number of high-end jewellery and watches as a store of wealth, with the criminal obtaining independent valuations on each piece to authenticate and value the wealth stored. In a similar case, police uncovered a large quantity of jewellery as part of a raid on a methamphetamine lab

(Ross, personal knowledge). Traded between drug traffickers and producers in exchange for more drugs; the jewellery was traced back to a particular break-and-entry crime that had occurred one week prior, at a jewellery store approximately 250 km away. A further method of payment at several transaction levels within the criminal enterprise, is through jewellery accumulated by mid-level drug dealers through previous drug exchanges (Financial Action Task Force, 2013). In a further drug production investigation, several pieces seized from the criminal enterprise were traced back to robberies of both business and residential premises. The criminal enterprise both stored the jewellery as a repository of wealth and subsequently sold it to generate profits, some of which were used to purchase further high-end jewellery for the personal adornment of those who headed the criminal organisation.

Higher-ranking criminals often incorporate high-value jewellery and watches into their criminal organisations by wearing and/or gifting it to close associates (Ross, 2010). Criminals may also own or exchange bespoke jewellery that denotes the organisation they are affiliated to. These displays are a function of jewellery as a status symbol within the criminal hierarchy, and in the cognition of other criminals (Venkatesh, 2001). In a further case of the same pattern, a mid-level drug dealer and member of a large criminal enterprise, sold and traded drugs to street-level dealers within the same organisation. The lower-level dealers sold and traded drugs for jewellery with thieves that were stealing jewellery from homes. The street level drug dealers in turn traded the jewellery up the proverbial chain, to a mid-level dealer, acquiring further drugs for sale and/or debt repayment. The jewellery was then sold as scrap to a local jeweller who paid with a cheque, effectively laundering the proceeds of crime. The jeweller also gave the criminal in-store 'credit', which was used to buy further high-end watches and jewellery for personal adornment (Financial Action Task Force, 2013, p. 87).

These cases highlight various utilisations of jewellery for status, wealth accumulation, alternate currency, and profit. What remains elusive to both law enforcement and academics, is the ability to evidence the connectivity of jewellery to criminal organisations as proceeds of crime. In cases where jewellery cannot be tied to the criminal organisation, law enforcement may have no choice but to return it to the criminal as the asset's 'rightful' owner, if they even succeed in seizing it in the first place. In the drug production investigation discussed previously, the suspect was arrested at the location where the drugs were being produced. On arrest and subsequent personal search, the suspect was found to be carrying approximately $4,000 USD in cash and $60,000 USD worth of jewellery—both proceeds of crime—upon their person. Recognising the obvious nexus of cash to the drug production enterprise, the attending officers seized the cash, but did not recognise the value of the jewellery or how the jewellery was connected. As such, the jewellery was given back to the suspect when they were released from custody.

3 Killer Objects: The Human Cost of Jewellery and Gem Crime

Sadly, criminal activity surrounding jewellery and gemstones is not restricted to theft or SWAP-crime alone. As both a targeted object and a fixture of criminal organisations, the very nature of jewellery and gemstones means that related crimes are often committed with weapons and can thus possess a tendency towards violence, resulting in serious physical injury or even death (Federal Bureau of Investigation, 2021). Due to the industrial context within which JAG crime often occurs, it is often jewellery industry personnel themselves who fall victim, as a result of retail store heists or robberies. Within the last decade, the Jewelers' Security Alliance (JSA) have recorded more than 124 homicides amongst the retail jewellery community across the United States alone (Jewelers' Security Alliance, 2019). Members of the public, too, are increasingly at risk of violence, injury, or death as a result of being targeted for their jewellery, whether through residential break-and-entry crimes or by being directly accosted in the street (Maclennan, 2018).

In addition to being the target of crime, jewellery and gemstones themselves may be implicated as weapons, and in turn, as an accidental or deliberate cause of death (Spears, 2017; Wainwright, 2001). In 1970, Deputy Prime Minister of Quebec, Pierre Laporte, was kidnapped and assassinated by French Canadian Nationalist terrorist group *Front de Libération du Québec* (Spears, 2017). A coroner's report concluded that Laporte was strangled using his own gold neck chain—a symbol of his Roman Catholic beliefs. Religious undertones were echoed in the homicide of Sister Helen Lynn Chaska, an orthodox Catholic nun who was sexually molested and strangled using her own rosary beads (AP News, 2003). An autopsy report detailed Sister Chaska's attacker(s) as having most probably used the beads to control Sister Chaska as he raped her before leaving her to die from ligature strangulation—a cruel application of the jewellery that otherwise stood to symbolise her purity and commitment to her faith. A further case in 2006 saw the rape and murder of local grandmother, Catherine Grosstephan, strangled by her long gold neck chain as she attempted to fight off an attacker. Following her death, Catherine's perpetrator(s) ripped off her necklace and two wedding and engagement rings worn around her fingers. Police described the incident as the callous murder of "a little old lady for a few trinkets that were of great sentimental value to her" (Edwards, 2006, p. 10).

Where jewellery and gemstones are concerned, however, the subject matter of the crime may in itself become the solution. Within the context of violence or death, it naturally follows that jewellery may harbour physical evidence such as biometrics, DNA, blood, or soft or hard tissue (Fisher, 2005; Lindsay et al., 1987; Rowe, 1997), acting as a conduit for trace evidence that may be further attributed to a victim or perpetrator (Starkie, 2012; Thompson & Puxley, 2007). Thompson and Puxley (2007) emphasise the importance and potential significance of trace evidence obtained from personal effects—particularly in cold case, missing person, or disaster victim identification enquires whereby the collection of primary evidence from an individual or their family is necessary for comparison purposes, but may be neither practical nor possible. Personal effects regularly laden with useful DNA include toothbrushes (Staiti et al., 2004; Tanaka et al., 2000), make-up (Webb et al., 2001), and unlaundered clothing (Budowle et al., 2005; Sasaki et al., 2007).

In the case of missing person Diane Chenery-Wickens; a watch, bracelet, wedding and eternity ring(s) were found at the cottage she shared with her husband (Luck, 2011). Friends insisted Diane wore her jewellery at all times, so when the items mysteriously reappeared without any sign of Diane, foul play was suspected. DNA specialists at the (now-defunct) Forensic Science Service (FSS) Laboratory in Lambeth were able to detect microscopic stains on the rings which had the visual appearance of blood. The FSS later proved that not only was the blood Diane's, but that the rings had been removed from her body whilst she was bleeding:

> At least some of the bloodstains present on the rings had formed as a result of small blood droplets landing on them... Given the appearance and location of the bloodstaining on the rings, it was most likely that they were being worn when they became bloodstained. This was particularly relevant to the investigation as the items were not present when the cottage was searched initially, but after her body was found. At the trial, the prosecution suggested that (Diane's husband, David) had revisited the body at the deposition site to remove the jewellery from Diane to prevent her being identified (Luck, 2011, pp. 14–16).

Consequently, just as the body may leave a trace upon an object, an object too, may leave its impression upon the body. A victim or perpetrator's skin may also tell a corresponding story through a visual or psychical discrepancy (Thompson & Puxley, 2007). Particularly distinctive patterns or shapes, such as neck chain impressions or the mark left behind by a ring, may even stand to substitute a now-absent item, acting as a proxy for both the jewellery and the crime itself. Furthermore, it may even be possible for police and/or jewellery experts to narrow down such markings to a specific individual or manufacturer design (Maclennan, 2020). In 2009, police returned to search the location where the homicide victim Teresa De Simone had been killed more than 30 years prior, in the hope of recovering discarded or concealed items of jewellery missing from her body at the time death (Mitchell, 2009). Raped, strangled, and her jewellery missing—a visible series of multiple abrasions had been observed upon Teresa's neck, appearing to match the description of a gold chain and crucifix which she had been said to be wearing that evening (Mitchell, 2009). Corroborated by the testimony of Teresa's friends and family, police were able to determine the cause of death as that of a long, slow strangulation, suspecting the neck chain may have been used as ligature by her 'Crucifix Killer' (Mitchell, 2009). In 2001, British newspaper *The Guardian* reported on the homicide of pensioner Alfred Wilkins (Wainwright, 2001). A suspected paedophile, Wilkins had taken cover in his home whilst hiding from a gang of paedophile-hunting vigilantes, many of whom police suspected included Wilkins' own neighbours. When police recovered Wilkins' body, it displayed multiple signs of injury thought to have been caused by the perpetrators' jewellery (Wainwright, 2001). Homicide detectives subsequently sought to compare the marks on Wilkins' body with that of the finger rings of some of Wilkins' neighbours.

Within this context of forensic human identification, jewellery holds the status of a 'secondary' identifier (Dorries, 1999): methods which utilise a range of factors that when combined, secondary identifiers can provide a high probability of identity. They can be used to temporarily supplement traditional 'primary' tools (such as DNA, fingerprints, or dental records), and can enjoy levels of success comparable to blood group and radiography (Dorries, 1999). Indeed, jewellery in particular can be an incredibly useful tool in assisting with the pre-emptive identification of the deceased in a variety of other ways, offering law enforcement contextual insight surrounding a range of incidents involving the loss of human life. This includes estimating the approximate date and time of death (Sincock, 2007), the location of death (Thompson & Puxley, 2007), and even nature of death—e.g., whether the result of accident, suicide, or homicide (Thompson & Puxley, 2007). Fisher (2005) notes how jewellery recovered with a body can be useful in identifying deceased persons at a crime scene, whereas Tsokos (2008) notes jewellery's strengths as an identifier at autopsy. In the mass fatality context, jewellery was regularly cited as a contributor to identification in the aftermath of September 11th, the 2004 Indian Ocean Tsunami, and the 7/7 London Underground bombings (Maclennan, 2018). The material strength of many precious metals and gemstones ensures jewellery can often withstand otherwise extreme environments or decompositional processes that the human body cannot (Thompson & Puxley, 2007), surviving through the scorching temperatures of fire, submergence in water, the degradation of burial, notable impact or force, corrosion, or contamination. The condition of jewellery may therefore also be of significance to a criminal investigation.

Although the direct loss of human life as a result of JAG crime may be an extreme outcome, it is not the only human loss incurred. Even in instances of simple theft; in stealing an item of jewellery, it is far more than solely the object that is lost. In that moment, criminals also take with them the lifetime of human memories embodied within an object; a devastating emotional loss unlike many other crimes of a similar nature. It is never just the object that is stolen; it is the sentiment, the heritage, the relationships, and the identities so inherently tied to a piece. The loss otherwise anchored to an item of jewellery cannot be removed simply by replacing the piece. This is especially true of jewellery bound up in death or disaster, whereby jewellery may be one of the last remaining and tangible links to a missing or deceased loved one. Personal objects can offer an intimate link to people living and deceased, and as a result may adopt a higher degree of meaning or symbolism following bereavement or tragedy. In this way, JAG-based investigations often go far beyond tracing objects, exposing criminals, and even identifying the deceased: returning jewellery and gemstones to their rightful owner(s), often a victim's family or next-of-kin, is often the true essence of jewellery and gemstone investigations.

4 Forensic Objects: The Evidential Value of Jewellery

Although the fundamental nature of jewellery implies its close proximity to the body; jewellery and gemstones do not necessarily have to contain trace evidence, or indeed, be co-located with an individual to offer contextual insight as to the persons, places, events, actions, or experiences that surround crime (Thompson & Puxley, 2007). Indeed, the inherent forensic qualities and physical properties of jewellery and gemstones mean that the very target or subject of crime may simultaneously come to be its solution.

Much like the human body, all jewellery has its own anatomical structure which can be dissected, with jewellery appraisers already prone to high volumes of 'detective' work through their ability to examine jewellery and gemstones at high magnification in order to identify microscopic markings. Many jewellery items are unique and may be identified by physical properties or characteristics, such as metal content or design; gemstone type, colour, or quality; personal inscriptions or engravings; hallmarks, trademarks, or serial numbers; representational symbols, such as those featured on medals, badges of office, or military insignia; in addition to religious, cultural, or genealogical indicators (Maclennan, 2018). Fisher (2005) notes that:

> inscriptions may often be found inside engagement, wedding, and other commemorative rings, while signet rings may carry initials, insignia, seals, crests, or other distinctive markings. In a number of countries, graduates of universities wear special rings. Orders, societies, and associations may use rings as marks of membership (p. 153).

The three distinct constructs of jewellery that have evidentiary value—markings, craftspersonship, and component parts—are unique to jewellery, setting it apart from other valued items, such as art. In its own right, each element can provide unique information about the item of jewellery, and in turn, the maker(s), owner(s), and/or wearer(s) of said objects. Markings on jewellery may include hallmarks, serial numbers, inscriptions, and engravings—both deliberate and accidental. These features may denote the type, quality, and/or purity of metal; the location or country of origin; the designer, maker, or manufacturer; and/or the year of production. Craftspersonship can denote the method of construction and potentially the tools or techniques utilised in bringing the item into fruition; the style, skill, or level of training of the craftsperson; the potential rarity of an item, whether mass-produced, a bespoke creation, and/or part of a limited series. Finally, the component parts of an item may include the materials and their rarity, any metal/alloy, plastic, or glass, which in turn may relate to the country of origin and/or method of production; any gemstone(s) present, which in turn may be laser engraved with a serial number or unique personal message; unique inclusions within each gem (microscopic internal markings, unique and specific to each individual gem), and/or any treatments applied, coupled with special optical features. Finally, signs of unique user personalisation—accidental scratches or marks, commissioned engravings, photographs concealed within lockets, self-sized adjustments—can often represent or encapsulate the direct interaction of the owner/wearer with other people and/or their surrounding environment.

The tools, techniques, and methodologies present within the jewellery industry—such as jewellery appraisal/valuation, authentication, servicing, and/or repairs—can help to establish all of the above. As many jewellery styles and models are also produced over a limited period, this can lend insight into not only timescales surrounding production and sale, but when a criminal may have acquired the item. This can assist in subject age assessment and in establishing a timeline when the piece was sold in relation to geographic location—potentially even an item's movement across continents, by reviewing its service history and/or detecting any repairs (Sincock, 2007). Serial numbers may provide clues as to the time or place of purchase, or indeed, the purchaser themselves (Sincock, 2007), whereas hallmarks may provide an indication as to where, when, by whom and for whom a piece was made. Particularly valuable gemstones are often laser engraved as a matter of course, concealing a microscopic series of serial numbers or even personal inscriptions otherwise unbeknownst to thieves. Many of these features can help to determine whether an item may be stolen, fake, or 'switched out' for a lesser quality imitation. In the case of bespoke or handmade items, these may be comparable to the records of the jeweller, appraiser, or insurance provider respectively.

Within the jewellery industry, there thus remains a relatively untapped yet potentially significant resource of knowledge that may assist law enforcement in utilising jewellery and gems themselves in the prevention, deterrence, and conviction of further incidents of that nature; providing law enforcement with much-needed insight to help contextualise criminal activity. Moreover, jewellery industry personnel regularly maintain and upgrade their knowledge and jewellery expertise through industry memberships and credentials and by virtue of conducting regular jewellery evaluations. In the United States, the Gemological Institute of America (GIA) regularly assists law enforcement with investigations using some of the aforementioned techniques. In a case reported in 2012, a suspected criminal was apprehended by the FBI in Florida after attempting to sell a stolen diamond (Burstein, 2012). The diamond was submitted to the GIA for examination, who were able to identify it as one they had previously valued by flagging it in their extensive appraisal database. Using the information associated with the stone, the FBI subsequently traced the diamond back to the suspect, who was convicted and subsequently sentenced for a variety of crimes involving major fraud. In a separate case, the GIA were able to identify the diamond in an engagement ring recovered on the remains of an unidentified body. Through the application of gemmological techniques, the diamond was eventually traced back to the jeweller who originally sold the piece, helping to establish the identity of the ring's original purchaser—the victim themselves (IDEX, 2012).

These analyses of jewellery and evidentiary observations made by jewellery appraisers have the potential to go beyond simple authentications and valuations, and when presented to law enforcement, could be of significant value to an investigation. In spite of this, police awareness and understanding of jewellery and gem crime remains limited (Financial Action Task Force (FTAF), 2013). So, what is stopping law enforcement from further tapping into the expertise of the jewellery industry?

5 The Challenges Faced by Law Enforcement

Like crime trends themselves, jewellery as a fixture of the criminal organisation has experienced an ebb and flow of interest within the law enforcement arena over the years, and until recently, had not found enduring interest (Ross, 2010). Despite being the second most costly item of theft in the United States after automobiles, jewellery is accompanied by one of the lowest police recovery rates of stolen property, second only to cash and coins (Duffin, 2021). This is rather remarkable given that many jewellery items possess such an array of highly identifiable features. In any case, most law enforcement professionals do not know enough about jewellery and gemstones to identify a stolen item, or indeed, to trace an item recovered with unidentified human remains. This lack of understanding and relatively poor knowledge of jewellery is something upon which criminals continue to exploit and rely (Ross, 2010).

Whilst law enforcement is accustomed to utilising the services of external jewellery appraisers and gemmologists to conduct authentications and valuations of jewellery seized in criminal investigations; the plausibility of employing these techniques and expertise in such settings often depends on both the type of investigation and the type of jewellery seized. This can vary from being an expensive and time-consuming process, to something that may be completed reasonably quickly at relatively little cost. Many identifiable features described may only be found on jewellery in instances where the jewellery or gems themselves are of significant financial value, given that it is generally higher-end items that possess hallmarks, serial numbers, laser engravings, or inscriptions. The geographical and/or cultural diversity once afforded by jewellery, too, is beginning to suffer from the homogenous trend led by high street stores, whereas an increased reliance on machines for production has contributed towards an inherent loss in individual hand craftsmanship, resulting in less variation between items. A simultaneous challenge is the concern that jewellery is removable, collectable, exchangeable, and interchangeable between individuals means that it may not necessarily belong to the individual from which it is eventually retrieved. Not only may pieces of jewellery become disassociated from a particular individual; in some instances, it may even come to be associated with a different person and thus identity altogether (Mackinnon & Mundorff, 2007). This may occur wilfully, in the case of legitimate borrowing; deliberately, in the case of criminal planning; or accidentally, in the case of external factors, such as a fight or struggle, or where there may be significant dispersion of debris as the result of impact or disaster.

In spite of this, international efforts to stymie money laundering and curb the sale of conflict diamonds have contributed to an increased awareness of commodity-specific legislation that has enshrined the need for law enforcement to know more

Table 1 Difference in stones covered by anti-money laundering legislation Canada and the United States

Canada	United States
Diamond, sapphire, ruby, emerald, tanzanite and alexandrite (Government of Canada, 2021).	Diamond, corundum (including rubies and sapphires), beryl (including emeralds and aquamarines), chrysoberyl, spinel, topaz, zircon, tourmaline, garnet, crystalline and cryptocrystalline quartz, olivine peridot, tanzanite, jadeite jade, nephrite jade, spodumene, feldspar, turquoise, lapis lazuli and opal (Financial Crimes Enforcement Network, 2005).

about the criminal manipulation of JAG commodities. Even amongst anti-money laundering proponents, however, the Financial Action Task Force (FTAF) only began to recognise the criminal use of JAG in the late 1990s and early 2000s. Globally, anti-money laundering legislation has only been in existence for 10–15 years, and remains absent entirely in many countries (Council of the European Union, 2022). Fewer still, are the countries which reference jewellery-specific legislation within their anti-money laundering regulations. For those that do, many guidelines still differ significantly, even among close trading partners such as the United States and Canada, which sees a significant difference in the gemstones covered under each country's respective anti-money laundering legislation. Table 1 outlines the difference in gemstones covered (controlled) in anti-money laundering legislation in both Canada and the United States (Financial Crimes Enforcement Network, 2005; Government of Canada, 2021).

Recent global developments in anti-money laundering also stand in contrast to the known use of jewellery and gemstones internationally by criminals and cartels, who have used these commodities within their criminal operations since the early 1900s, and particularly within the past 30–40 years. The Organisation for Economic Cooperation and Development (OECD) noted that during the 1980s and 1990s:

> gold was used by Colombian drug cartels to convert illicit cash from drug trafficking into stable legal and exchangeable assets. Gold bullions purchased on the international market with drug money were illegally imported into Colombia, then smelted and falsely declared as produced from local mines before being re-exported legally (Masse & Munevar, 2018, p. 6).

In addition to a vehicle for laundering the proceeds of crime, gold has additionally been used in complex tax recovery schemes to fraudulently generate money for the cartel by falsely reporting exports, recovering additional taxes for the gold exported from the government (Masse & Munevar, 2018). This inconsistency undeniably creates exploitable opportunities for criminals.

Whilst the knowledge and prosecution of predicate offences related to the proceeds of crime and money laundering as they specifically relate to jewellery remains relatively unknown; restrictions on the disclosure of important investigational information as a function of investigational confidentiality has additionally stymied the external analysis of jewellery and gemstones by non-police organisations (Ross, personal knowledge). One solution is to conduct such JAG analysis by the policing organisation itself: however, this presents its own hurdles on several fronts. In jurisdictions without specific jewellery, diamond, or precious metal laws, JAG commodities are investigated as a subsidiary to the crimes they are associated with, and as such, are less likely to be staffed with dedicated resources or subject matter experts:

> There is little specific enforcement of any crimes related to diamonds. Law enforcement looks at these crimes/commodities the same as all others and does not relegate specific resources towards it. In general, law enforcement has little knowledge about crimes and criminal activity involving these commodities/industry (Financial Action Task Force, 2013, p. 58).

The difficulties faced by law enforcement in maintaining a unit of officers highly trained in diamond, gemstones, and precious metal crimes are vast and complex. Both the size of a policing agency and numerous budget restrictions may impact the need for, and availability of, ancillary police services such as a dedicated JAG resource. A small policing agency may not be able to financially resource a dedicated JAG analyst position. Furthermore, the extent of training required for even a small resource is likely to be weighed against anticipated loss of expertise due to unit transfer, promotion, and attrition. A policing agency may additionally struggle with prioritising jewellery analysis as an internal position that is on the fringe of, or does not support, existing mandates. This is particularly important, as mandates alone are subject to fluctuation as a result of both government changes and criminal trends, and on a larger scale, are often influenced by external policies and guidance initiated by global organisations such as the FTAF. Perhaps one of the greatest overarching impasses, is the lack of available and specific data related to JAG crime on a local, regional, and global level, which may otherwise steer policy and mandate shifts.

Whilst pockets of jewellery crime expertise exist in several countries around the world, such expertise has generally been concentrated in locations that themselves are long-established global supply centres of jewellery, gold, or diamonds. In both Israel and Belgium, two of the world's leading suppliers of diamonds and gemstones, dedicated officers within the federal police service are specially trained in diamond and jewellery crimes. In Canada, the Royal Canadian Mounted Police (RCMP) established a dedicated Diamond Protection Unit (Freeze, 2004) after the country became known as a global diamond producer; however even as the world's third largest producer of diamonds (Government of Canada, 2021, 2022), the Unit was later disbanded due to resource restrictions and police mandate changes.

Whilst recognition of jewellery and gems amongst the law enforcement community is a move in the right direction; there remains no recognised international standard in place which assures a consistency and quality in the education, training, procedures, and standards in respect of evaluating jewellery related to crime. Although not every jewellery item seized by police will offer evidentiary value to an investigation; the potential evidentiary value contained in jewellery is often lost—or rather, underexplored—as a result of policy restriction and a lack of understanding on the part of police, pathologists, and prosecutors. This gap in expertise remains problematic at all levels, and represents a significant hurdle in the prevention, recovery, and prosecution of JAG-related crime (Ross, 2007). While law enforcement agencies must learn to further leverage the expertise held by jewellery industry professionals, police forces alone cannot curb jewellery and gem related crime. Understanding the criminal attraction to and use of jewellery, recognizing the challenges faced by law enforcement, and seeking proactive countermeasures through genuine and meaningful collaboration with the jewellery industry, represent some of the first steps to securing a solution.

6 A Collaborative Approach

The recognition of criminal targeting of JAG and the inherent forensic value of JAG items themselves, has led to prior (albeit limited) collaboration between law enforcement professionals and the jewellery industry. In the United States, a number of innovative partnerships have emerged between organisations such as the Federal Bureau of Investigation (FBI), New York Police Department (NYPD), Jewelers' Security Alliance (JSA), and Gemological Institute of America (GIA). As a non-profit organisation, the JSA regularly works closely with the FBI and other law enforcement agencies, collaborating on initiatives such as the Stolen Jewelry and Watches Website (Jewelers' Security Alliance, 2021a, b), which features thousands of case studies and public appeals related to JAG crime. In addition to providing frequent crime alerts and email updates to both jewellers and law enforcement, the JSA also offers regular seminars and events, consulting activities, and the publication of a comprehensive Annual Crime Report (Jewelers' Security Alliance, 2019).

In the aftermath of 9/11, independent jewellery valuers and appraisers throughout New York City together with experts from world-renowned New York jewellery brand, Tiffany & Company, collaborated with officers from the NYPD's Property Clerk Division to design an innovative World Trade Centre Jewellery Recovery Website (Dewan, 2004). Initiated in partnership with Dan McCaffrey, a former Director of Operations at Tiffany and Co. and retired FBI Special Agent in jewellery-related criminal cases, the website unveiled an online database as part of an extraordinary effort by agencies in New York City to ensure that any identifiable remnant of jewellery recovered from the disaster site was returned to its rightful next of kin (Dewan, 2004).

In 2012, a further collaboration led by Dan McCaffrey saw law enforcement officers from across several states of the United States attend GIA headquarters in California for a two-week programme of highly specialised training in the subjects of jewellery and gemmology (Bates, 2012). The result of unique collaboration between the GIA and FBI Major Theft programme, the course sought to enhance jewellery knowledge amongst the law enforcement community, from FBI Special Agents to Task Force Officers, providing practical training in jewellery and gemmology in an effort to more effectively solve JAG related crimes. By better understanding how the field of jewellery relates to their own investigations, the course encouraged officers to apply their new-found skills back into their own case work in order to identify stolen gems and jewellery and link them to a particular crime (Bates, 2012).

In Canada, a similar partnership has existed since 1996 between the Royal Canadian Mounted Police (RCMP) and Jewellers Vigilance Canada (JVC). The JVC regularly provides law enforcement with sponsorship, training, and investigational assistance in tracing and locating stolen or recovered jewellery. The sponsorship segment of the JVC programme includes both financial sponsorship of in-house police conferences and training, through to the provision of experts to attend and deliver presentations for robbery, property crime, and money laundering law enforcement events. The investigative arm of the JVC provides law enforcement with a 1000+ strong membership of jewellery expertise, including a dedicated 'Stolen Merchandise' section of the JVC website (Jewellers Vigilance Canada, 2022). This unique crime prevention programme provides the jewellery industry with vital and often time-sensitive information pertaining to stolen jewellery so that jewellers can be on the lookout for recently stolen items that criminals may attempt to sell. In late 2021, these efforts were expanded to include a new stolen diamond database to help assist police in tracking diamonds.

Since 2001, the JVC has also delivered hands-on JAG crime training to hundreds of officers annually across Canada and occasionally other nations. The programme offers a complete immersion in the end-to-end jewellery 'mine to market' supply chain, with an introduction to the opportunities exploited by criminals at every step. It includes gemmological and field identification techniques; jewellery tracing techniques; an introduction to the criminal utilisation of diamonds, gemstones, and precious metals; and investigation analyses from street level activities through to international money laundering investigations. In 2020, the JVC converted their diamond and gold valuation and jewellery tracking courses to online learning in response to the COVID-19 pandemic, so that learning can be undertaken by police at any time, from anywhere. In 2021, JVC expanded their outreach activities to include police and law enforcement preparatory colleges, delivering presentations on JAG crimes to officers in training. The ultimate goal is ensuring that when the students become police officers, they already have foundational knowledge of the jewellery-crime nexus.

Across the world, other law enforcement organisations are working to further collaborate within and across the jewellery industry. The Canadian Diamond Code of Conduct is working to create a diamond trademark database that would allow police to determine the manufacturer of a diamond, helping to facilitate the tracing of diamonds. In the United Kingdom, longstanding initiatives such as 'Safer Gems' (The National Association of Jewellers, 2021) also focus on facilitating collaboration between the jewellery and law enforcement industries to identify and trace international jewellery thieves and recover stolen jewellery often in the millions. Whilst initiatives like these are excellent and innovative demonstrations of knowledge exchange and collaboration between the law enforcement and jewellery industries; the majority of current and long standing approaches to JAG crime have arisen from outside of the jewellery industry itself, and have thus been largely rooted in crime prevention and deterrence, rather than identification or repatriation of items.

In most cases when law enforcement engages the services of a jewellery appraiser or gemmologist, it is to establish the authenticity or value of an item seized for the purpose of asset valuation. Occasionally, the seizure of a high value diamond or watch may result in law enforcement seeking a jeweller to glean a serial number to help trace the item and/or determine if it was stolen, but rarely has the police-jeweller investigative relationship expanded beyond these parameters. This has resulted in approaches which are not only narrow in their interpretation and scope in terms of the knowledge available to trace and identify jewellery and gemstones, but also an oversight as to the importance of the sentimental and interpersonal human relationships that often lie behind an object—especially if not immediately or outwardly perceived as 'valuable'.

In addition to achieving a greater literacy of understanding in the physical and technical properties of jewellery and gemstones and their inherent forensic value, law enforcement must therefore develop an ability to see beyond jewellery's outward sparkle; learning to 'read' and fundamentally respect the uniquely personal, sentimental, and anecdotal idiosyncrasies embodied within a piece, which may offer additional insight into whom the artefact belonged or related. To achieve a greater understanding of the criminal use of jewellery and the depth of criminal involvement within the industry, law enforcement must continue to tap into the incident and expertise of not only the jewellery industry itself, but endeavour to better understand the public's unique relationship with jewellery and gemstones. Yet, the jewellery industry too, must learn about law enforcement; of criminal behaviours and signatures, evidence preservation, and when and how to raise the alarm. Neither the police nor the jewellery trade acting independently can eliminate the criminal use of jewellery and gemstones.

Through embracing a collaborative approach to tackling JAG crime, shared priorities for both industries must include a mutual commitment to enhancing awareness surrounding the role and value of jewellery and gemstones in the criminal domain. Investigational outputs are material, and can include criminal charges, supporting evidence to co-existing criminal events, and an understanding of the criminal organisation and hierarchy. Whilst current partnerships serve to raise awareness, there is potential for greater engagement between the police and jewellery trade and the public. Opportunity exists for public engagement activities, educational outreach programmes, increased engagement with jewellery and law enforcement agencies internationally, and new stakeholder partnership such as with the insurance industry, to further illuminate and elevate the importance of jewellery itself, within jewellery specific criminal events. Open and transparent communication and collaboration across international borders and interdisciplinary boundaries is vital in order to share good practice and assist in the development of recognised and agreeable procedures, policy, standards, and legislation. Foundationally, there is also a need to undertake further research and to establish facts and findings, and to develop a much-needed evidence base of techniques for JAG crime investigations. Successive to this, through hands-on practical training and experience studying and handling jewellery and gemstones, law enforcement personnel may come to build first-hand experience in the subject matter of these crimes, translating knowledge and theory into relevant insight and appropriate practical expertise.

References

AP News. (2003, April 10). *Man who raped, strangled nun gets life.* Retrieved October 21, 2021, from https://apnews.com/article/c4d01aab3fc261480cbcf6b8a769dfad

Bates, R. (2012, May 19). School of rocks: The feds go to the GIA. *JCK Magazine.* Retrieved October 30, 2021, from https://www.jckonline.com/magazine-article/school-of-rocks-the-feds-go-to-the-gia/

Budowle, B., Bieber, F. R., & Eisenberg, A. J. (2005). Forensic aspects of mass disasters: strategic considerations for DNA-based human identification. *Journal of Legal Medicine, 7*(4), 230–243.

Burstein, J. (2012, January 30). Jewel thieves in South Florida's underworld behind the $15 million heist in Palm Beach County last year. *Colodny Fass.* Retrieved March 26, 2022, from https://www.colodnyfass.com/blog/jewel-thieves-in-south-floridas-underworld-behind-the-15-million-heist-in-palm-beach-county-last-year/

Clarke, R. V. (1999). Hot products: Understanding, anticipating and reducing demand for stolen goods. *Home Office Policing and Reducing Crime Unit, Police Research Series Paper 112.* https://popcenter.asu.edu/sites/default/files/hot_products_understanding_anticipating_and_reducing_demand_for_stolen_goods_clarke_1999.pdf

Council of the European Union. (2022). *Taxation: EU list of non-cooperative jurisdictions.* Retrieved February 12, 2022, from https://www.consilium.europa.eu/en/policies/eu-list-of-non-cooperative-jurisdictions/

Dewan, S. K. (2004, December 3). From 9/11 rubble, unclaimed mementos. *The New York Times.* Retrieved October 31, 2021, from https://www.nytimes.com/2004/12/03/nyregion/from-911-rubble-unclaimed-mementos.html

Dorries, C. (1999). *Coroner's courts: A guide to law and practice.* John Wiley & Sons.

Duffin, E. (2021, October 8). Recovery rate of stolen property in the U.S. 2020, by type. *Statista.* Retrieved October 29, 2021, from https://www.statista.com/statistics/252444/recovery-rate-of-stolen-property-in-the-us-by-type/

Edwards, J. (2006, May 23). Exclusive: Was gran strangled with her own necklace? *The Mirror.* http://www.mirror.co.uk/news/top-stories/2006/05/23/exclusive-was-gran-strangled-with-own-necklace-115875-17116052/

Federal Bureau of Investigation (FBI). (2021). *What we investigate: jewelry & gem theft.* Retrieved October 25, 2021, from https://www.fbi.gov/investigate/violent-crime/jewelry-gem-theft

Financial Action Task Force (FTAF). (2013). *Money laundering and terrorist financing through trade in diamonds.* https://www.fatf-gafi.org/media/fatf/documents/reports/ML-TF-through-trade-in-diamonds.pdf

Financial Crimes Enforcement Network. (2005, June 3). Anti-money laundering programs for dealers in precious metals, stones, or jewels. *Department of the Treasury Briefing.* Retrieved October 5, 2021, from https://www.fincen.gov/sites/default/files/shared/antimoneylaundering060305.pdf

Fisher, B. A. J. (2005). *Techniques of Crime Scene Investigation* (7th ed.). CRC Press.

Freeze, C. (2004, August 21) Organized crime eyeing Canada's diamond trade. *The Globe and Mail.* Retrieved, February 16, 2022, from https://www.theglobeandmail.com/news/national/organized-crime-eyeing-canadas-diamond-trade/article1002590/

Government of Canada. (2021). *Dealers in precious metals and precious stones.* https://www.fintrac-canafe.gc.ca/re-ed/dpms-eng

Government of Canada. (2022). *Diamond facts.* Retrieved October 31, 2021, from https://www.nrcan.gc.ca/our-natural-resources/minerals-mining/minerals-metals-facts/diamond-facts/20513

IDEX Online News (2012, April 12). GIA helps fight crime, holds course for special agents. *IDEX Online News*. Retrieved October 28, 2021, from http://www.idexonline.com/FullArticle?id=36658

Jewelers' Security Alliance (JSA). (2019). *Annual Crime Report 2019*. Retrieved October 25, 2021, from https://jewelerssecurity.org/wp-content/uploads/2020/12/2019-JSA-Annual-Crime-Report.pdf

Jewelers' Security Alliance (JSA). (2021a). *Jewelers' Security Alliance: Leading the war on jewelry crime since 1883*. Retrieved October 30, 2021, from https://jewelerssecurity.org

Jewelers' Security Alliance (JSA). (2021b). *Stolen jewelry and watches web site*. Retrieved October 30, 2021, from http://www.stolenjewelry.org/report/index_report.html

Jewellers Vigilance Canada. (2022). *Stolen merchandice web site*. Retrieved September 1, 2022, from https://jewellerycrimecanada.ca/stolen-merchandice.php

Lindsay, R. C. L., Wallbridge, H., & Drennan, D. (1987). Do the clothes make the man?: An exploration of the effects of lineup attire on eyewitness identification accuracy. *Canadian Journal of Behavioural Science, 19*(4), 463–478.

Luck, A. (2011, April 20). Britain's forensic scientists are the best in the world: so why is their elite force being disbanded? *The Daily Mail*. Retrieved January, 2022, from http://www.dailymail.co.uk/home/moslive/article-1377202/Britains-forensic-scientists-best-world-So-elite-force-disbanded.html

Mackinnon, G., & Mundorff, A. Z. (2007). Forensic human identification case studies: The World Trade Center – September 11, 2001. In T. Thompson & S. Black (Eds.), *Forensic human identification: An introduction* (pp. 485–499). CRC Press.

Maclennan, M. (2018). *Forensic jewellery: A design-led approach to establishing identity in forensic human identification* [Unpublished doctoral dissertation]. The University of Dundee.

Maclennan, M. (2020). Forensic jewellery: A marriage of two fields. *Journal of Jewellery Research, 3*, 41–58.

Masse, F., & Munevar, J. (2018). Due diligence in Colombia's gold supply chain: where does Colombian gold go? *The Organisation for Economic Cooperation and Development (OECD)*. Retrieved October 15, 2021, from https://www.oecd.org/corporate/Where-does-Colombian-Gold-Go-EN.pdf

Mitchell, B. (2009, September 23). Police search for 1979 murder jewellery. *The Independent*. Retrieved January 3, 2022, from http://www.independent.co.uk/news/uk/crime/police-search-for-1979-murder-jewellery-1791848.html

Nelson D., Collins L., & Gant, F. (2002). The stolen property market in the Australian capital territory. *Australian Institute of Criminology*. Retrieved February 16, 2022, from https://www.aic.gov.au/sites/default/files/2020-05/the-stolen-property-market-in-the-australian-capital-territory.pdf

Ross, K. (2007). Diamond and jewelry industry crime. *Federal Bureau of Investigation Law Enforcement Bulletin, 76*(2), 17–21.

Ross, K. (2008). *The Fifth C: The criminal use of diamonds*. Author House Books Inc.

Ross, K. (2010). *Undangling the karat*. [Unpublished master thesis]. Charles Sturt University.

Ross, K. (2021). Strengthening your DPMS toolkit. In *Proceedings of the Association of Certified Anti-Money Laundering Specialists Annual Conference*, September-November 2021, 20(4). ACAMS.

Rowe, W. F. (1997). Biodegradation of hairs and fibers in forensic taphonomy: The postmortem fate of human remains. In W. D. Haglund & M. H. Sorg (Eds.), *Forensic taphonomy. The post-mortem faith of human anatomy* (pp. 337–352). CRC Press.

Sasaki, M., Shiono, H., Fukushima, T., & Shimizu, K. (2007). Human identification by genotyping of personal articles. *Forensic Science International, 90*, 65–75.

Sincock, P. (2007). Forensic human identification case studies: The Rolex murder, Southwest England. In T. Thompson & S. Black (Eds.), *Forensic human identification: An introduction* (pp. 459–472). CRC Press.

Spears, T. (2017, August 12). Fifteen Canadian stories: the killing of Pierre Laporte by the FLQ. Retrieved October 5, 2021, from *The Ottawa Citizen.* https://ottawacitizen.com/news/national/fifteen-canadian-stories-the-killing-of-pierre-laporte-by-the-flq
Staiti, N., Spitaleri, S., Vecchio, C., & Saravo, L. (2004). Identification of a carbonized body by DNA profiling. *International Congress Series, 1261*, 494–496.
Starkie, A. (2012). *Body modifications as a tool to aid human identification* [Unpublished doctoral dissertation]. Teesside University.
Stevenson, R. & Forsythe, L. (1998). *The stolen goods market in New South Wales. New South Wales Bureau of Crime Statistics and Research.* New South Wales Attorney General's Office.
Tanaka, M., Yoshimoto, T., Nozawa, H., Ohtaki, H., Kato, Y., Sato, K., Yamamoto, T., Tamaki, K., & Katsumata, Y. (2000). Usefulness of a toothbrush as a source of evidential DNA for typing. *Journal of Forensic Sciences, 45*(3), 674–676.
The National Association of Jewellers (NAJ). (2021). *SaferGems.* https://www.naj.co.uk/safergems
Thompson, T., & Puxley, A. (2007). Identification from personal effects. In T. Thompson & S. Black (Eds.), *Forensic human identification: An introduction* (pp. 365–378). CRC Press.
Tsokos, M. (2008). *Forensic Pathology Reviews: Volume 5.* Humana Press.
Venkatesh, S. A. (2001). *Community justice and the gang: A life-course perspective.* Columbia University.
Wainwright, M. (2001, February 12). Jewellery marks 'clue' to pensioner's killer. *The Guardian.* Retrieved October 31, 2021, from https://www.theguardian.com/society/2001/feb/12/childprotection.martinwainwright.
Webb, L. G., Egan, S. E., & Turbett, G. R. (2001). Recovery of DNA for forensic analysis from lip cosmetic. *Journal of Forensic Sciences, 46*(6), 1474–1479.

Maria MacLennan is a Lecturer in Jewellery and Silversmithing at The University of Edinburgh in Scotland. A trained jewellery designer, for more than a decade Maria's award-winning research in Forensic Jewellery has helped pioneer new understanding of jewellery's role as an identification tool in instances of death, crime, and disaster. She occupies a hybrid role with the Police Service of Scotland, the United Kingdom's second-largest police force, and regularly provides advice and support to international law enforcement agencies on jewellery recovered with unidentified human remains.

Kelly Ross is a former police officer of the Royal Canadian Mounted Police (RCMP). He is a subject matter expert in jewellery and gem crime and a court-recognised expert witness in jewellery-related criminal activity. A trained gemmologist and rough diamond grader, Kelly's Masters degree and subsequent research has focused on the criminal use of diamonds, gemstones, and precious metals within drug trafficking organisations.

Design Crime in Context

Mass-Manufactured Design, Design-as-Art, and Chandigarh's Modernist Furniture

Petra Seitz, Nia Thandapani, and Gregor Wittrick

Abstract This chapter explores art crime in the context of design. Arguing that design is a discrete category, distinct from either fine art or antiquities, this chapter suggests that placement of mass-manufactured design objects within markets set up for art or archaeological material poses unique practical, conceptual, and moral questions and complications. This chapter explores and demonstrates these problematics through the specific context of the modernist furniture of Chandigarh, India.

1 Introduction

Over the past two decades, functional design objects have appeared with increased volume and frequency on the international art market, both in dealerships and as part of flagship sales at major auction houses (Lindemann, 2010). This chapter suggests that the placement of mass-manufactured design objects within commercial markets built for fine art and antiquities has created specific and unique logistical, conceptual, and moral problems which may create an environment rife for crime and related amoral activities. While this chapter problematises the placement of design on art markets, this critical analysis is not undertaken to legitimise or otherwise condone the morality or legality of current practices within these markets vis-a-vis art and antiquities, which are understood to have significant logistical, conceptual, and moral issues in and of their own right.

For the purposes of this chapter design objects are defined as objects with a functional purpose, whose conception has considered both aesthetic and functional

P. Seitz (✉)
Bartlett School of Architecture, UCL, London, UK
e-mail: petra.seitz.20@ucl.ac.uk

N. Thandapani
Design Historian, London, UK

G. Wittrick
British Museum, London, UK
e-mail: gregor.wittrick@network.rca.ac.uk

N. Oosterman, D. Yates (eds.), *Art Crime in Context*, Studies in Art, Heritage, Law and the Market 6, https://doi.org/10.1007/978-3-031-14084-6_3

value (Kaufmann Jr., 1969).[1] Design objects are contrasted with objects of fine art such as paintings, sculptures, and art photographs which contain predominantly aesthetic value and are not generally used for particular tasks outside of aesthetic appreciation (Walker, 1989; Lindemann, 2010, pp. 8, 18, 44). This chapter relates specifically to objects of mass-manufactured design—designed objects made on a large and standardised scale, frequently, but not always produced after the industrial revolution.

Design objects, and particularly objects of modern mass-manufactured design, have largely remained outside the scope of literature investigating operations of arts markets and related ethical and legal problems. Their particular physicality, production, quantity, and issues related to their functional use mean that much of the extant literature and laws dealing with fine arts and antiquities, while relevant, fall short of holistically addressing these objects. Literature exploring the actions of auction houses, such as Christos Tsirogiannis' (2016) *Something is Confidential in the State of Christie's* frequently limit their scope to antiquities, while literature investigating provenance such as Olivia Sladen's (2010) *Faking History: How Provenance Forgery is Conning the Art World* frequently limit inquiry to fine art, particularly paintings, and antiquities. While popular books such as *The Medici Conspiracy* (2006) and *Chasing Aphrodite* (2011) have explored controversies related to art and antiquities, particularly the case of the Getty Museum and its relationship to illicit materials, there are no such parallels for design objects.

Despite their frequently high financial value, mass-manufactured design objects are generally not covered by export stoppages related to cultural patrimony because of their more recent production dates (Amineddoleh, 2020, p. 29). As mass-manufactured objects gain a larger foothold within art markets and begin to be traded on a larger scale, the issues raised by their inclusion will become more pressing for the literature and related legal and ethical frameworks and bodies to address (Lindemann, 2010, pp. 29–31).

This chapter seeks to begin to fill this gap, introducing and defining the features of design objects and elaborating on the ways in which these features complicate operations on the art market, and in some cases, appear to incentivise or provide cover for illegal and amoral behaviours. Issues arising from the sale of design objects within the art market are illustrated by the case study of mid-century modernist furniture from the city of Chandigarh, India. The trajectory and treatment of these pieces of mass-produced furniture demonstrate the logistical, conceptual, and moral problems caused by the insertion of design objects on the art market. Further, the case study of Chandigarh's modernist furniture highlights the manifold connections between art markets, art crime, colonialism, and extractive capitalism, as well as the necessity of tackling these issues in a united and comprehensive manner.

[1] The field of Design History largely does not operate under a shared definition or understanding design. Issues surrounding the definition of design have been discussed at length by design historians such as Clive Dilnot, John Walker, Adrian Forty, Victor Margolin, and Kjetil Fallan, among others.

This chapter begins with an introduction to the history, context, and physicality of Chandigarh's modernist furniture. It then outlines three primary issues caused by the placement of design objects within commercial markets initially intended for the sale of fine art and antiquities: that the unique physicality of objects of mass-manufactured design poses issues regarding authenticity and authentication; that when subjected to the same market structures as fine art, design poses conceptual challenges to the notion of the 'original', and that conflation of design objects with works of art raises moral questions surrounding the role of particular actors. The chapter concludes by examining how, in the case of Chandigarh's furniture, placement of design on the art market has created a fertile environment for both illegal and immoral neocolonial actions, which continue in plain sight to this day.

2 Chandigarh's Modernist Furniture

Chandigarh's modernist furniture was designed and constructed to furnish the newly built city of Chandigarh, India in 1947. Developed immediately following the partition of India and the annexation of Lahore to Pakistan, Chandigarh was to serve as the Indian Punjab's new capital and administrative centre. It was to be, in then-Prime Minister Jawaharlal Nehru's words, "a new town symbolic of the freedom of India, unfettered by the traditions of the past" and "an expression of the nation's faith in the future" (Nair, 1950, p. 6, cited in Evenson, 1966, p. 6).

Together, American architect and planner Albert Mayer and Polish-American architect Matthew Nowicki formed the first planning and design team for the city of Chandigarh (Evenson, 1966, p. 4). After Nowicki was tragically killed in a plane crash shortly after the project began, Swiss/French architect Le Corbusier was recruited to take over the project (Evenson, 1966, p. 4).

While Corbusier re-designed the plan for the city and the Capitol Complex buildings largely from his office in Paris, his cousin, Pierre Jeanneret, along with British architects Jane Drew and Maxwell Fry, relocated to Chandigarh (Joshi, 1999; Rüegg & Spechtenhauser, 2012). Here, they became part of a larger team of Indian architects and planners including Aditya Prakash, Urmila Eulie Chowdhury and Jeet Malhotra, who executed the broader design of the city, designing everything from cinemas and private homes to day-care centres and hospitals, as well as much of the furniture which would be placed within these buildings (Evenson, 1966, p. 53).

Chandigarh's modernist furniture shares a broadly unified visual aesthetic. Comprising pared-back geometric forms, the pieces are constructed of angular, thick-cut joined native timber, with caning, leather upholstery, and glass added where appropriate for form and function (see Fig. 1).

The furniture remained in situ until roughly 1999 when two French antique dealers undertook their first trips to Chandigarh (Touchaleaume et al., 2010, pp. 10–11). This would be their first of over 30 trips to the city in the following seven years. During this time the dealers purchased an unspecified amount of the city's furniture, removed it to France, had the pieces professionally refurbished,

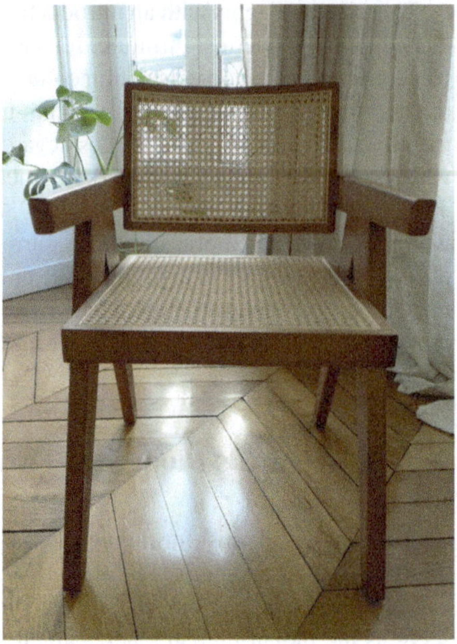

Fig. 1 Reproduction Chandigarh chair, manufacturer unknown, Paris. Image: Petra Seitz, 2022

exhibited them, began writing a book on the furniture, and finally put the pieces up for sale at auction (Artcurial, 2006; Touchaleaume et al., 2010, pp. 14–15).

From their initial entry into the market through to the present day, the furniture has continued to be sold at auction, fetching sums upwards of $300,000 USD (Phillips, 2008). The pieces have attracted popular media attention, which has largely maintained a consistent narrative of design, production, and use: that this furniture was the work of Swiss/French designer Pierre Jeanneret, and that it was undervalued in India until it was 'saved' by the French dealers in the 1990s. This narrative remains largely unquestioned in both the popular press and market literature. Today, pieces of Chandigarh's modernist furniture are some of the most coveted and ubiquitous modernist design objects on the art market.

3 Authenticating Mass-Manufactured Design

The unique physicality of mass-manufactured objects of design poses issues regarding authenticity and authentication when these objects are placed within markets set up for the sale and resale of fine art and antiquities. On the art market an object's value is built around its authenticity, rarity, and provenance (Sladen, 2010, p. 48). However, mass-manufactured design does not conform to this expected structure (Attfield, 2000, p. 102; Lindemann, 2010, pp. 8, 30–31, 208–209); mass-production makes accurate material and specialist observational identification between individual objects difficult, while these objects' initial proletarian status creates barriers to comprehensive provenance research and authentication (Dannehl, 2018, p. 174; P! Galerie, 2019). Combined, these challenges, as illustrated through the case study of Chandigarh's modernist furniture, can provide cover for the proliferation of illegal and amoral activity such as theft or fraud.

3.1 Mass-Manufactured Design

The production of mass-manufactured design objects relies on a clear separation of the design and production processes (Cardoso, 2010, p. 324). Once a designer has finalised their specifications, they are presented to a manufacturer to produce. The mass-manufacture process then entails replication of the identical objects in significant quantities following the same specifications.

For mass-production to function effectively, raw materials, component parts, and processes are made to standard dimensions and quality, facilitating uniform construction and assembly (Giedion, 1969, p. 49). Using standardised raw materials, near-identical component parts are created by repeating identical processes (Giedion, 1969). These parts are subsequently assembled to create near-identical end products in large numbers (Giedion, 1969). Standardisation, employed in both hand- and machine-production, increases production speed through the repetition of identical processes, and ensures the similarity of the end products assembled from identical component parts (Giedion, 1969). Unlike many works of fine art and antiquities, the end products of mass-production are not intended to be unique, nor are individual objects made to the same specifications easily identifiable from one another.

Chandigarh's modernist furniture broadly conforms to these principles of mass-production. During Chandigarh's construction, the team involved in planning the city designed numerous pieces of furniture to equip the new buildings. These chairs, tables and shelves were then produced by hand from local hardwoods in great quantities in workshops across Northern India (Seguin, 2014, p. 128). The hand-production of Chandigarh's furniture drew from practices of standardisation, with parts made to the same specifications to facilitate assembly. This mass-manufacture by hand has created a body of individual design objects with intense visual similarity.

However, certain aspects of the furniture's creation differ from the expected norms of machine-made European modernist furniture, with which Chandigarh's furniture is conflated on the art market. Chandigarh's furniture construction is visibly handmade, with pencilled assembly marks and tool marks visible on certain surfaces. While clearly constructed following relatively set designs, individual objects made to the same specifications may vary slightly in size and shape (Seitz et al., 2021). In addition, some individual objects have hand-painted serial numbers added to their frames, used by municipal governments to keep inventories of public furniture. Rather than facilitating the identification of so-called 'originals', as one might expect for objects of fine art or antiquities, these small differences within Chandigarh's mass-manufactured furniture instead *increase* the difficulty of distinguishing between 'original' and 'reproduction' items.

This obfuscation stems from the unpredictable and undocumented inconsistencies in manufacture across the whole body of Chandigarh's existing furniture. Differences between objects of the same design are only helpful for authentication purposes if these differences themselves can be verified. This verification would be incredibly difficult for Chandigarh's furniture for two primary reasons. First, inconsistencies between objects of the same design do not conform to or follow a discernible pattern. This means that any mark or size difference could be plausibly passed off as an 'authentic' difference, rather than a deliberately forged difference in a modern replica. Additionally, the large and unknown production scale of Chandigarh's furniture makes keeping accurate records of inconsistencies a challenging undertaking. Without verifiable records of individual object variations, any variation may be passed off as 'authentic' or original.

Differences between objects of the same design, then, are only helpful in authentication if markings and material differences are consistent throughout the large production runs, *and* if there are robust and reliable records to which differences can be compared. In the absence of these two elements, and the presence of variations between individual objects of the same design, there can be no standard in what a Chandigarh chair should actually look like—no standard dimensions or markings to tell an 'original' apart from a 'fake'.

3.2 *Material Analysis*

Facilitated in large part by technological advances, material analysis is an increasingly common method of authentication on the art and antiquities market. Material analysis provides specialists the ability to identify timelines and trajectories of art pieces through the age and substance of composite materials (Flescher, 2020, p. 40; Sladen, 2010, p. 48). While this approach can help identify distinctions between one-off or small run, handmade objects, differentiating between individual mass-produced objects of the same design is difficult, as these items are generally produced from the same materials at the same time. Identical materials means there can be no material differentiation between pieces from the same time period.

Additionally, decades of heavy use have meant that individual pieces of Chandigarh's modernist furniture have been repaired, with specific components altered or replaced over time (P! Galerie, 2019). This has resulted in the presence of many pieces of Chandigarh's furniture with elements, such as seat caning and legs which, when materially analysed, would date to different time periods. Combined with the sheer quantity of extant furniture, the handmade nature of its construction and its frequent repair and re-use challenge definite authentication of any given piece (P! Galerie, 2019).

While particularities of Chandigarh furniture exacerbate difficulties in identifying individual pieces, forms of standardisation remain inherent to the production of mass-manufactured design objects. These forms of standardisation in turn greatly increase the difficulty of authentication of 'original' and unique works.

3.3 *Provenance*

Mass-production, by definition, involves manufacture on a massive scale, with objects frequently created in their thousands to identical specifications (Hoban, 2001, p. 36). Because of their functional and reproducible nature, mass-manufactured design objects, including furniture, are generally purchased for use, rather than investment (Walker, 1989). Given the quantities of identical objects produced, and their frequently proletarian status, the scarcity of documented provenance creates a barrier to accurate and definite authentication (Dannehl, 2018, p. 174; P! Galerie, 2019). Unlike expensive artworks, few initial purchasers of utilitarian objects are likely to retain documentation, such as receipts, invoices, or purchase orders in the long term (Dannehl, 2018, p. 174). The frequent absence of detailed documentary evidence makes tracing the provenance of individual mass-manufactured objects to their initial point of sale or use exceedingly difficult.

Extant literature on Chandigarh's modernist furniture provides little documented evidence regarding the number of pieces of furniture produced by any given workshop, or in total.[2] Government records for production contracts are not referenced within the literature on Chandigarh's furniture, and the whereabouts of documentary evidence relating to the furniture's production are not currently known. However, photographic and anecdotal evidence suggests that since its original creation in the 1950s the furniture has been used as intended by the city's students and bureaucrats, that many pieces have been damaged and repaired, some sold for scrap, others destroyed, and others still removed from India, in many cases for resale in the West (Siegel, 2013). In addition, further examples have been made following the original designs since the first productions.[3]

The authors' research into Chandigarh's modernist furniture and its resale includes an ongoing cataloguing project, tracking pieces which have come up for sale at major auction houses in Europe and North America. The resulting database contains 1770 auction lots as of November 2021, including entries for lots containing multiple pieces of furniture (Seitz et al., 2021). This figure likely only represents a small fraction of the pieces produced for the city, as it excludes furniture sold in dealerships and smaller auction houses, furniture remaining in Chandigarh, and pieces which have been discarded or destroyed. Whilst not encompassing all

[2] The most frequently cited literature in auction listings, The Indian Adventure, does not provide names and locations of production workshops, and provides little evidence to support estimated production quantities.

[3] Examples of Chandigarh's modernist furniture being produced include upmarket items crafted by Bangalore-based Phantom Hands (https://phantomhands.in/products), and items produced by the Chandigarh Model Jail (http://chdmodeljail.gov.in/products/factoryproduct), among others.

sales of furniture to date, as many sales are not within public record, this data set illustrates the tremendous scale on which Chandigarh furniture was produced.

Together, the scale and materiality of these objects combine to create a vast, complex, and unclear picture regarding the specific origin, date, and provenance of any individual piece of Chandigarh's modernist furniture. The significant lack of available paperwork concerning original purchase, use, and transfer of ownership of pieces of mass-manufactured design, combined with the vast scale on which these pieces were produced makes authentication and verification of individual examples, even by the skeletal standards set by the art market, exceedingly difficult.

Such difficulty in sourcing provenance information is exemplified by publicly available auction listings for pieces of Chandigarh's modernist furniture, in which provision of information is typically sparse. Lots are generally afforded a photograph of the piece against a neutral backdrop, a short physical description, technical details, a brief bibliography, and briefer still provenance.[4] Bibliographic information is consistently limited in its scope, frequently only referring to *The Indian Adventure*, the lightly footnoted book written by the dealers responsible for initial extraction of Chandigarh pieces from the city (Seitz et al., 2021).[5] Similarly, descriptions of provenance are equally sparse, typically only stating the object's city and country of origin (Chandigarh, India) and occasionally an institutional location (i.e., 'Punjab University')(Seitz et al., 2021).

3.4 Illegal and Amoral Implications

The unique physical properties of objects of mass-manufactured design, their continued adaptation and replication over time, the sparse provenance information available regarding specific pieces, and the large scale on which these objects are produced create an environment which may provide cover and incentivise illegal and amoral market behaviours including, but not limited to, illegal extraction of objects from their original location, deliberate forgery, and unintentional confusion of contemporary iterations with 'original' pieces.

---

[4]A typical auction listing for a piece of Chandigarh's modernist furniture can be seen in the Christie's Interiors sale on 7 June 2011 at Christie's, London. Lot 344, "A PIERRE JEANNERET TEAK AND CANEWORK 'PUNJAB UNIVERSITY'". This lot includes a sole attribution of the armchair to Pierre Jeanneret, a sizeable date range for the object's production, and a sole bibliographic entry of The Indian Adventure. The lot does not include any information regarding the object's provenance (Christie's, 2011).

[5]Examples of such limited bibliographies abound in the authors' publicly available dataset tracking Chandigarh furniture at auction. The Indian Adventure began to be listed as bibliographic evidence even ahead of the volume's publication, as illustrated in the Important Design sale on 8 June 2010 at Wright, Chicago. A listing for a "pair of lounge chairs from Punjab University, Chandigarh" states "This design will be included in the forthcoming catalogue raisonné, Pierre Jeanneret/Le Corbusier: Oeuvres en Inde, Mobilier et Architecture by Touchaleaume and Moreau"' (Wright, 2010).

Much of this amorality is due to the fact that both forgeries—items manufactured in the present day and deliberately and artificially aged to simulate several decades of use—and 'original' pieces share the same nebulous physicality and lack of paperwork. Inconsistency within initial production of Chandigarh's furniture has made difficult the establishment of an archetype upon which to base authentication (P! Galerie, 2019). Further, the frequently repaired state of 'original' pieces, including insertion of newer replacement materials calls into question any dating methods which might be employed to separate the two categories of objects. Without the ability, even for experts, to differentiate material difference between 'original' and 'replica' Chandigarh furniture, there is a certain ease in passing the latter off as the former. This ease, in turn, may have allowed the art market and auction house sales to be populated with deliberate 'forgeries' (Medford, 2019).

Additionally, the vast scale on which objects of mass-manufactured design exist impedes the task of monitoring and ensuring the continued security and proper location of individual objects. Difficulty in monitoring in turn creates openings for illegal removal or resale of specific pieces. This is compounded by the lack of paperwork surrounding mass-manufactured objects: the specific trajectories of individual items are frequently incredibly difficult to trace and prove (P! Galerie, 2019).

The challenge of tracking individual pieces of furniture and ensuring their continued location in India are issues which have been recognised by several institutions within Chandigarh. As is common practice across many government buildings in India, numerous pieces of the city's furniture are painted with inventory codes, linking objects to institutions and locations. This practice ensures accurate tabulation of furniture, and its continued presence in proper locations. In 2017, the Chandigarh Heritage Conservation Committee, the body responsible for safeguarding the city's material heritage suggested attaching GPS tracking devices to the city's manhole covers in order to keep track of their whereabouts (Rohtaki, 2017; Yadav, 2022). Such methods of tracking and locating the city's objects demonstrate the difficulties faced in managing such quantities of material as well as the measures required to discourage illegal removal of objects of mass-manufactured design.

Desperate methods to keep account of Chandigarh's modernist furniture may be well-needed. Despite the export of this furniture being made illegal on 22 February 2011 by the Ministry of Home Affairs (Prashar, 2020a), items placed for sale since that date at prominent auctions provide no date of export, nor any indication or proof that the items were exported ahead of this cut-off (Seitz et al., 2021).

4 Conceptual Challenges to the 'Original'

When sold within the art market, items of design are frequently framed and treated as if they are objects of art (Lindemann, 2010). This treatment of design-as-art leads to conceptual challenges, as design objects, particularly those produced on a large scale, *are not art*, and have different properties to objects of fine art.

Authentication, as it is understood within the current framework of the art market, relies on the shared understanding that there is an identifiable 'original' object to authenticate. However, when subjected to the same market structures as fine art, design poses conceptual challenges to this notion of the 'original' object. The nature of replication through mass-manufacture, typical involvement of multiple actors in the design and production process, and the primary intended use of design objects all challenge currently held conceptions of the 'original' within art markets. These challenges call into question the financial value given to 'original' objects of mass-manufactured design.

Within the fine art market, an original work of art is typically considered to be a work conceptualised and created by an artist or their studio. The work 'belongs' to the artist and is made at an identifiable point in time. The work is singular or one of a limited edition: it is unique. In the case of reproducible mediums such as printmaking, financial value typically decreases as a greater number of copies increase, demonstrating the link between scarcity and financial value (Artsy, 2018; Lindemann, 2010, p. 18).

In contrast, objects of mass-manufactured design are typically not produced as distinct 'editions'.[6] While production runs may sometimes be identified and differentiated, they are not typically denoted on the product itself or within primary markets, as this information does not impact functional value of the object.[7] The scale of initial mass-manufacture is generally determined by the functional need for a given product, and expected market, rather than to create rarity (Lindemann, 2010, pp. 200–201, 269–271). A designer may create 'designs': drawings, plans, specifications, and prototypes (Collins Dictionary, 2022). These are often considered to be unique, but are not the end-product (Hoban, 2001, p. 17). Distinction must be made between these 'designs' and the mass-produced objects made following their specifications. The continued conflation of the two allows for mass-manufactured objects to be treated as original, singular, unique works at auction.

Given the distinction between artworks and objects of mass-manufactured design, the fine art model, wherein the execution of an original artwork by an artist is given primacy, cannot be easily or coherently applied to design objects (Fallan, 2010). The physical and temporal proximity of manufacture to the designer is irrelevant to an

[6]See collector Micheal Boyd and ex Senior Vice President of auction house Sotheby's James Zemaitis' comments in Lindemann's Collecting Design for reference to the uncertainty surrounding the number of mass-manufactured designs objects in circulation (Lindemann, 2010, pp. 30–31, 269–271).

[7]Miller's Collecting Modern Design, for instance, does not include specific production information (Date and location) for the individual object in question in its object listings. These listings instead include the designer's name, the piece name, and the year of design, in addition to estimated prices. Production information is not discussed as a feature of an object of design to interrogate before purchase. Miller's Collecting Modern Design highlights 'quality of design', 'scarcity' and 'condition of the piece' as factors most likely to impact price and financial value of designed objects (Hoban, 2001, p. 150). Likewise, the Sourcebook of Modern Furniture provides only Model name or number, year of design, Designer, Manufacturer, Materials, and Dimensions for each product presented (Habegger & Osman, 2005).

object's primary market value, as production contracts are often given to multiple manufacturers, in various locations, simultaneously or on different timelines, without the presence of the designer. In addition, design is commonly a collaborative process with multiple designers working on a single concept (Walker, 1989). The multiplicity of individuals involved in the conception and production of a design object means identifying an 'original' design object based on its artistic execution does not fit the same boundaries as an object of fine art (Walker, 1989).

On the market, the distinction of an 'original' piece of Chandigarh's modernist furniture follows the art market model, prioritising the role of the artist in an object's creation. In the case of Chandigarh's modernist furniture this has entailed establishing connections between individual furniture items and designers Pierre Jeanneret and Le Corbusier (Lindemann, 2010, pp. 30–31). This connection is built by attributing design of Chandigarh's furniture exclusively to Jeanneret and Le Corbusier, frequently only listing either of these two men as the objects' creators (Seitz et al., 2021). Such attributions appear to minimise, if not erase, the contributions of additional design team members, in addition to the network of manufacturers involved in physical creation and manifestation of the pieces.

While reproductions of artwork can be differentiated from original pieces, with different value assigned according to 'originality', such an ease of separation between earlier and later iterations is not the case for objects of mass-manufactured design, which are, by definition, intended to be infinitely reproducible. The core conceptual distinction between art and design is that the primary value of a design object is tied to its function—it has a use value (Walker, 1989). Following this, a design object can remain highly 'valuable' to its user irrespective of its financial or investment value. Assigning higher financial value to 'original' mass-manufactured design objects relies on the insistence that individual design objects have financial value *because* of their use-value, while simultaneously ignoring the identical use-value of reproductions. This leads us to ask upon what the financial value of mass-manufactured design is built.

The execution of Chandigarh's furniture, for example, was not only undertaken by a multitude of carpenters and caners at the manufacturing level, but also conceived within an office of architects, many of whom were involved in the furniture's design. As a result, the actual and precise attribution of particular designs for Chandigarh's modernist furniture remains unclear, with various styles seemingly manufactured in different locations to be used within different buildings. Pieces were repaired, as per the original intention for the furniture (Prakash, 2018), demonstrating that these were not to be treated as singular, unique objects, but rather reproducible, functional furniture. In this sense, their primary use value as functional furniture used in spaces across Chandigarh remains unchanged today, calling into question the basis for the high financial value which has been built at auction.

Conceptual issues regarding the use value of design thus problematise the high financial value of design objects on the art market. Despite the presence of such conceptual issues, there is little discussion of these topics in popular, market, or academic publications and networks. In the absence of any such discussions or examinations, market pressures for the maintenance of high prices seem to have prevailed, emphasising notions of scarcity by highlighting certain pieces as 'original', even when such conceptions contradict the very nature of design objects.

5 Moral Implications of Actors

Conflation of design objects with works of art also raises moral questions surrounding the role of several groups of actors within, and related to, the market. The existence of dealers writing foundational narratives on design pieces, and the unique presence of modern manufacturers of 'original' pieces gives rise to opportunities for intervention in the narrative creation surrounding objects of design.[8] This interference poses particularly strong moral questions given the loci of specialist knowledge with regards to items of design.

5.1 *Location of Design Historical Knowledge*

Unlike knowledge structures for objects of fine art and antiquities which are generally held in several locations including the academy, the market, and private collectors, knowledge regarding objects of design remains limited (Walker, 1989). As design history is a relatively recent discipline, there are fewer experts within the academy, and fewer still with specialist knowledge regarding objects of mass-manufactured design (Walker, 1989, p. 17). While this gap has historically been largely inconsequential due to the low financial value of objects of mass-manufactured design, the recent placement of such objects on the art market has dramatically increased the stakes and repercussions for generation and ownership of design knowledge. The recent dramatic increase in financial value of objects of design appears to have exacerbated repercussions of the limited knowledge base of design, creating a gap in information which dealers and contemporary manufacturers have eagerly filled (Lindemann, 2010, pp. 41–42, 191–192), to questionable results.

Intervention on the part of market actors in the construction of design knowledge is well illustrated in the case of Chandigarh's modernist furniture. In this instance,

[8] A striking example of the interconnectedness between design narratives and design sales is the establishment of the Design Museum, London, by Terence Conran. Prior to the launch of the museum, Conran rose to fame as both a designer in his own right, and a highly successful design retailer whose projects included the mid-market chain Habitat and the upper-market eponymous Conran Shop. The Design Museum has included pieces sold by Conran's retail businesses in their displays, published the book Terence Conran: Making Modern Britain (2021), and curated a 2022 display of Conran's design work. The museum itself features a carefully curated museum shop, which sells some Conran-related items. A broader discussion of potential influences on design by the field of Design History can be read in Design History: Understanding Theory and Method (2010).

the dealers responsible for initially bringing pieces to the European and North American art markets have, quite literally, written the book on the furniture. Éric Touchaleaume and Gerald Moreau's 2014 volume *The Indian Adventure* remains the most-cited volume in auction listings for Chandigarh's tables, chairs, couches, and daybeds (Seitz et al., 2021). This full-colour highly illustrated volume sets out both an overarching narrative of Chandigarh's furniture, as well as providing attributions and categorising individual pieces, infrequently supported by the standard of citation expected within the academic press.

Intervention on the part of dealers and manufacturers in the development of knowledge regarding Chandigarh's furniture has resulted in the creation of a narrative seemingly crafted to sell objects on the European and North American markets for higher prices (Medford, 2019). These narratives, emphasising the connection of Chandigarh's furniture to Europe, European modernists, and European modernism appear to omit key details about the deep connections of these objects to and within India (Seitz et al., 2020). Inaccurate histories such as these in turn play a role in minimising India's role in the development of modernism, in addition to the country's larger role on the world cultural stage, perpetuating neocolonial attitudes and beliefs.

Knowledge emanating from dealers is, of course, not unique to the instance of design. However, the lack of academic or non-market related experts to verify information or offer counter-narratives is unique. There are few individuals working within design history who are positioned to produce the well-cited, verifiable publications necessary to substantiate, complicate, or call into question Touchaleaume and Moreau's claims. Even if design history as a discipline were well positioned to deal with such issues, the quantity of popular literature produced on design would make the task of fact checking exceedingly laborious and difficult.

5.2 Contemporary Manufacturers

The unique makeup of knowledge creation and ownership regarding mass-manufactured design objects is compounded by potential interference in the creation of historical narratives by contemporary manufacturers. The inherent reproducibility of mass-manufactured design has led to a vibrant and profitable industry producing a steady stream of reproduction pieces, manufactured to designers' initial specifications. The existence of companies producing functionally identical pieces to those being auctioned or sold as 'originals' leads to unique issues of interference within the market for historic design. These corporate actors sponsor exhibitions and otherwise act to raise the profile and financial value of 'original' pieces of design (Proteau, 2018). This, in turn, enlarges the market for pieces produced in the present, and raises the profile and profits of the manufacturing company in question.

Such connections lead to morally questionable relationships between museums, manufacturers, dealers and auction houses, wherein all parties have a financial and reputational stake in increasing visibility and value of specific design objects.[9] As legitimate contemporary manufacturers definitionally cannot exist for items of fine art or antiquities, this triad is not present in most other sales situations.

The close relationships between these design-related bodies raises two primary problematics. First, involvement of directly related commercial entities in museum activity raises alarm bells regarding institutional 'firewall' policies, owing to the potential influence of corporate bodies on the impartiality of museum practice and the narratives they build (Proteau, 2018; Museum Association, 2016, p. 10). Additionally, unique to design, the simultaneous display of contemporary iterations of design objects alongside earlier examples complicates the understanding of what constitutes an 'original' object and raises issues regarding the promotion of pieces of historical design.

One company which has successfully tapped into the market for high-end furniture production is Cassina, an Italian manufacturer which has built its brand through the acquisition and production of early twentieth-century modernist chairs (Woodham, 2004, p. 71). Cassina's repertoire includes Le Corbusier's LC3 Grand Comfort chair, Charlotte Perriand's Nuage à Plots bookcase, and Gerrit Rietveld's Red and Blue chair, among many others (Cassina, 2021).

Cassina recently sponsored two blockbuster exhibitions on the French designer and architect Charlotte Perriand: *Charlotte Perriand: Inventing a New World* at the Fondation Louis Vuitton in Paris and *Charlotte Perriand: The Modern Life* at the Design Museum in London. In both cases Cassina donated furniture for use by visitors and produced reproductions of lost historic pieces. The existence of additional financial sponsorship or support provided by Cassina toward the two exhibitions and their host entities remains unclear.

Cassina's unspecified involvement in these exhibitions surrounding pieces for which it holds exclusive licensing rights demonstrates the problematics of commercial involvement in the creation of design narratives. Given that Cassina is the sole legal manufacturer of Charlotte Perriand furniture, can either the company or the two museums be trusted to put on an exhibit which critically and meaningfully engages with her work? Is Cassina exerting influence over how Perriand's works are represented in order to increase their covetability and sale price? When the Design Museum and Cassina praise Perriand's designs, are they speaking of the historical pieces, or the contemporary iterations? If no substantial difference between the two

[9]The Vitra Design Museum, for example, demonstrates the close connections between museums, manufacturers, dealers, collectors, and auction houses. The Vitra Design Museum acquired a major collection from the Charles and Ray Eames estate in 1988. Vitra is also a major contemporary furniture manufacturer which continues to produce the Eames' design objects including the 'Organic Chair' by Charles Eames and Eero Saarinen, under their 'Original selection' (Vitra, 2022). In Collecting Design (Lindemann, 2010) the modernist furniture dealer Ulrich Fiedler highlights the importance of his relationship with the collector and former director of Vitra Design Museum Alexander von Vegesack, whilst Richard Wright the Founder of Wright auction house, expresses his admiration for this 'outstanding company' whilst pointing out the importance of Vitra Design Museum's foundational place in the evolution of design collecting (Lindemann, 2010: pp. 94, 254–256).

can be gleaned, are shows such as those put on by the Fondation Louis Vuitton and the Design Museum simply glorified advertisements for Cassina?

In addition to its production of Charlotte Perriand pieces, Cassina manufactured Chandigarh furniture from 2019 to 2021 (Cassina, 2020).[10] The narrative employed to historicise and contextualise these pieces, as illustrated on the Cassina English-language webpage, follows the major points of the dealer's story regarding the pieces—that they were designed by Pierre Jeanneret, and that they belong to the European modernist canon while simultaneously being exotic pieces touched by the Indian subcontinent (Cassina, 2020).

No major exhibitions of Chandigarh's modernist furniture were held during the initial time in which Cassina's pieces were in production, however one can imagine a similar pattern being repeated as with the Perriand shows; Cassina manufacturing pieces while at the same time sponsoring a show dedicated to them, thus raising the profile of their own products and increasing the potential market for their sale.

The existence of modern manufacturers of historic design objects thus raises moral issues regarding the interference of contemporary manufacturers in the construction of furniture narratives, and the resulting profile and value of the pieces. These corporate actors, definitionally excluded from equivalent participation in the markets for fine art and antiquities, have the potential to act in unseen and unscrupulous ways in crafting narratives regarding design objects. Their involvement leads to the creation and dissemination of histories which are rooted in motivation for corporate profit, not by historians led by material evidence. This in turn leads to increased financial value for both 'original' items on the art market and contemporary pieces within commercial markets.

6 Conclusion

This chapter has illustrated how the production and use of mass-manufactured design raises physical, conceptual, and moral problems when such objects are placed within the art market. Further, inclusion of designed objects within art market structures creates conditions which may foster and provide cover for amoral and potentially criminal activity. The case study of Chandigarh's modernist furniture highlights these issues and exemplifies ways in which the issues of design within art markets can give rise to problematic activity.

The unique physicality of objects of mass-manufactured design poses issues regarding authenticity and authentication. Mass-production makes differentiation of individual pieces of design difficult. The quantities of any given design produced, combined with their frequently proletarian status, makes tracing the provenance of individual objects exceedingly challenging. Together these two factors, unique to

[10] At the time of writing in the spring of 2022, Cassina has re-launched a collection of Chandigarh designs, available for purchase.

design objects, may both encourage and provide cover to amoral or illegal market behaviours such as deliberate forgery of 'authentic' pieces, or confusion of contemporary replicas with 'original' iterations.

Further, when subjected to the same market structures as fine art, design poses conceptual challenges to the notion of the 'original'. As design objects are frequently intended to be mass-produced over long time spans, foundational questions are raised regarding the meaning of an 'original' design object.

Finally, the replicability of design objects poses moral questions regarding the involvement of specific actors, primarily dealers and contemporary manufacturers, in the creation of historical narratives and entanglement with cultural bodies and the art market. The lack of robust and prominent design historical knowledge has created unique opportunities for the creation of financially-motivated histories of design. Additionally, the continued production of design objects creates opportunities and pressures for design manufacturers to influence and mould historical narratives and understandings of design objects to increase their marketability and financial value.

Together, the physical issues of authentication, the conceptual issues caused by the definition of 'original' design objects, and the moral issues caused by knowledge distribution and the vested interests of various market actors have created an environment rife for the inception and encouragement of amoral and criminal behaviour.

As illustrated by the case study of Chandigarh's modernist furniture, incubation of amoral and potentially illegal behaviours vis-a-vis objects of mass-manufactured design are not purely hypothetical—the problematics of design on the art market have resulted in both tangible movement of pieces across borders and creation of histories shaped around financial interests, rather than historical truths.

The lucrative placement of Chandigarh's furniture on the fine art market has been made possible by the broader unique physical and conceptual problems outlined in this chapter. In particular, the positioning of mass-manufactured design objects as original art objects by privileging the furniture's connections to Pierre Jeanneret and Le Corbusier has perpetuated a neocolonial extraction of Chandigarh furniture and the whitewashing of its narrative. This has promoted a history of modernist design which has effectively erased the presence of South Asian people, knowledge, and labour.

This situation has created a number of damaging real-world implications that require urgent corrective intervention. The physical removal of Chandigarh's furniture from India into Western European and North American markets and collections has moved important pieces of Indian material culture out of reach of Indian people. Despite being paid for and designed by and for the people of Chandigarh, the last twenty years have witnessed a steady stream of Chandigarh's modernist furniture moving into the hands of the wealthy in the Global North. Not only does this movement deprive India and Indian people of key pieces of shared material culture and heritage, the movement of pieces and their commodification as art objects in private collections outside India also makes critical academic material analysis, by scholars well placed to write this history, particularly difficult to undertake. At the very same time, the continuing commodification of South Asian material culture continues to be narrated as protection of the furniture, continuing disturbing neocolonial attitudes of saviourism by collectors and heritage players, overshadowing local research into these pieces.

Removal from India has also broadly moved Chandigarh's furniture into a financially unaffordable realm for those it was originally intended to serve. Simultaneously, these objects have been heralded as fine examples of low cost, functional pieces of design by the very organisations increasing their financial value. Such a process embodies the worst of extractive capitalism, of a financial system foundationally rooted within a calculated intention to remove pieces at low cost from India and the Global South, build value for these pieces through specialist networks and infrastructures, and re-sell them in the West for prices unaffordable for the objects' original and intended owners and users. As this chapter has illustrated, however, the creation of value in the case of design objects within the art market is based upon conceptually unsound and practically problematic understandings of the nature of design compared to fine art. If accepted, the differences between objects of art and design have the potential to destabilise this market ecosystem.

At the same time as pieces have been extracted from India and moved out of reach of citizens of Chandigarh, the dramatic increase in financial value of these objects combined with pressure to counter neocolonial narratives of native 'underappreciation', have resulted in an unknown quantity of the furniture being placed under lock and key within Chandigarh itself (Prashar, 2020b). While this sequestering may help to prevent theft and may bolster the international reputation of Chandigarh in terms of preservation of cultural patrimony, it has also meant that even fewer pieces of furniture are available and accessible for daily use within the city. Additionally, this method of protection may hinder attempts to research and produce more accurate histories of the furniture broadly, and of individual pieces.

Scholarly research into Chandigarh's modernist furniture is further complicated by the predominance of historically and factually questionable narrative of the pieces created in the process of their sale. Such narratives have permeated many spaces, shaping both general and specialist knowledge regarding modernist furniture and Indian modernist design. This constructed narrative must both be comprehensively addressed and challenged in subsequent material on the subject in order to move toward a more accurate history and understanding.

The issues raised by this chapter are intended to be read as introductory, with further work needed in several complementary areas. Further study is needed on both the technical and material removal of these objects from India, as well as the legal and moral implications of movement which this chapter has raised. With the extraction of Chandigarh's furniture from India now illegal, questions regarding un- or under-provenanced furniture in sales and private collections abroad, and subsequent potential repatriation, can also begin to be addressed. Additional material-led research remains to be undertaken, ideally geared toward building a strong foundational base of the furniture's specific design and history.

Finally, broader design historical consideration of mass-manufactured design as it relates to the fine art market is desperately needed. Without additional acknowledgement and study of this phenomenon and its ontological and practical impacts on the nature of design and designed objects, the literature on these objects remains incomplete. Without critical and academic interrogation of the relationship between design and the art resale market new and less than accurate narratives of designed objects will continue to emerge, led by market interests rather than verifiable evidence and research. Further attention to market structures, opens up possibilities not only for greater understandings of design objects in and of themselves, but also how these objects are sociologically understood.

References

Amineddoleh, L. (2020). The role of provenance in resolving art-world disputes. In A. Tompkins (Ed.), *Provenance research today: Principles, practice, problems* (pp. 25–38). Lund Humphries.

Artcurial. (2006). *Pierre Jeanneret: Chandigarh Project*. Auction Catalogue.

Artsy. (2018). *What Determines the Value of a Print?* Retrieved October 29, 2021, from https://www.artsy.net/article/artsy-specialist-determines-value-print

Attfield, J. (2000). *Wild things: The material culture of everyday life*. Berg.

Cardoso, R. (2010). Craft versus design. In G. Adamson (Ed.), *The craft reader* (pp. 321–332). Berg.

Cassina. (2020). *Homage Á Pierre Jeanneret*. Retrieved May 11, 2020, from https://web.archive.org/web/*/https://www.cassina.com/en/jeanneret.

Cassina. (2021). *Products*. Retrieved October 16, 2021, from https://www.cassina.com/it/en/products/all-products.5.html

Christie's. (2011). *A Pierre Jeanneret Teak And Canework 'Punjab University' Armchair*. Retrieved March 4, 2022, from https://www.christies.com/lot/a-pierre-jeanneret-teak-and-canework-punjab-5444873/?from=salesummary&intObjectID=5444873&lid=1

Collins Dictionary. (2022). *Definition of 'design'*. Retrieved March 10, 2022, from https://www.collinsdictionary.com/dictionary/english/design

Dannehl, K. (2018). Object biographies: From production to consumption. In K. Harvey (Ed.), *History and material culture: A student's guide to approaching alternative sources* (pp. 171–186). Routledge.

Evenson, N. (1966). *Chandigarh*. University of California Press.

Fallan, K. (2010). *Design history: Understanding theory and method*. Bloomsbury.

Flescher, S. (2020). The challenges of provenance research. In A. Tompkins (Ed.), *Provenance research today: Principles, practice, problems* (pp. 39–53). Lund Humphries.

Giedion, S. (1969). *Mechanization takes command: A contribution to anonymous history*. The Norton Library.

Habegger, J., & Osman, J. (2005). *Sourcebook of modern furniture*. W. W. Norton & Company.

Hoban, S. (2001). *Miller's collecting modern design*. Mitchell Beazley.

Joshi, K. (1999). *Documenting Chandigarh: The Indian architecture of Pierre Jeanneret, Edwin Maxwell Fry, Jane Beverly Drew*. Mapin.

Kaufmann, E., Jr. (1969). *Introductions to modern design*. Museum of Modern Art and Arno Press.

Lindemann, A. (2010). *Collecting design*. Taschen.

Medford, S. (2019, August 14). 'Is your Jeanneret a fake?'. *Wall Street Journal*. Retrieved September 1, 2020, from https://www.wsj.com/articles/is-your-jeanneret-a-fake-11565785593

Museum Association. (2016). *Code of Ethics for Museums*. Retrieved March 10, 2022, from https://ma-production.ams3.digitaloceanspaces.com/app/uploads/2020/06/18145449/20012016-code-of-ethics-single-page-8.pdf

P! Galerie. (2019). *Authenticity: General Information About Provenance*. Retrieved March 10, 2022, from https://www.jeanneret-chandigarh.com/provenance.pdf

Phillips. (2008). *Pierre Jeanneret Illuminated library table, from Chandigarh, India*. Retrieved October 26, 2021, from https://www.phillips.com/detail/pierre-jeanneret/NY050108/86?fromSearch=pierre%20jeanneret&searchPage=3

Prakash, V. (2018, January 3). *Life and Work of Pierre Jeanneret with Maristella Casciato* (Architecture Talk). Retrieved November 2, 2021, from https://www.architecturetalk.org/home/11

Prashar, S. (2020a, October 11). Indian High Commission in London seeks copy of MHA orders with regard to heritage items' auction. *The Indian Express*. Retrieved November 2, 2021, from https://indianexpress.com/article/cities/chandigarh/indian-high-commission-in-london-seeks-copy-of-mha-orders-with-regard-to-heritage-items-auction-6720275/

Prashar, S. (2020b, November 23) Mumbai link: The challenge for Chandigarh Police in every case. *The Indian Express*. Retrieved March 10, 2022, from https://indianexpress.com/article/cities/chandigarh/mumbai-link-the-challenge-for-chandigarh-police-in-every-case-7061915/

Proteau, J. (2018). Reducing risky relationships: Criteria for forming positive museum-corporate sponsorships. *Museum Management and Curatorship, 33*(3), 235–242.

Rohtaki, H. (2017, November 2). UT heritage panel wants GPS chips on Corbusier's manhole covers. *The Indian Express*. Retrieved September 26, 2021, from https://indianexpress.com/article/chandigarh/ut-heritage-panel-wants-gps-chips-on-corbusiers-manhole-covers-4918357/

Rüegg, A., & Spechtenhauser, K. (2012). *Le Corbusier: Furniture and Interiors 1905-1965*. Foundation Le Corbusier.

Seguin, P. (2014). *Le Corbusier and Pierre Jeanneret – Chandigarh, India*. Galerie Patrick Seguin.

Seitz, P., Thandapani, N., & Wittrick, G. (2020, September 24). *Chandigarh Chairs: Missing Histories*. Recorded Lecture. Bangalore International Centre. https://bangaloreinternationalcentre.org/video/chandigarh-chairs-missing-histories/

Seitz, P., Thandapani, N., & Wittrick, G. (2021, November 1). *Chandigarh Furniture Auction Tracking Database*. Retrieved November 2, 2021, from https://docs.google.com/spreadsheets/d/1eufPduy5rjQxFruyClYPdC97euOuuU-GCQiYWTJ7GU0/edit#gid=0

Siegel, A. (2013). *Provenance*. [HD Video].

Sladen, O. (2010). Faking history: How provenance forgery is conning the art world. *Journal of Art Crime, 3*, 47–60.

Touchaleaume, E., Moreau, G., & Vigo, M. (2010). *Le Corbusier, Pierre Jeanneret: l'aventure indienne*. Gourcuff Gradenigo.

Tsirogiannis, C. (2016). Something is confidential in the state of Christies. *Journal of Art Crime, 9*, 3–19.

Vitra. (2022). *Organic Chair*. Retrieved March 13, 2022, https://www.vitra.com/en-as/about-vitra/original/organic-chair

Walker, J. (1989). *Design history and the history of design*. Pluto Press.

Woodham, J. (2004). *A dictionary of modern design*. Oxford University Press.

Wright. (2010). *Pierre Jeanneret: pair of lounge chairs from Punjab University, Chandigarh*. Retrieved March 4, 2022, https://www.wright20.com/auctions/2010/06/important-design/580?search=pierre+Jeanneret

Yadav, D. (2022, March 8). MC weighs geo-tagging heritage manhole covers. *The Times of India*. Retrieved March 10, 2022, https://timesofindia.indiatimes.com/city/chandigarh/mc-weighs-geo-tagging-heritage-manhole-covers/articleshow/90064041.cms

Petra Seitz is a PhD candidate at the Bartlett School of Architecture, UCL, a lecturer at the University of Greenwich, and a freelance design researcher. Her doctoral work explores the history and evolution of commercial office interiors through a Marxist Labor Process lens. She holds a MA in History of Design from the Victoria and Albert Museum/Royal College of Art and a BA in Politics from Oberlin College.

Nia Thandapani is a design historian based in Bangalore. Her research interests include late nineteenth century to mid twentieth century South Asian design, with a focus on book and furniture objects. Nia holds an MA in History of Design from the Victoria & Albert Museum and Royal College of Art and a BA in Graphic Design from Central Saint Martins.

Gregor Wittrick is an independent design historian and Assistant Collections Manager at the British Museum, London. He holds an MA in History of Design from the Victoria & Albert Museum and Royal College of Art, London, and a BA in Ceramics from Gray's School of Art, Aberdeen. His research interests include twentieth and twenty-first century product design and manufacture, particularly furniture and ceramics. He is one third of the ongoing Chandigarh Chairs project.

The Evolution of the Belgian Art and Antiques Unit

Richard Van Herzeele

Abstract Since the 2001 police reform, the Belgian federal Art and Antiques police unit has faced successive budget and personnel cuts, a dynamic that culminated in the 2015 decision to operationally discontinue the unit. Currently there is no dedicated police capacity for art crime in Belgium. Belgium nonetheless remains an important link in the international art trade and faces the concomitant illegal activity. This chapter charts the evolution of the Belgian federal police's Art and Antiques unit and examines how its decreasing resources have impacted art crime policing in the country, particularly with regards to the relationship between the police and private actors. This fact-finding is framed by the criminological theory of fiscal constraint, the basic hypothesis of which is that as public institutions prove unable to meet policing demand, private participation in policing grows, making for a pluralised policing landscape. The chapter aims to highlight challenges to art crime policing in a context where it is given a low priority by public institutions, spotlight the Belgian situation specifically, situate art crime policing in Belgium within broader criminological policing theory, and look towards the future of art crime policing.

1 Introduction

"The downsizing of the Art and Antiques Unit of the Federal Police to a single police officer has brought the clearance rate for art theft in Belgium to zero percent" (Van De Velden, 2017, para. 1). This was that single officer's message to the Belgian Senate during its hearings on policing art theft in 2017, a few years after the official announcement of the unit's closure on 26 March 2014 (Belgian Senate, 2018b, p. 20). Despite that decision, that one sole police officer nonetheless still dealt with art crime in Belgium at the time of the hearings owed to an operational rather than a political decision. In January 2017, Claude Fontaine, then Director-General of the Belgian Federal Police, and Patrick Ludinant, then-Director of the police's Central

R. Van Herzeele (✉)
Queen Mary, University of London, London, UK
e-mail: richardvanherzeele@gmail.com

N. Oosterman, D. Yates (eds.), *Art Crime in Context*, Studies in Art, Heritage, Law and the Market 6, https://doi.org/10.1007/978-3-031-14084-6_4

Directorate for Serious and Organised Crimes, unilaterally decided to (re)instate a point of contact at the Federal Police level to support art crime investigations: this reference officer was to liaise with other forces and coordinate art crime policing (Belgian Senate, 2018a; Biourge & Huysen, 2022). It is in the wake of this decision the closing of the unit was publicly reframed as a downsizing, although the appointment of the reference officer was not an official or full reinstatement of the unit. Be that as it may, the responsible Minister indicated that "a relatively small phenomenon like art theft could be handled by one person, certainly if they had extensive experience and expertise in the matter" (Bové, 2020, para. 8). However, it was made apparent in the Senate hearings that one officer functioning as a point of reference would not be enough to effectively counter art crime in Belgium (Belgian Senate, 2018b, pp. 25–26).

This short introduction begs the question of what happens to art crime policing when the police disengage. In layperson's terms: who will pick up the slack? Private entities, perhaps? At first glance, the art crime policing situation in Belgium aligns with what is in policing literature known as fiscal constraint theory. Fiscal constraint theory suggests a causal relationship between states' inability to meet policing demand and the expansion of private policing (Button, 2019, p. 33). The basic hypothesis of fiscal constraint theory is that policing gaps emerge when states fail to meet policing needs, and that those gaps are filled by private entities. The theory is part of the broader discussion surrounding plural policing, which is the idea that the police are no longer the sole provider of policing, and that other agencies and institutions, including private actors, engage in policing activities. This chapter applies these ideas to art crime policing in Belgium.

Given the absence of reliable statistics, this chapter draws upon interviews with the sole reference officer, Belgian politicians involved with the Senate report, an art security consultant, two art insurers, a former unit member now working as a consultant, and a heritage professional, all of whom active in Belgium, as well as official reports, newspaper articles, and the academic literature on policing and art crime. The chapter begins with an introduction of fiscal constraint theory, before profiling the Belgian police's art crime efforts. The interaction between police and other art crime policing entities is subsequently discussed. Theory is then applied to practice, the main takeaways from which are presented at the end of the chapter.

2 Fiscal Constraint

Before discussing fiscal constraint theory in more detail, the concept of policing itself needs explanation. In the common vernacular, policing is often understood to be "*what the police do*" (Button, 2019, p. 7; Crawford, 2014, p. 173; Jones & Newburn, 1998a, p. 2). This is a relatively recent development, resulting from the police institution successfully taking the mantle of the legitimate and sole guardian of society during the nineteenth century (Livingstone & Hart, 2003; Shearing & Stenning, 1987). In the latter half of the twentieth century, however, academic researchers observed a surge in private policing. This led to an understanding of policing independent from the police, thus opening the door for plural policing discussions (Johnston, 1992; Shearing & Stenning, 1987). Reiner (2010) defines policing as "the set of processes and activities with specific social functions aimed at the protection or continuation of a particular social order, or social order in general" (p. 5). In this view, the police are indeed a specific entity "tasked with a broad mandate of crime control, order maintenance and some negotiable social service functions" (Reiner, 2010, pp. 3–4), but while they have that task, they are other actors that perform those "processes and activities" that secure a social order (Button, 2019, p. 8; Johnston, 1992, pp. 4–7; Reiner, 2010, p. 3–8).

The criminologists of the latter half of the twentieth century also looked to explain private policing. Fiscal constraint theory is one of the main frameworks developed in this regard (Button, 2019; Jones & Newburn, 1998a; Johnston, 1999). Essentially, fiscal constraint theory explains the rise of non-police or private policing as a result of states' increasing inability to (continue to) meet policing demand. This inability comes as a result of a lack of funds, due to for example austerity policies, or the effects of globalisation, or as a result of a lack of expertise in the police force, especially when confronting new types of crime (Button, 2019; Jones & Newburn, 1998b). These developments necessitated a more flexible approach, which private policing was more suited to than traditional, hierarchical public systems, and private actors can have the expertise and capabilities the police lack (for example cybercrime, Button, 2020). States can then respond to emergent private policing by attempting to draw it in to shore up state legitimacy, making them junior or in some cases equal partners to the police force (Button, 2019; Garland, 1996; Jones & Newburn, 1998b). The state and police may however also actively resist private policing, even when policing needs are not being met. Thus, fiscal constraint can drive independent private enterprise, and/or prompt states to more explicitly leverage private expertise. These two interpretations of fiscal constraint theory are both intimately connected to the idea of plural policing, whereby a sometimes-motley patchwork of entities come together to meet policing needs.

Art crime policing is not a stranger to fiscal constraint. As recent academic surveys of art crime policing show, art crime is, at least in Europe, not prioritised by governments and police forces (Block, 2014; Oosterman, 2019; Kerr, 2020). While there are exceptions, perhaps most notably the Italian Carabinieri Headquarters for the Protection of Cultural Heritage, [1] which can call upon around three hundred officers (Oosterman, 2019, p. 222), most countries run relatively small art and antiques police units of up to five officers, or no dedicated unit at all. Moreover, some of the units that do exist have been under staffing and financial pressure. For example, the London Metropolitan Police's Arts and Antiques squad was reassigned to the Grenfell Tower Fire investigation in the summer of 2017, triggering fears it was to be closed, as the unit had been under consistent pressure for years (Bailey, 2017; Block, 2014; Chesters, 2017). This was averted after public pressure from

[1] Comando Carabinieri Tutela Patrimonio Culturale or Carabinieri or TPC.

academics and professionals, but the episode shows the precarity of even the higher-profile art crime units operating today (Kerr, 2020). A lack of dedicated police personnel carries risks for effective art crime policing.

A lack of budget deprives police forces of the necessary expertise to effectively combat art crime as well as the personnel. While a police investigator dealing with art crime does not necessarily need to be a fully qualified art historian, they do need a basic skillset in art (Belgian Senate, 2018b; Interpol, 2016; Interpol, 2017; Kerr, 2020; Willems-Hirsch, 2012). They need to know the applicable national and international legislation, the primary ways in which art is affected by crime, how art is trafficked, and how to recognise and handle objects. They also need to know how to move in the art world with all of its specific customs. As a former member of the Belgian unit put it, investigators need to "remain in regular contact" with the art world, visit regularly, and approach it with "understanding" (personal communication, 2020). This is not a skillset the average police officer or detective possesses. It requires training, or stability of employment and funding so that institutional experience can be built and transferred. A police force without that stability or the funds to equip its personnel with that art crime expertise will find it difficult to effectively police art crime, which leads to the policing gaps fiscal constraint theories sees private entities fill (Kerr, 2013; Interpol, 2017; Willems-Hirsch, 2012).

3 The Bureau for Art and Antiques

The Belgian specialised arts and antiques police unit was known as the *Cel Kunst & Antiek*, which translates to the Bureau of Art and Antiques. The unit was established in 1991 as part of the Judicial Police with four employees (Belgian Senate, 2018b; personal communication, 2017). Its activities were supported by officers of the precincts of the Belgian Judicial Police. At the time, most Belgian Judicial Police precincts, located in cities such as Antwerp, Namur, and Arlon, had at least one officer with a modicum of art crime expertise in their ranks, typically working as part of the precinct units dedicated to financial crime (personal communication, 2017). These precinct officers were not specifically assigned to deal with art crime, but voluntarily dealt with cases alongside their other responsibilities and investigations. In 1998, the Bureau of Art and Antiques started using its own digital stolen arts database called ARTIST (ART Information SysTem), and three extra members joined the team, alongside a Customs Office attaché (Belgian Senate, 2018b). These were the halcyon days for the unit.

The thorough and wide-ranging 2001 reform of the Belgian Police replaced its threefold structure of Municipal Police, Judicial Police, and Gendarmerie with a twofold structure comprised of the Local and Federal police. Together the latter two formed the new Integrated Police Force (Devroe & Ponsaers, 2013, p. 3). The reform retained the Bureau of Art and Antiques, which became part of the Federal Police. Meanwhile, the Judicial precincts were remapped. The officers at precinct level with art crime experience were redistributed across these new districts. Their numbers would however dwindle in the years following, as the precinct officers redeployed to other services, or retired (Belgian Senate, 2018b; personal communication, 2017). Eventually, the Bureau of Art and Antiques was left as the only centre of art crime policing expertise in the Belgian police force. Nonetheless, the unit's numbers also dropped in the years following the police reform. In 2004, two officers left the unit, and so did the Customs attaché (Belgian Senate, 2018a). In 2006, art crime policing was removed from the *Nationaal Veiligheids Plan* (National Security Plan), which determines which criminal phenomena are a priority for the Belgian police. The unit was left with but two members of staff remaining (Belgian Senate, 2018b; personal communication, 2017). One of these two was exclusively dedicated to the upkeep of the ARTIST database (Block, 2014). This creeping decline in police resources for art crime policing and its impact did not go by unnoticed, however.

In 2010, politicians Bart Tommelein and Martine Taelman tabled a proposal for the establishment of a publicly accessible database for stolen art. The duo opined such a database would have an "important preventative effect" by complicating the sale of stolen art (Belgian Senate, 2010, p. 6). They lamented the "unfortunate" reality that police forces did not register all art and antiques thefts, and stated police services conducted "no active policy in matching the database with the supply of dealers and auction houses" (Belgian Senate, 2010, pp. 1–2). The following year, senators Ludo Sannen and Bert Anciaux introduced a bill to incorporate specific art crime offences into the Belgian Criminal Code (Belgian Senate, 2011). The two senators disapproved of how "the Belgian police services have systematically disinvested from tackling art crime", and claimed the employment of the two remaining officers of the Bureau of Art and Antiques was not secure (Belgian Senate, 2011, pp. 1–2). In 2013, senator Martine Taelman, this time joined by senators Jean-Jacques De Gucht and Armand De Decker, announced the intention to table a follow up bill to her previous proposal with Tommelein, to grant all police units access to the ARTIST database (Bruzz.be, 2013). None of these proposals were enacted, ostensibly due to a lack of political momentum, but they show concern for art crime policing. Taken together, they contain elements that align with plural policing and fiscal constraint theory: the identification of a policing gap and in the case of the Tommelein-Taelman proposal overtures towards private involvement as a way to fill it.

Regrettably, Sannen and Anciaux' fears about the future of the unit proved to be well-founded. The unit was audited between 2012 and 2013 (Belgian Senate, 2018a). The closure of the unit was announced not long after (Belgian Senate, 2018a). Officially, this decision was made to "maximise human resources" (Dendooven, 2016, para. 3). Policymakers wished to "optimise" the police force, which needed to become a more flexible and versatile organisation (Maerevoet, 2016; personal communication, 2020; Werkgroep Optimalisatie Federale Politie, 2013). This meant, amongst other measures, the discontinuing of units that were not incorporated in the National Safety Plan, including the Bureau of Art and Antiques. The Bureau's tasks were to be taken up by the Local Police. However, Local Police forces were unwilling to do so: they had limited constraints themselves and no art crime expertise (Belgian Senate, 2018a). This led to the Kafkaesque situation where internal police procedure guidelines still required local forces to report art crime cases to a unit which no longer existed (Belgian Senate, 2018b; personal communication, 2017).

The situation provoked responses both nationally and internationally. Concerned cultural organisations and citizens sounded the alarm, with Edouard Planche [2] describing Belgium as a "weak link" in European art crime policing (Belgian Senate, 2018a: p. 92; Le Soir, 2017; Maerevoet, 2016). This prompted the aforementioned reinstatement of a point of contact for art crime police within the Federal Police (Belgian Senate, 2018a). This 'reference officer', a former member of the Bureau for Art and Antiques, was tasked with providing other elements of the police with support through offering expertise, advice, referrals, or other forms of support when they dealt with an art crime. This should however not be considered a reinstatement of the unit itself, as it is a matter of record Belgium have no "coordinating department specifically tasked with fighting art theft and the illegal trade of cultural objects, which does exist in other countries such as Italy, France or the Netherlands" (Belgian Senate, 2018b, p. 23). Shortly after the reinstatement of a point of contact the situation made it to the political agenda. The Belgian Senate held hearings on art theft and art crime policing late 2017 (Belgian Senate, 2018a). The resultant Senate report contained 97 recommendations, including the establishment of cooperation agreements between police and cultural stakeholders and, perhaps most importantly, the full reinstatement of the Bureau (Belgian Senate, 2018b).

All Belgian political parties supported the report and its recommendations, save for the Flemish-nationalist New Flemish Alliance [3] (NV-A), at the time of writing the majority party in Flanders, currently the most populous and economically powerful of Belgium's federated regions. On the one hand, the party refrained from supporting the report for a lack of clear figures on art crime (Van Boxelaere, 2018). Finding statistics on art crime is indeed notoriously difficult, though the question can be asked whether such statistics can be generated without police investment (Brodie & Yates, 2019). A vicious cycle where states deprioritise art crime because there are no statistics on the subject as none are generated due to states deprioritising art crime lurks around the corner (Belgian Senate, 2018b). Political considerations also played a role. N-VA representatives considered some recommendations of the report an infringement against the federal balance of power (7sur7, 2018). Belgium has been through an often-contentious process of federalisation and the country's division of competences between the various regional and federal levels is complex and sensitive. The issue with regards to art crime policing is that while the detection and punishment of art theft and the illegal art trade are a federal competence, i.e., a Belgian state competence, the (protection of) cultural heritage is a competence of the federal states, e.g., Flanders or Wallonia (Belgian Senate, 2018b). The N-VA considered the recommendation to set up

[2]Then in charge of the programme for the fight against illicit traffic of cultural objects at the United Nations Educational, Scientific and Cultural Organisation (UNESCO).

[3]Nieuw-Vlaamse Alliantie.

interfederal cooperation agreements in the context of art crime to be an attempt to broaden the federal level's mandate at the expense of the regional authorities.

In the immediate years after the Senate report the status quo was left unchanged. The reference officer continued his work alone (Belgian Senate, 2018a; Le Soir, 2017). However, in February 2020, then-Minister for the Interior Pieter De Crem announced that the Bureau of Arts and Antiques was again operational with two members of staff. At the same time, he voiced the intention to hire additional personnel and update the database (Bové, 2020). When interviewed in November 2020, the reference officer confirmed that there were plans to hire an individual to work on the database (personal communication, 2020). In March 2021, senator Stephanie D'Hose asked a parliamentary question about the status of the unit. Annelies Verlinden, the newly sworn-in Minister for the Interior, replied that the unit had been strengthened further with one additional full-time employee, bringing its total personnel to three individuals (Belgian Senate, 2021). However, in e-mail correspondence, a member of the Belgian police contested this version of events, stating that although two individuals were assigned to support the reference officer, this was not the type of robust strengthening the Minister's reply implied (personal communication, 2021). Of these two, one was not a police officer, but a programmer who was hired to work exclusively on the ARTIST database.

COVID-19 scuppered initial plans to train this individual to be able to also carry out operational duties. The other addition was, according to the Belgian police member, a police officer with no art crime expertise who no longer had an immediate function within the police force, and who was thus free to be detached to services in need. However, this individual was imminently retiring, and moreover, so was the reference officer himself, on 31 December 2021.

On 20 January 2022, the retirement of the officer became public knowledge (Loore, 2022). When again asked about the matter, Minister Verlinden now stated that the directorates of the Federal Judicial Police would carry out highly specialised tasks such as art crime policing, though adding that the updating work on the ARTIST database was progressing. Nonetheless, an internal memo produced by the Belgian Directorate General of the Judicial Police accessed by Belgian journalists indicated that in the absence of new budgetary resources art crime would no longer be monitored centrally, the ARTIST database will no longer be fed, and that the relay of information from and to foreign police forces, Europol, and Interpol would no longer be guaranteed (Loore, 2022). This was thereafter corroborated by the now-retired reference officer, who said that foreign services and Interpol still contacted him for information instead (Lelong, 2022).

Predictably, public outcry followed (e.g., Biourge & Huysen, 2022; Blue Shield Belgium, 2022). And much like in the aftermath of the unit's closure in 2016, the outcry provoked a U-turn. In early February, Minister Verlinden stated she had requested the Commissioner General of the Belgian Federal Police to "evaluate" the decision to discontinue art crime support, while Belgian Finance Minister Vincent Van Peteghem stated "We will make sure that this decision is reversed" in the Belgian Chamber of Representatives, while acting for Minister Verlinden (Biourge & Huysen, 2022, para. 12; La Libre, 2022; Lelong, 2022). At the time of writing what the substance of that evaluation will be, and whether dedicated resources will again be devoted to the Belgian police's art crime efforts, is unclear. What is clear, however, is that the way in which policymakers have treated art crime policing in general and the reference officer in particular has not been edifying. The reference officer repeatedly warned about the implications of his retirement in the years running up to it, but little was seemingly done to prepare (Biourge & Huysen, 2022; De Standaard, 2017; Huybrechts, 2018).

4 The Belgian Art Crime Policing Network

The police's capacity to combat art crime has unquestionably been damaged. Per the Senate report, the single reference officer within the DJSOC was no longer able to:

- coordinate the fight against the theft and trafficking of art;
- provide operational support to police forces in the field;
- provide specialised training for inspectors;
- maintain the ARTIST database;
- keep the art sector up to date of art crime via the alerts system;
- keep statistics on art theft nor conduct trend analysis of art crime; or
- maintain an expertise network in which there is regular consultation with research centres and art historians (Belgian Senate, 2018b, pp. 25–26).

The Bureau for Art and Antiques indeed relied on a network within the art world, ranging from museum experts to insurance companies to gallerists (Belgian Senate, 2018a, 2018b). Gallerists and museums have aesthetic and art historical knowledge crucial for art crime investigations which police forces nonetheless typically lack, such as for example the ability to identify whether an object is likely looted and if so, from where. Art crime investigators are first and foremost trained to be good detectives, rather than art connoisseurs (Belgian Senate, 2018a; personal communication, 2020). In a similar vein, private actors are part of information networks the police might find more difficult to penetrate as an outsider. A Belgium-based art security consultant specialised in museum security stated that his firm "assists using our worldwide network [...] So the questions we receive [...] are often about whether we can put the police in touch with certain people" (personal communication, 2020). A Belgian art insurer with years of experience said much the same: "when there is a theft of object(s) by artists we know we have been called and asked whether we might have heard something or have any idea on what other insurers may be involved" (personal communication, 2021).

But many private actors are more than just information sources. They are policing actors in their own right. The Belgian art insurer talked extensively about the client compliance checks they run, which act as a "filter", and also mentioned their involvement in due diligence trainings for other organisations (personal communication, 2021). The art security consultant assisted museums in "various areas, including architectural, organisational, electronic, and reporting facets [...] We identify possible risks and risk classifications and start discussions with the museum staff [to develop security solutions]" (personal communication, 2020). They moreover collaborated with the police when providing security knowhow for museums staging blockbuster exhibitions. Sometimes private actors are former police officers, as was the case for a Belgium-based private consultant, who was formerly a police officer working at the Bureau for Art and Antiques. This consultant utilised their previous police experience to "advise private and corporate clients on all matters regarding art purchase and securitisation" (personal communication, 2020). There are also organisations like the Art Loss Register and Artive, which provide stolen arts databases for users to check their items against as well as consultancy services. Finally, art market participants are expected to perform due diligence on their purchases, which adds another layer against art crime (Gommans, 2016). All of these actors can thus institute processes and activities contributing to the fight against art crime, which is to say policing activities.

As such, Belgian art crime policing has been plural policing for decades. The police have not been the sole actor policing art crime. And they have recognised as much. By developing this network with private actors, the police implicitly acknowledged private actors' expertise in the context of art crime policing and the reality the police cannot deal with the complex and specialised issue of art crime alone. This "expertise network" (Belgian Senate, 2018b, pp. 25–26) is thus a testament to plural policing, or as the security consultant put it: "we have certain insights the police do not [. . .] because of the way they are trained" (personal communication, 2020). While the upkeep of this network was severely affected by the closure of the unit, the reference officer still endeavoured to maintain it as much as possible (Belgian Senate, 2018a; personal communication, 2017). An important thing to note when using the word 'network' here is that in most cases these relationships between police and private sector were informal and ad hoc rather than formal and continuous. Plural policing does not necessarily imply intense, consistent networks within formalised frameworks.

There were some exceptions, however. Of particular note is the unit's relationship with the *Centrum voor Religieuze Kunst en Cultuur* (Centre for Religious Art and Culture, CRKC). This Centre was an expertise hub for religious heritage, founded by the Flemish diocese in 1997 but later officially recognised and partially subsidised by the Flemish government (Crkc.be, 2018). It was thus a partly public, partly private hybrid organisation. Since its foundation, the CRKC registered thefts from churches and other religious sites. In 2008, a module was added to the Centre's website that allowed users to directly notify the Bureau of Art and Antiques of thefts via a virtual form. This measure led to a large increase of registered cases: in 2009 nine thefts of thirty-six pieces were registered, whereas previously the annual maximum of registered thefts had been three (Belgian Senate, 2018a). This setup was thus a formalised, direct channel of communication between the unit and an external, non-police entity, together improving the policing of art crime (Belgian Senate, 2018a, 2018b). After the unit's closure, the CRKC and its functions were succeeded by the new religious heritage expertise centre PARCUM, which also runs a museum in Leuven, Belgium, with its own collection of art and religious heritage

(PARCUM, 2021). The reference officer maintained a good relationship with PARCUM's experts (personal communication, 2020; 2021).

Nevertheless, the closure of the unit had a negative effect on the upkeep of this network (Belgian Senate, 2018a). The outreach officer for PARCUM confirmed the police's engagement has been complicated by lack of resources (personal communication, 2021). The Belgian art insurer stated that they "have very good contacts with the unit, albeit a little less now than in the past" (personal communication, 2021). Previously, the insurer had been part of a regular meeting with "an expert, a restorer, and a policeman [of the unit]", but they indicated these monthly meetings ended after the closure of the unit (personal communication, 2021). The Belgian art security consultant indicated they still "have very good contacts with the [reference officer]", albeit "less now than in the past, because there are simply far fewer people working [on art crime within the police]" (personal communication, 2020). The private consultant who previously worked for the unit went as far as stating that "the police neglect the subject [of art crime] [. . .] they leave a gap" (personal communication, 2020). This comment brings us to fiscal constraint theory. To reiterate, this theory suggests that where policing gaps emerge, private policing flourishes, either because these gaps drive private enterprise to meet policing demand, or because it prompts states to draw in private expertise (Kerr, 2013). The question is whether the period of deprioritisation and eventual non-operation of the Bureau of Art and Antiques led private actors to fill the policing gap and/or the state to more explicitly look towards private policing involvement to protect cultural heritage. The answer to that question is even more relevant at the time of writing, when there is ostensibly no police officer dedicated to art crime.

5 Bridging Gaps

It is difficult to ascertain whether there have been more private policing initiatives since the Bureau of Art and Antiques was closed. The International Platform for Art Research and Conservation (IPARC), located near Leuven and established since 2008 has developed activities across the art spectrum, ranging from storage to conservation to research (IPARC, 2021). IPARC indicated to this researcher an interest in deploying their tools towards the prevention of art crime. It is also notable multiple Belgium-based private security firms now advertise tailored art securitisation on their websites. For example, SERIS developed a tailored security system for the soon to reopen Museum of Fine Arts in Antwerp (SERIS, 2021). Yet none of the interviewees considered themselves to be filling a policing gap. Many echoed the sentiment the unit's closure had opened a policing gap, but they considered themselves unable to fill that gap, because the police have unique investigatory and rule-enforcement capabilities the private sector does not. The private security consultant stated that "In the private sector, we [. . .] make risk analyses, but we can only do limited police work, such as identifying trends in terrorism and how art crime is organising itself" (personal communication, 2020). The private investigator emphasised the fundamental difference their and the police's toolkits, and so did both art insurers interviewed. All interviewees indicated a full reinstatement of the unit was desirable.

On the policy level, there have been some moves towards private involvement to bridge the policing gap. The Tommelein-Taelman proposal mentions a request by the Justice and Home Affairs Council (made up of justice and home affairs ministers from all the European Union member states) to the European Commission to "ensure that partnerships and greater cooperation are established between the private and public parties involved" (Belgian Senate, 2010, p. 4). The proposal approached the art trade as a partner in preventing thefts: the theory was that given access to an official stolen arts database the trade could check objects on the market for theft, disincentivising thefts overall (Belgian Senate, 2010). The Belgian Senate report specifically recommends cooperation with the insurance sector regarding an inventory of stolen objects, and generally advises strengthening private actors' own prevention programmes (Belgian Senate, 2018b, recommendations 73 and 96). It also recommends to actively keep centres of expertise involved with the police's art crime policing efforts, as well as the set-up of "public-private partnerships" (Belgian Senate, 2018b: pp. 33, 41–42, recommendations 15, 24, 46, and 71). There is thus a demonstrable subtext to these policy documents that private involvement is considered a potential boon to art crime policing in Belgium. More broadly, the new *Vision for the Police 2025* policy guidelines intend to shift the police's approach to a more networking-oriented collaborative approach (Allaerts et al., 2014). All of this aligns with fiscal constraint theory.

However, none of the interviewees indicated that the unit and reference officer became more inclined to work with private entities as their resources declined. The security expert emphasised the limitations of the law, stating

> when there is a real suspicion [of criminal activity], they [the police] do not give any information about any existing dossiers [. . .] The unit is very formal in its communication when dealing with thefts". He added that "more could be done [. . .] if the police were supported better [. . .] If the police could take us into their confidence a bit more, we could do more together, where it is legally possible (personal communication, 2020).

A second art insurer stated they have:

> an excellent working relationship with the police [. . .] nurtured over a period of many years [. . .] before you can obtain information from the police, you need to gain their trust (personal communication, 2020; 2021).

The former-unit-member-now-private-consultant was the most negative in their assessment of the situation: the relationship between police and private was in their opinion "very difficult". In their opinion, the Belgian police "is not ready for private policing" (personal communication, 2020).

The reference officer did not deny their reservations towards the private sector: "the Belgian police has a totally different view and culture than for example in the Netherlands and in England [. . .] we are a little bit more suspicious of partnerships with the private sector [. . .] I am careful" (personal communication, 2020). Previous negative encounters with private entities, also experienced by police colleagues abroad, had further fostered this suspicion (personal communication, 2017). The Belgian authorities are not likely to go as far as the London Metropolitan Police's Art and Antiques squad's ArtBeat programme, in which art professionals were trained as Special Constables to support the police (Block, 2014; Kerr, 2016). This however did not mean the reference officer excluded the possibility or even likelihood of more collaboration in the future (personal communication, 2020). On the other hand, the private side's trust was also damaged, by the police intervention at the 2020 edition of the Brussels Antiques and Fine Arts (BRAFA) fair, where agents of the Belgian customs office, the Federal Public Service for Economy, and Interpol publicly seized thirty-four artefacts (Cascone, 2020; Pryor, 2020). The intervention caused quite a stir. Thus, although policymakers have taken an interest in public-private engagement, legal factors, police culture, and trust issues complicate harmonious public-private interaction.

6 The Future of Art Crime Policing in Belgium and Beyond

In sum, art crime policing in Belgium is plural policing—as is art crime policing generally—and fiscal constraint has had a significant impact on its dynamics. It is nonetheless clear that other factors beyond fiscal constraint are at play, which brings to mind Johnston's (1999) assertion that private policing research needs to integrate a multi-factor approach that looks for connections with larger societal trends. What is also clear, is that art crime does need genuine police engagement, and that dedicated art crime police units need stable backing. Belgian policymakers' flip-flopping on art crime-priority has severely disrupted art crime policing in Belgium, opening up considerable policing gaps. The initial closure and then semi-revival of the unit in the form of the reference officer, the reframing of what was a closure as a downsizing of the unit, the calls for engagement with the private sector without fully engaging with the situation on the ground, the failure to act more quickly on the Senate report's recommendations, and the most recent about-facing in the wake of the reference officer's retirement have all been unedifying, unhelpful episodes.

The Belgian case shows that trust between the members of any putative public-private partnership is key, and that attitudes take time to evolve, complicating swift pivots to private engagement. Mere complementarity of skills itself will not be enough to build lasting relationships to the benefit of the fight against art crime. That Belgium's approach is noticeably different to, for example, counterparts in the Netherlands and the United Kingdom, implies their distinctive police cultures also impact specialised policing areas such as art crime. The Dutch unit was also closed between 2001 and 2009 (Oosterman, 2019), and a follow-up report was published as well, also recommending private outreach (Willems-Hirsch, 2012), but in the Netherlands the now reinstated unit *is* open to private interaction. Further establishing precisely why the experiences of the Netherlands and Belgium have diverged and what is precisely necessary for successful private outreach is key for policymakers in the field thinking about police-private cooperation in art crime policing. This invites further research into the complex dynamics of art crime policing, whether it be those shaping the relationship between art crime police units and the private sector, or those shaping policymaking towards art crime (see, on the latter point, Kerr, 2020). Additionally, the Belgian case shows crime policing builds upon information exchange, making it an example of broader shifts to intelligence-led policing as well as plural policing. Police and private databases could play an important role in this respect.

This chapter's charting of the Bureau of Art and Antiques' history and the interviews it is based on paint a relatively grim picture of art crime policing in Belgium. This is not for a lack of effort on the part of the reference officer or his colleagues and predecessors, and nor does it seem any actor mentioned in this chapter is necessarily averse to a well-functioning, active police engagement. This chapter, as a whole, is a statement in favour of a true and full reinstatement of the Bureau of Art and Antiques of the Belgian Federal Police, confident and equipped to engage with external partners. Re-establishing the unit however requires political will, and thought-through decision-making, with attention paid to the specific dynamics of Belgian politics and art crime policing. Yet, as the quote attributed to Dutch philosopher Erasmus, who spent many years in what is now Belgium, goes: *"to prevent is better than to cure"*.

References

Allaerts, D., Barbier, A., Bruggeman, W., Crispel, M., De Witte, L., Easton, M., Lemaître, A., Loyens, K., Maesschalck, J., Massei, A., Maurer, T., Ponsaers, P., Simonis, M., Van Den Broeck, M., Van Ryckeghem, D., & Wanderstein, H. (2014). *Een visie voor de politie in 2025*. Retrieved March 11, 2022, from https://www.law.kuleuven.be/linc/studiedagen/visiepolitie.pdf/

Bailey, M. (2017, August 16). Scotland Yard's Art and Antiques Unit heading for closure. *The Art Newspaper*. Retrieved August 31, 2022, from http://theartnewspaper.com/news/scotland-yards-art-and-antiques-unit-heading-for-closure

Belgian Senate (2010). Voorstel van Resolutie ter Oprichting van een Nationale Publiek Toegankelijke Databank voor Gestolen Kunst en Antiek van de heer Bart Tommelein en mevrouw Martine Taelman; *Stuk* 5–29. Retrieved March 11, 2022, from https://www.senate.be/www/?MIval=/publications/viewPub&TID=83888270&LANG=nl

Belgian Senate. (2011). Wetsvoorstel tot Aanvulling van het Strafwetboek wat de Diefstal van Kunst- en Cultuurgoederen Betreft ingediend door de heren Ludo Sannen en Bert Anciaux. Retrieved March 11, 2022, from https://www.senate.be/www/webdriver?MitabObj=pdf&MicolObj=pdf&MinamObj=pdfid&MitypeObj=application/pdf&MivalObj=83887360

Belgian Senate. (2018a). *Verslagrapport Bestrijding van Kunstroof*. Belgian Senate. Retrieved March 11, 2022, from http://www.senate.be/informatieverslagen/6-357/Senaat_verslag_kunstroof-2018.pdf

Belgian Senate. (2018b). *Informatieverslag betreffende de Optimalisering van de Samenwerking tussen de Federale Overheid en de Deelstaten inzake de Bestrijding van Kunstroof*. Belgian Senate. Retrieved March 11, 2022, from https://www.senate.be/www/webdriver?MitabObj=pdf&MicolObj=pdf&MinamObj=pdfid&MitypeObj=application/pdf&MIvalObj=100663917

Belgian Senate. (2021). Schriftelijke vraag nr. 7-1033. Retrieved March 11, 2022, from https://www.senate.be/www/?MIval=/Vragen/SchriftelijkeVraag&LEG=7&NR=1033&LANG=nl

Biourge, C., & Huysen, I. (2022). Faute de moyens, la lutte contre le trafic d'œuvres d'art au sein de la police fédérale est en suspens. *RTBF.be*. Retrieved March 11, 2022, from https://www.rtbf.be/article/faute-de-moyens-la-lutte-contre-le-trafic-doeuvres-dart-au-sein-de-la-police-federale-est-en-suspens-un-open-bar-pour-les-trafiquants-10925235

Block, L. (2014). Policing Art Crime in the European Union. In D. Chappell & S. Hufnagel (Eds.), *Contemporary perspectives on the detection, investigation and prosecution of art crime: Australasian, European and North American Perspectives* (pp. 187–205). Routledge.

Blue Shield Belgium. (2022, January 31). Open brief aan de Minister van Binnenlandse Zaken Annelies Verlinden. Retrieved August 31, 2022, from https://blueshieldbelgium.be/nl/open-brief-aan-de-minister-van-binnenlandse-zaken-annelies-verlinden/

Bové, L. (2020, February 26). Politie maakt geautomatiseerde databank over kunstdiefstallen. *De Tijd*. Retrieved March 11, 2022, from https://www.tijd.be/politiek-economie/belgie/algemeen/politie-maakt-geautomatiseerde-databank-over-kunstdiefstallen/10210708.html

Brodie, N., & Yates, D. (2019). *Illicit trade in cultural goods in Europe: Characteristics, criminal justice responses and an analysis of the applicability of technologies in the combat against the trade: final report*. Publications Office of the European Union.

Button, M. (2019). *Private policing* (2nd ed.). Routledge.

Button, M. (2020). The "New" private security industry, the private policing of cyberspace and the regulatory questions. *Journal of Contemporary Criminal Justice, 36*(1), 39–55.

Cascone, S. (2020). After authorities raided a Brussels antiquities fair, some dealers are calling the agents' widespread confiscations "Theft". *Artnet News*. Retrieved March 11, 2022, from https://news.artnet.com/market/antiquities-seized-brafa-art-fair-1791129

Chesters, L. (2017, December 14). Scotland Yard Art and Antiques Unit re-formed. *Evening Standard*. Retrieved August 31, 2022, from https://www.standard.co.uk/news/london/scotland-yard-art-and-antiques-unit-reformeda3719641.html

Crawford, A. (2014). The police, policing and the future of the 'Extended Policing Family'. In J. M. Brown (Ed.), *The future of policing: Papers prepared for the stevens independent commission into the future of policing in England and wales* (pp. 173–190). Routledge.

CRKC. (2018). *The Centre for Religious Art and Culture*. Retrieved March 11, 2022, from https://web.archive.org/web/20180917174734/http:/crkc.be/missie-en-opdracht

Dendooven, L. (2016, April 12). La cellule Art de la police fédérale supprimée, une aubaine pour les terroristes?. *RTBF Info*. Retrieved March 11, 2022, from https://www.rtbf.be/info/belgique/detail_la-cellule-art-de-la-police-ferale-supprimee-une-aubaine-pour-les-terroristes?id=9266654

Devroe, E., & Ponsaers, P. (2013). Reforming the Belgian police system between central and local. In N. R. Fyfe, J. Terpstra, & P. Tops (Eds.), *Centralizing forces? Comparative perspectives on contemporary police reform in Northern and Western Europe* (pp. 77–98). Eleven International Publishing.

Garland, D. (1996). The limits of the sovereign state—strategies of crime control in contemporary society. *British Journal of Criminology, 36*(4), 445–471.

Gommans, L. (2016). Art crime law. In A. Tompkins (Ed.), *Art crime and its prevention* (pp. 72–80). Lund Humphries.

Huybrechts, J. (2018). *Merendeel van de kunstdiefstallen blijft onopgelost*. Vrtnws.be. Retrieved March 11, 2022, from https://www.vrt.be/vrtnws/nl/2018/04/26/merendeel-kunstdiefstallen-blijft-onopgelost/

Interpol. (2016). Protecting Cultural Heritage; an Imperative for Humanity. Retrieved March 11, 2022

Interpol. (2017). *Creating a National Cultural Heritage Unit*. Retrieved March 11, 2022, from https://www.interpol.int/News-and-media/Publications2/Leaflets-and-brochures/Creating-a-National-Cultural-Heritage-Unit

IPARC. (2021). *IPARC: Conservatie & restauratie voor musea, verzamelaars, kerkfabrieken en kunstliefhebbers*. Retrieved March 11, 2022, from https://www.iparc.eu/en/home/

Johnston, L. (1992). *The rebirth of private policing*. Taylor & Francis US.

Johnston, L. (1999). Private policing in context. *European Journal on Criminal Policy and Research, 7*(2), 175–196.

Jones, T., & Newburn, T. (1998a). The sociology of policing. In *Private security and public policing* (pp. 1–27). Clarendon Press.

Jones, T., & Newburn, T. (1998b). The growth of private security. In *Private security and public policing* (pp. 95–117). Clarendon Press.

Kerr, J. (2013). *The securitization and policing of art theft in London* [Unpublished doctoral dissertation]. City University of London

Kerr, J. (2016). The role of the police in the co-production of art security in London. In N. Charney (Ed.), *Art crime: Terrorists, tomb raiders, forgers and thieves* (pp. 105–117). Palgrave Macmillan.

Kerr, J. (2020). The state of heritage and cultural property policing in England & Wales, France and Italy. *European Journal of Criminology, 17*(4), 441–460.

Kunstdiefstallen in België blijven onopgelost. (2017). De Standaard. Retrieved March 11, 2022.

Le gouvernement veut faire annuler le démantèlement de la cellule trafic art et antiquités. (2022). *La Libre*. Retrieved March 11, 2022, from https://www.lalibre.be/belgique/judiciaire/2022/02/03/le-gouvernement-veut-faire-annuler-le-demantelement-de-la-cellule-trafic-art-et-antiquites-XOWIPSMOVZBHJNMAJCNOWALGVU/

Le trafic d'œuvres d'art sème le trouble au Sénat. (2018). *7sur7.be*. Retrieved March 11, 2022, https://www.7sur7.be/belgique/le-trafic-d-oeuvres-d-art-seme-le-trouble-au-senat~a9c0b39f/

Lelong, J. (2022). *Roofkunst verkopen kun je voortaan best in België: Centrale dienst kunstcriminaliteit wordt opgedoekt*. De Morgen.

Livingstone, K., & Hart, J. (2003). The wrong arm of the law? Public images of private security. *Policing and Society, 13*(2), 159–170.

Loore, F. (2022). *Trafic d'art et d'antiquités: la police judiciaire fédérale dépose les*. Paris Match.

Maerevoet, E. (2016, May 2). Wegvallen van Kunstcel catastrofe voor ons land. *vrtnws.be*. Retrieved March 11, 2022, from https://www.vrt.be/vrtnws/nl/2016/05/02/_wegvallen_van_kunstcelcatastrofevooronsland-1-2645331/

Museumroof: Politie heeft nog geen toegang tot databank gestolen kunst. (2013, July 18). *bruzz.be*. Retrieved March 11, 2022, from https://www.bruzz.be/samenleving/museumroof-politie-heeft-nog-geen-toegang-tot-databank-gestolen-kunst-2013-07-18

Oosterman, N. (2019). Regional overviews of the policing of art crime in the European Union. In S. Hufnagel & D. Chappell (Eds.), *The Palgrave handbook on art crime* (pp. 213–237). Springer.

PARCUM. (2021). About. Retrieved March 11, 2022, https://www.parcum.be/nl/over-parcum

Pryor, R. (2020, March 2). Aggressive seizures by police at Brafa leave dealers feeling 'assaulted'. *The Art Newspaper*. Retrieved August 31, 2022, from http://www.theartnewspaper.com/news/dealers-felt-assaulted-by-seizures-at-brafa

Reiner, R. (2010). *The politics of the police*. Oxford University Press.

SERIS (2021, March 1). *Beveiliging van het Koninklijk Museum voor Schone Kunsten Antwerpen*. Retrieved March 11, 2022, from https://seris.be/nl/beveiliging-van-het-koninklijk-museum-voor-schone-kunsten-antwerpen

Shearing, C. D., & Stenning, P. C. (1987). Reframing policing. In C. D. Shearing & P. C. Stenning (Eds.), *Private policing*. Sage Publications.

Trafic d'Oeuvres d'art: La Belgique est trop Laxiste. (2017, July 13). *Le Soir*. Retrieved August 31, 2022, from https://www.lesoir.be/104396/article/2017-07-13/trafic-doeuvres-dart-la-belgique-est-trop-laxiste

Van Boxelaere, M. (2018, July 13). Roofkunst versjacheren doe je best in België (II). *Apache*. Retrieved March 11, 2022, from https://www.apache.be/gastbijdragen/2018/07/13/roofkunst-versjacheren-doe-je-best-in-belgie-ii/
Van De Velden, W. (2017, November 6). *Ophelderingsgraad Kunstdiefstallen Tot 0 Procent Gedaald*. De Tijd. Retrieved March 11, 2022, from https://www.tijd.be/politiek-economie/belgie/algemeen/ophelderingsgraad-kunstdiefstallen-tot-0-procent-gedaald/9950372.html
Werkgroep Optimalisatie Federale Politie. (2013). *Rapport Optimalisatie Federale Politie*. Retrieved March 11, 2022, from https://images.sypol.be/201351392744541_130121-rapport-officiel-vernl-optimalisatie-federale-politie—def-2001-15-30.pdf
Willems-Hirsch, E. (2012). *Kunst- en antiek- gerelateerde -criminaliteit: Verslag van een onderzoek voor het Nationaal dreigingsbeeld 2012*. Retrieved March 11, 2022, from https://www.politie.nl/binaries/content/assets/politie/onderwerpen/nationaal-dreigingsbeeld/2012/ndb-kunst-en-antiek.pdf

Richard Van Herzeele holds a master's degree in Law from the Catholic University of Leuven (Cum Laude), during which he enrolled in the optional course art and cultural property law ("Kunst- & cultureel-erfgoedrecht"), as well as a master degree in Art Business (Distinction with the Director's Recommendation) from Sotheby's Institute of Art London, for which he wrote a thesis comparing art crime policing in Belgium, Italy, and the UK. After the completion of his studies at Sotheby's Institute, he interned at various art galleries in Belgium, before commencing a PhD study on the topic of public-private art crime policing at Queen Mary University in September 2018. He has presented at the 2018 Transatlantic Cultural Property Crime Symposium that took place at Queen Mary University, has taught on art business and art crime related subjects at Sotheby's Institute as a guest lecturer for their master in Art Business, master in Art Logistics, and semester programmes, and was also a teaching assistant for the criminal law course at Queen Mary University London.

Fossil Trafficking, Fraud, and Fakery

Nussaïbah B. Raja and Emma M. Dunne

Abstract The fascination with ancient flora and fauna is a centuries-old phenomenon and is one of the main drivers of fossil crimes. Fossils have been sought by the rich and famous since the advent of colonialism, propelling development in the field of palaeontology but also in how fossils make their way through various, sometimes illegal, corridors to end up in museums and collections across the world. As demand for fossils increased in the nineteenth century, so did commercial avenues for these objects that were being sold not only to private individuals but also to scientific institutions. The most complete and visually impressive fossils in terms of size or uniqueness determine the market value of these fossils with some selling for millions of United States dollars. This has also led to the tampering or forging of fossils by many dealers in an attempt to inflate prices. While fossil crimes have been prevalent for centuries, the legal frameworks within which these crimes can be controlled or stopped are regularly challenged or even circumvented not only due to the lack of enforcements of these regulations but also due to how paleontological objects are classified in the first place as well as other legal loopholes.

1 Introduction

Fossils, the remains of ancient and extinct organisms preserved in rock, are the basic units of palaeontology, and represent our only direct evidence for the evolution and past biodiversity of life on Earth. Studies of fossils allow ancient environments to be reconstructed and reveal how species responded to past climate change, which is particularly pertinent in the face of the ongoing global climate crisis. But fossils today are not only important scientific objects; they are also used in art, construction, and for recreation purposes (Sookias, 2011). Fossils have had cultural importance since Palaeolithic times (Henriques & Pena dos Reis, 2015; Mayor, 2005) in the

N. B. Raja (✉) · E. M. Dunne
GeoZentrum Nordbayern, Department of Geography and Geosciences, Friedrich-Alexander University, Erlangen, Germany
e-mail: nussaibah.raja.schoob@fau.de; emma.dunne@fau.de

N. Oosterman, D. Yates (eds.), *Art Crime in Context*, Studies in Art, Heritage, Law and the Market 6, https://doi.org/10.1007/978-3-031-14084-6_5

form of jewellery, tools, and offerings (Dembard & Néraudeau, 2001; Peresani et al., 2013). Extinct animals also appear in the traditions of several Native American tribes which tell tales of giant creatures that once roamed the Earth (Mayor, 2005). Nowadays, fossils have become highly prized among the rich and privileged, who spend a considerable amount of money in order to own these items. This shows how the value of fossils is multifaceted and inherently depends on the body appraising its value (de Lima & de Souza Carvalho, 2020) Regardless of how they are perceived, the increasing market demand for fossil specimens over decades and centuries has also contributed to increasing theft, smuggling, and falsification of these objects (Di Maggio, 2018). The parallels between fossil and art crime are indisputable. In this chapter, we show how fossils, similar to art and other cultural objects, have come to represent a collectible and expensive good, closely associated with money, class, reputation, and power since the early days of European colonialism. We then present case studies on how fossils are viewed instead by the palaeontological community and society at large, how their perceived value has led to legal and ethical transgressions. We also summarise the legal frameworks that concern fossils and how they are disputed and used as a justification for those who choose to operate outside the law.

2 Colonial Looted Fossils

Developments in the field of palaeontology are closely linked with European colonialism, whose legacies persist to this day (Cisneros et al., 2022; Raja et al., 2022). Similar to several colonial looted artefacts such as the Benin Bronzes or the Parthenon (Elgin) Marbles, fossils were collected from around the world and transported to the colonial state to fill the *Wunderkammer*, the 'cabinet of curiosities'', which stood as a sign of social status among the elite in the mid-sixteenth century (Adas, 1998; de Lima & de Souza Carvalho, 2020). These cabinets would later be transformed into museums to allow public access and scientific enquiry (for some objects).

The story of how the famous sauropod dinosaur, *Giraffatitan brancai,* (Fig. 1) ended up as the centrepiece of the Museum für Naturkunde (MfN) in Berlin is one of colonialism and nationalism with a clear political agenda (Maier, 2003; Stoecker, 2019). In the early 1900s residents living near the Tendaguru Formation of German East Africa, now part of present-day Tanzania, contributed to its 'discovery'. Local workers at a mining company brought the large, exposed bones to the attention of a German engineer and a scientific expedition by German palaeontologists followed. This was funded mostly by the German Empire's upper class and nobility who firmly believed in the campaign, which comprised terms such as "rescue" and "national honour" (Maier, 2003). The newly united Germany at the time was known for its achievements ranging from music and philosophy, to industry, technology, and military breakthroughs, but not in the field of natural history. The United States on the other hand was making considerable progress in the palaeontological enterprise,

Fig. 1 The Giraffatitan brancai on display at the Museum für Naturkunde, Berlin. Photo by Shadowgate from Novara, ITALY, CC BY 2.0, via Wikimedia Commons

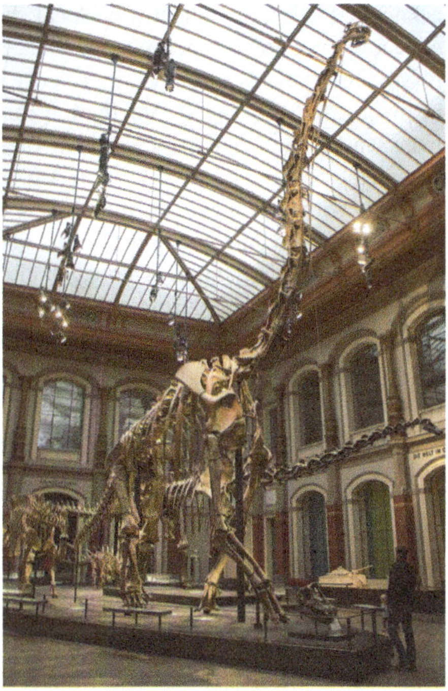

and was uncovering extraordinary specimens, including *Diplodocus carnegii*, nicknamed Dippy, recovered during an expedition funded by the industrialist and philanthropist Andrew Carnegie [1] and then believed to be the largest terrestrial animal to have ever lived (Maier, 2003; Nieuwland, 2010; Nieuwland, 2019). It was therefore necessary for Germany to demonstrate that it was equally capable of possessing such resources (Maier, 2003).

In the space of approximately four years, more than 200 tonnes of fossils made their way from Tanzania to Germany, including the bones of the *G. brancai* that usurped Dippy's record and became the tallest mounted skeleton assemblage in the world. [2] Because of the remote location and rough conditions of the Tendaguru site, more than 500 local workers were enlisted to help with the excavation and transport of these fossils—this contribution along with the colonial aspect of this expedition had until recently been completely written out of the history of these fossils in favour of lauding the achievements of the museum's former staff that contributed to it being known as a 'world class' institution. To this day, *G. brancai* remains central to the identity of the MfN (Fig. 1; Stoecker, 2019). These extractive practices are still observed today in the form of 'parachute science', where researchers, generally from higher income countries, conduct research in lower income countries without any

[1] Hence why Dippy's species name honours him.

[2] After it was remounted in 2007, it was recorded as being the tallest dinosaur skeleton mounted in the world in the Guinness Book of Records.

acknowledged involvement from local scientists, creating a global skew in knowledge accumulation (Cisneros et al., 2022; Stefanoudis et al., 2021). When it comes to fossils, the impacts of parachute science on many countries is exacerbated by the availability of thriving commercial avenues for their fossils (Raja et al., 2022). In many cases, the legal frameworks of these source countries are often devalued or completely dismissed (See section "At odds with legal classifications"), drawing parallels with how these specimens were acquired during the colonial era.

G. brancai is only one of numerous specimens that were collected under colonial propaganda and plunder. The legal circumstances under which natural history objects were acquired during colonial times remain questionable. In the case of the *G. brancai*, the Tendaguru hills were 'unclaimed land' absorbed by the German Empire and then declared to be 'crown land' (Stoecker, 2019). As this was in accordance with German law at the time, the procurement of this specimen is not considered to have been stolen, but rather was the 'translocation' of German property from Tendaguru to Berlin. However, circumstances such as these do not address issues of legalities from the perspective of the source country or that of the local people. It is known that the locals were suspicious of the Germans' activities and that they considered the bones to be their assets or wealth, although it is unclear whether these narratives remain in modern-day Tendaguru (Stoecker, 2019). Requests for the restitution of Tanzanian fossils and financial support for establishing adequate local infrastructure to care for them were first made in the 1980s and repeated in the late 2000s, but in 2018 the Tanzanian government announced that the logistics of returning the fossils were "complicated" and that instead, plans for a museum to raise the profile of the Tendaguru village through tourism and promote the local palaeontological heritage were underway (Qorro, 2018). The 2021 Tanzanian-German joint expedition to Tendaguru, funded by the German Foreign Office, finally took place after several delays due to the Covid-19 pandemic (Knauer, 2021).

Given the significance of the *G. brancai* to the field of natural history in Germany, the skeleton assemblage is now considered to be part of Germany's cultural assets and has been protected under the Act to Protect Cultural Property (*Kulturgutschutzgesetz*) since 2016 (Stoecker, 2019).

3 Commercialisation of Fossils in the 19th Century

In the nineteenth century, as more museums were being established, the demand for new fossil objects or material also increased. In England, the commercial market for fossils was developing rapidly, with specialised artisan fossil collectors regularly supplying museums with new fossils. Although most fossils were sold for a modest sum, some finds could prove to be lucrative, such as that of an almost complete

Archaeopteryx, the first 'missing link' [3] identified between dinosaurs and modern birds, which was sold to the Natural History Museum in London in the early 1860s for £700 GBP (equivalent to ~£85,000 GBP in 2021). The field was also expanding considerably across the Atlantic in the United States in the later half of the nineteenth century coinciding with the rise of American capitalism globally (Rieppel, 2015). In 1877, three major quarries in Wyoming were discovered to contain dinosaur fossils and were put up for sale, leading to a radical shift in the economic status of American dinosaurs and an emerging market for them. Demand for fossils, especially dinosaurs, was also being driven by a feud, dubbed the 'Bone Wars', between two notable palaeontologists at the time, Othniel Charles Marsh and Edward Drinker Cope. In an attempt to outcompete each other in uncovering new species and publishing scientific papers, they relied on anyone who could supply information regarding potential finds or valuable fossil specimens. Both men were wealthy and spent a considerable amount of their fortunes acquiring fossils: Cope is said to have spent $100,000 USD by 1888 (almost $3 million USD in 2021), and Marsh had spent twice the amount between 1868 and 1882 (Cope, 1888; Rieppel, 2015; Schuchtert & LeVene, 1940). The steady supply of fossils from the American West and the demand for them by many wealthy palaeontologists presented the perfect conditions for white settlers who were increasingly moving westwards to turn their attention and energy towards digging dinosaur bones for profit (Bradley, 2014).

The decades that followed the 1877 dinosaur discoveries marked a major change in the field of natural history, with capitalists and philanthropists, including Andrew Carnegie, investing in the founding of natural history museums and other cultural institutions, that generated social capital for these individuals just like they did for the elite class in Europe. This also led to fossil hunting—a line of work that persists today—becoming a more established and recognised profession, driven by emerging natural history museums supported by rich patrons who could afford to buy specimens for their exhibits. Fraud and deception, which had the potential to compromise the knowledge that was being produced from these specimens, were also prevalent, as they are to this day.

4 Demand for Fossils Drives Smuggling

Just like fossils have adorned the cabinets of the elite during colonial times, some fossil specimens, especially dinosaurs, have now become a symbol of social status among the rich and famous, who collect or invest in fossils like they would a piece of

[3] A non-scientific term used for referring to organisms that act as a bridge between two different high-level taxonomic groups, e.g., apes and humans, or dinosaurs or birds. The Archaeopteryx with its preserved feathers, fan-shaped but long and bony tail, and sharp teeth have features similar to both reptiles and birds.

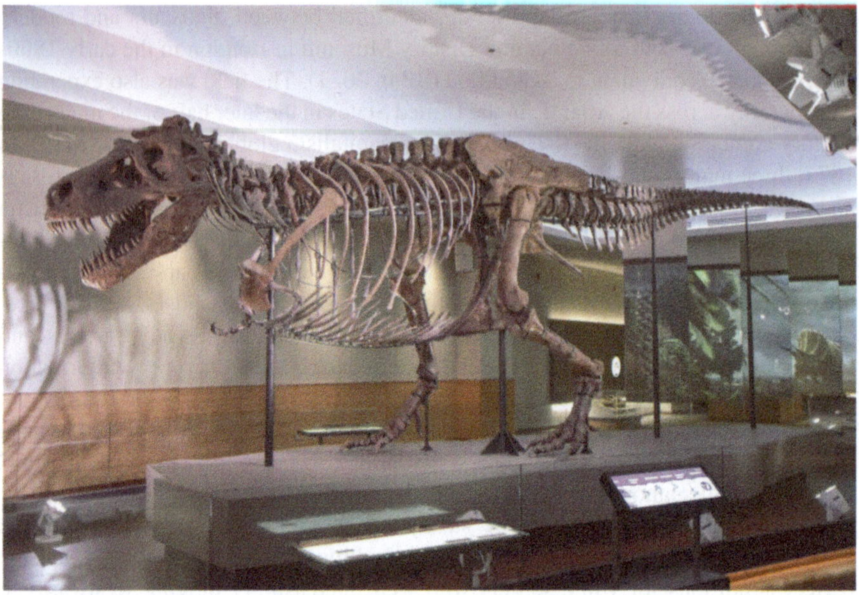

Fig. 2 SUE, the *Tyrannosaurus Rex*, on the display at the Field Museum of Natural History in Chicago, Illinois. Photo by Evolutionnumber9, CC BY-SA 4.0, via Wikimedia Commons

art (Gold, 2019; Reynolds, 2018). The most common market countries for fossils are the United States, the United Kingdom, France, and Germany. The success of the *Jurassic Park* film franchise put palaeontology firmly on the map by inspiring a new generation of palaeontologists and increasing the public's interest in fossil collecting (Sakurai, 1994; Webster, 2009). After the first film was released in 1993, fossil poaching on federal land in the United States increased (Sakurai, 1994), but at the time the United States lacked specific legislation to protect palaeontological material, except for the 1906 Antiquities Act, which is most applicable to archaeological material (Jones, 2019). One of the cases where the 1906 Antiquities Act was applied involved 'SUE', one of the world's largest, most complete, and best-preserved *Tyrannosaurus rex* specimens to have ever been found (Fig. 2).

SUE was found in South Dakota on the ranch land of Maurice Williams and sold in 1990 for $5,000 USD (equivalent to ~$10,000 USD in 2021) to the Black Hills Institute of Geological Research (BHI), a private company that deals with commercial collecting, preparation, and sale of fossils. In 1992, the Federal Bureau of Investigation (FBI) raided the BHI to seize SUE, citing the 1906 Antiquities Act, which stipulates that the dinosaur had been found on federal land and as such was federal property. Williams was a member of the Cheyenne River Sioux Tribe, and his land was part of the Cheyenne River Indian Reservation under the trust of the United States Department of Interior. A legal dispute over the ownership of the fossil began and ultimately Williams was declared the rightful owner of SUE. Williams was later granted permission to sell SUE, and the fossil was ultimately sold in 1997 for \$8.36 million USD (equivalent to ~\$13.5 million USD in 2021) to the Field Museum in Chicago, Illinois, supported financially by corporations such as McDonald's, The Walt Disney Company, and several other patrons, and setting a record at the time for highest price for which a fossil had ever been sold. [4] In the same year as SUE was confiscated, the issue of unregulated fossil collection on federal land was introduced to Congress to create a uniform policy for fossil collecting, but was only signed into the law in 2009 requiring permits (except in some cases [5]) for fossils collected on federal land (Fossils protected in US land legislation, 2009). SUE's record was broken three decades later, when 'Stan', another *T. rex* specimen also excavated by the BHI in 1992, was sold for \$31.8 million USD in 2020 to an anonymous bidder. Like SUE, Stan's sale also stems from a court ruling. In 2018, a judge ruled that Stan must be sold in order to pay the stake of one of the major shareholders of the BHI (Greshko, 2020).

High-profile fossil auctions have also served to highlight the extent to which fossils are smuggled across transnational borders. The most prominent and egregious case involves a fossil of *Tarbosaurus bataar*, a close relative of *Tyrannosaurus rex* that lived in what is now the Gobi Desert in Mongolia. Mongolian law enacted in 1924 criminalises the unauthorised export of fossils from the country. In 2012, a New York city auction advertised its star lot as a 75 percent complete "*Tyrannosaurus bataar*" specimen from Central Asia (Black, 2013; P. Williams, 2018). It is believed that the auction house advertised the dinosaur as *Tyrannosaurus* instead of *Tarbosaurus* to increase the hype around the specimen given the widespread popularity of the former (Black, 2012). Mongolian palaeontologist Dr Bolortsetseg Minjin, who was working at the American Natural History Museum, noticed an advertisement for the auction and immediately suspected that the specimen had been smuggled out of Mongolia (Black, 2013). With only two days until the sale, Minjin contacted a friend at the Mongolian government who alerted the Mongolian president about the issue. A letter from the president requested the auction be halted, but the auction house's lawyer asserted that there was no legal obligation to stop this auction as no United States laws had been violated by putting this specimen on sale (P. Williams, 2018). This highlights that while many countries have laws that stop the illegal excavation or export of fossils, they do not have powers to prevent any illegally acquired specimens being sold in other countries. The fossil was eventually sold to an anonymous bidder for \$1 million USD (Jacobs, 2013). However, just before the sale, a temporary restraining order forbidding the company to sell the specimen was issued holding the fossil in limbo until its ownership was legally proven in court (P. Williams, 2018). This resulted in the case *United States vs. one T. bataar skeleton*, which led to the arrest of Eric Prokopi, a fossil smuggler who had taken the specimen from Mongolia to the United States through the United Kingdom by falsifying customs documents. Prokopi was the same individual who smuggled a

[4] For a more complete discussion of this complicated case, see Jones (2019).

[5] See the Paleontological Resources Preservation Act (16 USC 470aaa, Sec. 6304).

T. bataar skull [6] that was purchased by actor Nicholas Cage in 2007 for $276,000 USD after he outbid Leonardo DiCaprio (Reuters, 2015).

Many fossils illegally coming out of China tend to come through routes encompassing Greater China, i.e., Taiwan, Macau, and Hong Kong (Liston & You, 2015). Hong Kong is a free port, a legacy of colonial rule, meaning there is little or no duty on goods coming in and out, and the authorities are lenient when it comes to antiquities trade, making it attractive for collectors and dealers (Gallagher, 2017). Many 'more sensitive' relics were smuggled through the Portuguese enclave of Macau before its retrocession to China, where officials are believed to be more corrupt than those in Hong Kong (Lo, 2009). In 2007, dinosaur eggs from Taiwan were seized en route to an auction house in California where they were to be sold for $420,000 USD (Vara-Orta, 2007). However, the original shipper could not provide documentation for the fossils, and the eggs were sent back to China. Experts even believe that these fossils might have been faked to fetch a higher price (Cheng, 2012). A package containing dinosaur eggs, shipped from Malaysia but originally believed to be from China, was discovered during a routine check at Milan Bergamo Airport, Italy in 2021 (Geiger, 2021). The eggs were accompanied by a certificate of authenticity issued by an organisation that apparently did not exist and the intended recipient turned the shipment over to the Italian state.

The fall of the Soviet Union in 1991 and the resulting economic collapse of Russia also proved to be a turning point for Russian palaeontology. In the early 1990s, the Paleontological Institute, Russian Academy of Sciences (PIN) in Moscow experienced financial difficulties and many staff members established fossil selling businesses as an alternative source of personal income (Abbott, 1996). At the same time, several important specimens went missing, without any sign of forced entry. Some of these mysterious disappearances seemed to have occurred when fossils were being sent abroad for display in other institutions, one of the legal ways in which the PIN was making money (Lundgren, 1998). In 1999, a German fossil dealer was arrested while attempting to take 1000 kg of minerals and fossils from Russia to Finland, due to irregularities in his export documentation (Abbott, 1999). The export certificates had been issued by the Ministry of Culture and countersigned by directors of the PIN, who advised the ministry on the scientific value of fossils. Information provided by staff members who had been made redundant from the PIN following a restructuring by the directors, linked the directors to the theft of the fossils (Abbott, 1998). The dealer was eventually let go without any charges and still operates a fossil selling business to this day.

[6]The specimen was later repatriated to Mongolia.

5 Falsifications and Forgeries

Fossil dealers cater to both professional palaeontologists and museums, as well as private individuals and organisations. Many factors determine the price at which a fossil can be sold. As a result, there are several cases dating back to the 19th century where dealers have tampered with fossils, such as in the case of the dinosaur nest above, to make them more visually impressive, or to complement incomplete or damaged specimens with plaster—all ultimately to increase their commercial value (Rieppel, 2015). In 1912, palaeontologist Arthur Smith Woodward and amateur archaeologist Charles Dawson announced the discovery of a fossil that was supposedly the missing link between apes and humans. The publication describing a human-like skull from Piltdown, England generated considerable interest. However, the initial celebrity of the 'Piltdown man' has long been overshadowed by its subsequent infamy as one of the most famous fossil frauds. Although there were some initial doubts about the authenticity of the skull, the specimen was broadly scientifically accepted for several decades until it was definitively demonstrated to be a hoax in 1953 (Spencer, 1990). Modern genetic and chemical analysis recently revealed that the Piltdown man skull is actually composed of a single orangutan specimen and at least two human specimens, and was most likely constructed by Dawson in his "hunger for acclaim" (De Groote et al., 2016). Another chimaera, *"Archaeoraptor liaoningensis"* was described in a 1999 edition of *National Geographic* as the missing link between dinosaurs and birds (Dalton, 2000). However, the fossil also turned out to be constructed from various other fossil pieces.

In the 1990s, the tampering and smuggling of a Brazilian fossil caused confusion among the research community when it was discovered that two groups of palaeontologists were working separately to erect a new taxonomic name for the same animal. One group, composed of British and German researchers, worked with a specimen that was likely smuggled out of Brazil and tampered with by fossil poachers, then sold to a museum in Germany (Cisneros et al., 2022). The group named the animal *Irritator challengeri,* after the painstaking restoration work, which apparently caused them much irritation. The second group, composed of Brazilian palaeontologists, unaware of *Irritator,* were working on a similar fossil and named it *Angaturama limai* (Kellner & Campos, 1996). These turned out to be the same animal, with the British-German group having 'priority' on the name by only a few days, as outlined by the International Code of Zoological Nomenclature. Had one fossil not been smuggled from Brazil, in violation of national laws, this clash likely would not have happened. Brazilian law states that fossils require export permits issued by Ministério de Ciência Tecnologia e Inovação (Cisneros et al., 2022). This case outlines the direct link between laws which have the purpose of protecting fossil heritage and the impact of breaking these laws has on science.

There are also rare occasions where fossils are treated with extreme suspicion, despite their validity, on account of previous cases of fraud and smuggling. *Halszkaraptor escuilliei,* a dinosaur labelled as being from "Central Asia" at a fossil exhibition (Fig. 3) was so unusual that it was first believed to be a chimaera just like

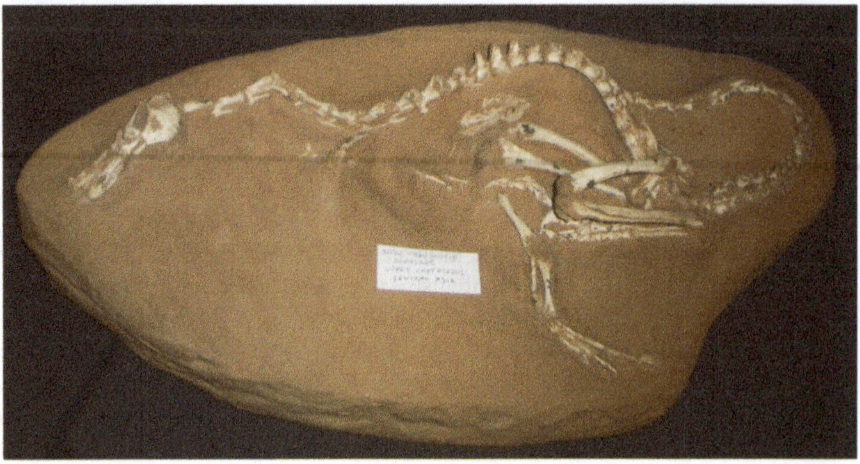

Fig. 3 Fossil of the *Halszkaraptor escuilliei* at the 2011 Fossil Show in Munich. Label reads "NEW TROODONTID DINOSAUR, UPPER CRETACEOUS, CENTRAL ASIA". Photo by Ghedoghedo, CC BY-SA 3.0, via Wikimedia Commons

"*Archaeoraptor*". The fossil was purchased in France in 2014 by a private collector, after it has made its way from China, through Japan, Germany, and the United Kingdom, and changing hands so many times that it is impossible to trace the fossil back to the poachers (Pickrell, 2020). Notes attached to the specimen (Fig. 3), probably by poachers and other dealers, provided more information about its provenance and it was later confirmed to be genuine fossil from the Gobi Desert of Mongolia. Researchers ran into further difficulty when attempting to publish their findings in a scientific journal as many reviewers thought that the fossil was too strange to be authentic. Ultimately, the fossil was taken to the European Synchrotron Radiation Facility in Grenoble, France where the first synchrotron scan (more commonly performed in physics, chemistry, and materials science) of an entire dinosaur fossil was obtained (Cau et al., 2017). This authenticity test stemming from fossil smuggling activity not only proved definitively that the fossil was genuine but also revealed unusual details about the animal's semiaquatic mode of life and ignited exciting future avenues of palaeontological research (ESRF, 2017).

6 At Odds with Legal Classifications

In many countries, fossils fall under the umbrella of 'cultural goods', particularly after the 1970 UNESCO *Convention on the Means of Prohibiting and Preventing the Illicit Import, Export and Transfer of Ownership of Cultural Property*. The 1970 UNESCO Convention lists objects of palaeontological interest in their definition of cultural property, and many signatories adopted similar definitions in their national legislations, such as Brazil (signed in 1973), China (1989), Mongolia (1991) and

Myanmar (2013). Many of these fossil protection laws use a variation of the term "of scientific value" to describe fossils that fall under their regulation, without a strict or universal definition. The scientific value usually varies, depending on the evaluating scientific body, but it is generally accepted that rare, complete, and unique fossils are most highly sought after and fall into this category.

Despite the existence of national and international laws for the protection of fossils, unregulated movement of fossils has persisted for decades, due to inadequate or improper implementation, corruption, and in many cases, loopholes being exploited by individuals wishing to circumvent administrative and financial responsibility (Cisneros et al., 2022; Dunne et al., 2021; Stewens, 2021). Many palaeontologists have criticised the conventions and legislation that apply to matters of fossil sale and export, and even view these laws as a barrier to pursuing their scientific interests (see discussion in Cisneros et al., 2022). One major claim that is frequently made is that fossil material is wrongfully treated the same as archaeological objects or other cultural artefacts (Endere & Prado, 2015; Liston & You, 2015; Martin, 2018). While archaeological remains and cultural artefacts have a clear relationship with humans, in terms of art, beliefs, customs, and mortality, fossils, with the exception of some hominid fossils, [7] do not. Fossils which existed long before humans appeared, therefore, seem ill-fitted to legislation referring to archaeology or culture (Martin, 2018). Many also oppose the idea of a fossil object 'belonging' to one country, as many fossil legislations declare, as modern geopolitical borders did not exist at the time that the organisms represented by these fossils were alive (Martin, 2018; Ulph, 2018).

Using these arguments to justify their actions in engaging in the illegal fossil business, many palaeontologists have amassed a long list of publications that have served their personal and academic interests at the expense of scholars and communities in fossil-rich countries. Peer-reviewed publications are considered the currency of academic science, with funding and job opportunities relying heavily on their quantity and the impact factor of the journal in which they are published. This pressure to publish plays an enormous role in enticing some palaeontologists towards illegal and unethical behaviour in order to get exclusive access to scientifically valuable fossils (Raja & Dunne, 2021). The case of "*Ubirajara jubatus*", [8] a Brazilian dinosaur fossil described and named in a scientific article in 2019 (Smyth et al., 2020), has recently ignited fierce discussion over the recent prevalence of fossil smuggling. The specimen of "*Ubirajara*" was allegedly exported from Brazil by German palaeontologists for study in 1995 (Pérez Ortega, 2021). However, the export of holotypes (the specimen upon which a species' name is based), such as this one, is explicitly prohibited under Brazilian law (Cisneros et al., 2022). Further investigations revealed that the export information provided in the study describing

[7] Consists of any of the groups of erect, bipedal primates, i.e. human-like, whose only living members are modern humans.

[8] The name of the fossil is in quotation marks as it is now an invalid name due to the retraction of the article originally describing it.

"*Ubirajara*" was in fact fabricated; instead of the specimen being "without commercial value" as stated on the permit supplied by the article's authors, the fossil was actually imported by a private company in 2006, and then later purchased by the museum where it presently resides (Pérez Ortega, 2021). Conflicting information recently came to light where it was stated that the museum where the fossil is currently reposited bought the fossil from Brazil but did not directly handle customs documentation (Lamm, 2022). Following efforts by the Brazilian scientific community and investigative journalists in bringing the unethical behaviour of the researchers involved to light, the scientific article describing the specimen was retracted by the journal, rendering the description and name of the fossil irrelevant and unusable to science—yet another example of how illegal activity directly impacts scientific research (Cisneros et al., 2021).

Interestingly, the *Kulturgutschutzgesetz* (that provides legal protection to the *G. brancai* at the MfN) was used to deny repatriations requests of *"Ubirajara"* in September 2021, right before it was revealed that the researchers had provided fraudulent information regarding the provenance of the fossil specimen (Pérez Ortega, 2021). The justification behind this claim was that the fossil was "legally acquired" under German law, overlooking the fact that Brazil has been regulating the acquisition of fossil material since 1942. This capture and imprisonment of natural objects in higher income countries, during the colonial era and thereafter, allowed museums and academic institutions in those countries to enrich their collections, in turn facilitating scientific research and attracting visitors to their exhibits (Cisneros et al., 2021). However, the profits, whether in terms of money or knowledge, are rarely, if ever at all, shared with the countries from which these resources were extracted. The colonial plunder of such objects is cited as one of the reasons that several Latin American countries adopted rigid laws to not only regulate the extraction of these resources but also the actions of foreign researchers (Cisneros et al., 2021). These laws in turn increase access of these materials to the local population, promote local scientific endeavours, and may even attract tourists to visit museums exhibiting these specimens, like *G. brancai* in Berlin or Dippy in several other countries. [9]

In the case of Birk Knowles fossil site in Lanarkshire, Scotland, the absence of geographical or geological contextual information that usually accompany fossil objects if collected by palaeontologists was used to deny repatriation requests (Birk Knowes Affairs, 2021. Birk Knowes is a designated Site of Special Interest (SSI) containing exceptionally preserved fossil fishes and arthropods. As an SSI, collectors are required to apply for permits from NatureScot, formerly Scottish Natural Heritage (SNH), although due to its remote location, the site was visited by some unauthorised fossil dealers. One such dealer was close with the site warden, which allowed him to collect fossils unimpeded despite reports from other palaeontologists to SNH about his activities. Due to this mismanagement and collusion, the site was

[9]Replicas of Dippy are exhibited in several countries across Europe and also in Argentina and Mexico, with the original one at the Carnegie Museum in the United States.

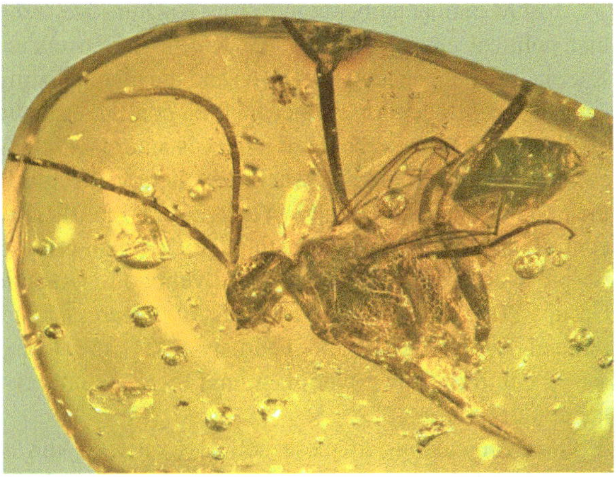

Fig. 4 Wasp entombed in amber. Photo by George Poinar, Oregon State University, CC BY-SA 2.0, via Wikimedia Commons

plundered for decades, causing permanent damage. The site was ultimately closed in 1995 after a series of actions that led to the dealer being caught, although they were not formally charged. A few years later, some researchers came to know about the purchase of Scottish fossils by the MfN in Berlin (MacFadyen, 2001). The fossils' locality information apparently never mentioned the Birk Knowes site, but rather Logan Water and Logan Farm, both alternative names for Birk Knowes (Birk Knowes Affairs, 2021. The SNH were alerted and the process to repatriate the fossils began. The MfN apparently agreed to repatriation in 2000 but changed its stance a year later (Hamilton, 2001), justifying themselves by saying that it was impossible to determine the exact origin of the fossils—a convenient excuse. In 2006, SNH eventually gave up and said that they were not considering legal action as European legislation had not yet been tested in courts and the proceedings would be too expensive (H. Williams, 2002).

One particular case where the human dimension cannot be disentangled from the fossils is that of Myanmar amber (Fig. 4), fossilised resin which preserves the remains of insects, plants, and small lizards that lived alongside the dinosaurs. This might bring the film *Jurassic Park* [10] to mind, where dinosaur DNA was apparently extracted from a mosquito entombed in a piece of amber. This association with the dinosaurs, combined with the exquisite preservation of the fossils, renders studies on Myanmar amber exceptionally popular (Dunne et al., 2021). In recent years, alarming information has emerged regarding the questionable premises under which Myanmar amber is acquired and the links between this material and human rights abuses by the national military forces, the Tatmadaw, against the ethnic population in the northern state of Kachin (Sokol, 2019).

[10] Myanmar amber was actually confirmed to be of mid-Cretaceous age (~99 million years old) in 2000, 10 years after the science fiction novel, Jurassic Park, was published upon which the movie franchise is based.

Most Myanmar amber comes from Kachin state, a region rich in natural resources that political entities, mainly the Kachin Independence Organisation through the Kachin Independence Army (KIA) and the national army, the Tatmadaw, compete to control and profit from, further fuelling conflict in the region (Combs, 2021; Sokol, 2019). Much of the recovered amber is smuggled across the border to China to be sold on the amber market, where jewellers, collectors, and palaeontologists source their amber material (Rippa & Yang, 2017). In 2017, the Tatmadaw seized complete control of the amber mines ousting the KIA—an offense that displaced thousands of people who lost their homes and livelihoods (Kachin Development Networking Group, 2019) and involved tactics of torture, abductions, and sexual violence (United Nations, 2019). In February 2021, the Tatmadaw launched a coup and seized control of the government and there are concerns of a potential civil war in the country.

Occurring alongside these ethical issues are the complex (il)legal aspects of exporting Myanmar amber with fossil inclusions. Myanmar has national antiquity laws that ban the permanent export of any fossil material. However, under other national laws amber is classified as a gemstone and can be legally exported provided certain conditions are fulfilled. Fossils trapped in amber therefore fall into a legal grey zone, as the fossils themselves cannot be legally traded or exported, but the amber surrounding them can. The interests of the Tatmadaw have defined the stance of the governmental body with respect to this situation, where the gemstone law is illegitimately given primacy over the antiquities law that concerns fossils (Stewens, 2021). However, while this situation remains unaddressed by legal experts and/or the Myanmar government—a difficult feat given the current coup—some palaeontological societies and scientific journals have released statements and guidelines regarding Myanmar amber research and publications with the aim of reducing the impact of palaeontological research on the ongoing conflict (Fossils protected in US land legislation, 2009; Theodor et al., 2021).

While these ethical and legal concerns of Myanmar amber are now widely known, the rate at which scientific articles describing these fossils are being published has not waned; instead it is increasing year on year (Dunne et al., 2021). Many palaeontologists remain of the opinion that the priceless scientific value that these fossils represent, that is the new plant and animal species being uncovered from Myanmar amber, is enough to justify their acquisition and research, or else they would end up in the hands of jewellers and private collectors and may be forever lost to science (Haug, Reumer, et al., 2020; Haug, Azar, et al., 2020; Sokol, 2019). They also argue that the contributions most palaeontologists make to the Myanmar amber economy is negligible (Haug, Reumer, et al., 2020; Haug, Azar, et al., 2020). Vertebrate fossil inclusions in amber are generally very rare and are sold for thousands of United States dollars—an alleged "partial bird wing with three claws" was priced at ~$23,000 USD on eBay and a dinosaur tail could potentially bring up to $100,000 USD in sale (Cooley, 2017). The remaining bulk of amber that have inclusions generally contains insects or plants and has relatively low commercial value, but remains scientifically valuable nonetheless. Most amber that contains insects, with a few exceptions, is generally sold for less than $5 USD on eBay, with most coming from Chinese traders, but a few also from Canada and Israel. [11]

7 Conclusion

Fossil crime, including fossil trafficking, fraud, and fakery by members of the palaeontological community and the public alike, has a centuries-long history. Given their high scientific and commercial value, fossils are afforded protection under several international conventions, as well as national laws in many countries. However, their perceived scientific and commercial value continues to trump legal and ethical concerns, and individuals frequently exploit loopholes in legislation, especially as there are few repercussions for engaging in this kind of illegal or unethical behaviour. As noted in several examples above, such as "*Ubirajara*", "*Archaeoraptor*", and *Halszkaraptor*, much of this illegal activity can actually harm the scientific processes, for example, by rendering taxonomic names invalid or eroding trust in expert opinion. Frequently, when fossil crimes are uncovered, such as when they are about to be sold or after the publication of a manuscript, it is too late. Prominent fossils, such as *T. bataar,* brought attention to the issue but several other 'less important' fossils make it through these illegal routes undetected. While legalities and technicalities are being discussed and disputed, the demand for fossils is far from waning and high-value fossils are attracting more and more the attention of palaeontologists, collectors, and dealers drawn to the extensive scientific, reputational, and financial rewards.

References

Abbott, A. (1996). Missing dinosaur skulls raise new fears of smuggling in Moscow. *Nature, 384*(6609), 499. https://doi.org/10.1038/384499a0

Abbott, A. (1998). Moscow's 'missing fossils' come under new scrutiny. *Nature, 391*(6669), 724–724. https://doi.org/10.1038/35681

Abbott, A. (1999). Fossil dealer charged over Russian cache. *Nature, 397*(6716), 189–189. https://doi.org/10.1038/16528

Adas, M. (1998). Imperialism and colonialism in comparative perspective. *The International History Review, 20*(2), 371–388. https://doi.org/10.1080/07075332.1998.9640829

Birk Knowes Affairs. (2021). https://birkknowesaffairs.com/

Black, R. (2012). *You Say Tyrannosaurus, I Say Tarbosaurus*. Smithsonian Magazine. https://www.smithsonianmag.com/science-nature/you-say-tyrannosaurus-i-say-tarbosaurus-142897656/

Black, R. (2013). The Million-Dollar Dinosaur Scandal. *Slate*. Retrieved June 27, 2022, from https://slate.com/technology/2013/01/tarbosaurus-bataar-smuggling-case-dinosaur-fossil-dealers-steal-bones-from-china-and-mongolia-to-sell-at-auction.html

[11] Based on a search for "burmite amber" on eBay.com on 11 October 2021.

Bradley, L. W. (2014). *Dinosaurs and Indians: Paleontology resource dispossession from Sioux lands*. Outskirts Press.

Cau, A., Beyrand, V., Voeten, D. F. A. E., Fernandez, V., Tafforeau, P., Stein, K., Barsbold, R., Tsogtbaatar, K., Currie, P. J., & Godefroit, P. (2017). Synchrotron scanning reveals amphibious ecomorphology in a new clade of bird-like dinosaurs. *Nature, 552*(7685), 395–399. https://doi.org/10.1038/nature24679

Cheng, Y. (2012). Smuggled dinosaur nest may be a fake. *China Daily*. Retrieved June 27, 2022, from http://www.chinadaily.com.cn/china/2012-02/09/content_14564865.htm

Cisneros, J. C., Ghilardi, A. M., Raja, N. B., & Stewens, P. P. (2021). The moral and legal imperative to return illegally exported fossils. *Nature Ecology & Evolution, 6*, 2–3. https://doi.org/10.1038/s41559-021-01588-9

Cisneros, J. C., Raja, N. B., Ghilardi, A. M., Dunne, E. M., Pinheiro, F. L., Regalado Fernández, O. R., Sales, M. A. F., Rodríguez-de la Rosa, R. A., Miranda-Martínez, A. Y., González-Mora, S., Bantim, R. A. M., de Lima, F. J., & Pardo, J. D. (2022). Digging deeper into colonial palaeontological practices in modern day Mexico and Brazil. *Royal Society Open Science, 9*(3), 210898. https://doi.org/10.1098/rsos.210898

Combs, D. (2021). *Until the world shatters: Truth, lies, and the looting of Myanmar*. .

Cooley, S. (2017, January 26). Dodging rumour and insurgency: The hunt for Burmese amber goes to the heart of Myanmar's turbulent north. *Financial Post*. Retrieved June 27, 2022, from https://financialpost.com/commodities/mining/dodging-rumour-and-insurgency-the-hunt-for-burmese-amber-goes-to-the-heart-of-myanmars-turbulent-north

Cope, E. D. (1888). *Cope to Jesup, 9 April 1888, Early Administrative Records, Archives of the American Museum of Natural History*.

Dalton, R. (2000). Feathers fly over Chinese fossil bird's legality and authenticity. *Nature, 403*(6771), 689–690. https://doi.org/10.1038/35001723

De Groote, I., Flink, L. G., Abbas, R., Bello, S. M., Burgia, L., Buck, L. T., Dean, C., Freyne, A., Higham, T., Jones, C. G., Kruszynski, R., Lister, A., Parfitt, S. A., Skinner, M. M., Shindler, K., & Stringer, C. B. (2016). New genetic and morphological evidence suggests a single hoaxer created 'Piltdown man'. *Royal Society Open Science, 3*(8), 160328. https://doi.org/10.1098/rsos.160328

de Lima, J. T. M., & de Souza Carvalho, I. (2020). Geological or cultural heritage? The Ex Situ scientific collections as a remnant of nature and culture. *Geoheritage, 12*(1), 3. https://doi.org/10.1007/s12371-020-00448-5

Dembard, F., & Néraudeau, D. (2001). L'utilisation des oursins fossiles de la Préhistoire à l'époque gallo-romaine. *Bulletin de La Société Préhistorique Française, 98*(4), 693–715. https://doi.org/10.3406/bspf.2001.12570

Di Maggio, R. M. (2018). Preventing art and antiquities crimes using forensic geology. In P. M. Barone & W. J. M. Groen (Eds.), *Multidisciplinary approaches to forensic archaeology: Topics discussed during the European Meetings on Forensic Archaeology (EMFA)* (pp. 239–249). Springer International Publishing. https://doi.org/10.1007/978-3-319-94397-8_18

Dunne, E., Raja, N. B., Stewens, P., & Thein, Z. M. M. (2021). Ethics, law, and politics in palaeontological research: The case of Myanmar amber. *OSF Preprints*. https://doi.org/10.31219/osf.io/awjex

Editorial. (2009). Fossils protected in US land legislation. *Nature, 458*(7238), 562–562. https://doi.org/10.1038/458562e

Endere, M. L., & Prado, J. L. (2015). Characterization and valuation of paleontological heritage: a perspective from Argentina. *Geoheritage, 7*(2), 137–145. https://doi.org/10.1007/s12371-014-0124-x

ESRF. (2017). *Synchrotron sheds light on the amphibious lifestyle of a new raptorial dinosaur*. Retrieved June 27, 2022, from https://www.esrf.fr/home/news/general/content-news/general/synchrotron-sheds-light-on-the-amphibious-lifestyle-of-a-new-raptorial-dinosaur.html

Gallagher, S. (2017). "Purchased in Hong Kong": Is Hong Kong the best place to buy stolen or looted antiquities? *International Journal of Cultural Property, 24*(4), 479–496. https://doi.org/10.1017/S0940739117000224

Geiger, G. (2021, June 15). Italian Customs Authorities Seized a Dinosaur Egg Hidden In a Package. *Vice*. Retrieved June 27, 2022, from https://www.vice.com/en/article/akgkba/italian-customs-authorities-seized-a-dinosaur-egg-hidden-in-a-package

Gold, H. (2019, August 7). Why Are Male Actors So Obsessed With Acquiring Dinosaur Skulls? *The Cut*. Retrieved June 27, 2022, from https://www.thecut.com/2019/08/nicolas-cage-and-leonardo-dicaprio-owned-dinosaur-skulls.html

Greshko, M. (2020, October 12). 'Stan' the T. rex just sold for $31.8 million—And scientists are furious. *National Geographic*. Retrieved June 27, 2022, from https://www.nationalgeographic.com/science/article/stan-tyrannosaurus-rex-sold-at-auction-paleontologists-are-furious

Hamilton, J. (2001, May). Fossil fury as Germans refuse to give back Lanarkshire's fish. *Sunday Herald*.

Haug, C., Reumer, J. W. F., Haug, J. T., Arillo, A., Audo, D., Azar, D., Baranov, V., Beutel, R., Charbonnier, S., Feldmann, R., Foth, C., Fraaije, R. H. B., Frenzel, P., Gašparič, R., Greenwalt, D. E., Harms, D., Hyžný, M., Jagt, J. W. M., Jagt-Yazykova, E. A., et al. (2020). Comment on the letter of the Society of Vertebrate Paleontology (SVP) dated April 21, 2020 regarding "Fossils from conflict zones and reproducibility of fossil-based scientific data": The importance of private collections. *PalZ, 94*(3), 413–429. https://doi.org/10.1007/s12542-020-00522-x

Haug, J. T., Azar, D., Ross, A., Szwedo, J., Wang, B., Arillo, A., Baranov, V., Bechteler, J., Beutel, R., Blagoderov, V., Delclòs, X., Dunlop, J., Feldberg, K., Feldmann, R., Foth, C., Fraaije, R. H. B., Gehler, A., Harms, D., Hedenäs, L., et al. (2020). Comment on the letter of the Society of Vertebrate Paleontology (SVP) dated April 21, 2020 regarding "Fossils from conflict zones and reproducibility of fossil-based scientific data": Myanmar amber. *Paläontologische Zeitschrift, 94*(3), 431–437. https://doi.org/10.1007/s12542-020-00524-9

Henriques, M. H., & Pena dos Reis, R. (2015). Framing the palaeontological heritage within the geological heritage: An integrative vision. *Geoheritage, 7*(3), 249–259. https://doi.org/10.1007/s12371-014-0141-9

Jacobs, D. L. (2013). *Stolen Dinosaur, Bought For $1 Million At New York Auction, Will Be Returned To Mongolia. Forbes*. Retrieved June 27, 2022, from https://www.forbes.com/sites/deborahljacobs/2013/05/06/stolen-dinosaur-bought-for-1-million-at-new-york-auction-will-be-returned-to-mongolia/

Jones, E. D. (2019). Assumptions of authority: The story of Sue the T-rex and controversy over access to fossils. *History and Philosophy of the Life Sciences, 42*(1), 2. https://doi.org/10.1007/s40656-019-0288-4

Kachin Development Networking Group. (2019). *Blood Amber Military resource grab clears out indigenous peoples in Kachin State's Hugawng Valley*. Retrieved June 27, 2022, from https://www.burmalibrary.org/en/blood-amber-military-resource-grab-clears-out-indigenous-peoples-in-kachin-states-hugawng-valley

Kellner, A. W. A., & Campos, D. d. A. (1996). First Early Cretaceous theropod dinosaur from Brazil with comments on Spinosauridae. *Neues Jahrbuch Für Geologie Und Paläontologie - Abhandlungen*, 151–166. https://doi.org/10.1127/njgpa/199/1996/151

Knauer, R. (2021, October 20). Tendaguru: Revival des Dinosaurierhügels. *Spektrum*. Retrieved June 27, 2022, from https://www.spektrum.de/news/tendaguru-revival-des-dinosaurierhuegels/1939360

Lamm, L. (2022, January 14). *Paläontologie: Herrscht in der Forschung immer noch Kolonialzeit?* National Geographic. https://www.nationalgeographic.de/geschichte-und-kultur/2022/01/palaeontologie-herrscht-in-derforschung-kolonialzeit-kolonialismus

Liston, J., & You, H.-L. (2015). Chinese fossil protection law and the illegal export of vertebrate fossils from China. *Journal of Vertebrate Paleontology, 35*(2), e904791. https://doi.org/10.1080/02724634.2014.904791

Lo, S. (2009). Cross-Border Crime between Taiwan and Mainland China: The response from the Taiwan Government. *American Journal of Chinese Studies, 16*(1), 15–32.

Lundgren, G. (1998). Protecting federal fossils from extinction comment. *Boston College Environmental Affairs Law Review, 26*(1), 225–262.

MacFadyen, C. (2001). Getting to grips with asset strippers. *Earth Heritage, 15*. http://www.earthheritage.org.uk/wp/wp-content/uploads/2018/03/EH15-2001.pdf

Maier, G. (2003). *African Dinosaurs Unearthed: The Tendaguru Expeditions (Life of the Past)*.

Martin, J. (2018). Dodgy fossils: International legislation and the meaning of 'cultural property'. *The Geological Curator, 10*.

Mayor, A. (2005). *Fossil legends of the First Americans*. Princeton University Press. https://doi.org/10.1515/9781400849314

Neues Jahrbuch Für Geologie Und Paläontologie - Abhandlungen, 151–166. https://doi.org/10.1127/njgpa/199/1996/151

Nieuwland, I. (2010). The colossal stranger. Andrew Carnegie and Diplodocus intrude European Culture, 1904-1912. *Endeavour, 34*, 61–68. https://doi.org/10.1016/j.endeavour.2010.04.001

Nieuwland, I. (2019). *American dinosaur abroad: A cultural history of Carnegie's plaster diplodocus*. University of Pittsburgh Press.

Peresani, M., Vanhaeren, M., Quaggiotto, E., Queffelec, A., & d'Errico, F. (2013). An Ochered Fossil Marine Shell From the Mousterian of Fumane Cave, Italy. *PLOS ONE, 8*(7), e68572. https://doi.org/10.1371/journal.pone.0068572

Pérez Ortega, R. (2021). 'It's like a second extinction': Retraction deepens legal and ethical battle over rare dinosaur. *Science, 374*. https://doi.org/10.1126/science.acx9223

Pickrell, J. (2020). The curious case of the stolen dino-swan. *New Scientist, 245*(3269), 40–43. https://doi.org/10.1016/S0262-4079(20)30314-6

Qorro, E. (2018, March 14). Germany to help Tanzania promote Tendaguru dinosaur. *IPP Media*. Retrieved June 27, 2022, from https://www.ippmedia.com/en/news/germany-help-tanzania-promote-tendaguru-dinosaur

Raja, N. B., & Dunne, E. (2021). Publication pressure threatens the integrity of palaeontological research. *EarthArxiv*. https://doi.org/10.31223/X5V32Z

Raja, N. B., Dunne, E. M., Matiwane, A., Khan, T. M., Nätscher, P. S., Ghilardi, A. M., & Chattopadhyay, D. (2022). Colonial history and global economics distort our understanding of deep-time biodiversity. *Nature Ecology & Evolution, 6*(2), 145–154. https://doi.org/10.1038/s41559-021-01608-8

Reuters. (2015, December 22). Nicolas Cage returns stolen Mongolian dinosaur skull he bought at gallery. *The Guardian*Error! Bookmark not defined.

Reynolds, M. (2018). The dinosaur trade: How celebrity collectors and glitzy auctions could be damaging science. *Wired UK*. Retrieved June 27, 2022, from https://www.wired.co.uk/article/dinosaur-t-rex-auction-sale-private-fossil-trade

Rieppel, L. (2015). Prospecting for dinosaurs on the mining frontier: The value of information in America's Gilded Age. *Social Studies of Science, 45*(2), 161–186. https://doi.org/10.1177/0306312715570650

Rippa, A., & Yang, Y. (2017). The Amber Road: Cross-Border Trade and the Regulation of the Burmite Market in Tengchong, Yunnan. *TRaNS: Trans-Regional and -National Studies of Southeast Asia, 5*(2), 243–267. https://doi.org/10.1017/trn.2017.7

Sakurai, D. S. (1994). Animal, mineral, or cultural antiquity the management and protection of paleontological resources. *Loyola of Los Angeles International and Comparative Law Journal, 17*(1), 197–243.

Schuchtert, C., & LeVene, C. M. (1940). *O.C. Marsh, Pioneer in Paleontology*. Yale University Press.

Smyth, R. S. H., Martill, D. M., Frey, E., Rivera-Sylva, H. E., & Lenz, N. (2020). Temporary removal: A maned theropod dinosaur from Gondwana with elaborate integumentary structures. *Cretaceous Research, 104686*. https://doi.org/10.1016/j.cretres.2020.104686

Sokol, J. (2019, May 23). Troubled Treasure: Fossils in Burmese amber offer an exquisite view of dinosaur times—And an ethical minefield. *Science | AAAS*. Retrieved June 27, 2022, from https://www.sciencemag.org/news/2019/05/fossils-burmese-amber-offer-exquisite-view-dinosaur-times-and-ethical-minefield

Sookias, R. (2011). *Sustainable Fossils: Past Life for the Present and Future* [Unpublished master dissertation]. Uppsala University https://www.diva-portal.org/smash/get/diva2:451040/FULLTEXT01.pdf

Spencer, F. (1990). *The Piltdown papers, 1908-1955*. Natural History Museum Publications. http://archive.org/details/piltdownpapers1900spen

Stefanoudis, P. V., Licuanan, W. Y., Morrison, T. H., Talma, S., Veitayaki, J., & Woodall, L. C. (2021). Turning the tide of parachute science. *Current Biology, 31*(4), R184–R185. https://doi.org/10.1016/j.cub.2021.01.029

Stewens, P. P. (2021, June 24). Burmese Amber: Palaeontology's Blood Diamonds Through the Lens of International Law. *Völkerrechtsblog*. Retrieved June 27, 2022, from https://doi.org/10.17176/20210624-192927-0

Stoecker, H. (2019, April 10). The Brachiosaurus brancai in the Natural History Museum Berlin. *Boasblogs.*. https://boasblogs.org/dcntr/the-brachiosaurus-brancai-in-the-natural-history-museum-berlin/

Theodor, J. M., Lewis, M. E., & Rayfield, E. J. (2021). Amber specimens acquired from Myanmar following military coup. *Society of Vertebrate Paleontology*. Retrieved June 27, 2022, from https://vertpaleo.org/wp-content/uploads/2021/06/SVP-Letter-to-paleontological-community-on-Myanmar-Amber_FINAL.pdf

Ulph, J. (2018). Acquiring Fossils: A complex picture. *Geological Curator, 10*(10), 657–670.

United Nations. (2019). *The economic interests of the Myanmar military: Independent International Fact-Finding Mission on Myanmar. UN Doc. A/HRC/42/CRP. 3.* https://www.ohchr.org/EN/HRBodies/HRC/MyanmarFFM/Pages/EconomicInterestsMyanmarMilitary.aspx

Vara-Orta, F. (2007, February 16). Agency quashes sale of Chinese dinosaur eggs. *Los Angeles Times.* Retrieved June 27, 2022, from https://www.latimes.com/archives/la-xpm-2007-feb-16-me-eggs16-story.html

Webster, D. (2009). The Dinosaur Fossil Wars. *Smithsonian Magazine*. https://www.smithsonianmag.com/science-nature/the-dinosaur-fossil-wars-116496039/

Williams, H. (2002). Fish fossils prove bone of contention. *BBC News*. http://news.bbc.co.uk/2/hi/uk_news/scotland/1855456.stm

Williams, P. (2018). *The dinosaur artist: Obsession, science, and the global quest for fossils*. Hachette Books.

Nussaïbah B. Raja received a Bachelors in Geography from King's College London, a Masters in Physical Geography at Ankara University in Turkey, and another Masters in Palaeobiology from the Friedrich-Alexander University Erlangen-Nürnberg, Germany where she currently is a PhD candidate. She engages with research at the intersection of palaeontology and humanities and applies a data-driven approach to topics on social justice, ethics and colonial legacies with regards to modern palaeontological practices.

Emma M. Dunne is an Assistant Professor in palaeobiology at the Department of Geography and Geosciences of Friedrich-Alexander-Universität Erlangen-Nürnberg, Germany. Her primary research focuses on deciphering the mechanisms that drive patterns of biodiversity, evolution, and extinction in the fossil record. Stemming from this research in palaeobiology, she also researches in how illegal and unethical research practices impact the wider discipline of palaeontology and, in turn, our understanding of the history of life on Earth. Recent case studies that she has led and collaborated on include fossils in Myanmar amber, the illegal export of Brazilian fossils, and the legal argument for fossils to be considered cultural objects.

Illicit Excavations and Trade in Antiquities

The Unsettled Challenge for Jordan

Ziad al-Saad and Stefan Simon

Abstract Illicit excavation and trade in antiquities represents a major and unsettled challenge for Jordan. The recent past has witnessed a phenomenal increase in the number of people involved in these illicit activities which result in the destruction of a significant part of Jordan's cultural legacy. Illegal diggers make a big mess of the sites and consequently, they destroy the archaeological record and with it: thousands of years of well-preserved layers of history. Due to these illegal activities, Jordan has lost irreplaceable parts of its cultural heritage, of which some are being circulated in the black market. This chapter investigates the various aspects of this phenomenon including its causes, with emphasis on the legal, social, and political circumstances that enable and explain it, the scale of the problem, and how it can be curtailed. The chapter will investigate the roles that should be played by key players such as the local communities, private sector, government, and non-governmental organisations and international organisations to alleviate this problem. Issues like promotion of ethical standards and raising awareness about threats posed by looting of cultural property will be highlighted.

1 Introduction

Jordan's diverse legacy of antiquities and archaeological sites attests to its rich history as a crossroads of ancient and modern Middle Eastern civilizations, many of which left their unique mark behind. Collected over thousands of years, this

The original version of the chapter has been revised. A correction to this chapter can be found at https://doi.org/10.1007/978-3-031-14084-6_14

Z. al-Saad
Faculty of Archaeology and Anthropology, Yarmouk University, Irbid, Jordan
e-mail: zalsaad@yu.edu.jo

S. Simon (✉)
Rathgen Research Laboratory, National Museum Berlin, Berlin, Germany
e-mail: s.simon@smb.spk-berlin.de

N. Oosterman, D. Yates (eds.), *Art Crime in Context*, Studies in Art, Heritage, Law and the Market 6, https://doi.org/10.1007/978-3-031-14084-6_6

legacy represents the origin and evolution of several religions, cultures, economies, and societies (MacDonald et al., 2001; Peterman, 1994). It is Jordan's heritage which lends the country the unique characteristic of an open-air museum and offers the potential for deeper multicultural and religious understanding through its study. Jordan's heritage is one of its strongest economic assets, and the relics left behind as a result of this vibrant past are irreplaceable treasures. Heritage tourism is an important driver of the national economy and accounts for about 13 percent of the country's gross domestic product (Ministry of Tourism of Jordan, 2021). The potential of Jordan's tourism sector, however, is not being fully utilised. The international tourism sector is both source of prosperity and decay. While tourism may advance development; many heritage sites are struggling with its negative impact on many levels. It is one of the largest and fastest growing economic sectors in the world, accounting for almost 10 percent of global gross national product and employment. In a 2016 report on World Heritage and Tourism in Climate Change, UNESCO and UNEP point out that tourism is responsible for around five percent of global carbon dioxide emissions, and this share is likely to double over the next 25 years. (UNEP—UNESCO—Union of Concerned Scientists, 2016). Yet, much potential exists to increase this contribution by improving the tourism products through the implementation of more effective management systems of Jordan's rich and diverse cultural heritage assets, (The World Bank, 2015).

The rich archaeological heritage of Jordan is constantly eroded by illegal excavations and illegal trade in antiquities carried out to meet an escalating demand for antiquities (Alshami et al., 2007; Al-Manaser & Atal, 2020). Unfortunately, these illegal activities have recently been systematic and have intensified to reach an alarming scale (Contreras & Brodie, 2010b; Kersel & Hill, 2019). These activities deprived Jordan of some of its most outstanding archaeological treasures, representing a major and unsettled challenge for the country (Contreras & Brodie, 2012; Kersel & Chesson, 2013; Kersel, & Hill 2020).

This article focuses on discussing and analysing the phenomenon of illicit excavations and trade in antiquities in Jordan in terms of its scale, root causes, and key players. The main aim of the chapter to explore new approaches and methods that can be used to fight and curtail this pressing and dangerous challenge. Capacity building of the concerned organisations, public awareness, and international cooperation are particularly stressed. It emphasises the roles that should be played by key players such as the local communities, private sector, government and non-governmental organisations and international organisations to alleviate this problem.

2 Situation Analysis

2.1 Nature and Extent of Illicit Excavations and Trade in Cultural Objects

Since the 1930s Jordan archaeological sites have been targeted by illicit excavations and smuggling of excavated cultural objects. Despite the existing legislative and policy interventions and efforts of the Department of Antiquities of Jordan (DoA), the illegal excavations and trade continue to thrive, resulting in considerable damage: physical, financial, social, and cultural.

Important archaeological sites that are dated to different periods, particularly Roman-Byzantine, Bronze Age, and Iron Age sites, were heavily looted and their archaeological strata were severely interrupted. Important sites such as Wadi Faynan, Abila, Bab adh-Dhra', and Ghawr as-Safi, are some examples of highly significant sites that have been heavily looted. It has been estimated (Contreras & Brodie, 2010a, 2010b) that from the Early Bonze site of Bab adh-Dhra alone, 28,084 pots were looted. Many of the artefacts looted from these sites were illegally smuggled and found their way to the international market. Another example of a site that suffered extensive looting is the Iron Age site of Fifa on the Dead Sea Plain. Based on data from aerial drones, a total of 3723 pits were looted over a period of 27 years resulting in a potential number of looted pots between 22,338 and 111,690 (Kersel & Hill, 2019, 2020).

The past two decades witnessed an exponential increase in the scale of looting of archaeological sites fuelled by economic hardship and turmoil in some neighbouring countries. As a result, the rich archaeological heritage of Jordan is being constantly depleted. The comprehensive proof of recent large-scale looting of Jordanian archaeological sites is provided by several studies that employed different documentation techniques such as site monitoring, archival spy photographs, and aerial and satellite surveillance and imagery (Hammer & Ur, 2019; Kersel & Hill, 2020).

Further evidence on large scale looting of Jordan's archaeological sites is provided by Jordan's database of archaeological sites, The Middle Eastern Geodatabase for Antiquities–Jordan (MEGA-Jordan). Currently the MEGA-Jordan database lists 425 sites, ranging from the Palaeolithic to the Islamic periods, that have been subject to looting, theft, or illegal digging (MEGA-Jordan, 2021).

Data on import and export transactions is collected by the World Bank and the United Nations is accessible through the World Bank's *World Integrated Trade Solution* (WITS) database. [1] This data captures trade categorised according to Harmonised System (HS) Codes which aggregate the data on specific classes of goods. Gross imports in Constant Dollars (k$) from both Jordan and Israel for the combined HS Codes 970500 (Collections and collectors' pieces; of zoological, botanical, mineralogical, anatomical, historical, archaeological, paleontological, ethnographic, or numismatic interest) and 970600 (Antiques; of an age exceeding one hundred years) are presented in Figs. 1 and 2. Obviously, there are shortcomings of this data, as they do not directly reflect the illicit trade, and there are also noticeable discrepancies in the reporting between various countries over the years.

However, we see an overall increasing trend of 'licit' trade of 'antiquities' over time with a major export route to the United States from both Israel and Jordan. The gross import from Israel exceeds the overall import from Jordan by a double-digit

[1] https://wits.worldbank.org/Default.aspx.

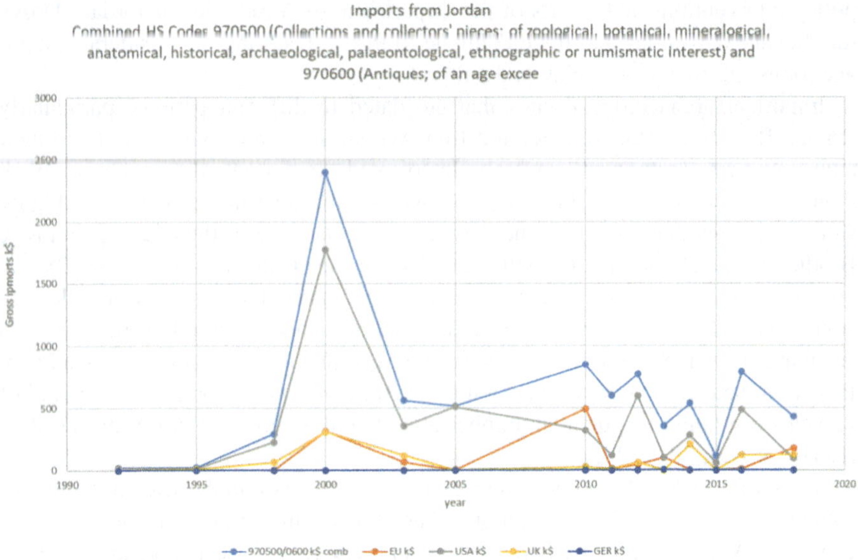

Fig. 1 Gross imports for combined codes 970500 and 970600 from Jordan (k$) as a function of time according to the https://wits.worldbank.org

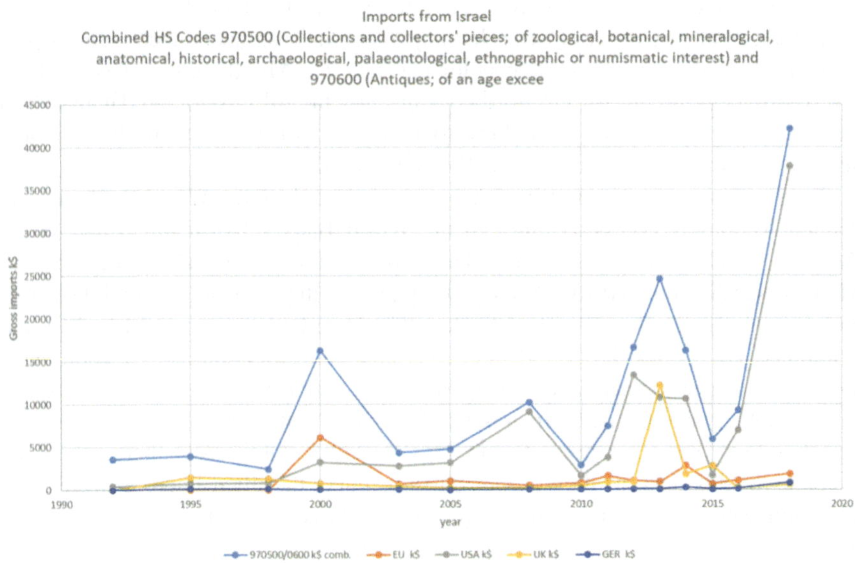

Fig. 2 Gross imports for combined codes 970500 and 970600 from Israel (k$) as a function of time according to the https://wits.worldbank.org

factor. This does not need to, but may mirror trends in illicit trade that deserves a more thorough analysis. Traditionally, an important pathway of illicit traffic from Jordan goes through Israel (Times of Israel, 2016), where a network of 60 plus licensed antiquities dealers (Kersel, 2022, pers. communication) is feeding the international market. The 1978 *Antiquities Law of the State of Israel* restricts dealing in antiquities except with written approval by the Israel Antiquities Authority (IAA).

Incidents of looting number up to the thousands in Jordan, ranging from minor metal detecting to aggressive excavation. A recent example of illegal smuggling of antiquities is the loss of 400 priceless Hellenistic gold coins that were stolen from the Citadel Museum in Amman and, despite government efforts, have not been recovered yet (The Jordan Times, 2016). More recently, in March 2022, United States authorities have returned nine looted artifacts to Jordan that were seized from collector and billionaire hedge fund founder Michael Steinhardt, as part of a landmark deal to surrender trafficked artifacts and avoid prosecution. (Times of Israel, 2022).

3 Jordan's Effort to Fight and Curtail Illicit Excavations and Trade in Antiquities

The Department of Antiquities of Jordan (DoA) is the public institution that is mandated to protect Jordan's cultural heritage mainly archaeological sites. Among an estimated number of archaeological sites of about 100,000, only 25,000 are registered and documented. DoA has taken a number of measures to prevent and curb looting and to protect archaeological sites and objects (Al-Saad, 2021). It has closely cooperated in implementing preventive measures with several national and international partners. At the national level the main partners are the Public Security Department, Customs Department, and a number of national cultural heritage NGOs and societies. Internationally, DoA has established close working relations with UNESCO and other IGO's such as ICCROM, and also International NGOs such as ICOMOS.

Archaeological site monitoring and protection has always been a priority of DoA irrespective of the limited resources available and the vast number of archaeological sites. The most important tool for site monitoring was the Jordan Antiquities Database and Information System (JADIS), developed by the DoA in 1990, which included an inventory of known archaeological sites (through published and unpublished reports) and maps of grid coordinates (Palumbo, 1992). In 2010, JADIS was replaced by a state-of-the-art database system called the Middle Eastern Geodatabase for Antiquities–Jordan (MEGA-Jordan). MEGA-Jordan was a result of a collaboration between the Jordanian DoA, the Getty Conservation Institute, and the World Monuments Fund. The web-based MEGA-Jordan system has the ability to track reported threats, disturbances, and legal violations involving the illegal excavation of sites and removal of artefacts (MEGA-Jordan, 2021). In addition to

MEGA-Jordan, a variety of techniques have been used to monitor site illegal disturbances including archaeological site survey and ground-truthing, and satellite and aerial imagery.

DoA has implemented a number of public awareness campaigns in cooperation with local partners such as the Higher Council for Youth targeting school and university students to help raise awareness of youth on the importance and significance of the country's cultural heritage. In addition, DoA publishes an annual magazine, Athar, to increase public awareness about the value and significance of cultural heritage, particularly archaeology. The DoA's Museums Directorate also organizes workshops and meetings with local communities and schools. The Jordan Museum and the Museum of Jordanian Heritage at Yarmouk University have regular programs for raising awareness of the public with special focus on schoolchildren. Most of the public awareness activities deal with the importance of cultural heritage and rarely is the issue of illicit trafficking is covered. There is no specific information policy or strategy relating to trafficking in cultural property in Jordan and limited sectors of the society are involved in these activities.

In 1974 Jordan ratified the 1970 UNESCO Convention on the Means of Prohibiting and Preventing the Illicit Import, Export and Transfer of Ownership of Cultural Property (UNESCO, 2021). DoA has been working closely with UNESCO on the effective implementation of the UNESCO Convention and other international agreements. Jordan partnered with UNESCO through a series of joint efforts and training programs to combat looting and trafficking. In June 2011, the DoA was among the Signatories of the Amman Declaration on the prevention and response to theft and looting of cultural objects from museums and sites, recommending a range of actions to be implemented to prevent and respond to situations putting heritage at risk (Amman Declaration, 2011). A recent effort on the part of Jordan to fight illicit trafficking of artefacts was a signature of a Memorandum of Understanding (MoU) with the United States. The MoU restricts the import of designated Jordanian cultural property into the United States in the absence of proof that it left Jordan legally. Objects covered include all sorts of artefacts under high threat of looting (United States Department of State, 2019). Further bilateral agreements with other antiquities receiving countries are under consideration.

Despite these efforts and achievements, the protection of Jordan's cultural heritage is still only partial and limited to a number of sites. The illicit excavation and looting of Jordan's archaeological sites continue at grow on an alarming rate. The huge responsibility of protection vast number of archaeological sites exceeds the human and financial capacity of the DoA. The Department is understaffed, underfunded, and in need of more specialised and technologically qualified human resources. As a result, many sites in remote locations are not effectively patrolled and protected.

4 Methodology

Three methods of data collection were used in this research to cover the various dimensions of the issue of illicit excavations and trafficking in cultural objects in Jordan. The first method consisted of desk review and the critical analysis of reports, documents, strategic plans, operational plans, national and international legislations, and study programs of the various Jordanian institutions concerned with cultural heritage protection and promotion with special focus on their role of the fight of illicit excavations and trafficking of cultural objects. The desk research provided the background information needed for the next method of this research which was conducted by using two instruments of data collection, namely questionnaires and interviews. Questionnaires were distributed to representative samples of the following target groups: staff of institutions responsible for protecting the cultural heritage including the Department of Antiquities, Ministry of Tourism and Antiquities, and municipalities, members of police and customs services; museum curators and staff; schoolteachers and children; university students and faculty members; and local community members of selected cultural heritage sites. Structured interviews were conducted with decision makers in the aforementioned institutions and organisations.

5 Root Causes of Illicit Excavations and Trade in Cultural Objects

Jordan's archaeological objects have attracted the attention of international antiques markets, museums, and private collectors, particularly in Europe and United States. Part of the attraction of Jordan's artefacts is their association with biblical history, and they are often identified as themselves biblical or from the Holy Land, which is reflected in a high demand from the international market (Kersel & Hill, 2020).

There is a long tradition of treasure hunting in Jordan mostly driven by a gold fever myth that is believed by large percentage of Jordanians, even among the highly educated (The World Post, 2013). Based on the analysis of the questionnaire responses and content of the interviews and other data collected in this study, it can be concluded that searching for gold treasures is the prime target of most looters because of the expected high monetary return. However, other archaeological objects such as ceramics, glassware, lamps, coins, and masonry are collected due to high demand on these objects from the international antiquities market.

Police and criminal court records indicate that illicit excavations and looting in Jordan is more and more becoming an organised activity with significant increase over the past few years in the number of people indicted for offenses related to this issue. Illegal excavators are mostly 'subsistence looters' who dig as a way of surviving poverty and unemployment. Interviews with locals involved in illegal excavations reveal that local these people do not receive more than one percent of the final retail value of their finds. The collected data in this research reveal some important information about the vicious cycle of illicit trafficking. The local looters are in most cases employed by shadowy middlemen, who buy the looted objects for cheap prices. The middlemen sell looted objects to some influential persons, who are known as antiquities dealers to many people as they even do not care to conceal their identity. The dealers use their connections and power to illegally smuggle the looted objects outside the country, largely to Israel as a transit station, where they manage to get dubious documents of authenticity through local dealers before the objects are moved onwards to the international markets.

The study results indicate that in addition to poverty of local people and greed of middlemen and influential stakeholders, there are a number of other factors that facilitate illegal excavations and looting in Jordan. These include the inadequacy of control mechanisms of this activities, weak security of archaeological sites especially the remote ones, poor documentation and registration of artefacts, and poor public awareness of the value and significance of cultural objects.

6 Critical Assessment of Jordan's Implementation of 1970 UNESCO Convention

Jordan was among the first countries that ratified the 1970 UNESCO Convention. Measures and activities that have been adopted and implemented by Jordan for controlling and fighting clandestine excavations and illicit trafficking of artefacts in response to 1970 UNESCO Convention have been critically examined and assessed. The assessment is based on content analysis of relevant reports and documents of various concerned government organisations in addition to the analysis of interviews performed with key personnel in these organisations.

Article 10(a) of the 1970 UNESCO Convention requests member states to regulate the trade in cultural objects in order to prevent trafficked products from being sold on the legal market and to monitor transfer of ownership of cultural objects more effectively (UNESCO, 2021). Jordan has responded to this request in its Antiquities Law (Law of Antiquities n°21, 1988, as amended by Law n°23, 2004) in two well-articulated articles establishing the prohibition of trade in antiquities. Article 23 argues that:

> Trading in antiquities shall be prohibited. All licenses for trading in antiquities shall be considered as cancelled upon the execution of this Law.

Whereas article 24 argues that

> Subject to Article 23 hereof, no transport, export, or sale of moveable antiquities outside the Kingdom shall be permitted without the approval of the Cabinet on the recommendation of the Minister based on the commendation of the Director.

Furthermore, all moveable cultural objects are considered public property, as stated in article 5a of the Antiquities Law:

> Ownership of immovable antiquities shall be exclusively vested in the state. No other party may own these antiquities in anyway or challenge the state's right to such ownership by delay or any other means.

The law generally bans illegal export and import of movable archaeological objects. The legal system of ownership and transfer of ownership of these objects is sufficiently regulated. However, these rules are insufficient to meet the obligations stated under Articles 6 and 7 of the 1970 UNESCO Convention. The scope of the export and import prohibition, control regulations, and procedures need to be clearly spelled out and effectively communicated to the general public. Furthermore, it is important to keep trade regulations up to date to cover commercial transactions through the Internet. At the moment, such transactions are taking place in a legal vacuum that must be filled as soon as possible. Over 80 percent of the interviewed people in this study have no clear understanding of these regulations and procedures. Many have not heard about them at all. The discrepancy between reality and the legislative texts is hardly conducive to the prevention and combating of trafficking.

Some may argue that the blanket prohibition on the export of antiquities may be one of the key factors for the large increase in illegal dealing with antiquities. The export ban 'encourages the desirability' of these artefacts on the international market because their scarcity increases their value. This, in turn, creates a strong financial incentive to engage in the illicit trafficking of antiquities. In order to enable the competent authorities to track cultural objects involved in commercial transactions, it is important to control transfers of ownership and ensure that illegally excavated items do not find their ways to the international market. This requires, in addition to the strong and well detailed legislations, competent authorities that can effectively enforce the regulations. The assessment study of the capacity of the administrative unit at the Department of Antiquities that is tasked with fighting illicit trade in antiquities in cooperation with the security agencies indicates that it lacks the necessary human and financial resources to ensure that the legislations are effectively enforced.

6.1 Regulation of Archaeological Excavations

Article 5 (d) of the 1970 Convention calls on Member States to control archaeological excavations. Jordan's Antiquity law responds to this request through two articles that deal with clandestine excavations:

Article 14: Despite the provisions of any other law, no person or entity will be allowed to carry out any excavations in antique sites in search of gold or any other hidden treasures.

Article 16: (a)-Only the Department may excavate for antiquities in the Kingdom, and allow by a special permission organizations, committees, scientific societies, and archaeological missions to excavate; according to the provisions of this law, and after ascertaining their abilities and qualifications; provided the excavation is carried out according to conditions set by the Director.; (b)- Subject to the provisions of item (a) of the article, it is forbidden for any person, whether natural or legal, to excavate for antiquities in any location in the Kingdom, even if it were his own private property.

The law clearly bans individuals from excavating for antiquities. The law states that only scientific institutions with the required skills and the necessary financial resources can obtain an excavation authorisation. The conditions for granting an authorisation and the rights and obligations of the holder of an authorisation are also laid down in the law, which also regulates the monitoring of excavations, the security measures to be implemented on sites during excavations, the conditions and procedure for revoking an authorisation, ownership of the scientific results of the excavations, and ownership of the objects unearthed during the excavations.

6.2 Bilateral Agreements

Article 9 of the 1970 UNESCO Convention calls on Member States to participate in international operations to safeguard the cultural heritage of any Member State that falls victim to archaeological or ethnological pillage and suggests that they conclude bilateral agreements to protect cultural objects that face a particular threat from trafficking, such as archaeological objects. As previously mentioned, Jordan has recently used a bilateral means to protect its cultural heritage against trafficking by signing a bilateral agreement with United States (DoS, 2019). Jordan should seek to sign similar agreements with neighbouring countries which act as a transit hub for smuggled artefacts and European countries, which are a main destination.

The outcome of these aforementioned legal measures has so far been much less than expected as evident by the recent significant increase of looting and pillage of archaeological sites (Vella et al., 2015; Al-Manaser & Atal, 2020). Recent data obtained from drone surveys, the national database of archaeological sites, and field archaeologists prove that clandestine excavations and looting have dramatically increased in scale and expanded to new sites (Kersel & Hill, 2020). There is no doubt that much remains to be done to ensure optimal implementation of the 1970 UNESCO Convention and to combat trafficking in cultural property effectively. The following are essential measures that are either missing or not adequately implemented and therefore need significant improvement:

6.2.1 Artefacts Inventory System

Although Jordan has developed with MEGA-Jordan an inventory system of its archaeological sites, it is yet to establish a national inventory system of its vast and diverse collection of artefacts. All archaeological collections in Jordan are owned by the Department of Antiquities which is the public institution mandated by law to collect and preserve these collections. The reality of the matter is that these collections are distributed among a number of institutions and museums that work separately with no clear coordination mechanism. Different institutions have partially registered some of their collections using different registration systems which are incompatible in most cases. No national register has so far been developed, which makes the registration and documentation efforts ineffective. The importance of the inventory as a means of proving ownership of a stolen or illegally exported cultural object goes without saying: under Article 7(b) of the 1970 UNESCO Convention, only cultural objects listed in an inventory can be seized and returned to their country of origin, one of the well-known short-comings of the convention and reasons why it fell short to efficiently curb illicit traffic over the past five decades.

6.2.2 Institutional Framework

States Parties are encouraged under Articles 5 and 14 of the 1970 UNESCO Convention to set up one or more national services for the protection of the cultural heritage, with qualified staff and an adequate budget. The DoA was established as early as the establishment of the modern state of Jordan and is mandated with the protection and management of Jordan cultural heritage. However, the DoA is currently suffering from the lack of qualified staff and sufficient funds to enable an effective curtailing of illicit excavation and looting Jordan's vast number of archaeological sites. It has no administrative division dedicated exclusively to combating trafficking in cultural property. Instead, Jordan has set up a special division within its police narcotics squad to seize illicitly trafficked antiquities.

6.2.3 International Cooperation with Police and Customs

Jordan has not yet made full use of the INTERPOL Stolen Works of Art Database. Such an effective working instrument is not used or supplied regularly with data by the concerned authorities. Cooperation with the World Customs Organization (WCO), particularly on its activities geared to preventing illicit imports and exports of cultural property, is almost absent.

Jordan has not set up specialised training programs for police and custom officers dealing with cultural heritage in order to properly implement the Convention.

6.2.4 Public Awareness

Under Article 10 of the 1970 UNESCO Convention, States Parties are required to undertake to restrict, by information in particular, the movement of cultural objects illegally removed from any State Party and to endeavour "to develop in the public mind a realization of the value of cultural property and the threat to the cultural heritage created by theft, clandestine excavations and illicit exports". Although public awareness activities on the importance of cultural heritage are frequently held by the concerned institutions, Jordan has not developed a specific information policy or strategy relating to clandestine excavations and trafficking in cultural property.

6.2.5 Restitution of Stolen Cultural Objects

Despite the fact that Jordan has lost significant numbers of its cultural properties due to looting and smuggling, it does not make use of UNESCO's *Intergovernmental Committee for Promoting the Return of Cultural Property to its Countries of Origin or tis Restitution in Case of Illicit Appropriation* (ICPRCP) for the restitution of its lost treasures. The Committee's task is to find ways and means of facilitating bilateral negotiations with a view to the restitution and return of cultural property to its countries of origin. The responsible national authorities in Jordan have little knowledge about the committee's working procedures and methods, particularly mediation and conciliation procedures (Al-Saad, 2021). It would be in the interests of Jordan to work closely with the committee and make better use of its methods and procedures with a view to upholding the right to the restitution or return of cultural objects stolen during occupation or by illicit trafficking.

7 Preventive Measures for Combating Clandestine Excavations and Illicit Trade in Cultural Property

The increasing demand by antiquities markets in importing countries, particularly in Europe and North America, have led to a spike in illicit excavations and looting of archaeological sites in Jordan. Despite all efforts exerted so far, Jordan is still far from effectively curbing these illegal activities which pose serious threats to its cultural patrimony and cause irreparable damage to its archaeological sites. Illicit excavations and trafficking are very complex phenomena that have many dimensions. Therefore, the combatting of illicit trafficking of cultural property can be best approached by implementing multidimensional preventive measures. Preventing the illicit trafficking of cultural objects is a fundamental necessity for the protection of Jordan's cultural heritage.

As explained earlier in this chapter, the assessment study performed in this research has identified serious weaknesses and flaws in a number of key areas which hinder Jordan's efforts to fight and curtail the crimes of looting and illicit trafficking. Serious weaknesses and gaps have been identified in the following areas based on content analysis and analysis of interviews and response to questionnaires: legislations, public awareness efforts, knowledge and skills of the competent authorities, artefacts inventory system, and utilisation of international cooperation. Effective fighting of this crime requires serious improvements in these areas. Jordan has an urgent need to develop a number of practical tools to effectively prevent, raise awareness of, and encourage the fight against illicit excavations and trade in antiquities. Below are the most urgent preventive measures as identified in the study:

7.1 Development of a National Inventory System

The lack of proper unified national registration and documentation system of artefacts makes it easier for thieves to steal valuable objects from museums and storage facilities without being discovered. The most recent example is the loss of 400 priceless Hellenistic gold coins that were stolen from the Citadel Museum in Amman and replaced by fake ones (The Jordan Times, 2016). The incident was discovered only by accident and a long time after its occurrence which significantly complicated the process of their retrieval.

It is a well-established fact that one of the best means to protect and recover stolen objects are proper inventories. Jordan is in urgent need to establish a comprehensive register of all artefacts in museums, storerooms, and private collections. Without this documentation, artefacts are at risk of theft and illicit trafficking, and it is very difficult to recover them. Proper registration and documentation facilitate the identification of artefacts and supports all concerned authorities to monitor their movement, determine their provenance and claim their restitution and return (ICOM, 2021). The national artefacts inventory and documentation system should be designed in a way to serve as effective tool in the fight against theft and illicit trafficking in cultural property.

In order to serve its purpose as a security measure the national registration and documentation system should fulfil certain requirements and be in congruity with the Object Identification (Object ID) specifications that are agreed upon by the International Council of Museums (ICOM), INTERPOL, custom authorities, insurance industry, and database experts. Object ID is an internationally recognised documentation standard developed to identify and record archaeological, cultural and artistic objects and launched in 1997. The standardised identification of artefacts provided by the Object ID is a very effective instrument for object identification and recovery in case of theft and illegal movement. It facilitates INTERPOL investigations to identify and apprehend stolen objects. The inventory system should provide the legal evidence for the ownership of the artefacts, which is vital for claiming the restitution and return of illegally smuggled artefacts. Therefore, the inventory system should be designed in a way that artefacts are recorded in accession files and in an accession register capturing the accession number, date, source, method of accessioning, and a brief description of each artefact. Artefacts records should include a unique object number, object name, current location, and distinguishing features. In addition, information on each artefact, such as authentication of provenance with a photograph, a digital image, and drawing should be included. These are vital for security purposes in cases where the artefact is stolen or illegally moved. The emerging technologies of microchips implanting may provide an additional effective method for tracking illegal movements of artefacts (Suzanne, 1998). Unfortunately, most museum staff interviewed in this study are not fully aware of the Object ID and its usefulness as a security tool to prevent illicit movement of objects. However, the newly established ICOM Committee in Jordan may become instrumental to adopt and implement international museum standard in the country. Ethical challenges in respect to illicit traffic for conservators and heritage scientists, together with educational aspects for the younger generation, have been in the focus of various European projects such as "Witness the Past" (Argyropoulos et al., 2011, 2014).

7.2 *Legislations Reform*

There is almost a consensus among all key decision makers interviewed in this study that the prevailing Jordan Antiquities Law has many shortcomings and flaws when it comes to the protection of the country's cultural heritage. The majority pointed out to the weakness of the law in dealing with the issues of looting and illegal trade in antiquities. A sense of urgency of revising and reforming the law has been notified among all concerned parties. DoA announced that a modified law is being processed since 2016 with no precise date when this processing will be finalised. The legislative reform is of great importance and urgency in order to fill the gaps in the existing law and to improve measures to combat the illegal excavation and trafficking of antiquities. A comprehensive revision of the law is necessary for better harmonisation and synchronisation with the provisions and requirements of the international conventions.

The revised law should particularly take account of and addressing contemporary illicit trafficking issues. It should spell out measures to combat the illegal excavation and trafficking of antiquities and toughening punishments for trafficking crimes. The law should also cover, even if in general terms, the practical measures against illicit trafficking in cultural property such as the establishment of a national inventory system of cultural objects, establishment of national services focused on the protection of cultural heritage, in particular against illicit trafficking, and dealing with trade in antiquities especially sales of cultural objects on the Internet. The revised law should be supplemented by detailed regulations and implementation procedures to detail the legal and practical measures covered in the law to facilitate their effective implementation.

Jordan should take full benefit of the international legislations. While Jordan has ratified two of the three main international instruments, the 1970 UNESCO Convention and the 1954 Hague Convention, it has not yet acceded to the 1995 UNIDROIT Convention (UNIDROIT, 2021). Priority should be given to strengthen the implementation of the 1970 UNESCO Convention as explained above and seriously consider accession to the 1995 UNIDROIT Convention. The lack of proper implementation of the international legal instruments may explain the hard to believe reality that Jordan has not ever submitted a restitution application to the UNESCO Intergovernmental Committee despite the fact that significant parts of Jordan's cultural treasures have been illegally moved or stolen over the past decades. These include irreplaceable cultural treasures of universal significance such as the Dead Sea Scrolls, Rizqeh chalcolithic statues, and mosaics of Jerash, just to mention a few examples (Al-Saad, 2021). Clearly, Jordan does not make use of the Intergovernmental Committee and nor does it draw any benefit from its role as facilitator for restitution and conciliation processes.

7.3 Upgrading and Enhancing Public Awareness Activities

It is quite clear that tackling illegal excavations and trade in cultural property in Jordan cannot be effective without a strong support from the general public. Increasing the public understands towards more respect and appreciation of cultural heritage values and significance is essential and represent a key preventive measure. The study results demonstrate that the people of Jordan generally underestimate the criminal aspect of illicit excavation and trafficking of cultural property. Eighty one percent of the respondents to the questionnaire believe that hunting for buried treasures is legal and for them does not represent a violation of the law or a criminal act of any sort. They also believe that it is ethically accepted as a way to raise money especially for unemployed youth. What is more striking is that the economic motivation for illicit excavation and trade in antiquities is accepted by some interviewed officials. Most of the respondents of the general public sample are not fully aware of the meaning, value, and significance of cultural heritage for them personally or for their society at large. A surprising large percentage (31 percent) of the general public has negative perception of the value and significance of cultural heritage and some even consider it as a hindrance to urbanisation and development.

Raising the public's consciousness on the criminal aspect of illicit traffic in cultural goods is a real challenge for Jordan. While changing the attitude of illegal excavators' and collectors themselves may prove difficult, it is a cornerstone to change the general public's tolerance towards those people and their activities. As a signatory of the 1970 Convention and following its Article 10 Jordan must implement educational and awareness-raising measures to fight illicit trafficking of cultural properties.

Innovative approaches and tools should be adopted to inspire a new public mindset regarding the protection of cultural heritage and the rejection of illicit excavation and trafficking. Partnership and effective coordination between the different concerned government branches and non-governmental organisations should be formed to adopt a national policy for implementing an efficient awareness raising activities that are specifically tailored for different categories of people taking in consideration their age, level of education, and cultural background. Public communication becomes easier, quicker, and more effective thanks to the new communication technologies, particularly social media. The combination of traditional communication mechanisms such as videos, TV programs, and brochures with more innovative tools, such as social media and collaborative platforms should be adopted and spread the idea that protection of cultural heritage it is of interest for everyone. Visual materials and awareness-raising resources produced by international organisations such as UNESCO, ICOM, and INTERPOL are valuable sources and should be included in the national campaign.

7.4 *Effective Use of Education*

The younger generation plays a key role in sustaining heritage today and in the future, and therefore their full engagement in the fight against illicit excavations and trafficking of cultural property is of paramount importance. This can be best achieved through combining elements of formal and informal education. The curricula of schools and university programs contain brief knowledge about the archaeology of Jordan. However, the topic of illicit excavations and trafficking is still completely missing and therefore, youth and children are ignorant about this serious issue and its catastrophic consequences. This why it is of utmost importance take urgently the following measures:

- Incorporate into the school curricula and university programs at undergraduate and postgraduate levels teaching modules on the promotion, protection, and transmission of heritage in all its forms with special focus on the fight against its illicit trafficking.
- Educational materials and educational kits on the protection and promotion of cultural heritage should be developed to target different age groups of students at schools and universities.
- Collaboration with the World Heritage Education Program should be activated to get benefit of their rich educational resources and materials.
- Innovative teaching methods employing modern technologies should be adopted to educate children on cultural heritage in an interactive, educational and entertaining way (Haddad, 2016; Mariotti, 2021).

Five state universities in Jordan provide teaching programs in the field of cultural heritage. Graduate and undergraduate programs in archaeology, anthropology, conservation of cultural heritage, and cultural heritage management are offered by these universities. Unfortunately, very little, if any, research has been conducted by these universities on the challenge of illicit excavations and trafficking of cultural objects that face the country. The universities are obliged to promote interdisciplinary research needed to analyse and identify the root causes of the phenomenal increase of illicit excavations and trafficking of cultural objects in Jordan and to develop adequate counter measures on various levels. They are also obliged to organize seminars and public lectures on the topic to target students from different faculties.

7.5 Capacity Building

The prevention and combating of illicit excavations and trade in antiquities in Jordan require the empowerment and support of its responsible authorities and organisations. Jordan needs effective capacity building that includes supporting the responsible organisations with qualified personnel, sufficient funds, and intellectual resources.

7.5.1 Department of Antiquities

The DoA is responsible for the protection and management of sites and collections of cultural objects, as well as the initial investigations into instances of looting and other offences related to cultural heritage. DoA is currently understaffed, underfunded, and in need of more specialized and technologically qualified human resources. DoA needs to establish within its organisational structure a specialised directorate to prevent and combat illicit trafficking. This new directorate should be tasked with monitoring trafficking in cultural property nationally and internationally. It should take the responsibility for operational investigations into various acts against the national cultural heritage, including theft of and trafficking in archaeological objects, damage to and looting of archaeological sites, and detection of forgeries and fakes. The new directorate should be supplied with highly qualified personnel of multiple capacities and expertise in the fields of archaeology, anthropology, archaeometry, national and international legislation, business, and public communication. The directorate should actively participate in investigations conducted by other judicial police departments in illicit excavation and trafficking and coordinate between the police and customs services and appropriate international organisations such as INTERPOL, WCO, and UNESCO. The new directorate should be supplemented with a well-equipped state-of-the-art laboratory for the detection of counterfeits and forgeries as detection and unveiling of well-manufactured and forged pieces of art usually require expert rigor scientific analyses.

7.5.2 Police and Customs

The responsible security and custom authorities need to be supported with qualified specialised staff, that have the capability and know how to identify and examine cultural objects. Existing departments and staff often lack the knowledge and training to investigate and prevent offences against cultural heritage, and regularly cannot compete with the resources of professional looters and illegal antiquities dealers. Furthermore, serious capacity building efforts are needed for all other responsible authorities and organisations including security authorities, the border guards, and museum professionals.

Police and custom authorities dealing with the fight of illicit trafficking of cultural heritage should be trained to be aware of international legislations related to illicit trafficking, INTERPOL working procedures, and international cooperation in police matters. Cooperation between all authorities concerned with illicit trafficking should be institutionalised under a common strategy.

8 Conclusion

Illicit excavation and trade in antiquities remain a major and unsettled challenge for Jordan. Although Jordan has taken a wide range measures to protect its cultural sites and objects against the dangers of theft, clandestine excavation, and illegal trafficking, these measures have not so far achieved the intended outcomes as indicated by the alarming increase and proliferation of pillage to the country's cultural heritage. In order to enhance and optimise Jordan's efforts in combatting clandestine excavations and illicit trafficking the following steps are proposed.

National legislation should be aligned with relevant international standards and be reviewed to include the illicit traffic of cultural property as a serious crime. The law should be supplemented with well-articulated and detailed operational guidelines for effective implementation of the law. A comprehensive revision of the law is also necessary for better harmonisation and synchronisation with the provisions and requirements of the international conventions particularly the 1970 UNESCO convention.

National capacities should be strengthened. Institutionally, Jordan needs to reform and strengthen the authorities and administrative units responsible for the protection of cultural heritage particularly those responsible for combating clandestine excavations and illicit trafficking. The responsible authorities and units must have the necessary financial and human resources to pursue the agreed strategy and objectives for preventing and combating trafficking. Effective capacity building that includes supporting the responsible organisations with up-to-date qualified personnel, sufficient funds and intellectual resources must be given the highest priority.

A special unit should be established at the Department of Antiquities to be specifically tasked with preventing and combating clandestine excavations and illicit trafficking. A national contact point should be designated to collect domestic information to foster cooperation at the international level and ensuring coordinated action. The use of the existing tools such as the INTERPOL Stolen Works of Art Database, the WCO's ARCHEO platform, ICOM's red lists, UNODC's knowledge management portal SHERLOC, and the UNESCO Database of National Cultural Heritage Laws should be strengthened and further integrated.

Jordan should utilise more effectively Article 9 of the 1970 UNESCO Convention to widen the scope of bilateral cooperation to protect its cultural heritage against trafficking by signing a bilateral agreements. In addition to the agreement signed with the United States, Jordan should seek similar agreements with neighbouring countries, which act as a transit hub for smuggled artefacts. Jordan should ratify the

1995 UNIDROIT Convention and apply especially the concept of due diligence outlined in the Article 4 when determining the provenance of objects.

National inventories of cultural property should be completed in Jordan to ensure preparedness in case of conflict or natural disaster. The system should fulfil international requirements and standards particularly the Object ID system as specified by ICOM.

Finally, Jordan must work hard on raising the awareness and respect of cultural heritage among its citizens. Innovative approaches and tools should be adapted to impulse a new public mind-set regarding the protection of cultural heritage and the rejection of illicit excavation and trafficking. Modern communication technologies, social media and education system, should be fully utilised in addition to other means to achieve this goal.

Acknowledgments This research has been conducted with the support of the Fulbright Foundation and La Sierra University.

References

Al-Saad, Z. (2021). Legal and operational measures for the prevention and combat of illicit trade in Jordan's cultural heritage. In H. Hayajneh (Ed.), *Cultural Heritage: At the intersection of the humanities and the sciences*. LIT-Verlag.

Al-Manaser, A., & Atal, Y. (2020). Looting of antiquities in Jordan: a general overview. *Adumatu, 42*, 7–15.

Alshami, A., Haddad, N., & Arafat, A. (2007, 25 Feb-1 March). *The role of the Department of Antiquities of Jordan in preventing the illicit trade of cultural heritage, strategies for saving our cultural heritage* [Conference presentation]. International Conference on Conservation Strategies for Saving Indoor Metallic Collections, Cairo, Egypt.

Amman Declaration. (2011). Retrieved June 27, 2022, from https://www.smb.museum/en/museums-institutions/rathgen-forschungslabor/research/guidelines/amman-declaration/.

Argyropoulos, V., Aloupi-Siotis, E., Polikreti, K., Apostolides, R., El Saddik, W., Gottschalk, R., Abd el Nazeer, M., Vryonidou-Yiangou, M., Ashdjian, P., Yannoulatou, M.-C., Simon, S., Davis, W., & Kassianidou, V. (2014). Museum education and archaeological ethics: An approach to the illicit trade of antiquities. *Journal of Conservation and Museum Studies, 12*(1), 1–8.

Argyropoulos, V., Polikreti, K., Simon, S., & Charalambousa, D. (2011). Ethical issues in research and publication of illicit cultural property. *Journal of Cultural Heritage, 12*(2), 214–219.

Contreras, D., & Brodie, N. (2010a). Shining light on looting: Using Google Earth to quantify damage and raise public awareness. *SAA Archaeological Record, 10*, 30–33.

Contreras, D., & Brodie, N. (2010b). The utility of publicly available satellite imagery for investigating looting of archaeological sites in Jordan. *Journal of Field Archaeology, 35*(1), 101–114.

Contreras, D., & Brodie, N. (2012). The economics of the looted archaeological site of Bab edh-Dhra: A view from Google Earth. In P. K. Lazrus & A. W. Barker (Eds.), *All the kings horses: Looting, antiquities trafficking and the integrity of the archaeological record* (pp. 9–24). Society for American Archaeology.

Department of Antiquities of Jordan (DoA). (1988). Jordanian law of antiquities, No. 21, 1988.

Haddad, N. (2016). Multimedia and cultural heritage: a discussion for the community involved in children's heritage edutainment and serious games in the 21st century. *Virtual Archaeology Review, 7*(14), 61–73.

Hammer, E., & Ur, J. (2019). Near Eastern landscapes and declassified U2 aerial imagery. *Advances in Archaeological Practice, 7*(2), 107–126.

ICOM International Observatory on Illicit Traffic in Cultural Goods. (2021). Documentation: Inventory/Identification. *ICOM.* https://www.obs-traffic.museum/documentation-inventory-identification.

Kersel, M. M., & Chesson, M. (2013). Looting matters. Early Bronze Age cemeteries of Jordan's southeast Dead Sea Plain in the past and present. In S. Tarlow & L. Nilsson Stutz (Eds.), *The Oxford handbook of the archaeology of death and burial* (pp. 674–699). Oxford University Press.

Kersel, M. M., & Hill, A. (2020). Databases, drones, diggers, and diplomacy: The Jordanian request for a US cultural property bilateral agreement. *Journal of Field Archaeology, 45*(sup1), S101–S110.

Kersel, M. M., & Hill, A. (2019). The (W)hole picture: responses to a looted landscape. *International Journal of Cultural Property, 26*, 305–329.

MacDonald, B., Adams, R., & Bienkowski, P. (2001). *The archaeology of Jordan*. Sheffield Academic Press.

Mariotti, S. (2021). The use of serious games as an educational and dissemination tool for archaeological heritage potential and challenges for the future: potential and challenges for the future. *Magazén, 2*(1), 119–138.

MEGA-Jordan. (2021). The National Heritage Documentation and Management System. Retrieved June 27, 2022, from www.megajordan.org.

Ministry of Tourism and Antiquities of Jordan. (2021). Jordan Tourism Strategy 2021 to 2025.

Palumbo, G. (1992). JADIS (Jordan Antiquities Database and Information System): An example of national archaeological inventory and GIS applications. In J. Andresen, T. Madsen, & I. Scollar (Eds.), *Computing the past. Computer applications and quantitative methods in archaeology* (pp. 183–188). Aarhus University Press.

Peterman, G. (1994). Archaeology in Jordan. *American Journal of Archaeology, 98*(3), 521–559.

Suzanne, C. (1998). Collections management inventory. In R. A. Buck & J. A. Gilmore (Eds.), *The new museum registration methods* (pp. 117–120). American Association of Museums.

The Jordan Times. (2016, February 3). *House panel looking into museum artefacts after 400 ancient coins replaced with fakes*. Retrieved June 27, 2022, from https://www.jordantimes.com/news/local/house-panel-looking-museum-artefacts-after-400-ancient-coins-replaced-fakes.

The World Bank. (2015). Jordan - cultural heritage tourism and urban development project. *World Bank Group*. Retrieved June 27, 2022, from http://documents.worldbank.org/curated/en/862751468186252386/Jordan-Cultural-Heritage-Tourism-and-Urban-Development-Project

The World Post. (2013, July 30). Jordan Treasure Hunters Ruin Ancient Artifacts. Retrieved June 27, 2022, from https://www.huffpost.com/entry/jordan-treasure-hunters-ruin-artifacts_n_3676581

Times of Israel. (2016, June 6). Norway launches probe after envoy's driver caught smuggling artifacts, Retrieved June 27, 2022, from https://www.timesofisrael.com/norway-launches-probe-after-driver-busted-smuggling-artifacts-from-jordan/)

Times of Israel. (2022, March 2). US returns Michael Steinhardts looted antiquities to Jordan. Retrieved June 27, 2022, from https://www.timesofisrael.com/us-returns-michael-steinhardts-looted-antiquities-to-jordan/

UNEP – UNESCO. (2016). *World Heritage and Tourism in a Changing Climate*. UNESCO and UNEP. Retrieved June 27, 2022, from https://whc.unesco.org/en/tourism-climate-change/

UNESCO. (2021, September 4). *Convention on the means of prohibiting and preventing the illicit import, export and transfer of ownership of cultural property 1970*. Retrieved June 27, 2022, from http://www.unesco.org/new/en/culture/themes/illicit-trafficking-of-cultural-property/1970-convention/

UNIDROIT. (2021, June 4). UNIDROIT convention on stolen or illegally exported cultural objects. Retrieved June 27, 2022, from https://www.unidroit.org/instruments/cultural-property/1995-convention

United States Department of State. (2019). *Memorandum of Understanding between the UNITED STATES OF AMERICA and JORDAN*. Retrieved June 27, 2022, from https://www.state.gov/wp-content/uploads/2020/04/20-201-Jordan-Cultural-Property-12.16.2019.pdf

Vella, C., Bocancea, E., Urban, T. M., Knodell, A. R., Tuttle, C. A., & Alcock, S. E. (2015). Looting and vandalism around a World Heritage Site: Documenting modern damage to archaeological heritage in Petra's hinterland. *Journal of Field Archaeology, 40*(2), 221–235.

Ziad al-Saad is professor of cultural heritage conservation and management at the Faculty of Archaeology and Anthropology Yarmouk University. He obtained PhD in conservation and archaeometry from University of London in 1992. He was visiting lecturer at Camberwell College, London, served as Chair of Department of Archaeology from 1994 to 1999, then became the Director of the Institute of Archaeology and Anthropology at Yarmouk University becoming its first Dean for two terms until 2007. He then moved to the newly established German-Jordanian University as Vice President for Academic affairs for two years and led the university strategic planning and quality assurance programs for two years. In 2010 he returned to Yarmouk University as Vice President for Research and International Affairs. He was then appointed by the Cabinet as Director General of Department of Antiquities of Jordan until the end of 2011 when he returned to Yarmouk University. Prof. Al-Saad research interest generally is in the areas of conservation and scientific analysis of archaeological materials with a particular interest in the conservation and stabilisation of archaeological finds especially metallic artifacts and stone monuments. He has been actively involved in the preservation and conservation of stone-carved monuments of the Nabatean city of Petra. Prof. Al-Saad has been very active researcher and managed to get millions of grant dollars from various international funding agencies including EU, World Banks, USAID, JAICA and others.

Stefan Simon is, since 2005, Director of the Rathgen Research Laboratory with the National Museums Berlin. Trained as a heritage scientist, Simon earned his PhD in Chemistry from the Ludwig Maximilian University, Munich with a thesis on the weathering and conservation of marble. His research focus lays on preventive conservation, authenticity testing, climatology and non-destructive testing. He served as a Council Member and Vice President (2009–2011) of ICCROM, Rome. As Inaugural Director of Yale's Institute for the Preservation of Cultural Heritage and Director of the Yale's Global Cultural Heritage Initiatives (2014–2019), Stefan Simon prioritised the advancement of sustainable conservation strategies triggered by global climate change and the green museum debate, and questions of conservation documentation, authenticity and access in the digital age. At Yale University, he is also Senior Research Fellow in the Department of Chemistry and Fellow at the Yale Law School. Between 2001 and 2005 he led the Building Materials Section at the Getty Conservation Institute, Los Angeles. Simon is a corresponding member of the German Archaeological Institute and has been recognised with Honorary Professorships at X'ianJiaotong University, China, and the Technical University Berlin. He has co-authored and published more than 150 articles on the preservation of cultural heritage.

New Security Challenges at Museums and Historic Sites: The Case of Spain

Estrella Sanz Domínguez, Francisco José Rufián Fernández, and Isber Sabrine

Abstract Security at museums and heritage sites has been an issue that has traditionally been oriented towards the protection of buildings and their contents against theft, and the evacuation of people in the event of a fire. But nowadays, analysing the wide range of risks and threats that they may be affected by is becoming increasingly complex. While contemporary societies are continually changing in terms never seen before, the risks and threats are increasing and evolving faster. This article aims to analyse how other security-related areas can help to resolve these challenges, for example, the different perspectives prepared by the National Security Plans and Civil Protection Systems, making an analysis of Spain, as an example within the European Union, and how the COVID-19 crisis has made these shortcomings even more evident.

1 Introduction

Traditionally, security measures and protocols have been developed following specific regulations' implementation, addressing fire prevention or occupational safety problems.[1] However, despite applying these regulatory obligations, proper analysis and development of these measures are still pending within cultural heritage

[1] The regulations in these two areas have been broadly developed at international, European, and national levels due to the incident risk and social awareness in the previous decade. Their measures are compulsory in any building open to the public or with workers in it.

E. Sanz Domínguez
Facultad de Bellas Artes [Faculty of Fine Arts], Complutense University Madrid, Madrid, Spain
e-mail: essanz@ucm.es

F. J. Rufián Fernández (✉)
Autonomous University of Madrid, Madrid, Spain
e-mail: francisco.rufian@gmail.com

I. Sabrine
Heritage for Peace, Barcelona, Spain

N. Oosterman, D. Yates (eds.), *Art Crime in Context*, Studies in Art, Heritage, Law and the Market 6, https://doi.org/10.1007/978-3-031-14084-6_7

sites and museums. To use the correct measurements in these contexts, we need to consider the specific characteristics marked by the elements to be protected: cultural assets of diversified nature and a varying degree of fragility; historical-cultural values; different economic worth. Additionally, these assets can be housed in buildings that are themselves of cultural significance. When located in urban centres assuming control over them will be easier, whereas in rural or natural spaces protection difficulties will multiply (Clark et al., 2019).

We can describe three legislative areas traditionally involved in the security design of cultural heritage sites: protection of workers, fire prevention—especially in relation to construction—and the Civil Protection in Emergencies. The latter devised as a public service action tool for the protection of people and their properties against emergencies arising from natural causes or human activities (Spanish National Civil Protection Strategy, 2019). Neither have been appropriately developed by policymakers to be applied in cultural heritage sites, and their implementations have depended on the judgements of managers and specialists.

From a criminological perspective, little research focuses on the relationship between heritage sites or buildings, and emergency management. Maybe the study of heritage destruction in armed conflicts is the most similar area in this regard. Regarding cultural goods, we can find investigations about different criminological aspects of archaeological looters, illicit trafficking of cultural goods, or art crimes (Balcells, 2018); together with studies concerning natural heritage, an area where some criminological theories have been developed in recent years, which could be applied to that field, like, the conceptual framework of conservation criminology (Gibbs et al., 2010; Kahler et al., 2021). There are similarities between this framework and the study of risk management in heritage; both involve different legislations, many professional disciplines, and an important impact in local communities.

Other classical criminological aspects have not been studied in the prevention, reaction, and emergency management involving heritage sites, such as analysing the different risks and their prevention, or the social impact when a heritage element is damaged or lost after a catastrophe or an attack. On the other hand, the current victimology studies extend the concept of the victim beyond that of the legal asset holder, including those who experience a catastrophe or the society as a victim. Perhaps, the apparent difficulty of establishing a direct victim, together with the problematic estimation of an incident, and the problems of definition and transference between different legislations, are the main causes of the lack of study by criminologists in this area, as in its day happened with the crimes against cultural heritage themselves (Balcells, 2018).

We want to address the calls in the discipline by presenting how legal and criminological studies can aid policymakers and cultural heritage professionals by better defining, and understanding, challenges faced concerning the emergency management of museums and heritage sites. Therefore, we contribute to legal and criminological research by arguing the liability of preserving cultural heritage on a technical level, as obliged by Spanish legislation.[2] These concepts can be extrapolated to other states whose, with the ratification of different international conventions, principal aim is to comply with this duty of protection.

The continual news related to the incidence of various threats to heritage dramatically reminds us of the importance and the relevance of starting a debate regarding the legislation that reviews and updates existing procedures in the face of a continuous evolution of risks.

We want to highlight our professional experiences and perspectives for consideration in future studies, or applications in this field, such as the protection of the values of heritage assets, the specific risks for their use (both touristic and cultural), their location within environments that are unfamiliar to the vast majority of visitors (e.g., sites in the countryside, castles built-in high places, etc.) or the implementation of occasional or temporary uses, such as the holding of different events. All of them, among others, are not taken correctly into account currently in security protocols.

At the same time, these and other risks are beginning to manifest themselves as real threats or are even become significant catastrophes. These are: (1) devastating consequences due to the incidence of climate change; (2) greater online exposure of the use of collections; (3) massive storage of information—sometimes confidential—in the cloud; (4) the impact of new social movements on cultural heritage; and (5) maintenance work in buildings or restoration interventions performed by, for example, non-professional actors. Therefore, it is essential to analyse the presence and impact of some of these potential risks that may have an uncertain evolution if they are not considered in museums or historical sites' security plans and protocols.

2 Importance of Raising Awareness

An emergency or disaster is the materialisation of risk when we have not been able to control it because, for example, there has been no action in prevention to reduce the vulnerability and the degree of exposure to potential threats (Paolini et al., 2012). The importance of identifying, analysing, and evaluating risks, the probability of their occurrence, and also our ability to react to them, in order to prevent them or mitigate their impact is therefore fundamental. Similarly, having up-to-date information on the evolution of these risks, and the possible increase in threats will enable cultural entities to have a more appropriate response capacity, work on training aimed at specific objectives, and plan their organisational structure based on real needs.

Cultural institutions are not on the fringes of social and technological development, in which risks, and threats, can change at a faster pace than has been usual until

[2] Law 16/1985 of 25 June is the national law regarding Spanish Historical Heritage. The different autonomous communities, in total 17, have, in essence, the same obligations regarding heritage conservation, in their own laws.

now. One possibility to alleviate this problem is to rely on the National Security Strategies and Risk Analysis that all states update annually.[3]

The Spanish National Security Strategy,[4] discusses different threats and challenges, as well as dynamics of social transformation that can be disruptive in certain aspects of cultural heritage in general. The document recognises the importance of cultural heritage, calling it, the "backbone of 21st century Spain" (National Security Strategy, 2017). These risks and threats appear transversally throughout the document, which is why a more specific subsequent analysis is necessary, together with a commensurate specialisation on the part of professionals (Rufián Fernández, 2020).

Among the threats and risks set forth, we highlight climate change, already mentioned previously due to its direct relationship with cultural heritage, and possibly the one with the most dynamic and extensive impact on economic, social, or environmental effects. However, we also find other threats to be analysed from the perspective of cultural institutions by changing the degree of exposure based on other variables. Acting in prevention not only means identifying, analysing, and evaluating risks, but also working to reduce them with corrective actions to prevent their future development (Paolini et al., 2012). By the same token, it is also important to disseminate the importance of prevention and to provide information about the actions that are carried out in this regard, since otherwise they would go unnoticed.

Risks to historical heritage are real and diverse, ranging from environmental impact to the theft of works of art. There are current cases that underscore their vulnerability and prevalence to external threats (Council conclusions on risk management in the area of cultural heritage, 2020). To be able to guarantee comprehensive security, with these types of anthropic risks, it is essential to have cooperation between institutions and civil society. However, to achieve this collaboration, it is necessary to raise awareness about these risks to which cultural heritage is exposed, and to convey its value to the population that, due to their proximity, can act directly or indirectly to protect it from different threats, or even assist in evacuation or post-disaster recovery in an emergency situation. Lack of awareness about the importance of cultural heritage should be considered a key factor in the risk assessment. This is something that has also been confirmed through the *ICOMOS Cultural Tourism Charter* (1999), after indicating the individual and collective right and responsibility to understand, respect, value, and actively conserve cultural heritage, which, in addition, highlights the dynamic interaction between tourism and cultural heritage.

---

[3]The National Security Strategy of the Spanish Government: https://www.dsn.gob.es/es/estrategias-publicaciones/estrategias; National Security Reports: https://www.dsn.gob.es/es/documento/informe-anual-seguridad-nacional-2020; and at European level, the European Security Union: (https://ec.europa.eu/info/strategy/priorities-2019-2024/promoting-our-european-way-life/european-security-union_es).

[4]The one approved in 2017 is currently in force, although work is being done to update it. Order PCM/1028/2020, of 30 October, by which the Agreement of the National Security Council is published, by which the procedure for the preparation of the National Security Strategy for 2021 is approved. "BOE" no. 292, of 05/11/2020.

3 Existing and Novel Risks for Cultural Heritage: Current Situation and Recommendations

Our objective is not to review the existing regulations regarding the protection of cultural heritage during an emergency, but to rethink the weaknesses revealed in recent years. There is no doubt that there is a greater awareness in this regard that has been translated into different regulations and work schemes, but, as we have pointed out in the introduction, their interrelation and necessary adaptation to the characteristics of heritage assets is still lacking development in accordance with the importance of the assets to be protected. For example, the Spanish government approved Law 17/2015 of 9 July, regarding the National System of Civil Protection, as an actualisation of the previous law in the matter stemming from 1985. This law established the legal framework for the preparedness and response to situations of severe collective risk, public calamities, or extraordinary catastrophe.

In 2015, coinciding with the approval of Law 17/2015, the Spanish Ministry of Culture developed a *National Emergency Plan and Risk Management in Cultural Heritage*, with three fundamental objectives for a correct national management of cultural heritage: (1) to design measures or procedures for prevention and protection in the face of a catastrophe; (2) to establish in such cases a methodology of action to minimize the damages; and (3) to design the instruments of action and the mechanisms of coordination with different institutions.

Law 17/2015, together with the National Plan, gives the administrations the tools to create mechanisms for cultural protection in every kind of emergency. Still, it has not been successfully developed, and only after the Notre Dame and Brazil National Museum fires raised awareness of the real danger. After these events, some museums and ecclesiastical institutions started developing safeguarding plans for their objects.

In June 2021, a Draft Bill was published, modifying Law 16/1985 of 25 June, regarding Spanish Historical Heritage, and Law 10/2015 of 26 May, to preserve Intangible Cultural Heritage. A new article is added, which indicates the obligation to have Safeguard Plans within buildings containing Historical Heritage assets:

> Properties that serve as the headquarters of cultural institutions and which contain, guard or display Historical Heritage assets of any nature, must have a Safeguard Plan that defines both the necessary measures to prevent or minimize any potential risks and the consequences thereof, as well as the actions for the protection, rescue or recovery of said assets in the event that they are affected by any type of catastrophic episode. The correct and effective implementation of these plans will require their inclusion in the local, regional or state Civil Protection plans, as appropriate.

This Draft Bill is not approved at the time of writing. Therefore, currently, no law compels museums, ecclesiastical, or cultural institutions to develop safeguarding plans for their collections. In addition, Spain still has different legal obligations that apply to cultural institutions relating to fire prevention, evacuation, and work safety, whose correct integration as a whole is essential. Besides, a proper study on the work made so far shows a lack of adaptation between the Civil Protection mechanism, and the real needs in cultural heritage conservation regarding the correct object protection in an emergency. In the following paragraphs, we will comment on the most relevant aspects that currently affect heritage.

3.1 Tourism

Analysing the impact of tourism on heritage sites requires effort and constant updating. It plays an important role in the Spanish economy, representing a significant portion of the GDP (IMPACTOUR, 2020).[5] This fact implies that, in order to understand its relevance, we must approach the correct analysis of their significance for security both in heritage sites and museums from three perspectives:

3.1.1 Economic Dependency

Many institutions have seen their budgets, and therefore their scope for action, severely cut with the disappearance of direct cash income from visitors. In line with dependence on tourism, we have seen examples in press of how some American museums have had to cut their workforce or put part of their collections up for auction to alleviate the serious economic crisis, thus breaking the limitations imposed up to now by the American Association of Art Museum Directors (AAMD), which restricted the sale of assets, justified solely for the purchase of other works, now providing a margin of two years to use the proceeds from the sale of cultural assets for other matters related to the maintenance of the museum institution itself. In Spain, this would be something unthinkable as established by the regulations aimed at preserving cultural heritage and by the concept of public ownership of it, deeply rooted within the community. Therefore, it is the state, and by extension society, that ultimately bears the economic impact of the closure of museums or other historical sites.

3.1.2 Compatibility

This is between preservation and accessibility. Not all cultural assets, museums or historical sites are designed for the tourism of the twenty-first century (García-Hernández et al., 2017; Paolini et al., 2012). It is complex to implement the necessary technical security measures due to costs, or geographical location. The correct balance between a vast number of visitors and events (more income) and

[5]The Pontevedra Museum, the *Románico Palentino* or the *Camino de Santiago* are part of the Spanish representation in the European Commission's IMPACTOUR project, which aims to study and analyse the impact of cultural tourism on the economy of the European Union. The project will end in January 2023.

the conservation of the sites, together with the proper technical security measures, as well for visitors and workers, is a matter hard to get.

3.1.3 Linking

Linking self-protection plans and security regulations with plans for the protection of cultural assets in the event of emergencies. Until now, each field has primarily been developed separately, both normatively and operationally, and the very characteristics of the heritage asset or of the site as a space with cultural value are rarely considered.

The relationship between tourism and the economy to maintain museums and heritage sites is evident. This fact jeopardises their sustainability and resilience, so it would be expedient for this risk factor to be included in risk management. On the other hand, alternatives will be considered that will alleviate these circumstances as far as possible, that is, to incorporate financial management and protection as a measure to reduce this risk, ensuring the resilience and the continuity of the activity as part of security.

For the maxim of the duty of conservation and integrity of Spain's cultural heritage to truly be compatible with that of access to, and the enjoyment thereof, by society, both the routes and the number of visitors must be properly planned to guarantee the security of the assets and the safety of the visitors themselves (Merryman et al., 2007; Paolini et al., 2012; Román, 1999). Risk management needs to be an integral part of conservation practices and conservation and management plans (Paolini et al., 2012), where visitor control is one of the most relevant issues. Most institutions have developed those methods, but it is not the same as safeguard plans or emergency protection plans for cultural property, which must be a document included in the institution's self-protection plan. All the plans must be nurtured by the information they contain, contemplating the comprehensive management of risk and possible emergencies.

The COVID-19 pandemic has shown some new trends. From an economic perspective, the dependence on tickets, events and visits has been one of the serious problems that many cultural institutions have had to face (Teijgeler et al., 2020). The lack of foresight and the absence of precedents on such a scale had as a consequence the need to rapidly improvise parallel financing, even allocating financial means that were scarce at that time. Some of these alternative routes were implemented through virtual visits and other activities that do not require physical presence (Museum Booster, 2021).

However, to achieve this, most institutions had to reconvert all their computer platforms and redirect their activities online as quickly as possible, bearing new costs at a time when income had all but dried up (Teijgeler et al., 2020). This in turn has influenced the emergence of other risks, computer risks, to which we will refer when talking about the use and proliferation of new technologies and to which more attention must be paid, since the modifications implemented by cultural institutions during COVID-19 have potentially left them more exposed to cyberattacks.

3.2 Climate Change

The effects of climate change are becoming evident around the world (torrential rains, floods, heavy snowfalls, hurricanes, droughts, fires, etc.), although the type of threat, the combinations thereof, or their effects may vary substantially in each country and region therein. Its consequences and impact can affect aspects of cultural heritage, also linked to society and the economy, in addition to the always tragic possibility of loss of human lives.

Climate change can trigger significant changes at the social and economic level and therefore, the response must be comprehensive, relating all these dimensions to the Sustainable Development Goals (United Nations, n.d.). We must highlight the international initiative of the Climate Heritage Network, where work began to raise awareness about climate change and its effect on cultural heritage. This is a voluntary, mutually supportive network of arts, cultural, and heritage organisations committed to helping their communities to address climate change and to achieve the ambitions of the Paris Agreement.

Knowing the threats arising from this risk will enable us to identify our weak points and thus be able to plan correction and, or mitigation, of strategies in advance (Hermann, 2017). The protection of cultural heritage is already one of the indisputable objectives in the policies developed in Spain in relation to climate change, as reflected in the adaptation plan prepared in this regard by the Ministry for the Ecological Transition and the Demographic Challenge (Ministerio para la Transición Ecológica y el Reto Demográfico, 2020).

Taking this into account, a series of considerations arise that should be highlighted. First, we must understand how the threats arising from climate change are developing—the possibility of their occurrence and their scope——what the physical processes of destruction are (Sesana et al., 2021), and which cultural assets are most sensitive to its effects and what, social, physical, and economic damages derived from its action may be.[6]

One of the most challenging situations is faced with possible sudden changes in temperatures and rainfall levels. There may be a considerable increase in the cost of the environmental parameter control and maintenance systems established inside the buildings that preserve cultural assets. Not all of them have been designed to function with sufficient protective capacity in extreme weather conditions. On the other hand, that kind of risk needs increased spending on maintenance, or closure or disabling of areas due to the need for urgent repairs caused by a climatic agent.

All this change the conditions within buildings, forcing the security measures to be rapidly modified to work adequately in those new situations. So, there are some important aspects to consider when controlling risks related to climate change. One of them is a review and further development of the procedures, tools, and methodologies for the preservation of cultural heritage, with more cooperative approaches raised from multiple perspectives and more participation (ICOMOS, 2020). Another

[6] See for a more detailed approach (Orr et al., 2021).

aspect would be to make a history of natural disasters and evaluate the response or impact on the different structures or infrastructures of the buildings to identify weaknesses and apply corrections.

The information and conclusions drawn from this work need to be studied in a plan, and operate on different models, scenarios, and prevalence levels that enable quick adaptations and reduce the impact in an emergency, all from holistic models that consider risks, vulnerabilities, resilience and management.[7] All these measures and plans are ineffective if there is no adequately trained staff, so it is essential to train workers linked to heritage sites on the effect of climate change on cultural heritage and ways to mitigate these effects within their institutions.

3.3 Technological Risks

New technologies have emerged as valuable fundamental resources for museums and heritage sites for the dissemination of their collections and miscellaneous activities.[8] They have also been a platform to approach a much younger audience that demands new uses and habits of cultural consumption. At the same time, technology has become a fundamental technical and administrative management tool, storing sensitive information that sometimes concerns security issues for guarded cultural assets. This new way of displaying, which has experienced a great boost during the COVID-19 pandemic, and the already well-established use of new technologies in the management of collections, is not without threats. An attack on this network, a prolonged system crash or data loss, for example, has serious consequences.

In principle, we can point out that the security of the information requires a guarantee of confidentiality, restricting its accessibility according to previously established authorization levels, whilst ensuring its access to authorised users when needed. At the same time, it must consider the integrity of the data handled by the institution, protecting its accuracy and limitations of use (e.g., intellectual property rights, right of reproduction, and right of public communication).

The security management guarantee should thus contemplate: the analysis of the indicated requirements; the development of a plan that guarantees them; and their implementation and maintenance. In any updated security plan, the prevention of physical risks should coexist with technological risks. In this regard, we would like to mention some aspects to take into account when controlling technological risks; the principles in this specific security area have been extracted from the guide

[7] In the model proposed by the ICOMOS Climate Change and Heritage Working Group (2019), very interesting aspects are included for the design of work tools that pursue this holistic vision.

[8] As technology has been growing in society, cultural institutions, especially museums, had to adapt them to this. As a result of that, the use of new technologies in museums has been an important element in their cultural offers, as shown in the Museum Innovation Barometer 2019, which can be consulted at https://museumbooster.com/research/.

Security of Information Technologies and Communications, published by the National Cryptological Center of Spain. The first step is developing an institutional security policy regarding the use of technologies, creating security guidelines for employees and externals. After that, we need to analyse and evaluate specific risks and, if the institution is developing online activities, study how much and how these can affect the institution.

Then, it is necessary to develop defence and contingency strategies to mitigate the possible damage, which is probably the most technical issue. The correct management of the different steps showed needs to consider estimating the cost of implementation and maintenance of the measures and the legal considerations of use. Humans are considered the most fragile link in that system, so training workers on the importance of these risks and prevention is compulsory.

3.4 Social Movements and New Political Ideologies

Although the attack and destruction of cultural heritage has been present at different times throughout history (e.g., Classical Antiquity, the Reformation and Counter-Reformation, the French Revolution, the Holocaust, Suffragette Actions, etc.), linked to political, religious, or ideological reasons, currently the conduct of the different social movements normally remains within the limits we can consider consistent with coexistence. However, some recent cases, such as that which occurred in the United States with the Black Lives Matter movement and its impact on cultural heritage, in which there have been attacks on public monuments associated with slavery or colonialism, reveal a real threat that must be considered in the risk assessment to plan an appropriate response.

In Spain, in June 2020, following the wake of this movement, the pro-independence political party Catalunya en Comú proposed the removal of the statue of Columbus in Barcelona, considering the colonizing character of the figure to be unfavourable. After a historical review, the statue of Antonio López, Marquis of Comillas, had been removed in this same city, considering him a slaveholder. In Madrid, sculptures such as that of the socialist politician Francisco Largo Caballero appear continuously vandalised with red paint and "murderer" graffitied onto it.

Another example can be found in the exhibition in museums of objects that are connected to the colonial histories of some countries, and that in recent years have been arousing large international protest movements to achieve their return to their states of origin.[9] However, not only is the ownership or the suitability of the place of exhibition of these collections being questioned, the debate also arises about what is exhibited, who chooses it, based on what criteria and whether this reading and choice

[9] In recent years, we have several examples of this situation: e.g., How recent anti-racism protests have pushed a longstanding debate about colonial looting in Europe (theartnewspaper.com); To Protest Colonialism, He Takes Artifacts From Museums (nytimes.com).

of pieces that is being made is correct (German Museums Association, 2018). In this regard, the 31st General Assembly in 2019, the ICCROM Council decided to dedicate a debate to the 'Decolonisation of heritage'.

So, the aspects to take into account when we want to prevent risks arising from social movements are going to be related to the identification of heritage elements that are susceptible to this anthropic risk. From this we can establish specific protection protocols where appropriate, at the same time of a review, and rethink the suitability of the manner in which colonial collections or other controversial heritage assets are exhibited and consider new forms of the presentation related to different sensitivities, while at the same time enhance the integration of indigenous communities. Conforming to the idea of a museum and/or heritage institution as being close to society, its educational programmes can be, and are, used to connect locals and immigrants from European colonies to collections of colonial origin.[10] These activities allow visitors, researchers and museum's staff to see the objects from different perspectives and to seek dialogue with the communities of origin. An example in Spain can be seen in the Museum of America when reading its mission: "To contribute to the mutual knowledge of Ibero-American cultures and peoples through the conservation and dissemination of the collections in the museum"; and in its vision: "To be an essential point of reference in this matter, nationally and internationally, having as principles dialogue, mutual respect and collaboration with all interested parties" (Museo de América, s.d.) On the other hand, these activities could mitigate negative aspects of securitisation, for example, exclusionary consequences for minorities (Atkinson et al., 2020).

It is necessary to specify in the security plan the actions to be taken in the case of a demonstration or any kind of social unrest and to monitor the momentum of these social movements to anticipate potential emergencies. It is compulsory to contact law enforcement agencies to ensure that information about possible demonstrations is received in good time, to be alert, and if there is any necessity, to establish a specific protocol that provides for the rapid closure of access points, as well as safe routes for possible evacuations.

As a general rule, we need to study and assess this specific risk based on the significance of the institution and its location in those areas where demonstrations or gatherings of people are common.

---

[10] See for example initiatives Abuab (https://abuab.org/es/) and Multaka (https://multaka.de/en/startsite-en/).

4 Risks Associated with Maintenance Works or Archaeological Excavations

Recent incidents such as the fire at the Notre Dame Cathedral in 2019, or that of the National Museum of Brazil in 2018, have been associated with actions related to maintenance works in the former, and just the opposite in the latter, i.e., the lack of adequate maintenance of the facilities. Both events can serve as examples to analyse situations of risk to which due attention is sometimes not paid, seeing the catastrophic results that they can have.

In the case of maintenance work or restoration interventions in historic buildings or buildings that house cultural assets, threats can arise from various sources. For example, scaffolding installation during maintenance works represent new access points to the building, intensifying the risk of intrusion. On the other hand, the increasingly common placement of tarpaulins across scaffolding structures may shelter any potential intruders. Sometimes, the scaffolding installation needs to close some access, or change directions. That means that the security team must continuously revise the access and evacuation routes when scaffolding installations are in place, and vet personnel from outside the institution who are working in construction teams.

The associated risks represent a broad and diverse spectrum regarding the lack of maintenance. In accordance our professional experiences, and the *Handbook of Emergency Procedures* (Hekman, 2010), some of the most important are: (1) appearance of pests due to accumulation of waste, disorder, and lack of pest control; (2) emergencies related to water due to lack of maintenance of external pipelines and drainage points, poor condition of roofs, poor condition of rainwater downpipes and internal sewage pipes, etc.; (3) risks of fire caused by a lack of maintenance of the lighting and power supply systems within the building; (4) risks related to the efficiency and correct operation of the fire detection and extinguishing system, due to failure to conduct the relevant reviews or to respect the established recertification periods; and, (5) risks due to lack of control of environmental fluctuations. It is important to control the relative humidity and temperature parameters during maintenance, especially in museums.

The lack of maintenance is an essential issue for museums and institutions. In. I Spain, this issue often brings headlines in the news. For example, in 2013, *El Mundo* reported on an incident in the Prado Museum caused by a water leak in the warehouses of cultural goods; fortunately, with only minor impact on some paintings and drawings (Efe, 2013). Or, in 2018, the fall of a painting of Titian, *Christ Crucified*, in the monastery of San Lorenzo del Escorial. In this case however, with significant damage to the work, and resulting due to a lack of revision of the anchorage system to the wall (Olaya & García, 2018). This painting painting had not been treated in a way according to its importance, not. N only for the obvious conservation duty for the object, but also the responsibility to prevent damage more generally. As we discussed in the introduction, criminological research on catastrophe prevention is an important issue, especially concerning historical heritage.

However, equally important for criminological analyses is to establish criteria for investigating possible responsibilities when the damage has occurred (Fernández González, 2017), e.g., who and why in the institution's staff could be legally responsible for omitting an action, or plan prevention. It would be useful to analyse laws and the different administrative institutions involved in this regard, to solve that kind of problem.

Ensuring the security planning has been joined with those responsible for the work is compulsory to ensure its application. In terms of responsibility, if they do not know the risk and how to deal with it, there is no liability, for example. The modifications to the security plans and self-protection plan are needed to reflect the current situations where appropriate and provide this information to the external agents involved (e.g., firefighters, law enforcement agencies).

The following considerations can be made in reference to the risks associated with archaeological excavations. First, research on archaeological heritage presents a series of risks inherent to its very nature. The specific methodology that must be followed during the works, together with the risks posed by the archaeological remains themselves, makes specific planning necessary to implement them correctly. We can therefore find archaeological excavations that reveal relics and bring them into the public consciousness that are almost impossible to know about in advance and are, at times, under precarious protection. This has the effect of inviting detectorists or looters, particularly in rural areas (Rodríguez Temiño, 2012). These practices are more common in countries where there are few restrictions on the use of metal detectors (Rodríguez Temiño, 2012), using them within the vicinity of public works or excavations to increase the chances of finding archaeological objects. Spanish legislation is quite restrictive in this regard, which makes it difficult for these acts to be committed, although it is still a reality due to the enforcement difficulties and therefore must be considered. Mainly because of the lack of enforcement and resources. One example can be found in the news about the discovery of an Iberian sanctuary in Jaén (province of Spain), facilitated by a report about archaeological plunder (López, 2021).

These characteristics obliged professionals who want to research in this field or design a security plan to consider some aspects arising from archaeological excavations. Scientific literature remains relatively insufficient (Clark et al., 2019). The fact that archaeological remains have been looted in many countries and circumstances besides the protection makes it possible to determine some critical security factors to consider for improving real protection. For example, raising awareness among local communities living near archaeological excavations has been essential as a factor of protection.

5 New Heritage Risks

We want to focus on other issues than those mentioned previously that, due to their complexity, require a broad and more specific analysis. We are referring to buildings classified as historical heritage but which are empty or in a state of disuse and the risk that this poses to possible illegal occupation or theft.

Thefts due to disuse can currently be classified as sporadic, although we can point to some events in this regard that appeared in the press during the closure of institutions due to the COVID-19 pandemic. For example, the case for the theft of the painting *The Spring Garden* by Vincent van Gogh, from the Singer Laren Museum in the Netherlands in the early hours of 30 March 2020, when the criminals took advantage of closure of the museum.

In Spain, there is a considerable quantity of historical heritage, mainly buildings and archaeological sites, which are essential to the urban fabric, although equally important in rural areas. It is necessary to pay attention to that kind of heritage by applying targeted public policies, thereby contributing towards the conservation of areas traditionally degraded, like historic town centres. Thus, their conservation will be guaranteed, but it will also allow heritage integration into social life. In addition, those kinds of measures will help improve the subjective security of the inhabitants and visitors. In that sense, it is possible to follow the research lines opened in the field of environmental criminology, but focus on areas like historic town centres, where tourism, inhabitants, and heritage must coexist. Usually, those kinds of historic elements mentioned in the previous paragraphs are out of the radar of law enforcement agencies and society in general regarding cultural crimes, so it should be noted that there is a so-called 'dark figure': those crimes that remain unreported to the authorities.

On the one hand, we find many properties that have varying degrees of protection and which, either because they belong to public institutions or are funded privately, are in disuse. A common consequence of the enormous maintenance costs that they entail is that they are in poor conservation conditions, and therefore of security, increasing the possibility of being occupied illegally, with the consequent physical deterioration that may result, in addition to other risks associated with fires, or theft of items of furniture, which disappear forever as they are not inventoried or catalogued, going completely unnoticed by specialists.

These institutions generally have security measures in place and the pieces are properly catalogued, making their subsequent sale impossible, or very difficult. Quite the opposite continues to happen, in a trend that dates back many years, in hermitages or small museums that do not have adequate protection, and in which it is easy to take objects of all kinds, even architectural elements from the building itself (Terreros Andréu, 2014). However, we must not forget that there are many crimes or acts of vandalism that are committed by people who do not recognise the cultural value of these objects, or who are responding to the most varied interests, which can range from the search for easy money, even being able to disassemble or divide pieces in order to facilitate their sale, or with the intention of harming the institution itself for some personal or ideological reason (Escribano Velasco & Del Val Recio, 2018). That was the case of the theft of the Codex Calixtinus from the cathedral of Santiago de Compostela in 2011, which responds to that kind of intention. This case was extensively covered by the media in Spain, due to the relevance of the manuscript and the place where it was kept. The question that most professionals raised, about how something like this could happen, was clarified when the author, an employee of the Cathedral with full access, confessed that it was out of revenge against the institution itself. There was no economic motive to this crime, and the manuscript was found abandoned, about to disappear or suffer serious damage.

Although the geographic isolation of some heritage sites has ordinarily been a risk factor to take into account in terms of security (e.g., due to lack of surveillance, lack of adequate documentation, increased response times for emergency services), to this we must add the confinement derived from COVID-19, and the shutdown of tourism. The absence of both tourist traffic and of the nearby population has increased this problem.

On that point, some aspects to consider when controlling risks arising from geographic isolation are first the importance of conducting periodic security checks, both of the site itself and its surroundings. Also, paying attention to crimes or events in other enclaves of historical-artistic value in the region could be replicated within our environment. Second, collaboration in surveillance tasks with local entities or with nearby inhabitants. At the same time, we are raising awareness among the inhabitants of the area and collaboration in reporting and surveillance (Clark et al., 2019). Third, to develop security protocols tailored to the available resources and means, prioritising their use at those sites or for those assets with the greatest vulnerability. Fourth, to act with prudence when publicising finds or declaring the existence of cultural elements in tourist guides or similar publications if no previous security measures have been implemented. Fifth, to anticipate expenses intended for the protection of cultural elements in the annual budgetary allocations (or support). And lastly, to perform accurate and up-to-date documentation of the assets and their circumstances of vulnerability, transferring this information to all the agents involved in their protection.

6 Conclusion

It is impossible to think of total security when it comes to protecting cultural heritage, but that does not mean that we should assume that action is impossible. Throughout this text, an attempt has been made to give visibility to different issues related to the protection and conservation of the collections kept in museums, ecclesiastical, and heritage sites, highlighting the constant challenge of guaranteeing their security due to the appearance of new risks or the continuous evolution thereof, most of them observed in the experience of the authors.

Undoubtedly, the COVID-19 pandemic has forced cultural institutions to face new challenges and review and rethink their management policies. However, when we analyse some of the situations, we realise that most of the main problems came from previous intrinsic issues, such as the economic impact due to the dependence on visits and tourism or the greater vulnerability to theft or vandalism due precisely to this lack of human presence due to the confinements, not foreseen, accentuating, in addition, in places with greater geographical isolation.

However, the successful management of these risks, with the aim of not leading to a disaster or emergency, can only be achieved if we ensure that relevant administrations, society, and the knowledge of technicians and scientists all work in the same direction. In summary, we can say that proper management and protection of heritage environments should be aimed at guaranteeing their conservation, but making it compatible with their use and enjoyment.

Here, we can find an area of expertise where criminology may have significant growth. For example, exploring the necessities and discussing innovative approaches that allow making a more knowledgeable decision in heritage protection and studying the number of disciplines and law regulations.

On the other hand, institutions should raise awareness and participate in work that should be part of their prevention plans. This would enable the interoperability of the services involved in the protection of cultural heritage, interdisciplinary education, and training in shared intervention methods.

References

Atkinson, C., Yates, D., & Brooke, N. (2020). 'Now that you mention it, museums probably are a target': Museums, terrorism and security in the United Kingdom. *Museum Management and Curatorship, 35*(2), 109–124. https://doi.org/10.1080/09647775.2019.1683881

Balcells, M. (2018) Aspectos criminológicos del expolio y del tráfico ilícito del patrimonio arqueológico. In A. Yáñez and I. Rodríguez Temiño (Eds.), *El expoliar se va a acabar* (pp. 335–357) Tirant lo Blanch.

Clark, J.H., Sanz Marcos, R. & Carotenudo, R. (2019) Archeological site of Clunia Sulpicia. In KALAM & EKABA Foundation (Ed.), *Seguridad en el Patrimonio. Simposio Científico Internacional* (pp. 103–108). Madrid.

Council conclusions on risk management in the area of cultural heritage. 8208/20, (May 2020). Retrieved March 1, 2022, from https://www.consilium.europa.eu/media/44116/st08208-en20.pdf

Efe. (2013, April 9). Las goteras dañan catorce obras en el Museo del Prado. *El Mundo*.. https://www.elmundo.es/elmundo/2013/04/19/cultura/1366387748.html

Escribano Velasco, C., & Del Val Recio, J. (2018). Patrimonio arqueológico y expolio en Castilla y León. In A. Yáñez & I. Rodríguez Temiño (Eds.), *El expoliar se va a acabar* (pp. 196–214). Tirant lo Blanch.

Fernández González, C. M. (2017). *Planes de autoprotección y de emergencias*. Editorial Reus.

García-Hernández, M., de la Calle Vaquero, M., & Yubero, C. (2017). Cultural Heritage and Urban tourism: Historic city centres under pressure. *Sustainability, 9*(8), 1346–1359. https://doi.org/10.3390/su9081346

German Museums Association. (2018). Guidelines on Dealing with Collections from Colonial Contexts.dmb-guidelines-colonial-context.pdf (museumsbund.de)

Gibbs, C., Gore, M., McGarrell, E., & Rivers, L. (2010). Introducing conservation criminology: Towards interdisciplinary scholarship on environmental crimes and risks. *British Journal of Criminology, 50*(1), 124–144. https://doi.org/10.1093/bjc/azp045

Hekman W. (2010). Handbook on Emergency Procedures. *ICOM*. Retrieved January 11, 2022, from https://icms.mini.icom.museum/wp-content/uploads/sites/57/2018/12/English.pdf

Hermann, C. (2017). Assessing historic places regarding risks and vulnerabilities associated with climate change to inform conservation planning—development of assessment methods in Northern Europe. *Journal of Heritage Management, 2*(1), 32–52. https://doi.org/10.1177/24559296177269272455929617726927

ICOMOS. (2020). *Résolution 20AG 2020/15—Patrimoine culturel et urgence climatique*. Retrieved September 7, 2021, from https://www.icomos.org/images/DOCUMENTS/Secretariat/2020/Patrimoine_culturel_et_urgence_climatique-R%C3%A9solution_20AG_15.pdf

IMPACTOUR. (2020). Retrieved October 26, 2021, from https://www.impactour.eu/

Kahler, J. S., Rivera, J. W., Steele, Z. T., Morales-Giner, P., Rivera, C. J., Ahossin, C. F., Kaur, A., & Episcopio-Sturgeon, D. J. (2021). Advancing applied research in conservation criminology through the evaluation of corruption prevention, enhancing compliance, and reducing recidivism. *Frontiers in Conservation Science, 2*, 698755. https://doi.org/10.3389/fcosc.2021.698755

López, J. (2021, July 02). La denuncia de un expolio de exvotos de bronce propicia el hallazgo de un santuario ibero en Jaén. *ABC Andalucia*. Retrieved November 10, 2021, from https://sevilla.abc.es/andalucia/jaen/sevi-denuncia-expolio-exvotos-bronce-propicia-hallazgo-santuario-ibero-jaen-202106301901_noticia.html

Merryman, J. H., Elsen, A. E., & Stephen, K. U. (2007). *Law, ethics, and the visual arts* (5th ed.). Kluwer Law International.

Ministerio para la Transición Ecológica y el Reto Demográfico. (2020). *Plan Nacional de Adaptación al Cambio Climático 2021-2030*. Retrieved September 7, 2021, from https://www.miteco.gob.es/es/ministerio/plan-adaptacion-cambio-climatico-2021-2030.aspx

Museum Booster (2021) *Museum Innovation Barometer*. Retrieved January 7, 2021, from https://museumbooster.com/wp-content/uploads/2021/08/Museum-Innovation-Barometer-2021.pdf

National Security Strategy (2017) https://www.boe.es/diario_boe/txt.php?id=BOE-A-2017-15181

Olaya, V., & García, A. (2018, October 3). Un "tiziano" se cae al suelo de la sacristía de El Escorial. *El País*. https://elpais.com/cultura/2018/10/03/actualidad/1538572401_183608.html

Orr, S. C., Richards, J., & Fatorić, S. (2021). Climate change and cultural heritage: A systematic literature review (2016–2020). *The Historic Environment: Policy & Practice, 12*(3–4), 434–477. https://doi.org/10.1080/17567505.2021.1957264

Paolini, A., Vafadari, A., Cesaro, G., Santana Quintero, M., Van Balen, K., Vileikis, O., & Fakhoury, L. (2012). *Risk management at heritage sites: A case study of the Petra world heritage site*. United Nations Educational, Scientific and Cultural Organization. http://openarchive.icomos.org/id/eprint/1456/

Rodríguez Temiño, I. (2012). *Indiana Jones sin futuro. La lucha contra el expolio del patrimonio arqueológico*. JAG Arqueología Editorial.

Román, J. J. (1999). Seguridad. In J.C. Rico (Ed.), *Los conocimientos técnicos: museos, arquitectura, arte* (pp. 321–378). Sílex Ediciones.

Rufián Fernández, F. J. (2020). El patrimonio histórico en la Estrategia de Seguridad Nacional. In M. A. Caracuel Raya, J. Díaz Toribio, E. Sanchéz Mateos, A. Crespo Alcázar, & M. T. Sanchéz González (Eds.), *VI Congreso ADESyD* "Compartiendo (visiones de) Seguridad" (pp. 90–101). ADESyD. https://www.adesyd.es/doc/destacados/ADD_DFEWRRI4.pdf

Sesana, E., Gagnon, A., Ciantelli, C., Cassar, J., & Hughes, J. (2021). Climate change impacts on cultural heritage: A literature review. *Wiley Interdisciplinary Reviews: Climate Change, 12*(4). https://doi.org/10.1002/wcc.710

Spanish National Civil Protection Strategy. (2019). Retrieved September 3, 2021, from https://www.boe.es/boe/dias/2019/04/30/pdfs/BOE-A-2019-6348.pdf

Teijgeler, R., Sabrine, I., Halleb, Y., Barakat, M., & Korinth, E. (2020). Heritage Guidelines for COVID-19. Iraq, Libya, Syria, Yemen. *Heritage for Peace and Aliph Foundation*. Retrieved November 9, 2021, from https://icomos.es/wp-content/uploads/2020/12/Heritage-Guidelines-for-COVID-19-full-version.pdf

Terreros Andréu, C. (2014). El expolio de Patrimonio Cultural: problemas de conceptualización jurídica. *Revista Electrónica de Patrimonio Histórico, 14*, 72–97. https://revistaseug.ugr.es/index.php/erph/article/view/3503/3508

United Nations. (n.d.). Objectif 13: Prendre d'urgence des mesures pour lutter contre les changements climatiques et leurs répercussions. Retrieved September 7, 2021, from https://www.un.org/sustainabledevelopment/fr/climate-change-2/

Estrella Sanz Domínguez Conservator-Restorer of Cultural Heritage, Master in Preventive Conservation and PhD in Fine Arts from the UCM. She has obtained several scholarships in conservation and restoration at the Instituto de Patrimonio Cultural de España, and in Museology at the Museo Nacional del Prado. Professionally, she has worked in conservation and restoration for different public institutions, and has carried out several projects as a specialist technician in Preventive Conservation and Protection of Collections in Emergencies for the Prado Museum and for the Ministry of Foreign Affairs, European Union and Cooperation, within its Cultural Heritage Area. She currently teaches on the Degree and Master's Degree in Conservation and Restoration of Cultural Heritage at the Faculty of Fine Arts, Complutense University of Madrid.

Francisco José Rufián Fernández has a degree in History. He is an archaeologist, founder of Pequeños Arqueólogos didactic workshops and Arqueovuelos (www.arqueovuelos.com). He is a specialist in cultural management, sustainable development and Heritage protection and is currently working in a Law Enforcement Agency, and developing his PhD in "Law, Government and Public Policies," in the Autonomous University of Madrid, about the legal protection of heritage by local policies, illicit trafficking, and emergencies.

Isber Sabrine is a Syrian archaeologist specialised in Cultural Heritage Management, as well as a certified National Tourist Guide in Syria. He has been member of the Syrian Spanish team of the Spanish National Research Council (CSIC) since 2005. He is a member of the Department of Archaeology at Institución Milá y Fontanals, CSIC. He has been involved in the protection of cultural Heritage in many countries in conflicts and is currently chair and co-founder of the international NGO Heritage for Peace. Since 2015 he has been involved on cultural initiatives for the refugees in Germany and Spain.

Revisiting the Looting of Site Q Through Lidar

A Case Study of Illicit Digging in La Corona, Guatemala

Kirsty E. Escalante, Tomás Barrientos Q., and Marcello A. Canuto

Abstract The looting of La Corona, Guatemala is one of the most well-known examples of Maya archaeological looting. Known only as 'Site Q' before its location was positively identified, dozens of carved stone panels were looted from La Corona before the site was studied archaeologically. The recent application of a remote sensing technique called lidar enables the mapping of the ground surface in forested regions, which has been revolutionary for Maya archaeology. In addition to the thousands of archaeological features visible in lidar imagery, lidar also shows the devastating impacts of looting on Maya archaeological sites. This chapter revisits the looting of La Corona in light of new lidar data, combining geospatial analyses and an in-depth review of archaeological excavation records from 2005–2019. Through this preliminary analysis of looting at La Corona, we aim to demonstrate the immense potential of lidar for understanding looting practices in the Maya region.

1 Introduction

Among the numerous Maya sites that were looted in the 1960s and 1970s, the looting of La Corona is one of the more well-known examples. Known only as 'Site Q' and by the dozens of carved stone panels that appeared on the art market, the location of the looted site was a mystery for over 30 years. Archaeological and

K. E. Escalante (✉)
Department of Anthropology, Tulane University, New Orleans, LA, USA
e-mail: kescalan@tulane.edu

T. Barrientos Q.
Department of Archaeology and Anthropology, University of the Valley of Guatemala, Guatemala City, Guatemala
e-mail: tbarrientos@uvg.edu.gt

M. A. Canuto
Middle American Research Institute, Tulane University, New Orleans, LA, USA
e-mail: mcanuto@tulane.edu

N. Oosterman, D. Yates (eds.), *Art Crime in Context*, Studies in Art, Heritage, Law and the Market 6, https://doi.org/10.1007/978-3-031-14084-6_8

epigraphic evidence have now convincingly linked Site Q to La Corona in north western Petén, Guatemala, and research has continued to reveal the devastating impacts of looting on the site. Lidar, a remote sensing technique, has been recently used to map La Corona and its surroundings and clearly shows the physical evidence of looting across the landscape, illustrating lidar's value for analysing illicit digging practices.

This chapter uses a combination of lidar and archaeological excavation records to re-evaluate the persistent looting activity that has been documented at La Corona. This case study includes a contextual analysis of looting recorded in excavation records, a quantitative analysis of looting features, and preliminary conclusions about the site's looting based on both lidar data and previous excavations. Through this preliminary analysis, we aim to demonstrate the potential of lidar to expand current understandings of looting in the forested Maya lowlands.

Archaeological looting is the deliberate, unscientific, and unsanctioned removal of artifacts, typically to supply the demand of the antiquities trade, and entails the destruction of their archaeological context via digging, trenching, tunnelling, bulldozing, or a combination thereof. Despite the differences in the environments and locations of archaeological sites worldwide, looting has been a persistent global problem that has proved difficult to eradicate (Barker, 2018; Brodie & Renfrew, 2005; Elia, 1997). In non-forested desert regions, archaeologists have employed remote sensing techniques and satellite imagery to monitor illicit digging and manage cultural heritage. Because of the arid environmental conditions that enable unencumbered views of the ground surface, there is a robust literature on how remote sensing and spatial analysis of looting have impacted heritage management efforts in desert regions worldwide (Agapiou et al., 2017; Bowen et al., 2017; Cerra et al., 2016; Elfadaly et al., 2018; Hernandez et al., 2008; Lasaponara & Masini, 2018; Tapete & Cigna, 2019).

Although Maya archaeologists have long known about the looting of Maya sites in Belize, Mexico, Guatemala, El Salvador, and Honduras, the full extent of this activity is not exactly known due to the dense forest canopy obscuring the ground surface. Therefore, despite the substantial spatial analyses of looting in non-forested regions, these studies have not developed at the same pace in tropical areas. Visualising the earth's surface in forested environments had not been possible until the application of lidar, which has allowed archaeologists to identify thousands of previously unknown archaeological features as well as the trenches left behind by looters. Lidar offers the first opportunity to remotely visualise the physical evidence of looting, illustrating its potential to provide an empirical understanding of the threats facing Maya archaeology. Just as aerial- and satellite-based imagery enabled the development of looting databases and well-informed heritage management plans in desert environments (Bowen et al., 2017; Parcak, 2009, 2017, 2019), lidar has the potential to do the same for forested regions (Cowley et al., 2020; McNeary, 2014).

2 Background of Looting in the Maya Area

The looting of the Maya area first came to light in the 1960s and 1970s, when stone stelae and polychrome ceramics began appearing *en masse* on the art market and in museums worldwide (see Coggins, 1969, 1972). Nevertheless, while evidence of looting was emerging at the end of the trade network, the precise effect of this illicit antiquities trade on the archaeological record itself was and is not fully known. Archaeologists could only guess the level of devastation based on the quantity of artefacts being sold on the market, and the identification of looter's pits at the few sites that were subject to archaeological study. In fact, looters excavated multiple sites, many of them before being encountered and studied by archaeologists.

La Corona is one site that was famously looted before it was studied by archaeologists. The first clue that an unknown Maya site had been heavily looted was the appearance of dozens of carved stone panels on the international art market (Graham, 1997; Schuster, 1997). Peter Mathews (1979) was the first to notice that these stylistically similar panels all bore a distinct emblem glyph of a snake head, now known to be the emblem glyph of the *Kaan* kingdom centred at the sites of Calakmul and Dzibanché in modern Mexico. Mathews reasoned that these panels must originate from the same site, which he nicknamed 'Site Q', an abbreviation of the Spanish word *que?,* meaning 'what?'. Mathews documented potential Site Q panels at museums and private collections primarily in Europe and the United States, with several of these pieces fetching over $10,000 USD at auction. [1] Archaeologists proposed several Maya sites as the potential source of the Site Q monuments, notably El Perú-Waka' in Guatemala, the Usumacinta region in Mexico, and Calakmul itself (Schuster, 1997). However, the carvings that were being excavated archaeologically from El Perú indicated that the site had its own emblem glyph and did not match the epigraphic decipherments of the Site Q panels. Moreover, the limestone from Calakmul was significantly more porous and eroded than the superior marble-like limestone used for the Site Q carvings (Martin, 1993; Schuster, 1997).

The origin of the Site Q monuments continued to elude archaeologists until the site of La Corona was documented by scholars in the late 1990s (Graham, 1997). La Corona only became known to science after Carlos Catalán and Luis Morales, two former looters, tree gum extractors, and jaguar poachers, alerted authorities of the existence of a site in the north western Petén, near the temporary camp 'Lo Veremos' where gum extractors lived while working in the forest (Barrientos Q & Canuto, 2022; Graham, 1997). In 1989, the site was visited by a team of German archaeologists who noted evidence of large structures bisected by looting trenches (Grube et al., 1990), but they did not locate evidence of carved stone monuments at the site. The site was then visited by macaw conservationist Santiago Billy in 1996, who requested the area be studied with satellite imagery. This led NASA archaeologist Tom Sever and remote sensing specialist Dan Lee to investigate the site as part of a

[1] Approximately $75,000 USD adjusted for inflation at the time of writing.

remote sensing study to detect archaeological features, particularly ancient Maya roads (Graham, 1997; Sever & Irwin, 2003). In late 1996, an expedition was planned to La Corona which included Sever, Lee, Billy, and conservationist Jim Nations. There they encountered a carved stone panel, causing them to contact Ian Graham and David Stuart of the Harvard Peabody Museum's *Corpus of Maya Hieroglyphic Inscriptions* (Barrientos Q & Canuto, 2022; Graham, 1997).

Graham and Stuart visited La Corona in 1997, later describing the carved monuments littering the site and the proximity of La Corona to two gum-extraction camps (Graham, 1997). Among the inscriptions on the scattered monuments, Stuart recognised the name "Chak Kutz" (Great or Red Turkey), the same name that had been previously identified in a Site Q panel purchased by the Art Institute of Chicago in 1965 (Graham, 1997; Mathews, 1979; Schuster, 1997). Although the discovery of the Chak Kutz glyphs at La Corona was the first link to the unprovenanced panels that had appeared on the art market, it did not definitively identify La Corona as Site Q, and Graham noted his scepticism that the mystery had been solved.

Multiple lines of evidence now indicate that the majority of the Site Q panels were looted from La Corona. In 2000, a petrographic analysis of a Site Q panel in the University of Maine's Hudson Museum demonstrated it was not dissimilar to an in-situ stone block from a staircase at La Corona, leading Stuart to suggest that La Corona was the origin of the looted panels (Guenter, 2005; Hudson Museum, 2021; Stuart, 2001). In 2005, long-term archaeological investigations began with the first reconnaissance survey of the site. During this fieldwork, Canuto found two carved stone panels within a looter's trench [2] bearing glyphs matching the style and epigraphic context of multiple Site Q monuments first identified by Mathews (Canuto et al., 2005; Guenter, 2005). Since the start of archaeological investigations at the site by the *Proyecto Regional Arqueológico La Corona* (PRALC) in 2008, archaeologists have continued to find irrefutable evidence that the Site Q monuments were indeed looted from La Corona.

Over 100 looting marks have been recorded throughout La Corona and surrounding sites by PRALC archaeologists, demonstrating the severe impacts of illicit digging driven by the demand for Maya art. Unfortunately, PRALC researchers have noted that looting in the area continues to the present-day, with the most recent incidents recorded as recently as 2016 (Ponce, 2017), indicating the need for continued preservation efforts of Maya sites in the Petén.

[2] Structure 13R-5.

2.1 *Ethnographic Perspectives and Current Threats to Maya Heritage*

The remote forested environment and potential dangers of encountering looters in action have hindered a comprehensive understanding of illicit digging in the Maya area. Nevertheless, there are a handful of ethnographic and anecdotal accounts that provide glimpses into looting practices and the circumstances that lead to Maya site looting.

Sociocultural studies on Maya looting have focused on understanding the reasons that compel local people to participate in this activity, and in some cases have included observations and interviews with former looters. These studies have shed light on the processes that lead to archaeological depredation, particularly the practice of subsistence digging, where local people participate in the illicit digging and sale of ancient objects in order to supplement low wages and insufficient economic opportunities (Hollowell, 2006). Matsuda's (1992, 1994, 1998a, 1998b) ethnographic research in Belize and Paredes Maury's (1999) research in Guatemala suggest that local people consider archaeological resources as part of the assortment of harvestable forest resources, leading to the 'harvest' of archaeological materials from ancient Maya sites during times of economic precarity.

In the Petén, ethnographic studies have linked archaeological looting to the extraction of tree gum, also known as chicle, and multiple scholars have noted the presence of archaeological materials at temporary chicle camps (Devine, 2016; Matsuda, 1998a; Paredes Maury, 1999). Chicle is the resin of the sapodilla tree (*Manilkara zapota*), which was a common ingredient in chewing gum before synthetic ingredients became prevalent around 1944–1945 (Schwartz, 1990, p. 140). Chicle was exported primarily to the United States, and though the industry experienced decline around 1980, extraction has continued to the present day (Devine, 2016; Schwartz, 1990). As chicle workers, also known as chicleros, navigate the forest to find untapped sapodilla trees, they inevitably come across archaeological sites during their work. Since chicleros know the environment well, travel an average of 3 to 5 km from the camp, and work on sap extraction from 4:30 to 7:00 am, they are in a position that allows them a great deal of time to explore the forest and encounter archaeological sites (Paredes Maury, 1999, pp. 16–17; 2019). In fact, chicle workers discovered multiple important sites in the Mexican and Guatemalan forests before they were known archaeologically (Graham, 1997; Yates, 2014a, p. 25). As noted earlier, La Corona is located within a known chicle extraction region and anecdotal accounts from former looters and chicle extractors who were active in this area of the north-western Petén also suggest a link between chicle and looting. Therefore, based on ethnographic accounts and the prevalence of the chicle industry in this area, it is likely that some of the historical looting that occurred at La Corona from 1960–1970 was associated with chicle extraction.

Recent evidence indicates that looting in this region continues to the present-day and may be linked to increasing incidents of wildfires and deforestation. Some scholars have noted possible links between the illicit antiquities trade and the trafficking of exotic animals, people, and drugs (Golden & Scherer, 2006; Parks et al., 2006; Yates, 2014a, 2017). Though the connection between looting and other criminal activities is difficult to ascertain, forest conservationists have reported deforestation in this area connected with the illicit drug trade (Allen, 2012; Kolbay, 2008; Sieff, 2020), an indicator that archaeological sites may also be at risk. However, given the potential dangers involved in studying looting, particularly if it is entangled with the trafficking of drugs and people, researchers may not be able to get a clear picture of the issue on the ground using traditional archaeological and ethnographic survey methods.

3 Application of Remote Sensing to Heritage Management

As discussed above, the application of remote sensing to study illicit digging has been well established in arid regions with little vegetation. However, in heavily forested environments like the Maya area, lidar is the first method that allows us to visualise the ground surface and, by extension, analyse and monitor looting. Lidar is a remote sensing technique that calculates distance by pulsing lasers from a sensor and measuring the amount of time for the light to reflect to the sensor. Some of the lasers will collide with vegetation while others will reach the ground surface, making it possible to remotely map features beneath the forest canopy.

In desert environments, applying remote sensing to monitor looting has resulted in the development of well-informed heritage management plans and international collaborations to preserve archaeological sites. Scholars have used satellite and aerial imagery in non-forested regions as a tool to document and protect cultural heritage by assessing damage to sites, reporting new site damage, evaluating the impacts of looting incidents, and creating detailed inventories of archaeological sites and threats to their preservation (Danti et al., 2017). These efforts have been consulted by multiple stakeholders and used to develop strategies for heritage protection.

Just as satellite imagery has supported cultural heritage preservation initiatives in arid environments, lidar has begun to do the same in forested areas (see Cowley et al., 2020; McNeary, 2014). Although the application of lidar for archaeological resource management and preservation is in its nascent stages, similar studies in non-forested regions indicate that lidar is a promising technique for understanding looting practices. In addition, the application of remote sensing to monitor archaeological sites is valuable not only for its ability to map large swaths of land, but also because it does so from a distance and without the potential for violent encounters. Because of the illicit and clandestine nature of antiquities trafficking, archaeological looting has led to violent confrontations globally, and archaeologists have described encounters with armed looters, as well as murders and lynchings committed due to looting conflicts (Balestrieri, 2018; Hardy, 2015; Yates, 2014a, 2014b).

In the Maya area, archaeologists have warned about violent altercations since the earliest days of site looting. For instance, Sheets (1973) described groups of looters decimating sites and murdering several locals in Mexico and Guatemala, Graham reported the death of his assistant after they came upon a looting-in-progress at La Naya, Guatemala (Graham, 1986; Robertson, 1972), and Robertson (1972) was held up by six men with machine guns at the site of Itsimté in 1970 while recording stelae for the Middle American Research Institute at Tulane University. In 2003, a looted stela from Cancuén was recovered after researchers tracked the monument to local drug traffickers, exposing the network from looters to buyers (Wilford, 2003). More recently, conservationists working in northern Guatemala have described multiple threats to the natural and cultural resources of the Maya Biosphere Reserve, including forest fires and deforestation for ranching operations related to the illegal drug trafficking trade, and have even reported being held at gunpoint by armed looters (Allen, 2012).

Remote sensing techniques like lidar enable researchers to safely monitor and protect archaeological sites without violent encounters, providing an approach to heritage management that does not involve policing or confronting armed looters. Using lidar to remotely study the scale and intensity of looting provides the first opportunity to understand how the demand for antiquities has affected Maya archaeological sites on a large scale without the potential for direct harm to the researcher.

4 Looting in La Corona

It is likely that many of the looting features that were noted by Graham and Stuart in 1997 and later recorded by archaeologists beginning in 2005 were created during the 1960s and 1970s, around the same time the Site Q objects were first appearing on the art market. Given the proximity of the 'Lo Veremos' chicle extraction camp to La Corona, as well as anecdotal accounts from former looters and refuse left behind at the site, it is likely that La Corona's early looting is linked to the chicle industry. At the same time, the massive looting trenches and interior tunnelling that have been observed at La Corona must have involved considerable effort and could not have been made in a single day, revealing a level of planning and logistical coordination needed to loot a structure and remove saleable artifacts. Given that some looting trenches were utilised more than once and that archaeologists have recorded new incidents since investigations began in 2005, it is clear that the site has been looted repeatedly over decades (Figs. 1 and 2).

Based on previous archaeological excavation records, looters encountered valuable deposits in several structures. Looters found sculpted stone monuments in at least eight looted structures, polychrome ceramics in twelve, burials in eight, and both burials and monuments in at least five structures (Fig. 3). These numbers are certainly underestimates since there is no information about the deposits found in 29 of the 62 looted structures. Since there is a high demand for both sculpted stone monuments and burial goods such as polychrome vessels and jade objects, the discovery of these types of objects was likely a key driver of the intense looting of La Corona's core, and it is possible that looters placed more illicit digs in areas where

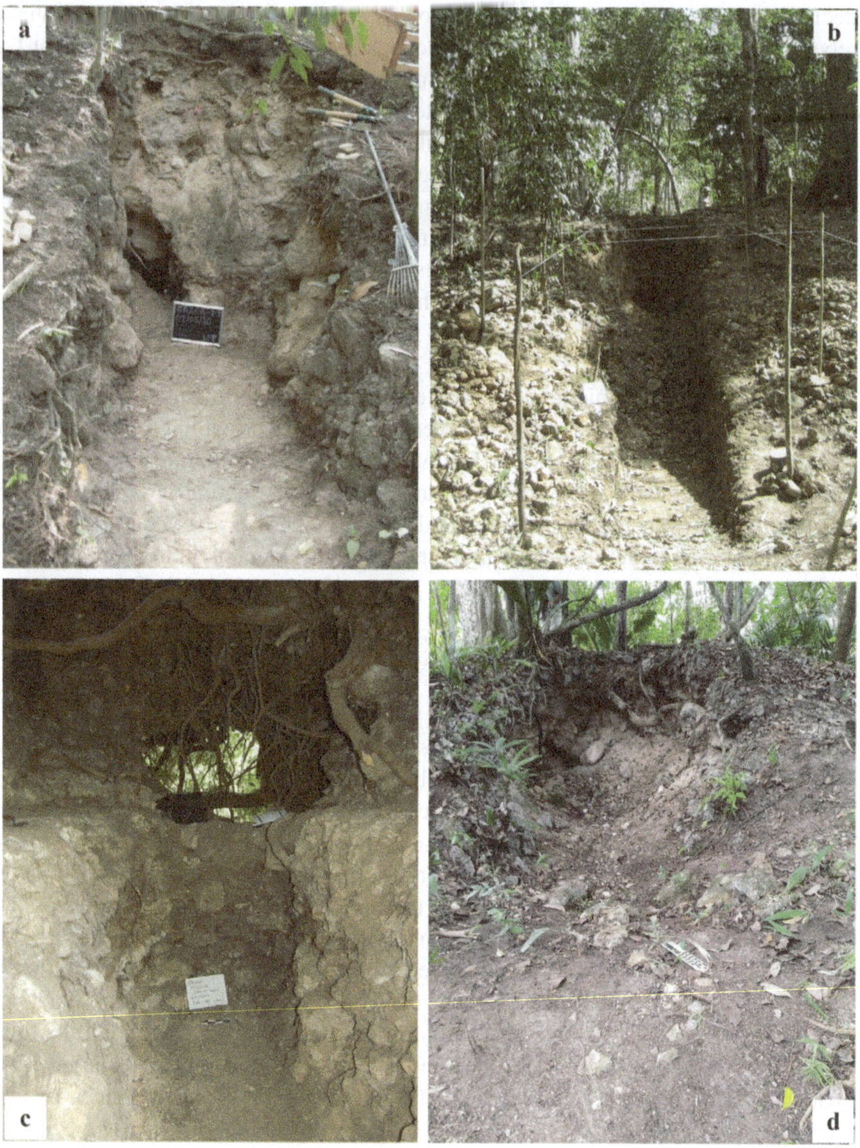

Fig. 1 Looting in La Corona: (**a**) Structure 13Q4-A (Padilla, 2011, p. 154); (**b**) Structure 13Q-5 (Desailly-Chanson, 2010, p. 112); (**c**) Structure 13R-2 (Baron, 2012, p. 234); (**d**) Structure 12P-30 (López & Escalante, 2019, p. 92).

they had previously encountered saleable objects. Evidence indicates that some trenches were looted more than once, while other trenches exhibited additional tunnelling in the structures' interiors, suggesting that looters may have found deposits that motivated them to keep digging in certain locations.

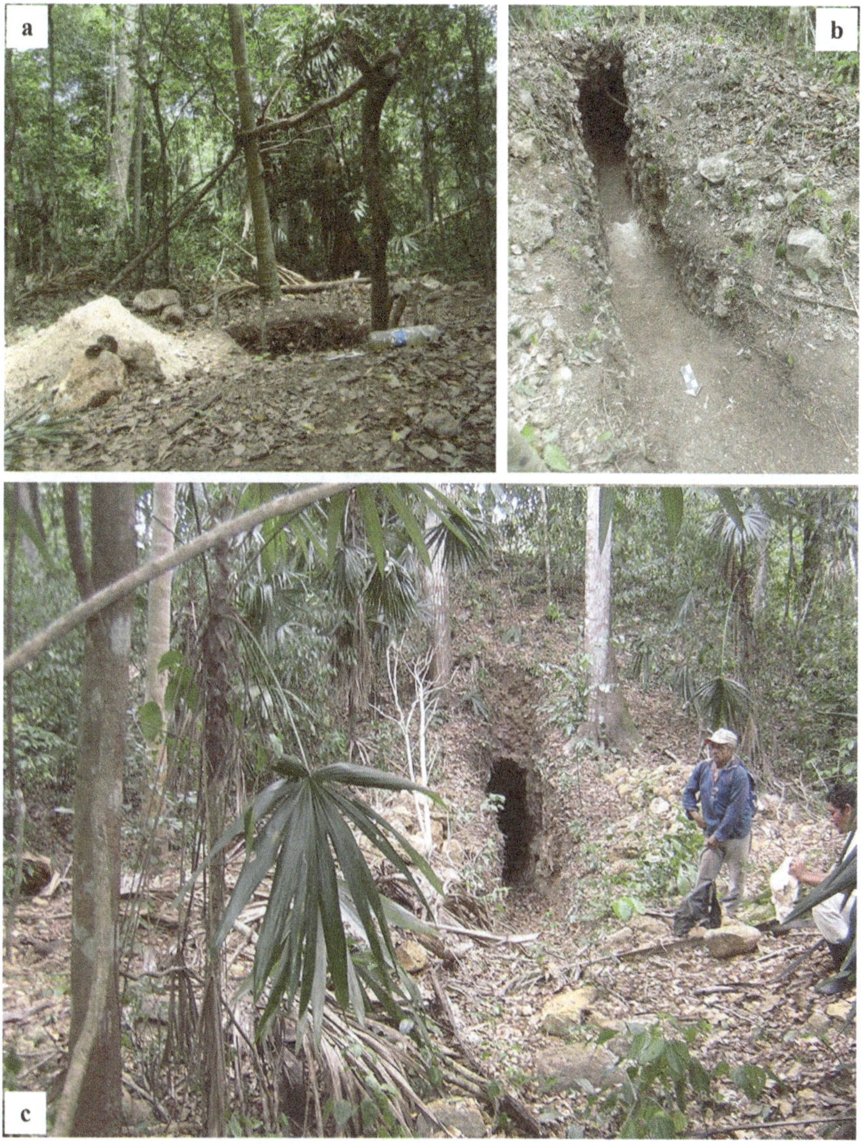

Fig. 2 Looting in El Jobillo: (**a**) Lift mechanism employed by looters in Structure 8M-13 (Ponce, 2017); (**b**) Structure 8M-9 (Ponce, 2020, p. 307); (**c**) Structure 8M-1 (Guzmán, 2011, p. 130)

PRALC has discovered the remnants of several looted monuments, left behind after the carved panels were removed from the larger stone for ease of transport. Like many looted Maya stone monuments, carved panels were removed from the larger stone to make them easier to transport, leaving behind discarded stone remains, the monument's carcass. Two carcasses have been matched to known Site Q monuments

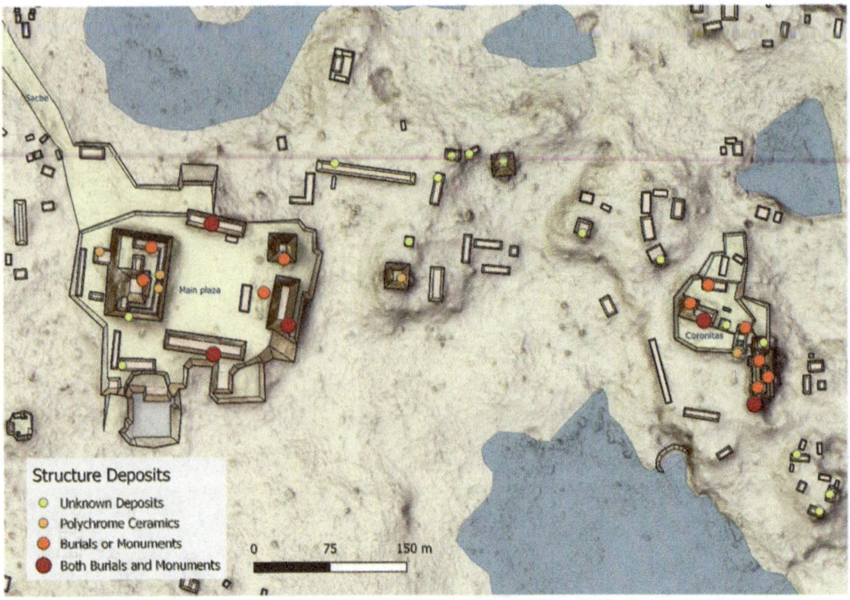

Fig. 3 Deposits encountered in looted structures in La Corona's central core

in private and museum collections. The remnant of La Corona Panel 6, also known as Site Q Altar 1 in Mathew's (1979) list of Site Q monuments, was discovered archaeologically in La Corona's core [3] (Ponce, 2013) (Fig. 4). The panel was in a private collection when it was first published in 1985 (Deletaille & Sonnery, 1985) and was later acquired by the Dallas Museum of Art in 1988. The structure was therefore looted sometime before 1985; additional research on when the monument appeared on the art market can offer a more specific date range for the structure's looting. Similarly, Element 3/Site Q Glyphic Panel 4, last known to be in the André Emmerich Gallery in Zürich, Switzerland (Coe, 1973; Mathews, 1998), matches a carcass found at La Corona.

Archaeological excavation records from La Corona also contained information about when looting may have occurred. For instance, Coronado-Ruiz (2009), Guenter (2010), and Perez (2020) found items left by looters that appear to date to 1960–1970. [4] Likewise, Ponce (2017) documented more recent refuse dating to between 2010–2016 at the nearby site of El Jobillo, including food packaging, water containers, clothes, and an improvised temporary shelter (Fig. 5). In addition, from 2005–2019 the archaeologists have occasionally recorded the appearance of new looting features. For example, three new looting incidents were noted in 2006 in the site's central plaza (Marken & Guenter, 2006) and both Guzmán (2012) and Ponce

[3] Structure 13R-10.

[4] Structures 13Q-4G, 13Q-6, and 12R-1, respectively.

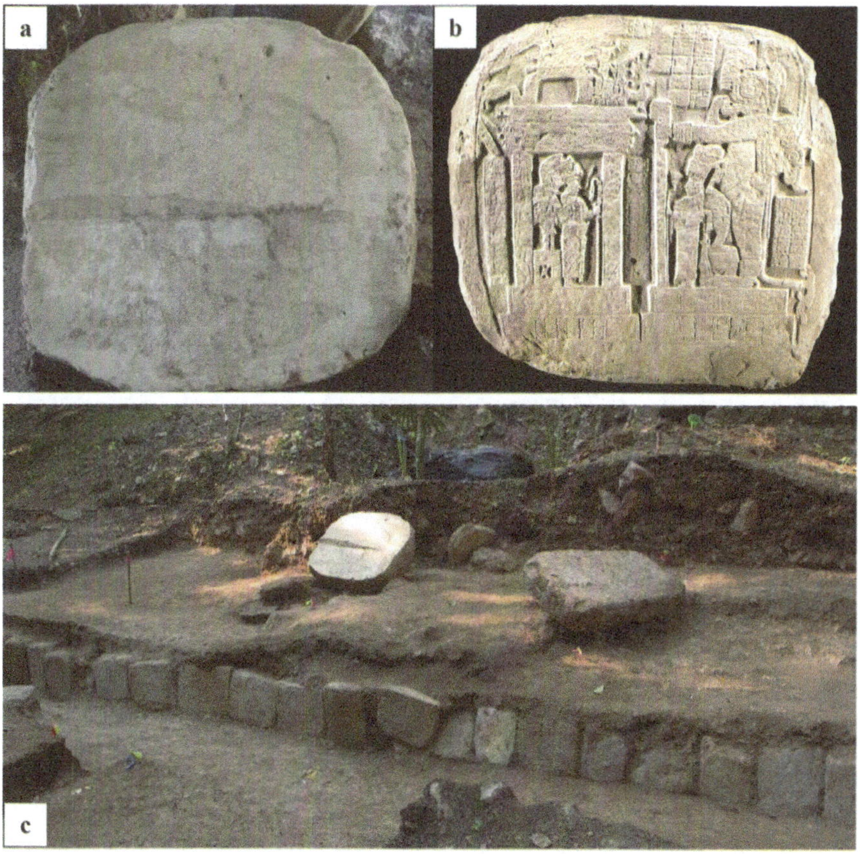

Fig. 4 (**a**) Carcass of La Corona Panel 6, Site Q Altar 1 (Ponce, 2013, p. 166); (**b**) Panel 6 in the Dallas Museum of Art; (**c**) Panel 6 carcass found in situ in La Corona structure 13-R10 (Ponce, 2013)

(2017) noted new trenches at El Jobillo in 2011 and 2016, respectively, that were not present when the site was first mapped in 2010 (Guzmán, 2011).

More recently, Ponce (2017) documented evidence of recent looting and wildfires at El Jobillo, indicating a possible link between looting, deforestation, and encroaching settlement. Several structures were burnt from forest fires and four new looting incidents were recorded at the site in 2016. In addition, Ponce noted the presence of a lift system made from branches cut from the surrounding forest that was placed over a still-open illicit excavation (Fig. 2). The lift was likely placed to facilitate the removal of soil from the pit, perhaps using a rope and pulley system, though these latter items were not left behind. Furthermore, the looters may have had previous archaeological experience (J. Ponce, personal communication, 2021). The illicit digs appear to have been laid out using archaeological methods, and the looters apparently used the presence of ancient stucco floors as a potential indicator for

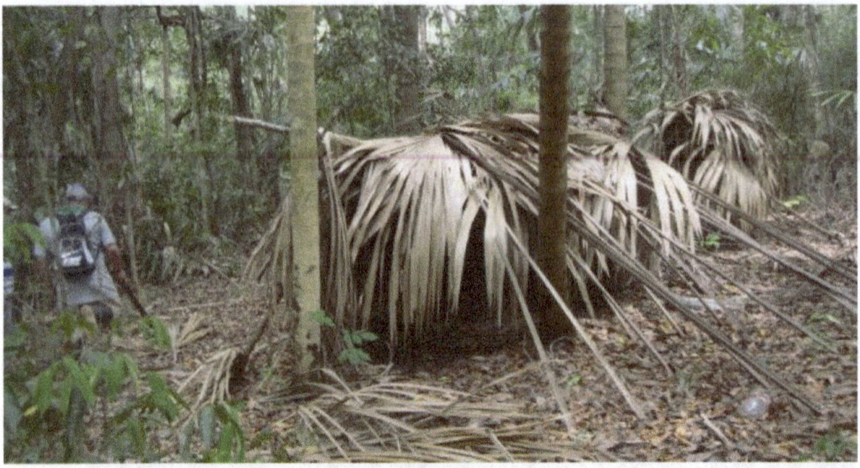

Fig. 5 Temporary camp used by looters near El Jobillo (Ponce, 2017, p. 202)

artifacts, as there were several intrusions in the profile walls just above the floor levels.

Over the past decade, wildfires and deforestation have increasingly threatened both forest conservation and archaeological preservation near La Corona, particularly in the Laguna del Tigre National Park where La Corona is located. Although much of the Petén is divided into community-managed forest concessions that exhibit lower rates of deforestation (Stoian et al., 2018), the Laguna del Tigre National Park is not part of a forest concession and is therefore subject to encroaching wildfires, illegal settlement, and land clearing for ranching related to drug trafficking (Devine et al., 2020; Sieff, 2020). Analyses of the fires in the Petén indicate a higher frequency of fires occurring within the Laguna del Tigre National Park compared to the adjacent forest concessions (Fig. 6), outlining the continued threats to the cultural and natural resources of this region and the need for empirically informed preservation strategies.

5 Lidar at La Corona

In 2016, the *Pacunam Lidar Initiative* (PLI) conducted a lidar survey of 2144 km^2 in Petén, Guatemala, including an area of 432 km^2 mapping La Corona and surrounding sites (Canuto et al., 2018). Using these data, an analysis was performed of the looting present in a 48 km^2 area centred around La Corona's central plaza. This analysis revealed a total of 100 field verified looting incidents and an additional 122 potential looting features visible in the lidar data (Fig. 7). The unverified looting features will be investigated in planned future field work that will focus on ground verification of potential illicit digs.

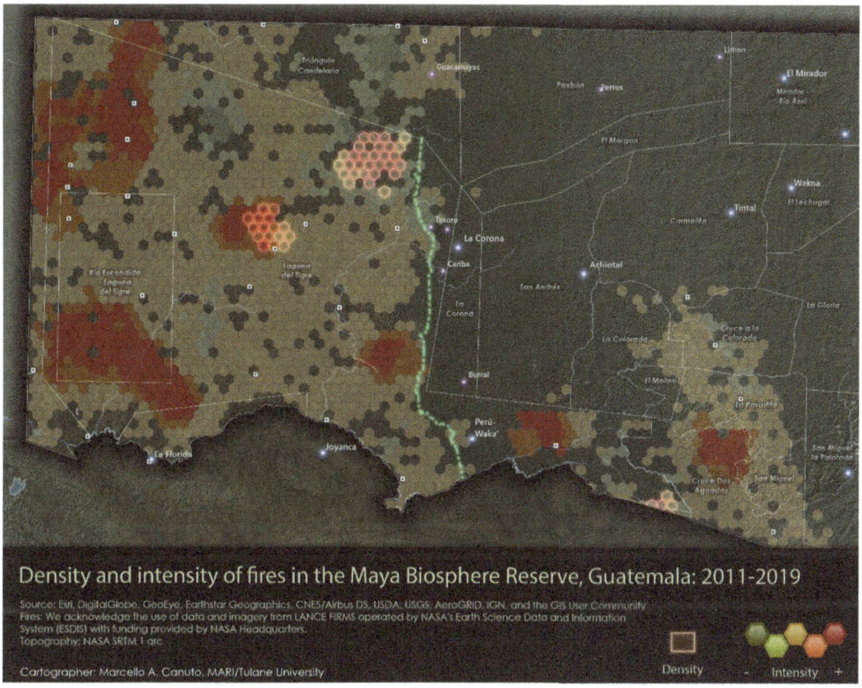

Fig. 6 Fires in the Maya Biosphere Reserve, Guatemala

A Kernel Density Estimation analysis [5] of the 100 verified looting incidents was conducted to determine clusters of activity. A point radius of 500 m around each looting feature shows that there are four distinct concentrations of looting activity in the study area, with the largest centred around La Corona (79%), and smaller clusters located in El Jobillo (9%), La Cariba (7%), and Conacaste (4%) (Fig. 8). The distribution of looting incidents indicates that, while La Corona was the focus of intense looting, surrounding sites were also targeted despite their relatively small size. A density map with a point radius of 100 m demonstrates that the large looting cluster around La Corona is composed of several smaller foci of activity. The largest cluster centred around La Corona's core shows a continuous concentration of illicit digs, with two dense accumulations in the central plaza and the Coronitas group (Fig. 9). The central plaza is the most looted structure group in the site with 36 looting marks, 22 of which are located in the palace structure complex. Coronitas is the next most looted group, with 18 recorded looting features. In addition, there are smaller concentrations of looting incidents dispersed across the site, including in the Tortugas Group (n = 3) and in an unnamed structure group to the northeast of La Corona (n = 6).

[5] Kernel Density Estimation calculates probability densities based on a given distance from the locations of known incidents, generating a map showing centres of activity.

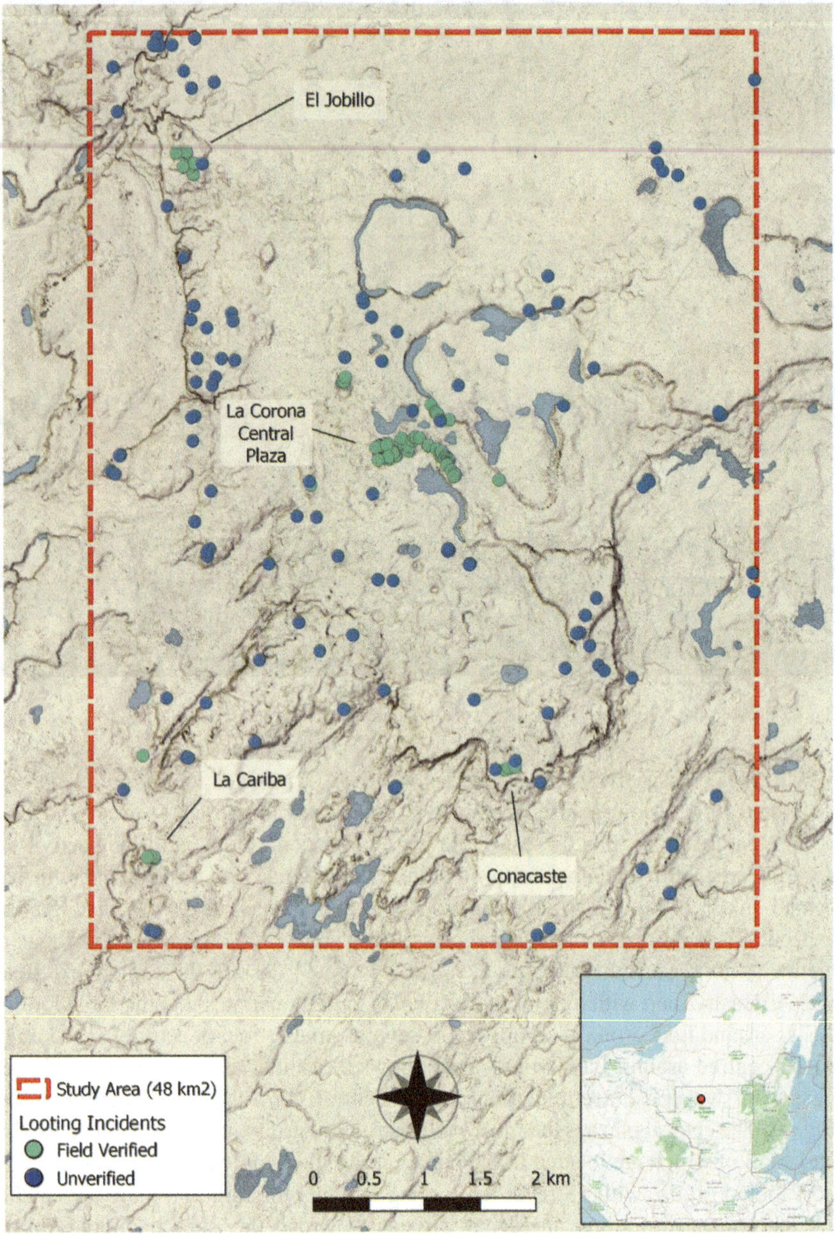

Fig. 7 Map of field verified and unverified potential looting features

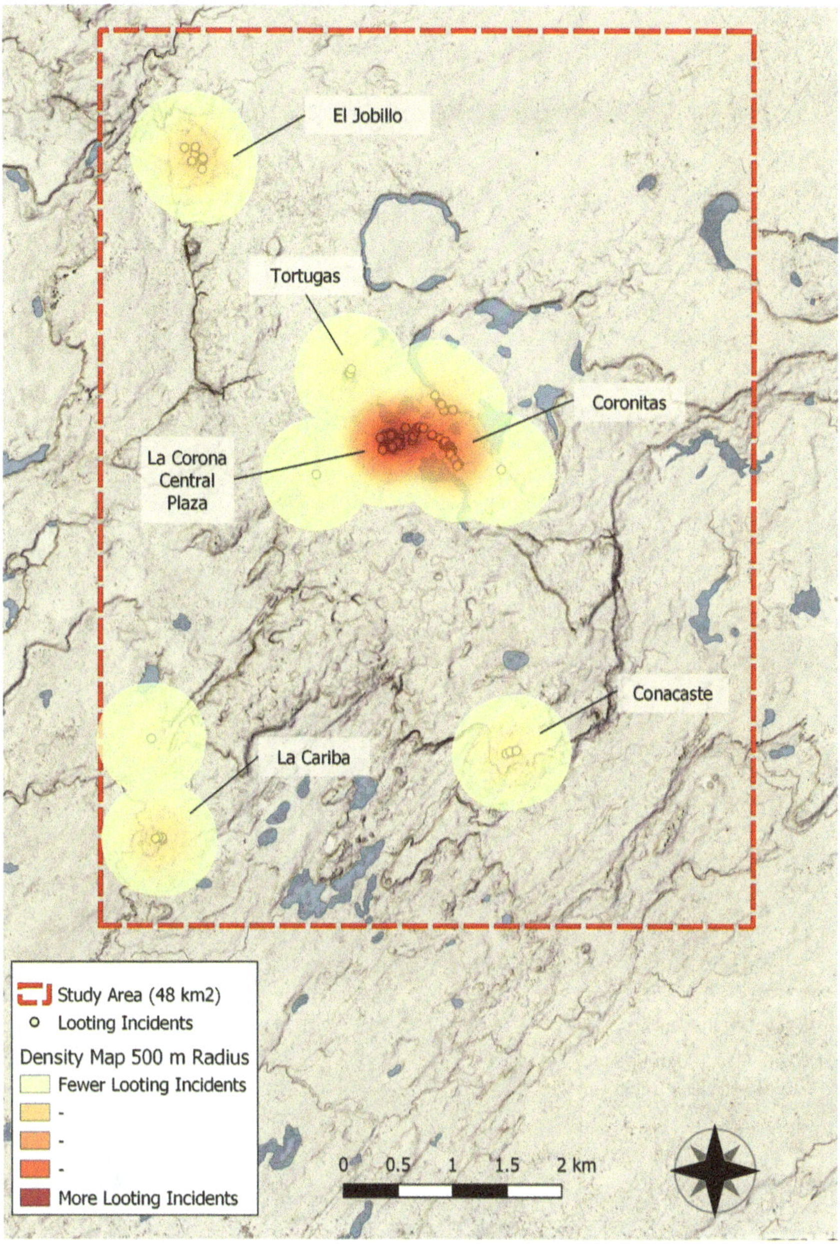

Fig. 8 Kernel Density Estimation with 500 m radius showing four clusters of activity

The 100 verified looting features occurred in 62 structures, an average of 1.61 features per structure. As noted above, La Corona's palace platform, comprised of

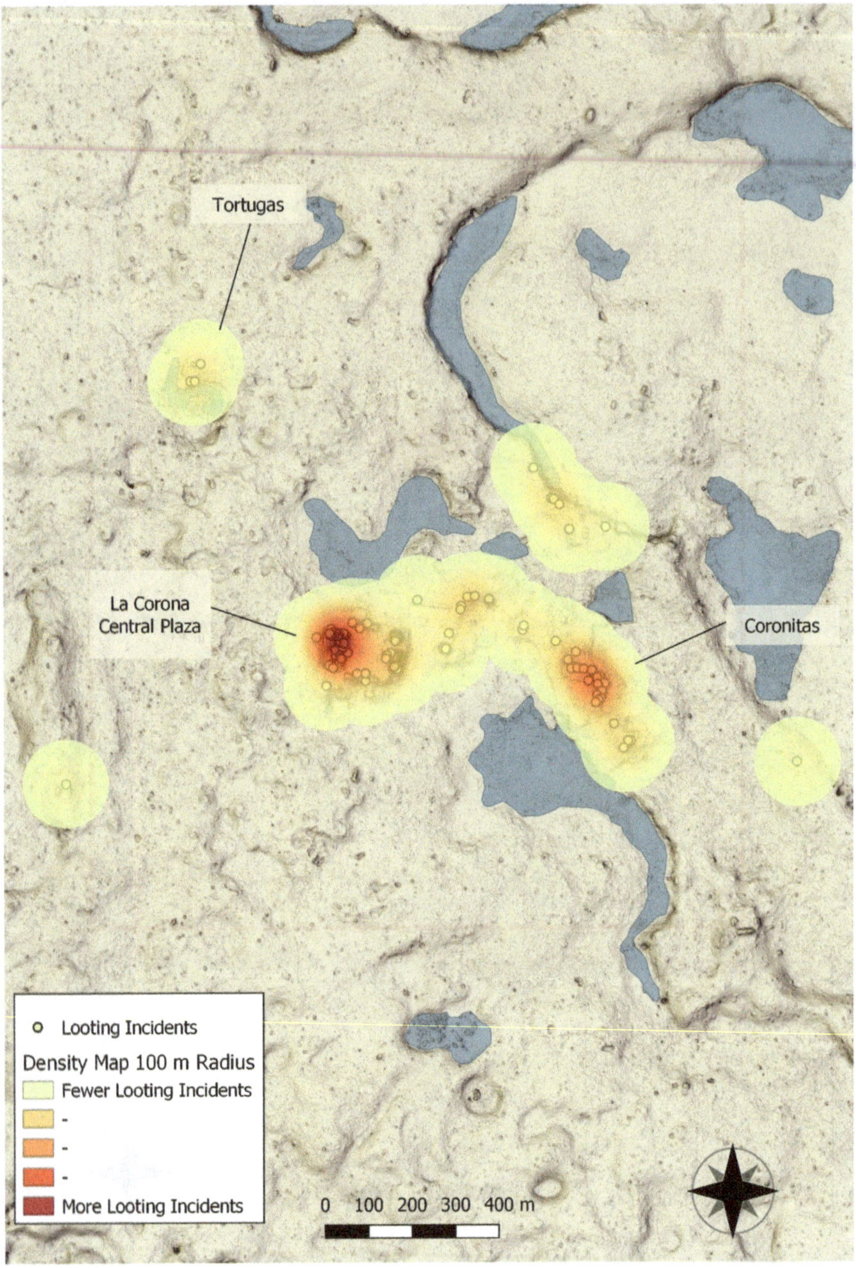

Fig. 9 Kernel Density Estimation with 100 m radius showing multiple looting clusters in La Corona's core

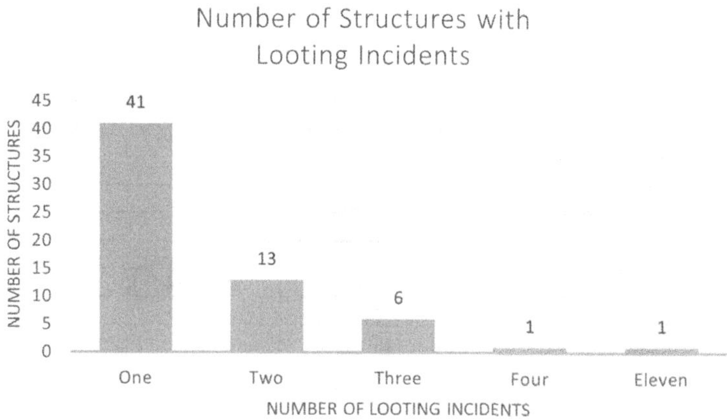

Fig. 10 Bar graph depicting the number of structures exhibiting looting features at La Corona

7 substructures [6] is the most looted portion of the site with a total of 22 recorded looting features. One of the palace substructures [7] has 11 looting features dispersed across its surface

A majority of the looted structures at the site, or 66% (n = 41) have only one looting incident, 21% (n = 13) have two, and 13% (n = 8) have three or more illicit digs, including the 11 looting features in the palace substructure mentioned above, a clear outlier in the data (Fig. 10). Although most of the looting marks are concentrated around La Corona's core, these features represent an average of two trenches per square kilometre over the 48 km^2 that was analysed for this study. The densest area of looting activity consists of 0.75 km^2 surrounding La Corona's core, within which there are 75 looting marks penetrating 40 structures. This area has a total of 150 structures, representing a looting rate of 27 percent. The looting features range in area from approximately 1.5 to 153 m^2 and have a mean area of 16.5 m^2. Despite the wide range of looting feature areas, 80 percent (n = 80) of the trenches are less than 20 m^2, with only 6 percent (n = 6) of the trenches measuring over 50 m^2.

The tallest structure in La Corona's central plaza also has the looting trench with the largest area, a massive trench extending from the ground to the summit, wrapping around the base of the structure and forming a large crater in the centre of the mound (Fig. 11). [8] The trench is deepest at the summit, where it is 4 m deep. Approximately 248 m^3 of soil and deposits were removed from this trench, an estimated effort of 700 person hours. Assuming a working day of eight hours/day and a looting rate of 0.35 m^3 per hour, looting this structure would have taken one person 87.5 days to

[6] Structures 13Q-4A–G.

[7] Structure 13Q-4G.

[8] Structure 13Q-1

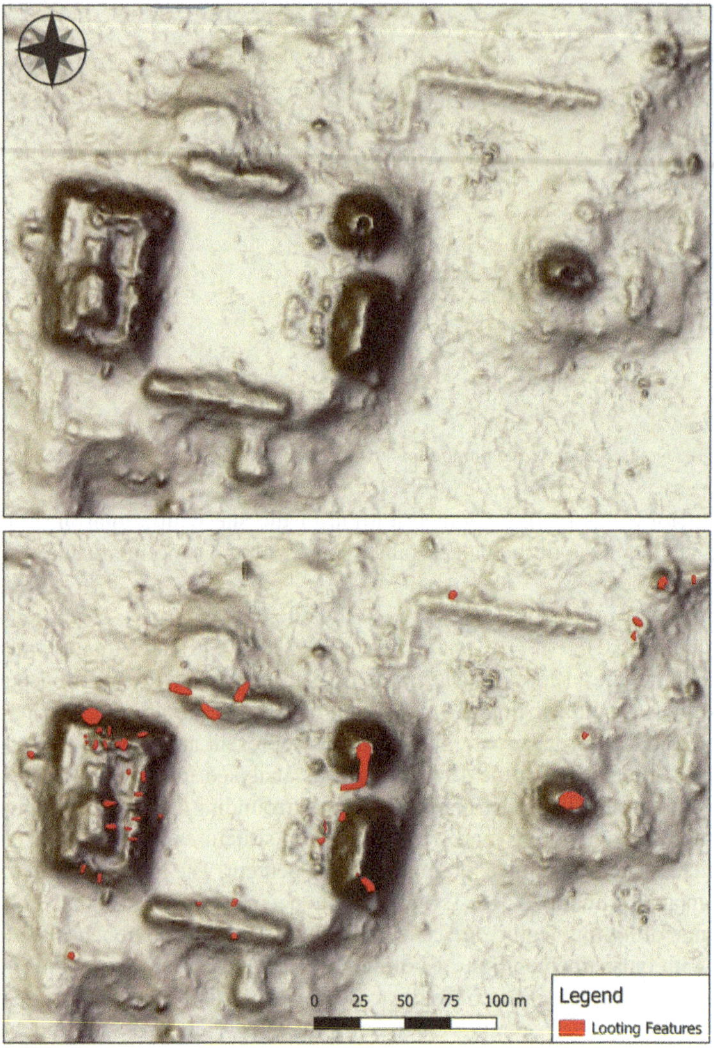

Fig. 11 Looting features in La Corona's central plaza

complete, or a team of six [9] a period of 15 days. A sample of nine additional trenches in La Corona and El Jobillo had a combined volume of approximately 264 m^3 of removed soils and deposits, an estimated effort of 754 person hours or 94 days. Looting La Corona was undoubtedly a massive effort that would have presented logistical constraints for food, water, and fuel, and required substantial planning and

[9] Based on anecdotes disclosed to the authors by former looters, organised teams of looters typically comprised 6–12 people.

coordination to loot and remove artifacts. Given that the 'Lo Veremos' camp was within 1 km of the site, the severe historical looting at La Corona could have occurred undetected over several years in conjunction with nearby chicle extracting activities.

Although the areal extent of many of the looting marks were considerably smaller than this trench, even marks with smaller areas exhibited devastating looting beneath the surface. For example, several of the looting scars contained tunnels or large intrusions branching into the interior of the structures, while others showed deep trenching beneath the ground level. These illicit excavations, left open and exposed to the elements for decades, have exacerbated the damage to the architecture and accelerated the structures' collapse.

6 Future Research

While the mystery of Site Q was solved over 15 years ago, lidar enables an analysis of looting patterns that was not feasible with traditional survey methods or aerial imagery. Future research will expand on this case study to other heavily looted areas of the Maya region, making use of a sample of 8359 km^2 of existing lidar data to record previous looting identifications, find potential looting incidents that have not been investigated, and analyse illicit digging in relation to the natural and built environment. Field verification and examination of excavation reports and other grey literature will supplement lidar analyses and reveal estimated looting dates, deposit types, and looting that is difficult to see on the surface, such as tunnelling.

The combination of geospatial lidar analyses, field verification, and grey literature, such as archaeological excavation records and archival imagery, contribute to understanding the effects of looting in the Maya area in multiple ways. This approach can facilitate the re-provenancing of looted objects, inform preservation methods for damaged sites, and enable the development of long-term policies for cultural heritage protection. In addition, spatial analyses of looting in the Maya area can help researchers understand the social behaviours and organisation of looting and the ways in which looting is linked to migration, deforestation, and other social patterns, both licit and illicit. This information can also be cross-referenced with existing research on the pre-Columbian antiquities market to track where looting has occurred geographically, the types of objects that were targeted, and how these patterns have changed through time. More broadly, conducting a thorough analysis of archaeological looting across a wide sample of Maya sites will result in data that can be used to inform cultural heritage protection policies and find solutions to curb the problem of Maya site looting.

References

Agapiou, A., Lysandrou, V., & Hadjimitsis, D. G. (2017). Optical remote sensing potentials for looting detection. *Geosciences, 7*(4), 98. https://doi.org/10.3390/geosciences7040098

Allen, W. (2012, October 8). In the Land of the Maya, A Battle for a Vital Forest. *Yale E360*. Retrieved January 30, 2021, from https://e360.yale.edu/features/in_the_land_of_the_maya_a_battle_for_a_vital_forest

Balestrieri, B. A. B. (2018). Field archaeologists as eyewitnesses to site looting. *Arts; Basel, 7*(3). Retrieved October 5, 2020, from http://dx.doi.org.libproxy.tulane.edu:2048/10.3390/arts7030048

Barker, A. W. (2018). Looting, the antiquities trade, and competing valuations of the past. *Annual Review of Anthropology, 47*(1), 455–474. https://doi.org/10.1146/annurev-anthro-102116-041320

Baron, J. (2012). Operaciones CR14, CR15 y CR17: Excavaciones en el Grupo Coronitas, Estructuras 13R-2, 13R-3, 13R-4 y 13R-5. In T. Barrientos Q, M. A. Canuto, & J. Ponce (Eds.), *Proyecto Regional Arqueológico La Corona. Informe Final Temporada 2011* (pp. 231–264). Instituto de Antropología e Historia.

Barrientos, Q. T., & Canuto, M. A. (2022). Descubriendo y Rescatando 'Ciudades Perdidas' en Petén: El 'Sitio Q' y La Corona. *Antropología e Historia de Guatemala, In Review*.

Bowen, E. F. W., Tofel, B. B., Parcak, S., & Granger, R. (2017). Algorithmic Identification of Looted Archaeological Sites from Space. *Frontiers in ICT, 4*. Retrieved May 27, 2020, from https://doi.org/10.3389/fict.2017.00004

Brodie, N., & Renfrew, C. (2005). Looting and the world's archaeological heritage: The inadequate response. *Annual Review of Anthropology, 34*(1), 343–361. https://doi.org/10.1146/annurev.anthro.34.081804.120551

Canuto, M. A., Estrada-Belli, F., Garrison, T. G., Houston, S. D., Acuña, M. J., Kováč, M., Marken, D., Nondédéo, P., Auld-Thomas, L., Castanet, C., Chatelain, D., Chiriboga, C. R., Drápela, T., Lieskovský, T., Tokovinine, A., Velasquez, A., Fernández-Díaz, J. C., & Shrestha, R. (2018). Ancient lowland Maya complexity as revealed by airborne laser scanning of northern Guatemala. *Science, 361*(6409), eaau0137. https://doi.org/10.1126/science.aau0137

Canuto, M. A., Guenter, S., Tsesmeli, E., & Marken, D. (2005). *El reconocimiento de La Corona, 2005*.

Cerra, D., Plank, S., Lysandrou, V., & Tian, J. (2016). Cultural heritage sites in danger—towards automatic damage detection from space. *Remote Sensing, 8*(9), 781. https://doi.org/10.3390/rs8090781

Coe, M. (1973). *The Maya Scribe and his World*. Grolier Club.

Coggins, C. (1969). Illicit traffic of pre-Columbian antiquities. *Art Journal, 29*(1), 94–114. https://doi.org/10.2307/775285

Coggins, C. (1972). Archeology and the art market. *Science, 175*(4019), 263–266.

Coronado-Ruiz, A. (2009). Operación CR 20G: Excavaciones en el Edificio G de la Estructura 13Q-4. In T. Barrientos Q. & M. A. Canuto (Eds.), *Proyecto Regional Arqueológico La Corona. Informe Final Temporada 2008* (pp. 57–74). Instituto de Antropología e Historia.

Cowley, D., Banaszek, Ł., Geddes, G., Gannon, A., Middleton, M., & Millican, K. (2020). Making LiGHT work of large area survey? Developing approaches to rapid archaeological mapping and the creation of systematic national-scaled heritage data. *Journal of Computer Applications in Archaeology, 3*(1), 109–121. https://doi.org/10.5334/jcaa.49

Danti, M., Branting, S., & Penacho, S. (2017). The American schools of oriental research cultural heritage initiatives: Monitoring cultural heritage in Syria and Northern Iraq by geospatial imagery. *Geosciences (2076-3263), 7*(4), 95. https://doi.org/10.3390/geosciences7040095

Deletaille, E., & Sonnery, J.-L. (1985). Rediscovered masterpieces of Mesoamerica: Mexico-Guatemala-Honduras. Editions Arts.

Desailly-Chanson, Y. (2010). Operaciones CR 33 y CR35: Excavaciones en las Estructuras 13Q-3 y 13Q-5. In M. A. Canuto & T. Barrientos Q. (Eds.), *Proyecto Regional Arqueológico La Corona. Informe Final Temporada 2009* (pp. 99–133). Instituto de Antropología e Historia.

Devine, J. A. (2016). Contesting global heritage in the chicle workers' museum. *Latin American Research Review, 51*(3), 101–122. https://doi.org/10.1353/lar.2016.0036

Devine, J. A., Currit, N., Reygadas, Y., Liller, L. I., & Allen, G. (2020). Drug trafficking, cattle ranching and land use and land cover change in Guatemala's Maya Biosphere Reserve. *Land Use Policy, 95*, 104578. https://doi.org/10.1016/j.landusepol.2020.104578

Elfadaly, A., Attia, W., Qelichi, M. M., Murgante, B., & Lasaponara, R. (2018). Management of cultural heritage sites using remote sensing indices and spatial analysis techniques. *Surveys in Geophysics, 39*(6), 1347–1377. https://doi.org/10.1007/s10712-018-9489-8

Elia, R. J. (1997). Looting, collecting, and the destruction of archaeological resources. *Nonrenewable Resources, 6*(2), 85–98. https://doi.org/10.1007/BF02803807

Golden, C., & Scherer, A. K. (2006). Border problems: Recent archaeological research along the Usumacinta river. *The PARI Journal, 7*(2), 1–16.

Graham, I. (1986). Looters Rob Graves and history. *National Geographic Magazine, 169*(4), 453–461.

Graham, I. (1997). Mission to La Corona. *Archaeology, 50*(5), 46–46.

Grube, N., Haase, E.-W., & Sattler, M. (1990). Vier neue archäologische Fundorte im nordwestlichen Peten. *Mexicon, 12*(3), 46–49.

Guenter, S. (2005). La Corona Find Sheds Light on Site Q Mystery. *The PARI Journal, VI*(2), 14–16.

Guenter, S. (2010). Operación CR32: Investigaciones en las Estructuras 13Q-2, 13Q-2A y 13Q-6. In T. Barrientos Q. & M. A. Canuto (Eds.), *Proyecto Regional Arqueológico La Corona. Informe Final Temporada 2009* (pp. 73–98).. Instituto de Antropología e Historia.

Guzmán, R. (2011). Reconocimiento Arqueológico y mapeo en La Corona. In T. Barrientos Q., M. A. Canuto, & M. J. Acuña (Eds.), *Proyecto Regional Arqueológico La Corona. Informe Final Temporada 2010* (pp. 127–150).. Instituto de Antropología e Historia.

Guzmán, R. (2012). Reconocimiento Arqueológico y mapeo en El Jobillo. In T. Barrientos Q., M. A. Canuto, & J. Ponce (Eds.), *Proyecto Regional Arqueológico La Corona. Informe Final Temporada 2011* (pp. 109–122).. Instituto de Antropología e Historia.

Hardy, S. A. (2015). Virtues Impracticable and Extremely Difficult: The Human Rights of Subsistence Diggers. In A. González-Ruibal & G. Moshenska (Eds.), *Ethics and the archaeology of violence* (pp. 229–239). Springer. https://doi.org/10.1007/978-1-4939-1643-6_14

Hernandez, M., Huth, U., & Schreier, G. (2008). Earth Observation from Space for the Protection of UNESCO World Heritage Sites: DLR Assisting UNESCO. *ISPRS Arch, XXXVII PT, B8*, 643–646.

Hollowell, J. (2006). Moral arguments on subsistence digging. In C. Scarre & G. Scarre (Eds.), *The ethics of archaeology: Philosophical perspectives on archaeological practice* (pp. 69–93). Cambridge University Press.

Hudson Museum. (2021). *The Search for Site Q - Hudson Museum—University of Maine*. The Search for Site Q Retrieved December 13, 2021, from https://umaine.edu/hudsonmuseum/collections/search/

Kolbay, B. (2008, May 30). Drug gang jungle fires threaten Guatemala ruins. *Reuters*. https://www.reuters.com/article/us-guatemala-maya-idUSN2727487020080530

Lasaponara, R., & Masini, N. (2018). Space-based identification of archaeological illegal excavations and a new automatic method for looting feature extraction in desert areas. *Surveys in Geophysics, 39*(6), 1323–1346. https://doi.org/10.1007/s10712-018-9480-4

López, M., & Escalante, K. (2019). Investigaciones en el Grupo Tortugas de La Corona: Operaciones CR-54 y CR-55, Temporada 2018. In T. Barrientos Q., M. A. Canuto, & M. López (Eds.), *Proyecto Arqueológico La Corona Informe Final Temporada 2018* (pp. 89–127). Instituto de Antropología e Historia.

Marken, D. B., & Guenter, S. (2006). Survey and Mapping of La Corona's monumental center. In M. A. Canuto, M. J. Acuña, E. E. Bell, S. H. Guenter, & D. B. Marken (Eds.), *Proyecto Arqueológico El Perú-Waka': Sub-Proyecto La Corona Informe No. 2, Temporada 2006.*
Martin, S. (1993). Site Q: The Case for a Classic Maya Super-Polity. *Mesoweb*, 17.
Mathews, P. (1979). *Notes on the Inscriptions of 'Site Q'*. Department of Archaeology, University of Calgary.
Mathews, P. (1998). *Site Q Sculptures*. Archaeology Magazine Archive. https://archive.archaeology.org/online/features/siteq/
Matsuda, D. (1992). *The Looting of Pre-Columbian Artifacts from Latin American Archeological Sites* [Master's Thesis, California State University]. http://dspace.calstate.edu/bitstream/handle/10211.3/126577/David.J.MatsudaThesis.PDF?sequence=1
Matsuda, D. (1994). Looted Artifacts. Seeds of change in Latin America. *Anthropos, 89*(1/3), 222–224. JSTOR.
Matsuda, D. (1998a). *Subsistence digging in and around Belize.* PhD Dissertation, Union University. https://www.elibrary.ru/item.asp?id=5488039
Matsuda, D. (1998b). The ethics of archaeology, subsistence digging, and artifact looting in Latin America: Point muted counterpoint. *International Journal of Cultural Property, 7*(1), 87–97. https://doi.org/10.1017/S0940739198770080
McNeary, R. (2014). Applications of Airborne LiDAR for cultural heritage management initiatives in Northern Ireland. In H. Kamermans & M. Gojda (Eds.), *A sense of the past: Studies in current archaeological applications of remote sensing and non-invasive prospection methods* (pp. 67–82). Archaeopress.
Padilla, L. (2011). Operación CR 20: Excavaciones en el Palacio de La Corona. In T. Barrientos Q., M. A. Canuto, & M. J. Acuña (Eds.), *Proyecto Regional Arqueológico La Corona. Informe Final Temporada 2010* (pp. 151–172). Instituto de Antropología e Historia.
Parcak, S. H. (2009). *Satellite remote sensing for archaeology*. Routledge.
Parcak, S. H. (2017). Moving from space-based to ground-based solutions in remote sensing for archaeological heritage: A case study from Egypt. *Remote Sensing, 9*(12), 1297. https://doi.org/10.3390/rs9121297
Parcak, S. H. (2019). *Archaeology from space: How the future shapes our past* (1st ed.). Henry Holt and Company.
Paredes Maury, S. (1999). Surviving in the rainforest: The realities of looting in the rural villages of El Petén, Guatemala. *FAMSI Reports*.
Paredes Maury, S. (2019). There and back again: Looting, trafficking culture, and the management of cultural heritage in Guatemala. In C. G. Tremain & D. Yates (Eds.), *The market for Mesoamerica: Reflections on the sale of Pre-Columbian antiquities* (pp. 61–86). University Press of Florida.
Parks, S., McAnany, P. A., & Murata, S. (2006). The conservation of maya cultural heritage: Searching for solutions in a troubled region. *Journal of Field Archaeology, 31*(4), 425–432.
Perez, F. (2020). Investigaciones Arqueológicas en La Estructura 12R-1, Temporada 2019. In T. Barrientos Q., M. A. Canuto, & M. López (Eds.), *Proyecto Arqueológico La Corona Informe Final Temporada 2019* (pp. 123–160). Instituto de Antropología e Historia.
Ponce, J. (2013). Operación CR16: Excavaciones en la Estructura 13R-10, Temporada 2012. In T. Barrientos Q., M. A. Canuto, & J. Ponce (Eds.), *Proyecto Regional Arqueológico La Corona. Informe Final Temporada 2012* (pp. 141–186). Instituto de Antropología e Historia.
Ponce, J. (2017). Investigaciones Arqueológicas en El Jobillo: Temporada 2016. In T. Barrientos Q., M. A. Canuto, & E. Bustamante (Eds.), *Proyecto Arqueológico La Corona Informe Final Temporada 2016* (pp. 191–212). Instituto de Antropología e Historia.
Ponce, J. (2020). Investigaciones Arqueológicas en El Jobillo, Temporada 2019. In T. Barrientos Q., M. A. Canuto, & M. López (Eds.), *Proyecto Arqueológico La Corona Informe Final Temporada 2019* (pp. 289–309). Instituto de Antropología e Historia.
Robertson, M. G. (1972). Monument Thievery in Mesoamerica. *American Antiquity, 37*(2), 147–155. https://doi.org/10.2307/278202

Schuster, A. M. H. (1997). The Search for Site Q. *Archaeology, 50*(5), 42–45.
Schwartz, N. B. (1990). *Forest Society A Social History of Petén, Guatemala*. University of Pennsylvania Press. https://go.openathens.net/redirector/tulane.edu?url=http://www.jstor.org/stable/10.2307/j.ctv4s7k6r
Sever, T. L., & Irwin, D. E. (2003). Landscape archaeology: Remote-sensing investigation of the ancient Maya in the Peten rainforest of northern Guatemala. *Ancient Mesoamerica, 14*(1), 113–122.
Sheets, P. D. (1973). The pillage of prehistory. *American Antiquity, 38*(3), 317–320. https://doi.org/10.2307/279718
Sieff, K. (2020, July 5). *The Guatemalan rainforest: Lush jungle, Mayan ruins and narco jets full of cocaine*. Washington Post. https://www.washingtonpost.com/world/2020/07/05/guatemala-cocaine-trafficking-laguna-del-tigre/
Stoian, D., Rodas, A., Butler, M., Monterroso, I., & Hodgdon, B. (2018). *Forest concessions in Petén, Guatemala: A systematic analysis of the socioeconomic performance of community enterprises in the Maya Biosphere Reserve*. Center for International Forestry Research. https://www.cifor.org/knowledge/publication/7163/
Stuart, D. (2001). Las ruinas de La Corona, Petén, y la identificación del 'Sitio Q'. *XV Simposio de Investigaciones Arqueológicas En Guatemala*. XV Simposio de Investigaciones Arqueológicas en Guatemala, Guatemala City, Guatemala.
Tapete, D., & Cigna, F. (2019). Detection of archaeological looting from space: Methods, achievements and challenges. *Remote Sensing, 11*(20), 2389. https://doi.org/10.3390/rs11202389
Wilford, J. N. (2003, October 30). Ancient Maya Altar Retaken From Looters in Guatemala. *The New York Times*. https://www.nytimes.com/2003/10/30/world/ancient-maya-altar-retaken-from-looters-in-guatemala.html
Yates, D. (2014a). Displacement, deforestation, and drugs: Antiquities trafficking and the narcotics support economies of Guatemala. In J. D. Kila & M. Balcells (Eds.), *Cultural property crime: An overview and analysis of contemporary perspectives and trends* (pp. 23–36). Brill. https://brill.com/view/book/edcoll/9789004280540/B9789004280540_003.xml
Yates, D. (2014b). Church theft, insecurity, and community justice: The reality of source-end regulation of the market for illicit Bolivian cultural objects. *European Journal on Criminal Policy and Research, 20*(4), 445–457. https://doi.org/10.1007/s10610-014-9232-z
Yates, D. (2017). Illicit cultural property from Latin America: Looting, trafficking, and sale. In F. Desmarais (Ed.), *Countering illicit traffic in cultural goods: The global challenge of protecting the world's heritage* (pp. 33–46). International Council of Museums International Observatory on Illicit Traffic in Cultural Goods. https://osf.io/preprints/socarxiv/ny7z6/

Kirsty E. Escalante is a PhD Candidate in Anthropology at Tulane University. She has worked on archaeological excavations in Guatemala, Mexico, Belize, South Africa, Peru, and in multiple states in the southern and north eastern United States. Her dissertation examines archaeological looting in the Maya area using a combined analysis of lidar imagery, previous archaeological excavation records, and field verifications of looting incidents to better understand illicit digging practices and organisation. In 2022, she won the Society for American Archaeology Student Paper Award and grants from the Lambda Alpha National Anthropology Honor Society and the Rust Family Foundation for her dissertation research on illicit digging in the Maya area. She is also an archaeologist for a cultural resource management firm in Atlanta, Georgia, managing over 100 archaeological surveys for transportation projects throughout the state of Georgia.

Tomás Barrientos Q. is a Guatemalan archaeologist who is currently co-director of La Corona Regional Archaeological Project (PRALC). He obtained a PhD in Anthropology at Vanderbilt University and has conducted archaeological research throughout Guatemala for the last 25 years in sites like Kaminaljuyú, Piedras Negras, Cancuén, Lake Atitlán and the Escuintla region in the Pacific Coast. His specialties include spatial analysis of architecture; socio-political and ancient geopolitics theory; lowland, coastal, and highland Maya archaeology; cultural astronomy, pre-Columbian gastronomy, and cultural heritage management.

Marcello A. Canuto is currently Professor of Anthropology at Tulane University. He has undertaken excavations in the Maya region, South America, India, north Africa, and the northeast US. His primary research interest in the Maya area has been on the integrative mechanisms that the ancient Maya used to build and maintain a socio-politically complex society throughout both the Preclassic and Classic periods. More broadly, his interests include household and community dynamics, the development of socio-political complexity in ancient societies, the definition of identity through material culture, and the modern social contexts of archaeology in Mesoamerica. His past research in Honduras investigated the nature of ethnic diversity at Copan. He now co-directs a project in the understudied Northwest Petén, Guatemala where he investigates the construction of social categories and the mechanisms by which complex socio-political organizations develop and were maintained. Among many publications are the edited volumes The Regimes of the Ancient Maya (in preparation with Cambridge, 2019), Understanding Early Classic Copan: New Research and New Themes (University of Pennsylvania, 2004), The Archaeology of Communities: A New World Perspective (Routledge, 2000). Canuto is also the Director of the Middle American Research Institute at Tulane University and was previously Assistant Professor of Anthropology at Yale University. He also serves on the U.S. Board of the Universidad del Valle Guatemala.

Securing Borders and Restraining the Illegal Movement of Cultural Property to, from, and within, the Island of Ireland

Ted Oakes

Abstract There are more border crossings on the island of Ireland between Ireland (a Member State of the European Union) and Northern Ireland (a constituent region of the United Kingdom, a non-European Union country) than the entire eastern boundary of the European Union. At almost 500 km long, the border has a complex history, and was previously a hotspot of terrorism and smuggling activities, including the smuggling of cultural heritage. Though the British withdrawal from the European Union has been a major test for the complex and delicate constitutional settlement in the region which ended decades of sectarian strife, it has also renewed the possibility of increased smuggling activities along the border, including the smuggling of cultural heritage. This chapter will spotlight the history of the Irish border and the movement of cultural heritage to, from, and within the island of Ireland. This research will show that the border has long been problematic for authorities seeking to protect cultural heritage, and that European Union membership has assisted (to some degree) in restraining illicit trade of cultural heritage, though not eliminating it entirely.

1 Introduction

In 1903, the Attorney General for Ireland brought a suit in London's High Court against the Trustees of the British Museum over the Broighter Hoard, a collection of gold Celtic ornaments unearthed at a small farm near Derry in the north of the island of Ireland (now Northern Ireland)[1] in 1896. Subsequently acquired by the British

[1]Note on terminology: Northern Ireland shall be used to refer to the devolved region of the United Kingdom established in 1921 which occupies the north-eastern most part of the island of Ireland; Ireland (also known as the Republic of Ireland and previously the Irish Free State) shall refer to the

T. Oakes (✉)
ICOM, Paris, France

IMT School for Advanced Studies, Lucca, Italy
e-mail: edward.oakes@imtlucca.it

N. Oosterman, D. Yates (eds.), *Art Crime in Context*, Studies in Art, Heritage, Law and the Market 6, https://doi.org/10.1007/978-3-031-14084-6_9

Museum, the Attorney General alleged that their removal from Ireland had been illegal (Bailkin, 2004). Although the island of Ireland had been united with the island of Britain as the United Kingdom since 1801, Irish treasure trove law, which governed the ownership of such historic finds, remained distinct from those laws in Britain (Webb v. Ireland, 1988) and the Attorney General argued the objects should be returned to Royal Irish Academy in Dublin who were in fact the rightful owners under Irish treasure trove law (Neill, 1993). The High Court agreed with the Attorney General that Irish treasure trove law had been broken, and the hoard was returned to the Royal Irish Academy (ibid.). Though a complex case in many other respects, Ireland being part of the same polity as Britain meant there were mechanisms to secure the return of the hoard. However, for most of the twentieth century following Irish independence and the partition of the island, there were no such mechanisms. Joint Irish and British membership of the European Union from the 1970s onwards would remedy these issues to some degree, but Brexit would in turn unravel it once more. Beginning with the complex division of the island along cultural lines, by tracing the evolution of heritage protection legislation of both North and South, and in taking into account examples of illegal movement of cultural heritage over the border and across the Irish Sea, this chapter will explore the evolution of heritage protection policies for moveable cultural heritage on the island of Ireland against the backdrop of crisis. Furthermore, this chapter will examine the potential impact of the new European Union import regulations on addressing the illicit trade of cultural heritage across the Irish border and the likelihood of increased smuggling activities in the aftermath of the Brexit. This analysis will demonstrate that, though Brexit has the potential to cause problems with respect to efforts to restrain illicit trafficking for the European Union as a whole, and the United Kingdom, protecting heritage on the island of Ireland has long been problematic.

2 Irish Heritage and Shifting Cultural Identities

At the start of the twentieth century, the island of Ireland was a constituent country of the United Kingdom, and not without concerns for the loss of cultural heritage. The example of the Broighter Hoard and subsequent court case had not been a unique experience, and since the 1850s, private actors in Ireland had been working to protect historic monuments across the island. Just like the rest of the United Kingdom, in Ireland the protection of heritage was guaranteed through the *Ancient Monuments Act (1882)* which mainly protected built and immovable heritage (Halfin, 1995). As demonstrated in the case of the Broighter Hoard, a certain amount of protection was afforded through Irish treasure trove law (Webb v. Ireland, 1988),

independent state established on the rest of the island of Ireland following its secession from the United Kingdom in 1922.

which by the nineteenth century had evolved from its original purpose and was now seen as a law for the retention—for the common good—of antiquarian objects of interest and value. These legal orders aside, there were no other protection for movable cultural property in Ireland or the rest of the United Kingdom, and by the beginning of the twentieth century, it was often private citizens that would raise awareness of the absence, as well as lead campaigns, to protect heritage.

Ireland was strikingly different from the rest of the United Kingdom. On the one hand, it was England's first and most closely integrated colony and it profited from Britain's extensive empire. Like Britain, Ireland too had its own 'gentleman scholars' who participated in the Grand Tour and amassed a heritage in Ireland that was, essentially, not of Irish origin, like those collections acquired by the 2nd Earl of Bantry in his Tour of Italy in the 1840s (Boggi, 2016), and by the late nineteenth and early twentieth century Ireland also developed a museum system, centred around one of Dublin's most affluent districts and mirrored heavily on the British museum institutions in South Kensington, which focused on collections of arts and science (Sawyer, 2011). Similarly to London, these museums too had their own burgeoning upper-middle class communities to develop, manage and valorise these institutions and their collections (p. 446). And just like London's museums, ethnographic cultural objects, looted from other parts of the empire, also found their way into these Dublin based collections (Artforum, 2021).

On the other hand, Ireland retained strong cultural traditions and heritage which set it apart from England, and indeed Britain. In fact, there were two traditions: one descended from the British Protestant settlers grouped mainly in the north of the island, the Unionists; and one of descendants from the mainly Gaelic and Catholic indigenous communities who occupied the rest of Ireland, the Nationalists. At this stage, neither was mutually exclusive and both saw themselves as equally Irish as the other (Sawyer, 2011, p. 442), though there were marked difference and oppositions. The Unionists cherished the cultural, economic, and political links with Britain, valorised a heritage that emphasised the industrial and commercial character of the North, while also stressing their roots as a Protestant-dissenter class (ibid., p. 435), commemorating events like the triumph of the Protestant William III over the Catholic James II (Cooney, 1996). The Nationalists, on the other hand, desired a weakening of these constitutional links. They called for the establishment of a Dublin based parliament to manage Irish affairs, all the while equally using heritage to strengthen their cause (pp. 155–157). Beginning in the late nineteenth century, Ireland was experiencing a renewed interest in the Gaelic language, culture and heritage, and both communities initially supported and encouraged this cultural movement (Pritchard, 2004). The Gaelic Revival also greatly impacted on collecting attitudes in the Dublin based museums where Ireland's Celtic past was celebrated as a Golden Age, and Gaelic and Celtic archaeology became privileged to the extent that the original collections of art and science became marginalised (Sawyer, 2011).

But as the Nationalists aspirations for a Dublin parliament became increasingly real in the first decades of the twentieth century, this Gaelic Revival was in turn commandeered by the Nationalists in their campaign for self-determination, and the Unionists—who vigorously opposed any prospect of parliamentary independence for Ireland—began to firmly reject any association with Irish culture, and refocused their efforts to protecting, promoting, and valorising their interests and heritage in the north of the island (Pritchard, 2004). These shifting cultural identities would impact greatly on the protection of movable heritage on the island and the reverberations would be felt for decades to come.

3 Partitioning Ireland and Protecting Heritage

By the 1910s, the political situation on the island was becoming tense. With the Nationalists tantalisingly close to achieving their aims of a Dublin based parliament, the Unionists took up arms to oppose it. The British Government in London, concerned by the threat of civil war, sought some form of exclusion for the Unionists to maintain peace (Ruane & Todd, 1996). And although the concept of partitioning the island was anathema to the Nationalists (Ferriter, 2019), as early as 1912 it was emerging as the most preferred option of the policy makers to avoid bloodshed (Mulvagh, 2019). Despite this, violence still exploded as Nationalist opinion shifted from moderate constitutionalism to outright militant republicanism. British forces quickly suppressed a rebellion in Dublin in 1916 where Nationalists declared a republic, but in 1919 Nationalists leaders reaffirmed their 1916 declaration of independence and launched a war of independence that would last until 1921. By then, any accommodation between the Nationalists and the Unionists would be impossible and the British Government partitioned the island. The *Government of Ireland Act (1920)* made the north-eastern, mostly Unionist, part of the island a devolved region of the United Kingdom, Northern Ireland, with its own internal administration and a Unionist dominated regional parliament; and in 1921 Nationalists and the British Government signed the Anglo-Irish Treaty which ended the war begun in 1919 and created the independent Irish State on the rest of the island (Mulvagh, 2019). Much valuable cultural heritage was lost during this violent period. The stately homes of those 'gentlemen scholars' were targeted in attacks carried out by zealous Nationalists who burnt many of these residences to the ground, often with their valuable artist patrimony inside (Harris, 2006). Additionally, an enormous and irreplaceable wealth of documentary heritage for the entire island, dating from the 1100s, was lost during a battle between Nationalists and British forces in Dublin in May 1921, which saw the Public Records Office nearly entirely destroyed along with its valuable historical artefacts (McCullagh, 2021).

Following the establishing of these two jurisdictions, for most of the twentieth century, tensions between Ireland and Northern Ireland would pivot from cool to largely non-existent as both administrations initially focused on state building processes with highly differing agendas. In Northern Ireland, with its devolved government based in Belfast, the power to legislate for the regulation of the movement of cultural heritage remained with the central British Government in London, and though heritage protection *per se* was a devolved issue, it was still never a priority for financially conservative Unionist Belfast ministers (Fry, 2003), despite speculative evidence to suggest that collectors were profiting from the lack protections, and concerns that heritage objects were being taken out of Northern Ireland (Evans, 1953). It has been suggested that identity politics largely drove the cultural policy of Belfast administration, and this can be inferred from the establishment of certain cultural institutions in the aftermath of partition (Cooney, 1996), but it was apathy and disinterest which required Belfast to enact the *Ancient Monuments Act (Northern Ireland 1926)* which was in reality only an extension of the United Kingdom-wide 1882 law, as it was not intended to strengthen existing protections, nor did it envisage the extension of protections to any type of moveable heritage (Fry, 2003). For moveable heritage, regulations would only arrive in 1939 when the Second World War saw the reorganisation of the British economy, and the movement of all resources (including cultural goods) being controlled to assist the war effort. The *Import, Export and Customs Powers (Defence) Act (1939)* ensured no items of cultural heritage could leave the United Kingdom during the conflict and, although planned as a temporary war time measure, it remained law in the United Kingdom—including Northern Ireland—for most of the twentieth century (Chamberlain & Hausler, 2014).

Cultural nationalism was most certainly on the agenda of the Dublin administration in independent Ireland where academics and museum professionals were conscious of the increasingly large quantities of archaeological materials leaving Ireland in the years before and after independence (Department of the Taoiseach, 1926). Irish civil servants in Dublin took a poor view of the British legislation they had inherited, which they did not consider fit for purpose (the Parliamentary Draftsman cited the British colonial era legislation as "clumsy and unhelpful") (Office of the Attorney General, 1928a), and rather than emulating the British legal order, Ireland's first legislators looked to continental Europe for inspiration, notably to Italy (Bourke, 1929) which only a few years previously enacted its own system of protection across the peninsula (Levi, 2008). In the mid-1920s, Dublin began drafting new legislation which, civil servants hoped, would keep certain cultural materials inside the new State to protect Irish identity (Office of the Attorney General, 1928b). Largely, this meant archaeological materials associated with Ireland's Gaelic past—precisely those types of materials cherished in the Gaelic revival—and though there were attempts made to include non-archaeological materials through a draft *Prohibition on Exportation from the Free State of Works of Art*—these efforts were eventually abandoned (Department of the Taoiseach, 1925).

Instead, the resulting *National Monuments Act (1930)* specifically protected objects that had an "association with any Irish historical event or person" (National Monuments Act, 1930) and prohibited the removal of these mainly archaeological materials from Ireland without a licence. The Act also prohibited the excavation of archaeological sites without a licence, and it built on constitutional developments which had seen the transfer of sovereignty from the Crown to the State, and with that, the transfer of ownership of undiscovered cultural heritage to the people (Webb v. Ireland, 1988). Yet, throughout the drafting process for the 1930 Act, the Attorney General raised concerns of infirmities, in particular that it "interfere[d] too drastically with the rights of private property" (Attorney General of Ireland, 1925), especially with respect for export regulation, and that it would create a potential burden on the State to provide compensation in cases of refusal of a licence for export (Department of the Taoiseach, 1925).

4 Heritage Protection and the Border

The concerns of Ireland's Attorney General were quickly proven correct and the loss or near loss of several important items of heritage from Ireland over the following decades after the passage of the 1930 Act demonstrated its infirmities. In the 1930s, export of the Galway City regalia (a silver guild sword and mace set) became a legal headache for the Irish Government that would drag on for nearly 30 years. In an explanatory letter to the Government, the Attorney General explained that even though that the terms of the 1930 Act had applied to the regalia, they were still illegally relieved from Ireland (apparently with the full knowledge of the Government, according to the Attorney General), and the entire debacle lead the Attorney General to declare the new law unenforceable (Attorney General of Ireland, 1931). The regalia were finally returned in 1961 through an act of goodwill from their subsequent American owner who had purchased them in the 1930s (NUI Galway Library, 2014). Events like this were not unique and for the rest of twentieth century, illegal happenings that threatened heritage in Ireland usually led to the amendment of the *National Monuments Act* (Conlon, 2014), or the adoption of new legislation entirely. Confusion over the exact coverage of the 1930 Act was apparent again in the 1940s with the near loss of the Ormond papers to buyers from abroad (Office of the Secretary of the President, 1945), and the resulting *Documents and Pictures (Regulation of Export) Act (1945)* was passed to extend protections to other forms of non-archaeological heritage. However, it was drafted hastily and soon recognised as wholly inadequate, and for a time, it inadvertently obliged banks to require export licenses to move necessary paperwork north of the border to Northern Ireland (Department of Justice, 1946).

The border was also becoming a more conspicuous problem. By the 1970s, the Unionist administration in Belfast had progressively strengthened its heritage protection system, making Northern Ireland the most regulated region of the United Kingdom, though still substantially less burdensome than the regime in the South (Cooney, 1996). The two Irelands therefore had competing protection regimes, with different levels of protection and though customs checkpoints existed since partition, the border had always been a relatively porous frontier by European standards Anderson, 2008). This fact was not lost on museum and heritage professionals in Dublin who noted that the largely unpatrolled border with Northern Ireland meant that valuable items of heritage could be easily moved north across it, and subsequently off the island and on to the international market elsewhere (Ryan, 1981). The lack of bilateral agreements between Ireland and the United Kingdom complicated matters further, and meant Ireland was reliant on goodwill to secure the return of any lost items of heritage, as demonstrated in the case of the Killymoon Hoard which was illegally removed from Ireland, and only brought to the attention of Irish authorities by British Museum officials who discovered the hoard on sale on the London market (Department of the Taoiseach, 1968). Indeed, this situation was precisely the reason why officials at the National Museum of Ireland encouraged the Irish Government to accede to the 1970 UNESCO Convention as a means to navigate the problems posed by the border.

Smuggling was, of course, not something new, and almost immediately after partition organised smuggling operations began, ranging from illicit trade of fuel, animals, medicine and food, both North and South, depending on which direction was more profitable (Ferriter, 2019). But at nearly 500 km long, with 208 official crossings (not including fields, farm paths or trails that have their own unmarked crossing, nor houses that straddle the border) it was, and remains, impossible for officials to patrol effectively. The situation was becoming much more volatile in the 1970s. Following partition, Northern Ireland had retained a large Nationalist minority, whom Unionists regarded as a threat to their administration and therefore made no effort to integrate (Anderson, 2008). But after decades of systematic discrimination, Nationalists began a peaceful campaign for civil and political rights. Attempts to suppress the campaign by the Belfast administration led to rioting, which in turn led the administration to request British troops in to support the Northern Irish police force. But it soon became clear that the Unionist administration had lost control of was becoming an increasingly unstable situation. In 1973 the British Government abolished the devolved Belfast administration and began ruling Northern Ireland directly from London.[2]

5 Towards European Integration and Peace

Shortly after the Unionist administration in Belfast was suspended, both Ireland and the United Kingdom joined the European Union (then the European Economic Community) and the potential role of the European project in remedying the complexities of the border and bringing peace, had not gone unrecognized (Ferriter, 2019). However, the political situation only deteriorated further. Attempts to establish a consociational regional government—where Unionist and Nationalists would share power in a reformed Belfast administration—were met with strong opposition from Unionist grass roots (Anderson, 2008) and throughout the 1970s and 1980s violence, what colloquially became known as The Troubles, only increased. The dangerous security situation necessitated the militarisation of the border, partly to hinder the north/south movement of paramilitaries and partly to contain violence within Northern Ireland. Still, violence often spilled over into Ireland and to Britain, and occasionally continental European. Paramilitary organisations, both Nationalist

[2]For more on history and origins of The Troubles, see Ruane and Todd (1996) The Dynamics of Conflict in Northern Ireland.

and Unionist, engaged heavily in organised crime to finance their activities and the line between criminal and paramilitary became increasingly blurred (Hourigan et al., 2018). These blurred lines were illustrated in several robberies of a prominent private art collection outside of Dublin in the 1970s and 1980s (RTE, 2001). Russborough House, a mansion outside of Dublin city containing one of the world's largest private art collections owned by a wealthy industrialist was repeatedly targeted by paramilitary groups and criminal organisations: in 1976 the Irish Republican Army (IRA) (along with British-aristocrat-turned-Irish-republican, Rose Dugdale) raided the house and stole several paintings which they intended to use as a ransom for their political aims (RTE, 2001); and the house experience another robbery in 1986 only this time it was orchestrated by Dublin crime lords, the stolen paintings were eventually retrieved in London and other cities elsewhere in Europe several years later, during which time they ended up in the hands of the IRA (Hourigan et al., 2018; Ní Chonaill, 2011).

But by the 1990s, the conditions for peace were emerging, facilitated in part (but not possible without) the European Union framework (Todd, 2015). In particular, the signing of the Maastricht Treaty would have profound implications for the movement of cultural property both North and South. The Treaty would formally establish the European Union Common Market on 1 January 1993 but with the internal borders between European Union Member States now unmonitored, mechanisms would be needed to ensure that protected items of cultural heritage in one Member State could not be moved across these open frontiers and into another Member State where less onerous laws could see them easily removed from the European Union altogether. European Union-wide customs rules were introduced to control the movement of cultural goods leaving the European Union with licences issued under *Regulation 116/2009* (originally *Council Regulation (EEC) No 3911/92*) and Member State issuing export licenses on behalf of the European Union (Conlon, 2014). To ensure the return of any cultural objects lost to another Member State across these now open internal borders, *Directive 2014/60/EU* (originally *Council Directive 93/7/EEC*) was enacted to assist with the return of certain cultural objects unlawfully removed from the territory of a Member State (Stamatoudi, 2011). With these instruments, there was now a mechanism for protection against the types of problems identified by the Irish museums experts in the 1980s.

The tensions between the two communities in Northern Ireland was also decreasing. An uneasy truce between the Nationalists and the Unionists was finally agreed in 1998 with the signing of the *Good Friday Agreement*, a broad and flexible settlement which established a Nationalist-Unionist power-sharing administration and parliamentary assembly in Belfast and normalised relations between Ireland and the United Kingdom. Though the European Union was not a major broker in bringing the Good Friday Agreement to fruition, the frameworks provide by European Union membership were beneficial. Joint membership of the European Union was referenced in the Agreement and with peace, European financial support was directed into the region to help reconciliation projects and bridge gaps between the two previously competing communities (Ferriter, 2019). It is also significant that some cross-border organisations established in the Good Friday Agreement failed to develop as originally envisaged precisely because joint European Union membership made them less necessary (Daly, 2017). Indeed, over 140 areas of North-South were enabled owing to the overarching European Union legal and policy framework, several of which were expressively aimed at countering the smuggling of cultural goods (Campbell, 2019). In the early years of the 2000s, imposing military infrastructure along the border was finally removed which had profoundly symbolic impact and though the border remained in place it became much less contentious with its demilitarisation (Ferriter, 2019). Peace and European Union membership was not a panacea, and evidence suggests that criminal organisations are using the open border as well as the close ethnic, cultural and national ties that link Ireland, Northern Ireland, and Britain, to smuggle materials to mainland Europe (Hourigan et al., 2018). The situation is similar to that on mainland Europe where officials have long been aware of the exploitation of the Schengen open borders policy to smuggle cultural materials from one jurisdiction to another (Roodt, 2015), and, it remains a constant battle for border officials and customs authorities and cross border cooperation is a key element for success (Somers Cocks, 2018). Indeed, the recognition of the security threats posed by criminal and terrorist organisations was a key reason behind the *European Union Regulation 880/2019* on the import of cultural goods (European Commission, 2018), and from 2025, the introduction of certain cultural goods into the European Union will be illegal without a licence (Somers Cocks, 2018).

6 Brexit and Re-Partition

Drafting for Regulation 880/2019 began in 2017, a year after the United Kingdom referendum on European Union membership on 23 June 2016. But the United Kingdom vote to leave the European Union was an unprecedented shock to the European project (Somers Cocks, 2018). The implications of the referendum for Ireland and Northern Ireland, where a majority of voters in Northern Ireland voted against Brexit (BBC, 2016a, b), were even more profound, given the extent to which European Union membership had facilitated in building peace, not to mention the shared mechanisms which secure the protection of cultural heritage. As negotiations began to untangle nearly fifty years of membership, maintaining the open border on the island of Ireland—an open border until now only possible because of joint-European Union membership—was identified as a priority for both Ireland and the European Commission. To maintain peace and stability in the region, this appeared to be something that the British Government agreed with (Elgot, 2017). But many aspects of the Brexit debate focused on cultural identity and the preservation of a national cultural exceptionalism, themes which are contrary to both the Good Friday Agreement and the European Union (Joannin, 2021), and throughout the Brexit debate, observers noted that the existence of the Border was never fully appreciated by Leave campaigners (Hayward, 2020). Indeed, efforts to avoid a hard border turned out to be the most complex issues throughout most of the withdrawal negotiations (Murphy, 2021).

But along with the threats to peace in the region, Brexit also raised doubts about the involvement of the United Kingdom—and with it Northern Ireland—in many European Union activities to address the illegal movement of cultural property, activities which had remedied some of the complexities of the border. Observers queried British participation under Directive 2014/60/EU (Hausler & Mackenzie-Gray Scott, 2017) and British involvement in European Union-wide policing operations was also in doubt as European police forces voiced their unease at the situation, highlighting the importance of intra-European Union border operations to fight illicit trade of cultural materials (Somers Cocks, 2018). The continuation of the European Union export licences system was also uncertain, and the European Union expressed concern that if the United Kingdom left the European Union common market, taking Northern Ireland with it in the process, an open border with Ireland would fatally undermine Regulation 116/2009 on exports (Council of the European Union, 2020). There were complex issues surrounding Regulation 880/2019 on imports too. Since it had not come fully into force, during the negotiations it became apparent to both the British (United Kingdom Parliament, 2019a, 2019b) and the European Union negotiators (Council of European Union, 2020) that a situation could accidentally emerge where the Irish Government would be required to implement checks along the Irish border for cultural goods entering the European Union from the United Kingdom via Northern Ireland. The Ireland/Northern Ireland Protocol in the final Withdrawal Agreement largely avoided these fears, by ensuring a hard border was avoided and included guarantees that the regional parliamentary assembly would vote to decide on the continuation of this compromise very four years (Institute for Government, 2021); this arrangement effectively ensures that Northern Ireland, while remaining a part of the United Kingdom, continues to be part of the European Union common market. The final agreement also stipulates that Northern Ireland will continue to implement Regulation 116/2009 (European Commission, 2020), and accommodations were made to ensure the United Kingdom continues to operate within the 2014/60/EU mechanism (Minister of State for Culture and Media, 2021). Separate concerns on Regulation 880/2019 on imports have also been remedied, and it has been decided that the Regulation will come into forced only in Northern Ireland with import licences issued by Northern Ireland Customs, when the law comes fully into force in 2025 (European Commission, 2020).

Still, the Withdrawal Agreement, and the Protocol, has been controversial. Given that a 'hard' border between Ireland and Northern Ireland has been avoided, only by placing a 'hard' economic border along the Irish Sea between Northern Ireland and the rest of the United Kingdom, Unionists believe their position in the United Kingdom has been fundamentally undermined, both economically and constitutionally (Murphy, 2021). And there remain potential risks to heritage. The United Kingdom's decision to repeal Regulation 880/2019 on import in 2021 (though retaining it for Northern Ireland, as per the terms of the Agreement) has dismayed observers who have raised fears this will lead to two systems of controls inside the one polity of the United Kingdom, which may increase the likelihood of smuggling (Rogers, 2021) or at the very least create confusion as to what rules apply and where (Pryor, 2021).

7 Conclusion

While there is increased focus on the potential for Brexit to turn the island of Ireland into a hot spot for smuggling cultural goods in and out of Ireland and the European Union, the reality is that this has long been a concern along the Irish border. Though the problems affecting the island are unique, especially those relating to the troubled history between the island's communities, these problems have long existed. Indeed, smuggling was only aggravated by the unique circumstances and tension upon which the border came into being in the first place. However, this case study of the island of Ireland demonstrates the ability of the European project to create a framework which can regulate the cross-border movement of cultural heritage. It is not perfect, and Brexit has stretched this framework to its breaking point, not to mention jeopardising the delicate constitutional settlement between the island's communities. But it is a framework that exists and works to some degree on one of the most controversial frontiers in Europe. Previously an internal border of the European Union, now an external border with a non-European Union country, by understanding the workings of this border we may better understand how to best protect the other frontiers of the European Union, and in doing so, mitigate to some extent the worst impacts of illicit trafficking of cultural heritage.

References

Anderson, J. (2008). Partition, consociation, border-crossing: Some lessons from the national conflict in Ireland/Northern Ireland. *Nations and Nationalism, 14*(1), 85–104.

Artforum. (2021, April 13). National Museum of Ireland makes plans to Return Benin Bronzes. *Artforum.* Retrieved October 24, 2021, from https://www.artforum.com/news/national-museum-of-ireland-makes-plans-to-return-benin-bronzes-85454

Attorney General of Ireland. (1925). *Letter to Mr Banam dated January 1925.* Ancient Monuments Protection Bill (Preliminary) (2002/14/338), National Archives of Ireland.

Attorney General of Ireland. (1931) *Correspondence to the Taoiseach.* Galway mace and sword (TSCH/3/S6076 A.), National Archives of Ireland.

Bailkin, J. (2004). *The culture of property: The crisis of Liberalism in modern Britain.* University of Chicago Press.

BBC. (2016a, 24 June). Brexit: David Cameron to quit after UK votes to leave EU. *BBC News.* Retrieved June 1, 2019, from https://www.bbc.com/news/uk-politics-36615028

BBC. (2016b, 24 June). EU referendum: Northern Ireland votes to Remain. *BBC News.* Retrieved June 1, 2019, from https://www.bbc.com/news/uk-northern-ireland-36614443

Boggi, F. (2016). Viscount Berehaven's tour of Italy in 1842–3: Collecting 'articles of taste' for Bantry House. *Journal of the History of Collections, 29*(2), 309–325.

Bourke, S.A. (Parliamentary Secretary to the Minister for Finance). (1929, 24 Oct). "National Monuments Bill, 1929—Second Stage." Ireland. *Dáil Éireann Debate,* Vol *3.2*. Retrieved June 10, 2019, from https://www.oireachtas.ie/en/debates/debate/dail/1929-10-24/16/

Campbell, J. (2019, June 20). Irish border: UK expert panel to advise on post-Brexit arrangements. Retrieved June 20, 2019, from *BBC News*. https://www.bbc.com/news/uk-northern-ireland-48702232

Chamberlain, K., & Hausler, K. (2014). United Kingdom. In J. A. R. Nafziger & R. K. Paterson (Eds.), *Handbook on the law of Cultural heritage and international trade* (pp. 460–505). Edward Elgar Publishing Limited.

Conlon, P. (2014). Ireland. In J. A. R. Nafziger & R. K. Paterson (Eds.), *Handbook on the law of cultural heritage and international trade*. Edward Elgar Publishing Limited.

Cooney, G. (1996). Building the future on the past: Archaeology and the construction of national identity in Ireland. In M. Días-Andreu & T. T. Champion (Eds.), *Nationalism and archaeology in Europe* (pp. 146–165). UCL Press.

Council of the European Union. (2020, 15 May). *Proposal for a Council Decision establishing the position to be adopted on behalf of the European Union in the Joint Committee established by the Agreement on the withdrawal of the United Kingdom of Great Britain and Northern Ireland from the European Union and the European Atomic Energy Community as regards the adoption of a decision to amend the Agreement*. Retrieved September 1, 2021, from https://eur-lex.europa.eu/legal-content/EN/TXT/?uri=CELEX%3A52020PC0195

Daly, M. E. (2017). *Brexit and the Irish border: Historical context* [Policy Paper]. Royal Irish Academy–British Academy Brexit. Retrieved June 7, 2019, from https://www.thebritishacademy.ac.uk/sites/default/files/BrexitandtheIrishBorderHistoricalContext_0.pdf

Department of Justice. (1946). *Export of Bank Documents*. Documents and Pictures (Regulations of Export) Act, 1945) (90/9/40), National Archives of Ireland.

Department of the Taoiseach. (1925). *Government Memorandum of 12 November*. National monuments and antiquities: Protection and prohibition of export (TSCH/3/S4633). National Archives of Ireland.

Department of the Taoiseach. (1926). *Letter from Director of National Museum, Mr Bremmer*. National Monuments (Amendment) Act, 1954 (TSCH/3/S8488 C), National Archives of Ireland.

Department of the Taoiseach. (1968). *Note on discovery of Killymoon Hoqrd 1967*. Killymoon Hoard of Irish Bronze Age gold ornaments, (98/6/966.) National Archives of Ireland.

Elgot, J. (2017, November). Ireland threatens to block progress of Brexit talks over border issue. *The Guardian*. Retrieved November 1, 2021, from https://www.theguardian.com/politics/2017/nov/17/irish-pm-brexit-backing-politicians-did-not-think-things-through

European Commission. (2018). *Security Union: Agreement to crack down on illicit trade in cultural goods*. http://europa.eu/rapid/press-release_IP-18-6733_en.htm

European Commission. (2020, 17 December). *Notice to stakeholders: Withdrawal of the United Kingdom and EU Rules on the Export and Import of Cultural Goods*. Retrieved September 1, 2021, from https://ec.europa.eu/info/sites/default/files/notice-brexit-export-cultural-goods_en.pdf

Evans, E. (1953). Archaeology in Northern Ireland, 1921–1951. *Ulster Journal of Archaeology, 3*(16), 3–6.

Ferriter, D. (2019). *The border: The legacy of a century of Anglo-Irish politics London*. Profile Books Limited.

Fry, M. F. (2003). Preserving ancient and historic monuments and sites in State Care in Northern Ireland, c1921 to c1955. Part One: Establishing a system of care. *Ulster Journal of Archaeology, 62*.

Halfin, S. (1995). The legal protection of cultural property in Britain: Past, present and future. *DePaul Journal of Art, Technology and Intellectual Property, 6*(1), 1–38.

Harris, L. (2006, January 1). 'The destruction of memory: architecture at war', by Robert Bevan. *The Art Newspaper*. Retrieved March 10, 2022, from https://www.theartnewspaper.com/2006/01/01/the-destruction-of-memory-architecture-at-war-by-robert-bevan

Hausler, K., & Mackenzie-Gray Scott, R. (2017). Outside the debate? The potential impact of Brexit for cultural heritage in the UK. *Art Antiquity and Law, 22*(2).

Hayward, K. (2020). Why it is impossible for Brexit Britain to 'take back control' in Northern Ireland. *Territory, Politics, Governance, 8*(2), 273–278.

Hourigan, N., Morrison, J. F., Windle, J., & Silke, A. (2018). Crime in Ireland north and south: Feuding gangs and profiteering paramilitaries. *Trends in Organized Crime, 21*(2), 126–146.

Institute for Government. (2021, 1 March). Northern Ireland protocol: Consent mechanism. Retrieved March 19, 2022, from https://www.instituteforgovernment.org.uk/explainers/northern-ireland-protocol-consent-mechanism

Joannin, P. (2021, February 8). "Brexit and the Irish Question" *Foundation Robert Schuman*. Retrieved November 1, 2021, from https://www.robert-schuman.eu/en/european-issues/0583-brexit-and-the-irish-question

Levi, D. (2008). The administration of historical heritage: The Italian Case. In S. Fisch (Ed.), *National approaches to the governance of historical heritage over time*. IOS Press.

McCullagh, T. (2021, May 25) How 'priceless' records were lost in burning of the Custom House 100 years ago. *Irish Independent*. Retrieved March 10, 2022, from https://www.independent.ie/regionals/dublin/how-priceless-records-were-lost-in-burning-of-the-custom-house-100-years-ago-40461984.html

Minister of State for Culture and the Media. (2021). Withdrawal of the UK from the EU. *Kultugut Schutz Deutschland*. Retrieved November 1, 2021, from http://www.kulturgutschutz-deutschland.de/EN/EverythingAboutTheProtectionOfCulturalProperty/LegalBases/EuropeanLaw/Brexit/Brexit_node.html

Mulvagh, C. (2019). Ulster Exclusion and Irish Nationalism: Consenting to the principle of partition, 1912–1916. *Revue Française de Civilisation Britannique, XXIV* (2). https://doi.org/10.4000/rfcb.3773

Murphy, M. C. (2021). Northern Ireland and Brexit: Where sovereignty and stability collide? *Journal of Contemporary European Studies, 29*(3), 405–418.

National Monuments Act 1930. Retrieved June 10, 2019, http://www.irishstatutebook.ie/eli/1930/act/2/section/2/enacted/en/html#sec2

Neill, K. (1993). The Broighter Hoard: Or how Carson caught the boat. *Archaeology Ireland, 7*(2), 24–26.

Ní Chonaill, S., Reding, A., & Valeri, L.L. (2011). *Assessing the illegal trade in cultural property from a public policy perspective*. RAND Europe.

NUI Galway Library. (2014, May 26). From Galway to California and Back Again—the Galway Civic Sword and Mace. *HardiBlog*. Retrieved October 17, 2021, from http://hardimanlibrary.blogspot.com/2014/05/from-galway-to-california-and-back.html

Office of Secretary of the President. (1945). *Notes, August 1945*. Documents and Pictures (Regulation of Export) Act, 1945 (2005/3/104), National Archives of Ireland.

Office of the Attorney General. (1928a). *Letter to the Attorney General from the Parliamentary Secretary of the Minister for Finance*. National Monuments Act, 1930 (2002/14/690), National Archives of Ireland.

Office of the Attorney General. (1928b). *Memorandum to the Government*. National Monuments Act, 1930 (2002/14/690), National Archives of Ireland

Pritchard, R. M. O. (2004). Protestants and the Irish Language: Historical heritage and current attitudes in Northern Ireland. *Journal of Multilingual and Multicultural Development, 25*(1), 62–82.

Pryor, R. (2021, October 19). Northern Ireland's art market mired in post-Brexit confusion. *The Art Newspaper*. Retrieved October 20, 2021, from https://www.theartnewspaper.com/2021/10/19/northern-ireland-dealers-confused-over-new-rules-art-market

Regulation (EU) 2019/880 of the European Parliament and of the Council of 17 April 2019 on the introduction and the import of cultural goods.

Rogers, F. (2021). Following the UK's Repeal of the EU Import Regulation in Great Britain, will Northern Ireland become a gateway to Europe for illicit cultural property? *The Antiquities Coalition*. Retrieved November 1, 2021, from https://thinktank.theantiquitiescoalition.org/following-the-uks-repeal-of-the-eu-import-regulation-in-great-britain-will-northern-ireland-become-a-gateway-to-europe-for-illicit-cultural-property-recommendations-for-the-uk-to-mitigate/

Roodt, C. (2015). *Private international law, art and cultural heritage*. Edward Elgar Publishing Limited.

RTE. (2001, June 26). Russborough House has history of art thefts. *RTE News*. Retrieved June 19, 2019, from https://www.rte.ie/news/2001/0626/16372-paintings2/

Ruane, J., & Todd, J. (1996). *The dynamics of conflict in Northern Ireland: Power, conflict and emancipation*. Cambridge University Press.

Ryan, M. (1981). *Reports from the Keeper of Antiquities at the National Museums of Ireland.* Documents and Pictures (Regulation of Export) Act, 1945. (2018/184/1) National Archives of Ireland.

Sawyer, A. (2011, April 28–30). *National Museums in the Republic of Ireland*. [Conference Paper] presented at the EuNaMus, European National Museums: Identity Politics, the Uses of the Past and the European Citizen, Bologna.

Somers Cocks, A. (2018, November 14). Will the UK be able to take part in antiquities busts after Brexit? *The Art Newspaper*. Retrieved June 19, 2019, from https://www.theartnewspaper.com/comment/will-the-uk-be-able-to-take-part-in-antiquities-busts-after-brexit

Stamatoudi, I. A. (2011). *Cultural property law and restitution: A commentary to international conventions and European Union law*. Edward Elgar Publishing Limited.

Todd, J. (2015). The vulnerability of the Northern Ireland Settlement: British Irish relations, political crisis and Brexit. *Études Irlandaises, Irlandaises, 40*(2), 61–73.

UK Parliament. (2019a, 30 January). Proposal for a Regulation of the European Parliament and of the Council on the import of cultural goods. *House of Commons Select Committee* https://publications.parliament.uk/pa/cm201719/cmselect/cmeuleg/301-lii/30113.htm

UK Parliament. (2019b, June 20). North-South Cooperation Scoping Exercise. *House of Commons Select Committee*. Retrieved June 20, 2019, from https://www.parliament.uk/documents/commons-committees/Exiting-the-European-Union/17-19/Correspondence/UK%20Government%20scoping%20document%20(1).pdf

Webb v. Ireland, I.R 353. (Supreme Court of Ireland 1988).

Ted Oakes is an historian and Heritage Protection Coordinator at the International Council of Museums (ICOM), Paris. A graduate in European history and cultural policy from University College Dublin, he is a PhD candidate at IMT Lucca, Italy, where his research is examining the historical evolution of European law to combat the illicit trade of cultural property.

Stealing Heritage in Canada

Cara Grace Tremain

Abstract This chapter presents a study of reported thefts of tangible cultural heritage from Canadian museums over a period of more than a century. Why a chapter dedicated to this topic? Because previous research into such crimes within Canada has been meagre, hindering the ability to understand which types of heritage are the most at-risk from theft. When any item of tangible heritage is stolen—regardless of value—the impact on history and culture is very real, and every attempt must be taken to avoid this from happening. Exposing the threats facing items of tangible cultural heritage in Canada, by revealing those that have been stolen from museums, is a means of demonstrating the need to improve protection of the nation's collections. At the outset of this research, the aim was to gather information about thefts of heritage from both media reports and law enforcement. Unfortunately, other than gaining access to the Interpol Stolen Works of Art database, it was not possible to acquire much information from police authorities. Canada lacks a standardised national crime management system, and has only one provincial investigative unit for art and heritage crime, which hinders the ability to obtain this information. Consequently, the study also demonstrates the need to establish a Canadian federal team (or at least more provincial units) specialised in the investigation of crimes relating to cultural heritage.

1 Protecting Cultural Heritage in Canada

The history of Canada's development as a colonial nation, which has roots in the arrival of Europeans as far back as the eleventh century, includes the imposition of western attitudes and traditions. Among these was the practice of collecting and

C. G. Tremain (✉)
Department of Sociology and Anthropology, Langara College, Vancouver, Canada
e-mail: ctremain@langara.ca

N. Oosterman, D. Yates (eds.), *Art Crime in Context*, Studies in Art, Heritage, Law and the Market 6, https://doi.org/10.1007/978-3-031-14084-6_10

displaying tangible heritage from non-western cultures, which led to items from the sophisticated Indigenous peoples of this region of the world (commonly referred to as First Nation, Inuit, and Métis) being especially sought-after by colonial settlers. This led to the systematic and widespread theft of Indigenous cultural heritage (Cole, 1985), facilitated by colonial laws such as the Potlatch ban under the *Indian Act* (Joseph, 2018). As Canadian museums developed, so too did the range of heritage items in their collections. Consequently, the origin of items within the 2600 museums, galleries, and heritage institutions across the country today reach far beyond the nation's borders.

Addressing the colonial nature of Canadian cultural organisations—especially museums—is becoming more commonplace (e.g., Logan, 2014; MacKenzie, 2009; Wrightson, 2017), but it is also important to look critically at the security that such organisations can, or cannot, offer to their collections. Protection of cultural heritage from theft is a responsibility that museums must manage in addition to safeguarding objects from destructive elements such as fire, pests, and humidity. The Canadian Conservation Institute provide resources to assist museums in preventing theft (e.g., Tremain, n.d.), and the International Council of Museums (ICOM) Committee for Museum Security has published various documents related to preventing, monitoring, and reporting thefts (Jirásek, 2010; Liston, 1993). Another resource is Artefacts Canada, a database containing more than four million object records and one million images from over 500 of the nation's museums. [1] The database has been described as "a valuable tool to protect those collections from the risks of misappropriation or theft because it establishes a clear publicly-accessible record of ownership and provenance" (Canada National Report, 2015, p. 3).

In addition to security guidelines to prevent theft, and digitised databases demonstrating ownership in case of theft, some Canadian legislation also exists to protect cultural heritage. In 1977, the federal Government adopted the *Cultural Property Export and Import Act* (CPEIA) in response to UNESCO's 1970 *Convention on the Means of Prohibiting and Preventing the Illicit Import, Export and Transfer of Ownership of Cultural Property.* [2] The CPEIA makes it illegal to import cultural property (including tangible heritage) into the country if the sale of such property is banned or controlled by the country of origin, and restricts the export of cultural property considered to be nationally important or otherwise significant without a permit. [3]

[1] https://app.pch.gc.ca/application/artefacts_hum/indice_index.app?lang=en, accessed 8 August 2021.

[2] https://laws-lois.justice.gc.ca/eng/acts/c-51/, accessed 6 August 2021.

[3] https://www.canada.ca/en/canadian-heritage/services/about-movable-cultural-property.html, accessed 6 August 2021.

2 Policing Cultural Heritage in Canada

Even with legislation that can be adhered to, and guidelines that can be followed, it is not always possible for museums to protect items from theft. When the best intentions fail, policing systems are in place to investigate thefts and (hopefully) locate stolen material. The history of policing in Canada—like the history of museums—is related to settler-colonial development. Indigenous processes of governance and social control already existed throughout the lands which later became known as Canada, but were not recognised by the burgeoning non-Indigenous population (Monchalin, 2016). Consequently, much of the structure and organisation of early policing was based on pre-existing European systems (Seagrave, 1997, pp. 14–21). The first federal police force was established in 1873 following an Act of Parliament, and in 1920 the North West Mounted Police (NWMP) became the nationwide federal law enforcement agency. The NWMP later became the famed Royal Canadian Mounted Police (RCMP) (Cooper, 1981; Royal Canadian Mounted Police, 1990; Seagrave, 1997). In addition to being Canada's national and federal law enforcement agency, the RCMP can be contracted by provinces and territories to act as a provincial police service. Eight of the ten provinces and all three territories in Canada currently contract the RCMP as a provincial force. The Sûreté du Québec and the Ontario Provincial Police take the place of the RCMP in those provinces. Various municipalities in Canada also choose the RCMP as a police force, making the RCMP a federal, provincial, and municipal police force.

In 2008, a specialised art crime unit was established within the Sûreté du Québec, part of the investigative department of economic crimes (Bruemmer, 2009; Schofield Sezgin, 2011; The Canadian Press, 2009). The unit was the first of its kind in Canada and remains the only such unit to this day. As such, the country "is considered a soft target by art thieves [. . .] because only one police force has a dedicated staff handling such crimes" (Ormsby, 2011, para. 19). The unit regularly sends out art-theft alerts and assist the RCMP, Interpol, and the Canada Border Services Agency with crimes related to art and heritage (Sandals, 2014). The Canadian National Central Bureau of Interpol, based in Ottawa, used to play a more prominent role in tracking heritage crime. In the 1980s they developed The Repository of Stolen Artifacts (ROSA), bringing together information traditionally documented in internal police files (Interpol Ottawa, 1984). They also published *Theft of Cultural Property in Canada* booklets from 1984 to 1995, featuring detailed information and statistics. In the 1995 booklet it was estimated that of all known cultural property thefts that have occurred since 1966, 8.2 percent (172 of 2086) were from museums or exhibitions (Interpol Ottawa 1995). After 1995, information about stolen cultural property was accessible via Interpol's Stolen Works of Art Database (which does not include statistical information akin to those published in the aforementioned booklets).

Other statistics related to crimes against cultural heritage in Canada are not easy to locate, due to lack of a national crime database. Retrieving this information from individual police agencies is also difficult because each has their own system for documenting crimes, and among these exist differences in terminology and descriptions of stolen goods. It is especially challenging for agencies to identify crimes against cultural heritage, because there is a lack of offence codes for reporting such crimes. In 2005 the CPEIA was amended to include Mischief in Relation to Cultural Property, and it became a reportable offence in 2014. [4] The Canadian Centre for Justice Studies, which provides public information about all reported crimes in the country, reveals that since 2015 there have been 244 violations of this offence. [5] The Canadian Police Information Centre's website also allows the public to search for stolen property, but is only applicable to property with a serial number. [6] Since heritage is not generally something that has a serial number, as automobiles or appliances do, the website is not particularly useful for searching for most stolen cultural heritage.

Outside of policing, the nation's museum associations also have a surprising lack of data available. Neither the Canadian Museums Association nor ICOM Canada were able to provide the author with data because they do not have these kinds of statistics available (personal communication, 2021). Compounding this problem is the likelihood that many thefts go unreported or unpublicised. As Gross (2021, para. 2) has explained, "museums have at times withheld information about thefts, fearing that revealing security weaknesses could make other institutions less likely to loan them art or that it could encourage other thefts." Other times, "museums can sometimes take years to realise that pieces in storage have been taken" (para. 9) and stolen goods go unreported because their absence is not noticed. Furthermore, the ICOM Code of Ethics for Museums suggests that "information about the security of the museum [...] must be held in strict confidence" (International Council of Museums, 2017, p. 42).

The secrecy surrounding museum thefts is not unique to Canada. Grove and Thomas (2016, p. 9) discovered in their interviews with museum personnel in Europe "what seemed to be the first rule of museum security: you do not talk about museum security." However, as Gross (2021) argues, reporting stolen goods can make it more difficult for thieves to sell them and there is also a chance they can be identified by the public. An example of the benefit of a public announcement is the 2019 theft of a hand from the *Residential School Totem Pole* outside the Montreal Museum of Fine Arts. The museum announced the theft via a press release and social media, gaining widespread attention (e.g., Montreal Gazette, 2019). The pole was carved by Kwakiutl artist and residential school survivor Charles Joseph, [7] and by announcing the artwork's significance the museum hoped to appeal to the culprit(s) to return the missing hand (Fig. 1). The tactic worked, and in less than two weeks the thieves returned the hand with an apology note explaining "at the time, we were not in a sober state of mind, and we had no idea what the totem pole was...we

[4] https://laws-lois.justice.gc.ca/eng/annualstatutes/2005_40/page-1.html.

[5] https://www.statcan.gc.ca/eng/subjects-start/crime_and_justice.

[6] https://www.cpic-cipc.ca/index-eng.htm.

[7] see https://www.charlesnativeart.ca/.

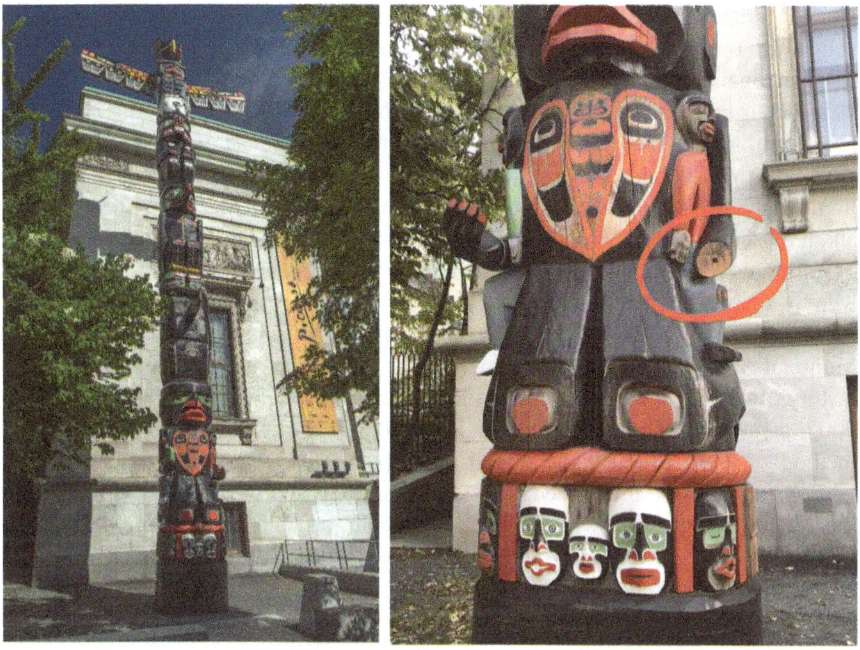

Fig. 1 Left: The pole with hand intact. Right: the pole with missing hand. Source: Charles Joseph. Born in Alert Bay, British Columbia, in 1959. *Residential School Totem Pole*. 2014–2016. Red cedar, acrylic paint. 1524 × 762 cm (including wings), 152.4 cm (diam.). The Montreal Museum of Fine Arts, on loan from a private collection. Acquisition No. 442.2017. Photographs reproduced with permission of Charles Joseph, the Montreal Museum of Fine Arts, and the artwork's owner

were simply ignorant of what it symbolized, and have decided we 100% needed to return it" [8].

Media reports also indicate that Canadian cultural property thefts are related to organised crime. For example, Bruemmer (2009) reported that organised criminal groups were using art stolen from Montreal to launder money, or in exchange for illicit drugs. Alain Lacoursière, the 'Colombo' of Quebec's art world and predecessor of Quebec's art crime unit, also uncovered evidence linking organised crime to stolen art: specifically that Montreal was being used as a gateway to the New York art market (Knelman, 2011). More than a decade ago, estimates put the number of organised criminal groups in Canada close to 1,000 (Sewell, 2010, p. 122). It is highly likely there are many more such groups today, which puts the safety of cultural property in the country at a higher risk.

Other than the information discussed above, "there is very little data publicly available in Canada to indicate just how widespread a problem theft in museums really is" (Tremain, n.d., para. 5). Rob Vingerhoets, a Detective Constable in the

[8] see https://nationtalk.ca/story/the-left-hand-of-charles-josephs-totem-pole-returned-to-the-mmfa-with-a-letter-of-apology, accessed 30 October 2021.

York Regional Police even lamented that "we can never hope to come up with a solution to our problem because we cannot even keep track of how bad a problem it is" (personal communication, 2021). Similarly, in 2006 Czegledi claimed that "Canada is a fantastic place to steal art…because no one is paying attention" (Knelman, 2007). The lack of data is not unique to Canada: studies focused on Australia (McCubbin, 2019), Europe (Grove & Thomas, 2016; Peek, 2011), and South Africa (Benson & Prinsloo, 2013) also reveal a general lack of information about museum thefts. Grove and Thomas (2016, p. 2) argue that because one quarter of museums may not have up to date records of their collections, even if such data were available, the true extent of loss or theft cannot be measured.

The most well-known Canadian museum theft by far is the 1972 theft from the Montreal Museum of Art. It is remembered as "the largest art heist in Canadian history" because the value of the stolen items was roughly $2 million (Knelman, 2005, para. 16). [9] The theft is often referred to as the 'skylight caper', based on the method of entry used by the thieves (Hampton, 2019). It is the only Canadian museum theft to be mentioned in *Museum of the Missing* (Houpt, 2006), despite the fact the book was written by a Canadian journalist. Museum thefts made headlines again across Canada when John Mark Tillmann was arrested in 2012: police uncovered roughly 10,000 works of art, antiques, documents, and other cultural objects in his home. He is remembered as quite literally creating "his own private museum by stealing from other museums" (Narcisse, 2015, para. 1).

Tillmann targeted a range of museums, universities, libraries, and antique shops in the eastern Atlantic provinces (including his native Nova Scotia) but also carried out thefts in Europe, particularly his wife's native Russia (Taber, 2014). In interviews he gave after his arrest, he revealed brazen tactics, including posing as a maintenance worker to remove artworks from walls in plain sight of staff (ibid.). In 2016, he was provided a platform to entertain audiences with tales of his life of crime, and boast of his success, in a special episode of *The Fifth Estate* (part of the national CBC television network programming). [10] He was granted parole that same year, after serving only a third of his nine-year sentence. After his death in late 2018 media interest peaked once again (CTV Atlantic, 2019), and his special episode aired for a second time. [11]

In reporting thefts of cultural heritage from a viewpoint that emphasises their daring and bold nature, such as has been the case with crimes carried out by Tillmann and culprits of the 'skylight caper', Canadian media outlets are downplaying their seriousness. This becomes even clearer from reports of a 2018 theft at the Gardiner Museum in Toronto, in which a woman stole a small rock from an exhibition created

---

[9] The theft is featured as number 23 of 'The 25 Greatest Art Heists of All Time' in a February 11, 2021, *ARTnews* article (https://www.artnews.com/list/art-news/artists/greatest-art-heists-of-all-time-1234583441/van-gogh-singer-laren-museum/).

[10] The Collector. (2016). The Fifth Estate, Season 41, April 2016. https://www.cbc.ca/fifth/episodes/2015-2016/stolen-treasures.

[11] The Collector: Still a Mystery. (2019). The Fifth Estate, Season 44, March 2019. https://www.cbc.ca/fifth/episodes/2018-2019/the-collector-still-a-mystery.

by Yoko Ono. The crime was berated in the media for the ease with which the woman was able to steal the object, and particularly because it failed to meet expectations of an elaborately planned crime (Mudhar, 2018). By not focusing on the negative impact museum thefts have for society, but instead sensationalising them, the media are implicit in creating a public palatability and acceptance of such crimes.

3 Data and Methods

Data collection for this study began with an investigation into museum thefts reported by Canadian media. Since the study is directed at cultural heritage, no art galleries were included. Unfortunately, a centralised source of Canadian digitised newspapers does not exist. Consequently, a variety of resources were consulted including Google News search, Newspapers.com, ProQuest Canadian Major Dailies, and various provincial and national media websites. Search results were limited to English language newspapers (based on the author's inability to read French language) and keywords included terms such as: Canada/Canadian; museum; steal/stole; thief/theft; and robbery. Incidents were recorded when they were specific to items of cultural heritage or clearly targeted museum property. [12]

To obtain data from law enforcement, requests for information about museum thefts were submitted to the RCMP and provincial police agencies (including the Sûreté du Québec Art Crime Unit and Ottawa, Toronto, and Vancouver Police). Only the RCMP were able to provide information, consisting of two pages of minimal data about six thefts in British Columbia. [13] Information about six additional thefts, in which 29 items were reported stolen, were obtained from Interpol's Stolen Works of Art Database. Though names of museums are not provided in Interpol's search results, the date and location of thefts is available. Using this information, it was possible to determine that three of the thefts had not appeared in the aforementioned media reports. Similarly, a theft from a museum in Whitehorse, Yukon, was identified in Interpol Ottawa's *Theft of Cultural Property in Canada* booklets (without which, the Yukon would not be represented in this study). [14]

[12] The 2019 theft of historic artifacts in a duffel bag that an employee of the North Vancouver Museum and Archives was carrying is not included for this reason. The thief may have "simply grabbed the bag without realizing what was inside" and therefore may not have been a crime directed at museum objects: https://globalnews.ca/news/5815611/priceless-artifacts-stolen-near-north-vancouver-museum/.

[13] Of those thefts, the majority were unrelated to this study because they targeted non-heritage items such as Christmas decorations, fuel tanks, tools from a storage container, and museum lights.

[14] Booklets from 1984 to 1988, and 1991 to 1995, were available for consultation.

The combined information from media reports, the RCMP, and Interpol, reveal that at least 1676 items have been stolen from a minimum of 50 Canadian museums since 1905 (see Table 1). Based on reported values, this represents a financial loss of at least $6.5 million CAD. In total, 76 separate thefts were identified in all locations across Canada except the Northwest Territories (this of course does not mean there have not been thefts of heritage in this part of the country). The total number of items stolen from the 76 thefts cannot be known with certainty, due to some reports approximating or omitting this information. What is known, however, is that heritage items have been continually stolen from Canadian museums over a period of almost 120 years.

On at least one occasion, an item has been stolen more than once from the same museum. [15] The number of thefts per decade is shown in Table 2 (which possibly indicates an over-representation of media reports from the last 20 years, rather than an increasing trend in museum thefts) and the location of thefts is shown in Table 3. While the number of thefts and timeframe is somewhat similar to McCubbin's (2019) findings from Australian museums (she identified 66 thefts over a period of almost 80 years, in which 91 items were stolen), the overall number of items stolen in Canada is more than 18 times greater.

To understand the types of items targeted by thieves, those reported stolen were categorised and Fig. 2 shows the known quantities of each (excluding stolen cash: of which several incidents were documented, totalling in the region of perhaps $5000–$6000 CAD). [16]

As the figure demonstrates, the highest quantities of items stolen are wartime items and currency (identified as coins and banknotes in a museum's collection, not including the aforementioned cash). However, these numbers are not reflective of the number of incidents of such thefts. Almost all coins were stolen in one incident from the Museum of Vancouver in 1908, and almost all wartime items were stolen over a period of several months in 2010 by a long-time volunteer of The Military Museums in Calgary. For a more accurate understanding of the most at-risk items, the number of individual thefts related to different categories is presented in Fig. 3.

This figure demonstrates there have been more incidents involving currency compared to war memorabilia, but there have been even more incidents related to art and items that do not fit neatly into any of the other categories. The following

[15] A medal was stolen in 2002 from the Cowicham Valley Museum and Archives and was later returned by an individual who purchased it. The medal was stolen from the museum again in 2015, along with several other items.

[16] Cash thefts included money stolen from a ticket counter, cash register, gift store, donation boxes, and directly from staff members. Since cash is not unique to museums, and therefore does not help understand what heritage items thieves are targeting from museums, it was not included in this figure.

Table 1 Thefts reported at Canadian museums from 1905–2020

Location	Number of museums who have reported thefts	Number of incidents	Number of items stolen	Value of items stolen in CAD	Items recovered
AB	5	At least 5	At least 609	At least $1,000,000	At least 66
BC	12	24	At least 751	At least $2,000,000	At least 25
MB	2	2	7	Unknown	Unknown
NB	1	1	4	At least $5,0000	2
NL	2	At least 2	At least 4	Unknown	Unknown
NS	5	5	8	At least $10,000	8
NU	1	1	7	$10,000	Unknown
ON	14	20	At least 141	At least $380,000	At least 16
PE	2	2	11	Unknown	At least 8
QC	6	11	132	At least $3,000,000	At least 69
SK	2	2	At least 2	$6000–$8000	Unknown
YT	1	1	1	Unknown	Unknown
Total	At least 53[a]	At least 76[b]	At least 1676[c]	At least $6,411,000[d]	At least 194[e]

[a] This number includes three unknown museums from the Interpol database
[b] This number is likely to be higher since the exact number of thefts that occurred at the Newfoundland Museum in the 1920s, and the number that occurred over several months at The Military Museums in 2010, is unknown
[c] This number is likely to be significantly higher considering that three volumes of stamps and currency were stolen from the Newfoundland Museum in the 1920s, and $6000–$8000 CAD worth of objects were stolen from the Sesula Mineral and Gem Museum and Rock Shop in Saskatchewan in 2018. Unfortunately, quantities of stolen objects were not provided in the media reports of either theft
[d] This number is likely to be higher considering that values were provided for 26 incidents only
[e] This number is based on reports of recovery found by the author in her search for data about museum thefts. Since the search criteria did not include terms related to recovery, the actual number could be higher

highest numbers of incidents relate to the theft of ethnographic objects, housewares, and jewellery.

4 Discussion

Based on the items in museums being targeted by thieves, it is perhaps not surprising that art is the number one choice. Crimes against art have clear ties to financial and socio-political goals (Houpt, 2006): stealing a painting by a well-known artist can not only earn you a tidy sum if sold, it can also put you in an enviable position if

Table 2 Identified thefts per by decade(s)

Decade(s)	Number of identified thefts
1990–1920	4
1921–1940	1
1941–1960	2
1961–1980	5
1981–1990	10
1991–2000	8
2001–2010	17
2011–2020	25
Unknown[a]	4
Total	76

[a]Four thefts by John Mark Tillman were mentioned in passing by media reports, without accompanying dates

Table 3 Location of items stolen from museums

Location of theft	Number of thefts
Display case	16
Inside museum[a]	13
Inside- unspecified area[b]	14
Outside museum	7
Storage/Archives	3
Unknown	23
Total	76

[a] This category includes items stolen from galleries/ exhibition areas, a gift shop, and a ticket counter
[b] This category includes thefts that were reported as having taken place inside museums, but lacked specific details about the location of the theft

hung on the wall of your home (akin to what Tillmann did with many of the artworks he stole, including a 130-year-old painting he hung above his bed [Taber, 2014]). Another popular category are items categorised as 'other', including things such as a wax head, chainsaw, and taxidermy animals. It also includes several items stolen by Tillmann including a telescope and inkwell. As discussed below, Tillmann specifically targeted unusual and inexpensive objects. While 'other' items are inconsistent in their nature, what is consistent is their low financial value. Furthermore, most were stolen from smaller museums that were likely considered easy targets by thieves.

While it is impossible to know what a thief might want with a wax head or taxidermy animal, in other instances items were undoubtedly stolen based on their raw properties. Stealing objects for material value is referred to as 'commodity theft', and according to some security personnel wasn't recognised as an issue at museums until the late 2000s (Mandel, 2008). Although the material value of objects may be significantly less than their artistic value, it is much easier to sell the raw material. For example, McCubbin (2019, p. 163) has argued that many items stolen from Australian museums—especially coins and medals—were taken for the market

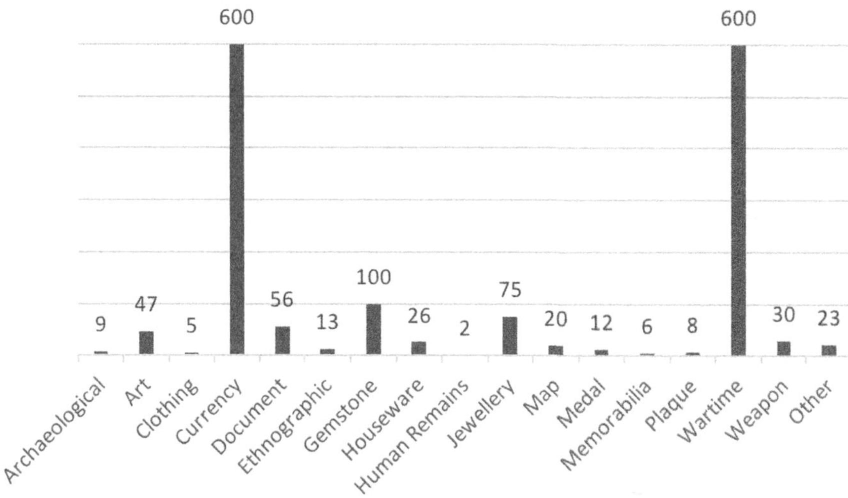

Fig. 2 Quantities of items reported stolen from Canadian museums from 1905 to 2020 (in some cases including estimates)

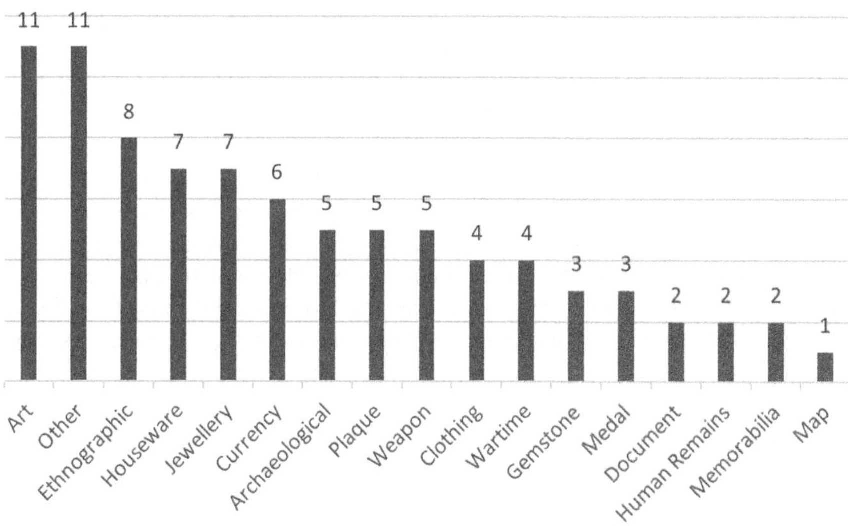

Fig. 3 Number of reported thefts from Canadian museums from 1905 to 2020 (some involved more than one category)

value of their material. Peek (2011) has also explained that precious materials like metals, gems, and jewellery have a high probability of being stolen from a museum but a low probability of recovery because they can be reshaped into unrecognizable objects. Even Mark Starling, president of fine art exhibition company PACART, has commented that "the Royal Ontario Museum probably doesn't have to worry that someone's going to go in and steal one of the mummies or dinosaurs [. . .] if they've got raw gold sitting around, I'd be more careful about that" (Battersby, 2017).

Combining stolen currency, gemstones, medals, plaques, and jewellery from Canadian museums amount to a total of almost 800 items. It is likely that a fair number were targeted for their material properties, as demonstrated by four bronze plaques stolen from the New Brunswick Museum in 2016, two of which were recovered after being sold to a scrapyard. The plaques were estimated to have been worth more than $1600 CAD each, based on the value of the metal alone (Cave, 2016). A higher profile crime was the 2006 theft of a pair of royal nineteenth century Indian shoes encrusted with diamonds and rubies, valued at $160,000 CAD, from the Bata Shoe Museum in Toronto. The thief targeted the shoes based on the perceived value of the gemstones, but ironically, they had "no street value because their decorative gems are cloudy and improperly cut" (Puzic, 2006, para. 7). In other instances, items have been pawned to fund illicit drug habits, as was the case with eight antique pocket watches stolen from the Royal BC Museum in 2014 (Harnett, 2014) and coins stolen from the Museum of Vancouver in 1907 (The Province, 1907). While weapons might also be stolen for their material properties, it seems more likely they are targeted because they are useful for criminals. For example, three men stole nine guns from the Canadian War Museum in 1945 and later used them to rob a gas station. Tragically, one of the men shot and killed a police officer after the robbery using one of the guns: this was "the first police officer killed in the line of duty in the City of Ottawa" (Burtch, 2010, p. 9).

Only a small number of the 76 identified thefts can be confidently asserted to have involved 'professional' criminals. These include the 'skylight caper' and six thefts carried out by Tillmann. We know that Tillmann was able to sustain his long-term career and avoid suspicion by limiting the number of items he stole at any one time, and by targeting unusual or inexpensive objects (Hutchins, 2014). However, as with the 'skylight caper', other professional-style thefts at Canadian museums have focused on expensive goods. For example, a 1981 theft of 70 opals—valued at more than $100,000—from the Royal Ontario Museum was carried out by an individual who managed to disengage a security alarm with their "extremely sophisticated grasp of electronics" (Johnson, 1981). Another professionally-planned theft took place in 2008 at the Museum of Anthropology in Vancouver, when thieves stole items valued at $2 million CAD in less than three minutes. The thieves were able to stop security cameras prior to the incident, and enter the museum by removing a glass panel at the rear of the building (Schofield Sezgin, 2012).

The overall lack of evidence of professional thefts aligns with the findings of both McCubbin (2019) and Peek (2011). It also bolsters the suggestion by Tremain (n.d.), who argued that the majority of museum thefts are the result of a seized opportunity. Even Houpt (2006, p. 100) has argued that "you don't need to be either graceful or well-informed to carry off a successful heist". He backs this up with the example of the 2004 theft of a version of *The Scream* from Norway's National Gallery, in which armed thieves crashed into a door on their way inside and reportedly dropped the painting twice on their way out. Fortunately, armed robberies are not the 'norm' for museum thefts in Canada. The 'skylight caper' thieves were the only ones to have armed themselves for a theft of non-cash-based goods. Only two other thefts from Canadian museums involved armed robbery, both targeting cash: a 1991 theft from the Royal BC Museum—in which two staff members were mugged at gunpoint for several thousand dollars (McLintock, 1991)—and a 2004 theft from the Museum of Civilization in Quebec, in which a thief with a knife stole $2000 CAD from staff members working at the ticket counter (The Ottawa Citizen, 2004).

The infrequency of armed robberies at museums coincides with the infrequency of thefts involving items of high value. As Czegledi has explained, thieves "won't steal something that they won't get money for" (Knelman, 2007). Thefts involving valuable objects in some cases are likely commissioned, while other times are carried out in the hopes of making a tidy profit. An unusual incident in this case was the 2011 theft of an ancient Persian sculpture from the Montreal Museum of Arts, valued at $1.2 million CAD. The sculpture was reportedly sold via a "friend of a friend" to an individual from Edmonton, Alberta, for just $1400 CAD (CBC News, 2014).

While the Persian sculpture was not in a glass display case, it was reportedly securely anchored down. Clearly, such security methods are no deterrent for thieves. This aligns with most cases of theft at Canadian museums, which shows that items have been stolen from all manner of locations regardless of security measures in place (Table 3). Of the 16 known thefts from display cases, information about the way items were removed from 12 of them was available. The majority ($n = 6$) involved thieves interfering with locks in some way (either picking or forcing open). Other incidents involved cases being smashed ($n = 3$), lifted to allow access to items ($n = 2$), and even stolen in their entirety ($n = 1$). The differences in approach are likely a reflection of the nature of security at a museum, the level of experience of the thieves, and the overall planning of the theft.

Thefts involving items stolen from storage or archives make up the smallest number of incidents ($n = 3$), which suggests that museum personnel in Canada are not stealing items 'behind the scenes': or if they are, these crimes are not being identified as such or are not being reported. Only five of the 76 thefts were reported as having been carried out by museum personnel. This includes Tillmann, who stole goods when he volunteered at the Halifax Citadel Museum in the 1990s. Considering such a small number of thefts appear to have been carried out by 'insiders', it is safe to say there is a lack of evidence that thefts of cultural property from Canadian museums are primarily conducted by those with inside access. This is in direct contrast to Battersby (2017), who suggested that most thefts from museums are carried out by employees, but aligns with the research by Grove and Thomas (2016): based on interviews with museum staff in England and Finland, they learned that most were restricted from accessing secure areas and therefore few personnel had the opportunity to carry out thefts.

5 Conclusion

While the majority of Canadian museum thefts tend not to attract much media attention, likely because they are the antithesis of Hollywood movie drama, they are happening on a consistent basis across the country. Thieves are targeting museums for a range of items and it seems that no museum is safe, and no location inside or outside of a museum is safe. Even more troubling is that current security measures can be easily overcome by thieves: display cases, locks, and guards are not successful deterrents. Quite simply, if a thief wants to steal something from a museum, they will take it whether there is a barrier in place or not. More than 45 years ago, Trondsen (1976) warned that the 'norms' of visitor compliance to museum security was on the decline and thefts were on the rise: the data from various museums around the world (including that shown here) demonstrates that thefts are indeed commonplace. The challenge for museums is to balance access to their collections with protective methods. Some have adopted the "crime prevention rational of 'removing objects' in order to reduce the potential reward to the offender" (Grove & Thomas, 2016, p. 5). Others are choosing to put public access first, in line with the rationale that "there will always be thieves and collections cannot simply be kept behind bars or in a safe" (Peek, 2011, p. 1).

So, what can be done if museums do not hide away their objects? How can these objects be protected? Museums can continue digitizing collections, to create accurate records that can be used as evidence in case of thefts. But this is a slow and expensive process, and will take many years and more funding to achieve. Other museums can invest in increased security measures, but this again is outside the financial capabilities of many museums. Another tactic is to report thefts to police and announce them to the public. As Czegledi (2012, p. 2) has argued, "secrecy only benefits the offender". There may be instances in which it might be thought inadvisable or impractical to publicly announce a crime, but if cultural heritage has any chance of being retrieved from criminals the police need to be informed. As Runhovde's (2021) sobering study of the illicit cultural heritage trade in Norway reveals, customs officers rely on police tips about museum thefts to prevent heritage leaving the country and entering the international art market. Runhodve's (2021) study also demonstrates the need for specialised cultural heritage units: something Canada needs more of. The creation of a federal art and heritage crime unit (or at least more provincial-based ones) would allow for a real difference to be made in tackling the theft of cultural heritage throughout the country.

The suggestions made here to better understand and track museum thefts are not novel since they also apply to other parts of the world. But the data introduced here provides new insight into Canadian museum thefts and demonstrates that the issue is real, ongoing, and potentially getting worse. Czegledi (2010, p. 112) has argued that Canada's "lax sentencing approach" to heritage theft plays a role in this, and that the time has come to realise the seriousness of these crimes. Quite simply, Canada needs to pay more attention to, and provide more resources for, tackling cultural heritage crime. Otherwise, the heritage being cared for in the nation's museums will continue to disappear at the hands of thieves.

References

Battersby, S. (2017, March 30). Is the theft of the 100-kilogram 'Big Maple Leaf' coin cause for concern at Canadian galleries? *Metronews*.

Benson, B., & Prinsloo, J. (2013). Thefts from museums and galleries in Gauteng: The value of accurate crime reporting. *Acta Criminologica: Southern African Journal of Criminology, 26*(1), 18–36.

Bruemmer, R. (2009, January 28). SQ, RCMP form squad to rub out art crime. *Montreal Gazette*.

Burtch, A. (2010). Dead Man's Gun: True Crime in Post War Ottawa, 1945-1946. *Ontario History, 102*(1), 1–19.

Canada National Report. (2015). *On the Implementation of the 1970 Convention on the Means of Prohibiting and Preventing the Illicit Import, Export and Transfer of Ownership of Cultural Property, 2011–2015*. https://en.unesco.org/sites/default/files/canada_2011-15natrep_1970_en.pdf. Accessed 2 August 2022.

Cave, R. (2016, August 2). Heavy Bronze Plaques Stolen from New Brunswick Museum. *CBC News*.

CBC News (2014, February 13). Stolen Artifact from Montreal Museum Recovered in Edmonton. *CBC News*.

Cole, D. (1985). *Captured Heritage: The scramble for northwest coast artifacts*. Douglas and McIntyre.

Cooper, H. S. (1981). The evolution of Canadian Police. In W. T. McGrath & M. P. Mitchell (Eds.), *The police function in Canada* (pp. 37–52). Methuen.

CTV Atlantic. (2019, February 13). Infamous Nova Scotia art thief dies, shrouded in mystery. *CTV News*.

Czegledi, B. (2010). Crimes against culture merit serious consquences. *Canadian Criminal Law Review, 15*(1), 111–127.

Czegledi, B. (2012). An introduction to art theft. *Canadian Criminal Law Review, 17*(1), 1–2.

Gross, J. (2021, March 16). We don't know how much art has gone missing from museums. *The New York Times*. Retrieved October 30, 2021, from https://www.nytimes.com/2021/03/16/arts/design/stolen-armor-louvre-returned.html

Grove, L., & Thomas, S. (2016). The Rhino Horn on display has been replaced by a Replica: Museum security in Finland and England. *Journal of Conservation and Museum Studies, 14*(1), 1–11.

Hampton, C. (2019, October 7). The Skylight Caper. *Canadianart*. Retrieved October 30, 2021, from https://canadianart.ca/features/the-skylight-caper/

Harnett, C. E. (2014, January 9). 'Priceless' watches returned to Royal B.C. Museum after theft. *Times Colonist*.

Houpt, S. (2006). *Museum of the missing: The high stakes of art crime*. Key Porter Books.

Hutchins, A. (2014, April 26). He's Turned into one of Canada's most infamous antique thieves. *Maclean's*. Retrieved October 30, 2021, from https://www.macleans.ca/society/life/hes-turned-into-one-of-canadas-most-infamous-antique-thieves/

International Council of Museums. (2017). *ICOM Code of Ethics for Museums*. Retrieved October 5, 2021, from https://icom.museum/wp-content/uploads/2018/07/ICOM-code-En-web.pdf

Interpol Ottawa. (1984). *Theft of Cultural Property in Canada*. Royal Canadian Mounted Police.

Interpol Ottawa. (1995). *Theft of cultural property in Canada*. Royal Canadian Mounted Police.

Jirásek, P. (2010). Theft. In W. Hekman (Ed.), *Handbook on emergency procedures* (pp. 11–14). International Committee on Museum Security.

Johnson, A. (1981, January 9). Alarm disconnected by 'clever professional': Museum finds opal display case empty. *The Globe and Mail.*

Joseph, B. (2018). *21 Things You May Not Know About the Indian Act: Helping Canadians Make Reconciliation with Indigenous Peoples a Reality.* Page Two Books.

Knelman, J. (2005, November 12). Artful Crimes. *The Walrus.* Retrieved July 19, 2021, from https://thewalrus.ca/artful-crimes/

Knelman, J. (2007, January 27). Art thieves, look out. *The Globe and Mail.* Retrieved April 30, 2022, from https://www.theglobeandmail.com/news/national/art-thieves-look-out/article678051/

Knelman, J. (2011, September 20). Police cracking down on a hotbed of hot art in Quebec. *The Globe and Mail.*

Liston, D. (1993). *Museum Security and Protection: A handbook for cultural heritage institutions.* Routledge.

Logan, T. (2014). National memory and museums: Remembering settler colonial genocide of indigenous peoples in Canada. In N. Eltringham & P. Maclean (Eds.), *Remembering genocide* (pp. 126–144). Routledge.

MacKenzie, J. M. (2009). *Museums and empire: Natural history, human cultures and colonial identities.* Manchester University Press.

Mandel, S. (2008, June 1). Insider Theft, Fires and Vandals Top List of Museum Concerns. *Security Management.* Retrieved August 19, 2021, from https://www.asisonline.org/security-management-magazine/articles/2008/06/insider-theft-fires-and-vandals-top-list-of-museum-concerns/

McCubbin, M. (2019). Purely Bent on Mischief: Theft from Australian Museums 1870s–1950s. In S. Hufnagel & D. Chappell (Eds.), *The Palgrave handbook on art crime* (pp. 149–185). Palgrave Macmillan.

McLintock, B. (1991, April 9). Museum boost security after dangerous lesson: police had urged safer method. *The Province.*

Monchalin, L. (2016). *The colonial problem: An indigenous perspective on crime and injustice in Canada.* University of Toronto Press.

Montreal Gazette. (2019, September 29). Vandal damages totem pole outside Montreal Museum of Fine Arts. *Montreal Gazette.*

Mudhar, R. (2018, April 16) Why Toronto museum heists look nothing like the movies. *Toronto Star.*

Narcisse, U. (2015, October 9). The Saga of the Canadian Museum Thief. *BC News Service.* Retrieved July 19, 2021, from http://journalism.blog.brooklyn.edu/the-saga-of-the-canadian-museum-thief/.

Ormsby, M. (2011, 21 August). 100 years ago, the Mona Lisa was stolen. *Toronto Star.* Retrieved June 27, 2022, from https://www.thestar.com/news/insight/2011/08/21/100_years_ago_the_mona_lisa_was_stolen.html

Peek, M. (2011). Theft in Museums in the Netherlands - Facts and Figures to Support Collection Risk Management. ICOM Committee for Conservation 16th Triennial Meeting. Retrieved August 19, 2021, from https://www.icom-cc-publications-online.org/1193/Theft-and-Vandalism-in-museums%2D%2D-facts-and-figures-to-support-Collection-Risk-Management

Puzic, S. (2006, January 25). Hunt on for Stolen Bata Shoe Museum Artifacts. *The Globe and Mail.*

Royal Canadian Mounted Police. (1990). *Fact sheets.* Royal Canadian Mounted Police.

Runhovde, S. R. (2021). On the front-line: Controlling the illicit cultural heritage trade in Norway. *International Journal of Heritage Studies, 27*(11), 1192–1205. https://doi.org/10.1080/13527258.2021.1950028

Sandals, L. (2014, January 14). 5 Ways Canada Can Fight Art Theft. *Canadianart Features.* Retrieved July 19, 2021, from https://canadianart.ca/features/5-ways-canada-can-fight-art-theft/

Schofield Sezgin, C. (2011, April 29). Q&A with Quebec's first art crime enforcement unit. *Art Crime Blogspot.* Retrieved August 5, 2021, from https://art-crime.blogspot.com/2011/04/q-with-quebecs-first-art-crime.html

Schofield Sezgin, C. (2012, October 29). Bill Reid Theft 2008: Postmedia News obtains RCMP and university campus security records to answer outstanding questions about the heist of UBC's Museum of Anthropology and the investigation that followed. *Art Crime Blogspot*. Retrieved October 30, 2021, from https://art-crime.blogspot.com/2011/04/q-with-quebecs-first-art-crime.html

Seagrave, J. (1997). *Introduction to Policing in Canada*. Prentice Hall Canada Inc..

Sewell, J. (2010). *Police in Canada: The Real Story*. James Lorimer and Company Ltd..

Taber, J. (2014, April 23). Police working with thief to recover thousands of stolen artifacts. *The Globe and Mail*.

The Canadian Press. (2009, January 31). Unit of RCMP and Quebec cops focused on art theft. *CTV News*.

The Ottawa Citizen. (2004, June 20). Knife-wielding thief robs museum. *The Ottawa Citizen*.

The Province. (1907, March 6). Will be sentenced for coin theft Thursday. *The Province*.

Tremain, D. (n.d.). Agent of Deterioration: Thieves and Vandals. Resource Document. *Government of Canada*. Retrieved August 6, 2021, from https://www.canada.ca/en/conservation-institute/services/agents-deterioration/thieves-vandals.html

Trondsen, N. (1976). Social control in the art museum. *Urban Life, 5*(1), 105–119.

Wrightson, K. R. (2017). The limits of recognitions: *The Spirit Sings*, Canadian museums and the colonial politics of recognition. *Museum Anthropology, 40*(1), 36–51.

Cara Grace Tremain completed her PhD in archaeology at the University of Calgary in 2017. She has long held an interest in museums and has experience of both working in, and research at, various museums in England and North America. Her interests also include the looting, trafficking, and sale of cultural heritage, and the manufacture of archaeological fakes and forgeries. She has published on the topics of looting, auction house sales, forgeries, and museum collections. She is an Instructor in the Department of Sociology and Anthropology at Langara College in Vancouver.

The Theft of Your Soulmate

Motivations for the Theft of Rare Violins

Summer R. Austin

Abstract Through a combination of criminology, ethnomusicology, sociology, and psychology, this study analyses the complex relationships between musicians and instruments and how these powerful relationships can motivate deviant behaviour. Using rare Cremonese violins as a case study, this chapter contextualises the complex values associated with rare violins before expanding on John Conklin's 1994 work with Routine-Actor-Theory and Simon Mackenzie's 2005 characterisation of art theft motivation to investigate cases of musicians as 'motivated offenders'. Taking an 'object-focused' approach, this initial research considers theoretical issues and presents an empirical case study for understanding violins as active in influencing crimes around them. Instrument theft is an incredibly intimate crime—both for the victims and the offenders. In a world where your instrument is an extension of your being, your voice, your soulmate, this highly personal crime warrants further examination.

1 Introduction to the World of Violins and Art Crime

Rare musical instrument theft is a particularly under-researched aspect of art crime. This chapter presents an empirical case study of the theft of rare violins and the varying motivations for this type of crime. By taking an 'object-focused' approach, this research aims to provide theoretical frameworks for understanding the complex relationships between offenders and violins and how violins may be active in influencing crimes around them. Expanding on John Conklin's (1994) work applying Routine-Activities-Theory (RAT) to artworks, in conjunction with Simon Mackenzie's (2005) characterisations of art theft, this study presents supplementary classifications of profit-motivated violin thefts followed by an in-depth examination of art-motivated theft and the relationships between object and offender, violin and musician. Two case studies are presented of musician offenders—musicians who

S. R. Austin (✉)
Institute of Archaeology, University College London, London, UK
e-mail: summer.austin.20@ucl.ac.uk

N. Oosterman, D. Yates (eds.), *Art Crime in Context*, Studies in Art, Heritage, Law and the Market 6, https://doi.org/10.1007/978-3-031-14084-6_11

commit criminal offenses involving instruments (violins in this case study)—that illustrate the complex relationship between musician and instrument which is deeply personal, as well as potentially influencing deviant behaviour. Instrument theft is an incredibly personal crime, both for the victims and the offender. Musical instruments are unique 'suitable targets' *because* they live their lives out in the world with both their musicians and the audience. Musicians become 'motivated offenders' due to the sophisticated socially constructed values that certain violins embody. Instrument theft is not a victimless crime; both musician and instrument suffer professionally and intimately.

The first section of this chapter contextualises the complex values associated with violins as historical entities, sacred musical individuals, authoritative status symbols, and high investment opportunities. The following section presents violins as active agents in their own lives, moving through time, influencing musicians, audiences, and society through their musical voices. As cultural, social, and financial entities, violins are never neutral, inanimate objects but encapsulate multi-layered meanings both social and profoundly personal. The relationship between musician and instrument is deeply intimate, becoming intertwined with their own identity, self-worth, and morality. It is vital to understand the multifaceted roles and values that violins inhabit in order to understand the motivations of offenders and the consequences for victims. This is followed by a section which outlines the criminological framework for this study supported by several supplemental case studies involving violin theft. Two expanded case studies of musicians as offenders are presented with detailed accounts of the crimes, victims and offenders followed by motivating factors and discussion. The aim of this initial research is to explore the relationship between object and offender, violin and musician; how some violins unintentionally influence deviant behaviour and the painful consequences of such crimes. In a world where your instrument is an extension of your being, your voice, your soulmate, this highly personal crime deserves further examination and offers a framework for considering other human-object relationship criminological behaviour.

2 Violins as Value

> My violin had seen off Napoleon, Queen Victoria, Stalin, Mao Tse-tung, two World-Wars, and the atomic bomb. People come, people go, violinists live, violinists die, empires rise and fall, and the violin lives on, washed from shore to shore on the tide of wealth, fortune and history. This is but a speck of time for my Strad. Min Kym (2017, p. 165).

2.1 Violins in Context

This section contextualises Cremonese string instruments as significant musical entities invested with emotion and a wide range of historical, cultural, musical and monetary significances. As seen in the quote above, these instruments exist independently of their owners or performers, with their own identities, social biographies, and cultural capital (Gosden & Marshall, 1999; Bourdieu, 1986). One need not be a world-class musician to recognise the name Stradivarius; the name is synonymous with the finest rare string instruments ever made. For the last 300 years, there has been a persistent mystique about the celebrated instruments. Violins, as we know them today, came to be crafted in Italy during the early 1500s by the father of violin making, Andrea Amati, consequently vaulting Cremonese violin makers (luthiers) to the forefront of violin making in Europe. Cremona served as an epicentre of knowledge and resources for the next four generations of renowned luthiers, including: Amati, Giuseppe Guarneri del Gesù, Giovanni Guadagnini, and the maestro, Antonio Stradivari (Cattani et al., 2013).

Antonio Stradivari (1644–1737) began making instruments in the 1650s, and in 1680 he opened his own workshop. He and his family produced an estimated 1100 stringed instruments in his 70-year career—predominantly violins but also violas, cellos, guitars, and one harp—of which only approximately 650 instruments still exist today. Stradivari died in 1737, and by the late eighteenth century, most of the Cremonese violin making knowledge had been lost (Cattani et al., 2013), leaving only the infinite Cremonese-mystique. Today, traditional Cremonese violin-making is included on the UNESCO's *Representation List of the Intangible Cultural Heritage of Humanity*.

Among musicians today, old Cremonese instruments are not merely renowned; they are legendary, mythical, sacred, and personal. Stradivarius instruments (often referred to as Strads) are not merely tools of the trade; they are divine individuals within the musical community, validating one's success while helping achieve a perfect sound together. Strads and other Cremonese string instruments are highly sought-after instruments reserved for the most elite musicians. The status of world-renowned musicians and the status of select Cremonese violins enhance each other producing a mutual halo effect (Moro, 2019); one cannot be great without the other being equal.

Debates about what makes Cremonese string instruments superior continue as science strives to unveil the secrets of Cremonese luthiers. Studies have tested a wide range of possible influencing factors, including: varnish, wood minerality, climate-change, river algae, acoustic variants, UV lighting, and tree-rings. Multiple double-blind studies have indicated that both violinists and audiences cannot distinguish between 'old' and 'new' violins (see Fritz et al., 2014, 2017). But most virtuosos will tell you that by simply comparing the 'old' versus the 'new' that you are missing the point. They will tell you that Strads have a special blend of superior materials, extended biographies, and an enigmatic psychological quality resulting in a more multifaceted relationship cultivated between performer and instrument which produces superior emotional and powerful music (Almond, 2017). This unique and intangible relationship is part of the faith-like devotion that motivates musicians to desire these rare and esteemed violins (Kym, 2017; Moro, 2019). It may be the very fact that science cannot answer the question about what makes a Stradivarius great, that enhances musicians' faith in these instruments, creating and enforcing the halo effect. Whether or not Strads are scientifically superior instruments is irrelevant;

musicians and society have accepted their superiority, thus they are highly sought after as both instruments and investments and as targets for crime.

The market for old Cremonese instruments is predicated on limited supply and increased demand resulting in astounding prices; a 'Great Strad' can sell privately for upwards of $15 million USD. Their increasing rarity and return on the market have attracted investors who see their acquisition as a safe investment. The elevated market for these instruments often makes them unobtainable for musicians, and increasingly these instruments are sold to banks, foundations, consortiums, and collectors, then either loaned out to prominent musicians, creating a form of forced patronage (Bucur, 2016; Campbell, 2008) or, isolated within bank vaults and museum cases as collector pieces. The prestige of Stradivari's instruments, these career validating and science defying entities, their cultural and economic significance, these elements contribute to the value and power of Cremonese violins which create a powerful motivation for crime.

2.2 *Violins as Active Agents*

The social agency of Stradivarius violins illustrates the complex relationships and networks that stem from some musical instruments and highlights the impact, roles, meaning, and motivations that violins play in today's society. The violinist Min Kym describe Strads as: "a touch of magic, the life [Stradivari] blew into these lumps of wood transforms them [. . .] you are holding immortality" (Kym, 2017, p. 88). This metaphor is useful when considering violins with theories of object agency and the social life of instruments. I propose one can equate 'magic' to *object agency* and 'immortality' to the *social lives* of violins. The magic of a Stradivarius is equivalent to its *agency*: capable of producing or promoting action. Gell (1998) argues that distinguished and iconic objects, such as a Great Stradivarius, can form their own social agency and occupy positions within networks and 'causes events to happen in their vicinity, not necessarily the specific events intended' (Gell, 1998). Strads form networks between contemporary actors (musicians, audiences, museum visitors, etc.) and connect back into history. Every famous performer, every distinguished listener, every emotion conveyed is imbued within that violin, further adding to its magic, to its agency. Ethnomusicologist Eliot Bates stipulates that musical instruments are social, active agents who have some degree of agency and are protagonists in their own stories—they are actors who facilitate, prevent, or mediate social interaction among other characters (Bates, 2012, p. 364). Thus, we can think of these violins not as passive, inanimate objects but as cultural, social, and financial entities, that embody multifaceted meanings both socially and personally.

The agency of Strads manifest in the synergy between instrument and musician. When a great musician plays a great Stradivarius: "we all know that feeling. It's the difference between a good violin and a great one. A good one, you have to work hard to make it sound right [. . .] but a great violin can never let you down. It knows [. . .] It inspires you, it carries you both across the line" (Kym, 2017, p. 97). Several themes are present here, a hierarchy of value—both in the violin and its agency, which directly correlates with its musical status, the collaboration between violin and musician, and the ability for the violin to actively carry the musician through the performance. Just as all Strads are not necessarily 'great Strads', not all violins have this magic, this agency (Bates, 2012) which further reduces an already limited supply of 'great' instruments available for musicians. This perceived power, partnership, and prestige of elite Strads draws musicians to these instruments and potentially motivates deviant behaviour. When we examine object-focused crimes involving rare violins, the powerful agency of a 'great Strad' and the complex networks that are interwoven within them, violins can be seen as actively and unintendedly influencing crimes committed against them.

2.3 *Violins as Social Lives*

As indicated in the section opening quote by Kym, Strads have lived long, diverse lives, lives that musicians hope to be a part of someday. The characteristic of immortality that Kym attributes to Strads is a fitting conceptualisation for their 300 years of *social lives*. Cremonese violins are highly anthropomorphised: they are named, described as living, having a soul, brimming with emotions, voice, and mannerisms (Almond, 2017; Kym, 2017). Musicians glorify the lived lives of their violins (e.g. when they were born, famous individuals who have passed in and out of the violins' life) and often see themselves as a mere chapter in these instruments' stories, never owning them, simply renting them from history for a brief time. Violins are seen as eternal entities, moving through time and space, bestowing their musical gifts upon a select few before moving on. According to Appadurai (1986), material objects have social potential and a social life, where 'things' such as musical instruments can have a 'career' (Appadurai, 1986; Dawe, 2001, p. 223). Career instruments live highly active and social lives. They travel the world with their musician, getting on planes, trains and automobiles and performing at concerts night after night. By looking at these concepts of magic and agency, immortality, and social lives, we start to understand the complex and personal networks that violins form and how these powerful relationships motivate both musical mastery and potentially crime. The extraordinary life of a Strad is part of the strong appeal to both musicians and musician offenders. Both wish to be part of that life, to hold immortality. However, the methods each use to go about inserting themselves into a violin's life illustrate the power violins have to influence morality and behaviors.

2.4 *Violins as Identities*

By examining how musicians' identities become intertwined with their musical instruments' identities, we can better understand both the motivations of musician as offenders and the trauma of loss for victims. Logically, a musician requires an instrument to perform, to make a living, to express the countless hours of practice, dedication, and emotion required to be an elite performer. At the same time, a violin requires a musician to allow its voice to be heard, to best display its musical prowess and artistic tone, thus creating a collaboration between musician and instrument (Simoens & Tervaniemi, 2013, p. 172). This relationship between musician and instrument is a deeply personal and profound connection built upon compatibility, synergy, and faith. Playing a Strad is every violinist's dream. It is a career validating experience that confirms the musician as a true master in the eyes of their peers (Campbell, 2008). The authoritative and validating power these instruments have cannot be overemphasised. Musicians describe a symbiotic relationship between instrument and player; one cannot be truly great if the other is not great (Almond, 2017). This relationship is both emotional and physical; the musician embraces the violin to their body, working together to create art, and it becomes an extension of their own physicality, their own self.

Musicians describe the profound emotional experience upon first meeting with 'their' instrument; Min Kym states:

> It was my violin [. . .] that all her life, my Strad had been waiting for me as I had been waiting for her [. . .] It was love at first sight, love and everything else: honour, obedience, trust, everything. All my life had been a rehearsal for when I would meet my violin, and we would begin (Kym, 2017, p. 84).

There is a spiritual-like experience when one meets their instrument, their musical soulmate which creates the impression that a musician is changed or perhaps, finally complete, finally whole. For these musicians, their identities (both professionally and personally) are interwoven with their instruments. It is vital to appreciate this intimate relationship between musician and instrument when we consider the consequences of this type of crime; the trauma of ripping away a part of yourself, a part of your soul.

This profound relationship motivates musicians to strive for perfection but can result in an obsessive relationship with their instrument from which they may find it difficult to separate; it validates their professional status but also their own identity and self-worth. Inferiority complexes sometimes manifest through an unhealthy degree to which musicians' self-esteem are tangled with their levels of success as a performer (Kemp, 1996, p. 106), resulting in the musician either believing they are disappointing their instrument or, inversely, that their instrument is an obstacle to their success (Simoens & Tervaniemi, 2013). Musicians personal and professional relationships with musical instruments are vital to understanding the motivations of musicians as motivated offenders. As we will see in the following section, how individuals and society engage with instruments can become complicated and traumatic. Bates (2019) argues that:

> We take seriously the ways people actually engage with instrument objects, we must grapple with the messiness of these encounters. In countless experiences, people regard their instruments as instruments of power, as influencing their owners for good and for evil, or as producing moral and ethical effects in both performers and listeners (Bates, 2019, p. 42).

Bates clearly articulates the power and active agency that violins have, and their ability to influence behaviours and morality. By examining how violins embody agency, live social lives, and are professionally and personally intertwined in musicians' identities, we can consider crimes involving violins in new ways—where violins potentially and unintendedly influence and motivate musicians to offend.

2.5 *Violins as Motivation*

The relationship between musician and instrument acts as the catalyst for musicians who commit violin theft. Here I will present the criminological framework and case studies to further analyse how these relationships influence deviant behaviour. Expanding on Conklin's (1994) work applying Routine-Activities-Theory (RAT) to artworks, in conjunction with Mackenzie's (2005) characterisations of art theft motivation, this section presents supplementary classifications of profit-motivated violin thefts, then turns its focus to art-motivated offenders. This particularly personal crime—for both the victims and the offender—deserves closer examination to understand what motivates a musician to steal another's musical soulmate.

Conklin's application of RAT states that art theft is more likely to occur where three factors are present: a suitable target, a motivated offender, and the absence of capable guardians (see, e.g., Cohen & Felson, 1979). Overwhelmingly, rare instrument theft parallels other types of art thefts; they are predominantly monetarily motivated and garner abundant media attention when committed (Mackenzie, 2005). Violins are considered suitable targets due to their size and ease of transport, frequent travel, and high monetary value. Once a Strad is stolen, it is nearly impossible to resell due in part to being so well-documented. As violinist Laurie Niles states: "famous Strads have been photographed from more angles than a porn star" (quoted in Rohrlich, 2014b). Rare musical instruments have little-to-no known black-market, and coupled with the small community of dealers, experts, luthiers, and musicians, there are few ways to profit financially from their theft. Despite the lack of a black market, rare string instrument thefts still occur. It is helpful to understand what motivates these crimes to better predict and protect both musicians and their instruments.

2.6 *Profit-Motivated Violin Thief*

The vast majority of instrument thefts are profit-motivated (Wittman, quoted in Wise, 2019). The profit-motivated theft is more likely to be committed by either an individual or a group of criminals who are often repeat offenders and may be connected to organised crime. Profit-motivated offenders are more likely to use violence and potentially damage the art. A suitable target for the profit-motivated thief is based purely on financial value (Mackenzie, 2005, p. 356). Mackenzie categorises art thefts by motivation: profit-motivated offenders and art-motivated offenders. I have further subcategorised profit-motivated thieves into opportunistic and targeted. Definitions and case studies with brief discussion follow.

2.6.1 Opportunistic Thief

This opportunistic offender does not know the social, cultural or financial value of what they are stealing before the crime is committed; they are not targeting a famous violin, rather they are seizing a random opportunity. Examples of the profit-motivated opportunistic violin thief include the following cases.

The theft of Min Kym's 1696 Stradivarius in 2010 was committed by three thieves at Euston station. Kym reflects on the loss of her violin, which sent her into debilitating depression and how interwoven her identity was and is with her violin in her book, *Gone—A Girl, A Violin, A Life Unstrung*. The emotions immediately following the loss of her violin are described as: "It's my violin and its gone! [. . .] I want to run back to a time when it was safe, when I was whole. [. . .]. It's gone! It's gone! But more than that. . . . I've gone too" (Kym, 2017, p. 123). The thieves were eventually caught, and the violin was retrieved in 2013 unharmed, but circumstances forced Kym to relinquish her beloved Strad, thus losing it yet again.

In 1980, musician Luigi Alberto Bianchi's car was broken into, and his 1595 *del Crocifisso* Amati viola was stolen. It was recovered in 2006 after a suspect tried to sell it in Milan. However, Bianchi and his insurance company's legal battle over ownership lasted until 2013, when a financial agreement was settled, and Bianchi was reunited with his viola 33-years later (The Strad, 2013a, b). In 1998 Bianchi suffered a second loss with the targeted theft of his 1716 *Colossus* Stradivarius violin, which has not been recovered yet (Daltas, 2018). Bianchi offers a unique example of repeat victimisation (Mackenzie, 2005).

In 2004, the 1684 *General Kyd* Stradivarius cello, owned by the Los Angeles Philharmonic, was stolen from the musicians' porch by a passing youth who abandoned it soon after. It was soon discovered in the rubbish and returned after widespread media coverage (Broder, 2004).

These cases illustrate thieves who saw an opportunity and took it (literally) without prior knowledge of the value (culturally, historically, financially) of the object they have stolen. They were motivated by the opportunity and the false prospect of quick profit and are the most common type of violin theft.

2.6.2 Targeted Thief

The second type of profit motivated thief is the targeted thief. A targeted thief is a criminal that targets rare instruments for their perceived resale value. Ambitious, if not foolish, they believe that they can profit from this crime. Examples of the targeted profit-motivated thief include the following.

The theft of the 1715 *Lipinski* Stradivarius violin by a self-proclaimed 'high-end art thief' who in 2014, tasered Milwaukee Symphony Orchestra concertmaster Frank Almond and stole his violin. The thief had waited in the carpark for the violinist, taser in hand, get-away driver ready, illogically believing they could profit from this crime. Almond remembers "being utterly traumatised and disoriented when it was stolen, and not just because I had been shot with a taser. It was as though a fundamental part of my life was gone forever" (quoted in Almond, 2017). The thief was arrested through a series of almost amateur mistakes, and the violin returned unharmed within two weeks (Bissinger, 2014; Rohrlich, 2014a).

Another famous case of targeted home-invasion is Erica Morini's 1727 *Davidoff* Stradivarius violin which was stolen in 1995 while the 91-year old violinist lay in the hospital dying. The theft entered Morini's Manhattan apartment undetected, unlocked the closet the *Davidoff* was in, took the violin in its case and replaced it with an empty case, relocked the closet, and left. When Morini requested her beloved Stradivarius one last time before she died, she actually clutched a stand-in violin as hers was already gone. Despite a suspect list that reads like the game *Clue,* the violin has not been recovered and is on the FBI's Top 10 Art Crimes list (Dickinson, 1999; Wise, 2019).

These two subcategories illustrate the variation in motivation, planning, and purpose, while both profit-motivated, opportunistic thieves are looking for a quick buck with no aspirations to steal something like a Strad. The targeted thief, while motivated by the instrument, is motivated by the financial value it represents. These nuanced variations within profit motivated theft reveal the ways that the violins themselves influence the crime, by inspiring the offender to target them because they are a 'great Strad'. Understanding the distinction between motivation, planning, and intent of these profit-motivated thefts may be useful to better protect both musicians and their violins through various forms of target hardening.

2.7 Art-Motivated Violin Thief

Art-motivated theft is rare and more likely to be committed by an individual. These individuals are usually not a professional criminals and the crime is usually low-tech. The lack of past criminal experience suggests two attributes: one psychological and one practical—the practical being that they enjoy privileged access or knowledge of the art; the psychological being their use of neutralisation techniques to justify their actions (Mackenzie, 2005). The art-motivated thief wants the art for themselves. They want to own it, to possess it, and thus the art is less likely to be damaged during the theft. A suitable target for an art-motivated thief is entirely personal; it "depends upon factors that have often gone under-analysed in relation to art theft: these are the possibility of a relationship between the offender and the object" (Mackenzie, 2005, p. 356). This relationship between thief and violin is central to cases of musicians as art-motivated thieves. The only known cases of art-motivated Stradivarius violin theft have been committed by fellow musicians, making these crimes particularly captivating and confounding. The two in-depth case studies below present the victims, the crime and the offenders with a detailed discussion.

2.7.1 The 1713 Gibson-Huberman Stradivarius

The Victims

Violin: The *1713 Gibson-Huberman* Stradivarius, named after its two most famous musical partners, the British violinist Alfred Gibson (1849–1924) and Polish violinist Bronislaw Huberman (1882–1947). The violin was made in 1713 during Stradivari's 'Golden Period' and is one of his finest creations.

Musician: Bronislaw Huberman was a child prodigy and world-famous virtuoso who purchased the *Gibson* Strad in 1911. While on tour in 1919, the *Gibson* Strad was stolen for the first time. Having been left in Huberman's hotel room in Vienna, it was stolen then recovered, unharmed, 3-days later (*The New York Times,* 29 February 1936a & 01 March 1936b). In the 1930s, with the rise of Hitler, Huberman used his celebrity to denounce antisemitism publicly and is credited with establishing the Palestine Orchestra in 1936, which helped Jewish musicians from Germany and Central Europe obtain exit visas, ultimately saving over 1000 Jews (Tsioulcas, 2013). Huberman helped raise funds for the musicians and their families by organising a United States fundraising tour in 1936. Headlining this tour was Huberman and his Stradivarius. The Strad was stolen in 1936. After the second theft of his Strad, Huberman was heartbroken. He died in 1947, never knowing what happened to his Stradivarius.

The Crime

At a fundraising performance at Carnegie Hall in February 1936, Huberman first performed on the Stradivarius, then switched to his 1731 Guarneri del Gesu violin, leaving his Strad in his dressing room. When the violin was discovered to have been taken, the police were notified. After the concert, Huberman returned to the dressing room and noted that the thief had left behind six high-end bows, each worth $1500 USD ($30,000 USD in 2021). This, Huberman stated, indicated that the thief was not a musician as they would have realised their value. No suspicious individuals were reported, and despite extensive media coverage and a $30,000 USD reward ($600,000 USD in 2021), the violin never surfaced.

The Offender

Julian Altman; according to Altman's widow, Marcelle Hall, Altman confessed to the theft on his deathbed in 1985. In subsequent accounts, Hall stated the crime and motivation as follows. The night of the concert, Altman, a young café musician, stole the Strad when he knew that Huberman would be playing a different violin. In the months before the concert, Altman became friends with the doormen at Carnegie Hall and covered for them while they went on breaks which was how he gained access backstage. Huberman was targeted because of the quality of his violin; Hall stated that Altman had always dreamed of becoming a great violinist, and that was his motivation for the crime. After the theft, Altman covered the Strad in black shoe polish to mask its iconic varnish, then performed publicly on it for almost 50 years. Altman and his disguised Strad's career progressed from pubs to presidents; at one point, Altman was a violinist with the National Symphony Orchestra in Washington D.C., where he was photographed performing before President Richard Nixon. Hall claimed that he never acted as if the violin was anything extraordinary, going so far as to allow his grandchildren to play it. Altman's last decades were turbulent, including a gambling addiction, depression, and legal problems subsequently resulting in Altman's conviction for child molestation. While in jail Altman was diagnosed with cancer, and before his death in 1985, he confessed his crime to Hall. Two years later, Hall reported the stolen violin to Llyod's of London, the owners of the Strad after the insurance pay-out, and received a finder's fee of $263,000 USD (Madden, 1987; *The New York Times,* 06 Nov 1996).

At the time of writing, the *Gibson-Huberman* Stradivarius is owned and played by world-renowned violinist Joshua Bell, who rescued the violin from being purchased as a collector's piece in 2001.

2.7.2 The 1734 Ames-Totenberg Stradivarius

The Victims

Violin: The *1734 Ames-Totenberg* Stradivarius, named after the British violinist Alfred Gibson (1827–1893) and Polish violinist Roman Totenberg (1911–2012). The violin was made in 1734 and is considered one of the great examples of Stradivari's later period.

Musician: Roman Totenberg, a child prodigy, acquired the *Ames* Stradivarius during the height of his career in 1941 and toured the world while recording extensively. By the 1960s, Totenberg started to focus on teaching, holding prestigious posts at several institutions, including Head of the String Department at Boston University (BU) from 1961 until 1978 and as the School Director at the Longy School of Music in Cambridge, Massachusetts, from 1978 until 1985. The Strad was stolen in 1980. On the loss of his violin, Roman's daughter, Nina Totenberg stated, "It was a crushing loss for my father. As he put it, he had lost his 'musical partner of 38-years.' And when he would ultimately buy a 1734 Guarneri violin [. . .] he'd have to rework the fingering of his entire repertoire for the new instrument. My father would dream of opening his violin case and seeing the Strad there again, but he never laid eyes on it again" (Totenberg, 2015). Roman Totenberg died in 2012 at the age of 101, never forgetting his beloved Stradivarius.

The Crime

On 13 May 1980, after a concert performed by Totenberg at the Longy School of Music, Totenberg left his violin in his office attached to the theatre and joined the crowd. When he returned, the Stradivarius and a Francois Tourte bow were missing. The case was retrieved nearby, but the violin was gone. Despite Totenbergs' strong suspicions of one individual, there was not enough evidence for a search warrant and the violin was not recovered (Edgers, 2016).

The Offender

Philip Johnson; a promising, but difficult, 27-year-old former student at Boston University. Totenberg and Johnson met while both were at BU. Johnsons' music teacher Joseph Silverstein recalled that Johnson, while naturally talented, was combative, dismissive, entitled, and generally unliked by the faculty; there had been discussions whether to keep him at the school (Edgers, 2016). The night of the crime, audience members recalled being surprised that Johnson attended Totenbergs' concert as he was a vocal critic of Totenberg's, stating that the ageing master did not deserve such a fine instrument. It was also noted that he had a violin case with him and was seen outside Totenbergs' office (Edgers, 2016). After the theft, Johnson left Boston and for 10 years tried to make a career as a violinist, taking gigs around the United States and Venezuela. However, his antagonistic personality prevented him from achieving his goal, even with a Stradivarius (Edgers, 2016). Acquittances remember that he did all the necessary maintenance to the violin himself. Johnson's later years were characterised by divorce, depression, gambling, and manic behaviour. He died in 2011 from cancer at the age of 58, leaving the *Ames-Totenberg* Stradivarius in a plastic crate in his closet. In 2014, Johnson's unsuspecting ex-wife decided to sell the violin and had it evaluated. Upon examining the violin, the violin expert recognised it was a stolen Strad and contacted the FBI. The FBI took possession of the violin and presented it to the Totenberg's daughters in July 2015. In 2018, the *Ames-Totenberg* Stradivarius was acquired by the *Rare Violins In Consortium, New York* and is currently on loan to the American violinist Nathan Meltzer.

2.7.3 Musicians as Art-Motivated Thieves

Common aspects in the cases discussed above reveal valuable reflections when considering musicians as both capable guardians and motivated offenders and violins as suitable targets. First, it needs to be recognised that, overwhelmingly, musicians do not lead lives of crime; they work incredibly hard physically, mentally, and emotionally to imbue the world with beautiful music (Kemp, 1996). Yet, as these two cases demonstrate, some musicians choose to steal another's musical soulmate. What makes this crime more intrusive is the recognition that, as fellow musicians, the offenders would assumably comprehend this profoundly personal relationship and trauma that they inflicted upon the victims. What is it about instruments that motivate these musician offenders?

Common aspects in the two cases include the locations of the thefts. Both were taken from semi-public performance spaces with lax to no security which gave the thieves their opportunity (Harvey & Shapreau, 1997). The victims—both musicians and violins—share similarities. Both musicians were well-established, mature virtuosos who were deeply affected by the loss and sadly died before their violins were recovered. Both violins were targeted because of their prestige and not because of their monetary value. Both Altman and Johnson were young, inspiring musicians and both had privileged access and specialised knowledge. Altman knew Huberman would switch violins during his performance and had access backstage, while Johnson had access to the music department and knew Totenberg's routines. Both crimes were straightforward, and the offenders had the knowledge and skills to remain undetected by performing their own maintenance on the instruments and neither seems to have revealed their crimes to anyone else. Both repeatedly performed on the stolen instruments, yet neither achieved the elite careers associated with Strads. Both had turbulent final years related to personal issues and mental illness; the potential link between art-motivated thefts and mental illness is outside the scope of this chapter but deserves further investigation. Finally, both Altman and Johnson retained the Strads until their deaths, potentially indicating a complicated relationship formed between the musicians and the kidnapped Strads. The desire for this private relationship felt between musician and violin discussed above may be both motivator for the offense, and motivation for retaining the instrument for life.

While it is impossible to know specific influences and factors regarding the offenders since their actions came to light post-mortem, we can make inferences based on what we know about art motivated thefts and the powerful relationships and values between musicians and their instruments.

3 Motivating Values

Both Mackenzie (2005) and Bates (2019) emphasise the relationships individuals have with objects. These relationships can be powerful, constructive, and intimate or messy, obstructive, and disenchanted but, when considering motivations for art-motivated instrument thieves, the relationship between thief and violin is essential. I will now consider several possible influencing motivations of instrument-motivated thieves including: neutralising techniques, forms of validation, the psychology of ownership, the identity between musicians and instruments, and barriers of access.

In order to justify their crimes, musician offenders may employ neutralisation techniques (Sykes & Matza, 1957). They may deny responsibility, claiming they would have never been able to obtain a violin of that status otherwise (both due to musical status and financial limitations) or deny injury, maintaining that no one was physically harmed in these thefts and dismissing the emotional and psychological trauma of loss. They may deny the victim, believing the musicians did not deserve their violins, as seen with Johnson's comments about Totenberg not deserving his Strad. Finally, they may appeal to a higher loyalty, claiming that the ends justify the means and that they deserve these violins and care for them. These psychological tricks help the musician offender justify their motivations and crimes against the victims.

Perhaps the most logical motivation for the theft of a rare violin by a musician would be validation. As stressed above, musical status and musical identity are correlated to the quality of the instrument; offenders may see their current instruments as a barrier and a Strad as the ladder to their success. By stealing these authoritative and prized entities, they are able to validate themselves, both in the ownership of the instrument and the ability to get away with such a shocking crime. However, this validation is entirely private and does not result in professional status which would otherwise be obtained through playing such a rare instrument. The very fact that these musicians do not achieve the public and professional validation associated with Strads and yet keep, care, and play the Strads signifies that the crime is not only about obtaining a rare violin for status and validation. It indicates that it is about the violin itself, what the violin embodies, the value of the violin, the relationship with the violin. It is about possessing the violin, even if the world never knows.

Another powerful motivator is the psychology of ownership, possessing something considered sacred, much the way musicians view Strads. Ownership can influence self-worth and self-potential; hence, offenders are likely to desire ownership over objects of significant social, cultural, and personal status (Pierce et al., 2003, p. 21). Developmental psychologists suggest that the feelings of 'mine' and 'me' are closely related and that possessions can come to play such a "dominant role in the owner's identity that they become part of the extended self" (Pierce et al., 2003, p. 85). Psychological ownership can lead to deviant behaviour that defies social constructs. Thus ownership, whether legal or not, can form a strong link between identity and the object, potentially resulting in immoral and illegal behaviour. While most musicians place themselves within the social lives of their Strads, these thieves kidnap the instrument from those lives, thus owning it entirely. They are now not only a chapter in these great instruments' lives, they are their masters.

Possibly the strongest motivation is the complex and personal relationships musicians have with their instruments. Musician offenders may be attempting to replicate the intimate relationship other musicians feel with their instruments; this is a type of appropriation of relationship, if they do not have a positive relationship with their own instrument (Simoens & Tervaniemi, 2013). This crime can be conceived as both violin theft and identity theft when one considers the powerful intertwinement of identity and instrument as previously described. It is difficult to assess these offenders' success in developing a relationship with the Strads; both offenders played the violin and retained the instruments till death, which could indicate a relationship was achieved.

The final motivator to consider is the barriers to access to these instruments due to limited supply, further constrained by a hierarchy of value and agency associated with selected violins based on provenance, prestige, and performance. This is further compounded by transforming these musical objects into museum objects, further restricting access and increasing financial barriers for musicians. While neither offender profited financially from their crimes, they also could have never accessed them due to their lack of both financial means and musical status.

These motivations, while theoretical, illustrate the complex, powerful, and messy relationships between musician offenders and violins and how the violins themselves motivate deviant behaviour. Without that validating agency or that social pedigree, the powerful intertwinement of instrument and identity, these violins would not be considered suitable targets for musicians.

4 Silence of the Violins

4.1 Not a Victimless Crime

As suggested throughout this chapter, there are two victims when a violin is stolen, the musician and the violin. Both are silenced through the crime: the musician through the loss of their musical partner, while the violin is muted in its social role. Kidnapped instruments are unlikely to be adequately maintained and may suffer lasting damage. Musicians suffer both personally and professionally. Personally, there is the initial trauma of the theft, which may include physical trauma as seen in the case of Frank Almond's assault. But even without physical trauma, there is always emotional trauma as seen in the case studies. Musicians equate the theft of their instrument to losing a limb, a piece of their soul, a void, emptiness. The loss of something so intimately tied to one's identity can result in the "shrinkage of personality, a partial conversion of [the victim] to nothingness and feelings of depression" (Pierce et al., 2003, p. 86). Self-blame and humiliation, both professionally and personally, are often reported. Professional musicians require an instrument to work, thus they must either acquire a substitute or face loss of income. Exacerbating the loss and trauma is the frensied media coverage which may result in a 'known quantity' for other instruments thefts (Tseloni & Pease, 2003). Musicians face public humiliation, victim-blaming, accusations, and loss of social and professional status with negative effects on their careers. Fresh out of the hospital, Frank Almond was required by his insurance company to take a polygraph test to clear him of suspicion of foul play (Vittes, 2016). Because of the monetary value these instruments represent, musician victims must go through countless police interviews, insurance depositions, private investigators, and media interviews, repeatedly forcing the victim to recount and defend their actions. Even if the violin is recovered, sometimes within hours, insurance premiums skyrocket, and if the violin is a loan, the owner may no longer trust the musician and remove the instrument from them, repeating the loss. However, all of these consequences do not compare to the loss of a musical soulmate. The final consequence to consider is the one we all experience, the silencing of violins when they are deemed too precious, too pricey to be played. Violins are increasingly thought of as an investment, not an instrument, and high-profile thefts increase the likelihood of violins being regulated to visual art within museums, bank vaults, and private collections.

4.2 Discussion: Musicians or Mausoleums

When considering the relationship between offender and art, violins offer a unique and valuable case study. Violins have been presented as suitable targets due to their high monetary and cultural value, their authoritative and sacred agency and as well as their social lives through collaborative careers. A profit-motivated offender may or may not know the financial worth of the instrument depending on their target, but the art-motivated offender will not care. For them, it is about the relationship, the connection they have with the instrument. They are compelled to possess the sacred, the immortal, in order to validate themselves and forge a relationship. How do musicians become capable guardians for their instruments? Musicians report the lengths they go to protect their instruments, including being in constant physical contact and dressing inconspicuously to disguise the fact that they have millions of dollars strapped to their backs. They use decoy cases, GPS trackers, and other technologies. However, all of these solutions require resources, often financial, which places a larger burden on the musician, and all of this does not change the fact that musicians are humans; they make mistakes, they are emotionally and physically exhausted from hectic schedules and intense travel, they get tired and fatigued, and no matter how much violins seem to have their own personalities, a kidnapped violin cannot call out when it is taken. Thus, the question remains, how do musicians secure the sacred when they are themselves human? Is it possible to prevent these types of crimes when the motivations differ between profit and art, or are we moving to a point where rare violins are too valuable to be in the world?

Passionate debate surrounds musical instruments that serve only as museum objects. Bates argues that "instrument museums are mausoleums, places for the display of the musically dead, with organologists acting as morticians, preparing dead instrument bodies for preservation and display" (Bates, 2012, p. 365). Yet it is an inevitable consequence that interacting with violins is to risk 'performance wear' at best, irreparable harm and loss at worst. Are these objects that should be silenced and preserved for posterity, or should they be allowed to 'live' and fulfil their purposes with the understanding that they will eventually be no more? If we think of instruments as social agents who have their own agency, who are the protagonists of their own stories, then silencing them within museums is disingenuous to their purpose and their lives.

5 Conclusion

The powerful relationship between instrument and musician is essential to understanding what motivates musician offenders. This incredibly personal crime—for both the victims and the offenders—illustrates the profound influence musical instruments have in society and on individuals. This research helps us consider how objects and our relationship with them affect our own identities, behaviours, and morality. The two case studies detailed above illustrate how violins themselves can unintentionally influence crime around them. While this chapter looks at cases of musician offenders who steal rare violins, the theories and discussions can be applied to a wide range of material studies and the powerful, and sometimes messy relationships we as a society and as individuals have with these entities. Violins theft is not a victimless crime; no matter the financial, historical, or monetary value of one's instrument, the love and the loss is universal for the victims as Kym poetically articulates:

> Suddenly I picture an island of stolen violins [. . .] waiting to be rescued, a host of lost violins that have been smashed from their homes, taken from those who love them. I imagine them gathered on the shore, playing furiously, in the hope that some passing distant ship will hear them, alter its course, rescue them all, restore them into the waiting arms. . . A violin stolen is an act of cruelty. The violins on these pages are all different. Some are like mine, instruments that possess greatness within their frame, but many do not. But they all speak to those who love them (Kym, 2017, p. 177).

The consequences of this crime are devastating. The status of Stradivarius as divine individuals ensures that they will continue to be coveted by musicians and the world, thus it is vital that we examine these powerful encounters and personal relationships between musician and instrument to better understand motivating factors for violin crime and their traumatic consequences. By taking an object-focused approach to this intimate crime, this initial research provides theoretical frameworks for understanding the complex relationships between musicians and violins and how violins influence crimes.

References

Almond, F. (2017, July 20). Blind testing Strads and Guarneris misses a fundamental point. *The Strad.* Retrieved June 27, 2022, from https://www.thestrad.com/blind-testing-strads-and-guarneris-misses-a-fundamental-point/6944.article

Appadurai, A. (1986). *The social life of things: Commodities in cultural perspective.* Cambridge University Press.

Bates, E. (2012). The social life of musical instruments. *Ethnomusicology, 56*(3), 363–395. https://doi.org/10.5406/ethnomusicology.56.3.0363

Bates, E. (2019). Actor-network theory and organology. *Journal of the American Musical Instrument Society, 44*, 41–51.

Bissinger, B. (2014, November). The Stradivarius Affair. *Vanity Fair.* Retrieved June 27, 2022, from https://archive.vanityfair.com/article/2014/11/the-stradivarius-affair

Bourdieu, P. (1986). The forms of capital. In J. Richardson (Ed.), *Handbook of theory and research for the sociology of education* (pp. 241–258). Greenwood.

Broder, J. M. (2004, May 8). Thief in Los Angeles Carries Off Priceless Cello, a Stradivarius. *The New York Times*. Retrieved June 27, 2022, from https://www.nytimes.com/2004/05/08/us/thief-in-los-angeles-carries-off-priceless-cello-a-stradivarius.html

Bucur, V. (2016). *Handbook of materials for string musical instruments*. Springer.

Campbell, R. A. J. (2008). Fine violins as an alternative investment: Strings attached? *Pensions: An International Journal, 13*(1), 89–96. https://doi.org/10.1057/palgrave.pm.5950065

Cattani, G., Dunbar, R. L. M., & Shapira, Z. (2013). Value creation and knowledge loss: The case of cremonese stringed instruments. *Organization Science, 24*(3), 813–830. https://doi.org/10.1287/orsc.1120.0768

Cohen, L. E., & Felson, M. (1979). Social change and crime rate trends: A routine activity approach. *American Sociological Review, 44*(4), 588. https://doi.org/10.2307/2094589

Conklin, J. E. (1994). *Art crime*. Praeger.

Daltas, K. (2018, January 9). Obituary: Viola and violin soloist Luigi Alberto Bianchi, 1945-2018. *The Strad*. Retrieved June 27, 2022, from https://www.thestrad.com/news/obituary-viola-and-violin-soloist-luigi-alberto-bianchi-1945-2018/7432.article

Dawe, K. (2001). People, objects, meaning: Recent work on the study and collection of musical instruments. *The Galpin Society Journal, 54*, 219–232. https://doi.org/10.2307/842454

Dickinson, A. (1999, May 9). The Case of The Stolen Stradivarius. *Washington Post*. https://www.washingtonpost.com/archive/lifestyle/1999/05/09/the-case-of-the-stolen-stradivarius/0170af90-9452-452b-9377-c3314899668f/

Edgers, G. (2016, March 17). The Violin Theft. *Washington Post*. Retrieved June 27, 2022, from http://www.washingtonpost.com/sf/style/2016/03/17/the-violin-thief/

Fritz, C., Curtin, J., Poitevineau, J., Borsarello, H., Wollman, I., Tao, F.-C., & Ghasarossian, T. (2014). Soloist evaluations of six Old Italian and six new violins. *Proceedings of the National Academy of Sciences, 111*(20), 7224–7229. https://doi.org/10.1073/pnas.1323367111

Fritz, C., Curtin, J., Poitevineau, J., & Tao, F.-C. (2017). Listener evaluations of new and Old Italian violins. *Proceedings of the National Academy of Sciences, 114*(21), 5395–5400. https://doi.org/10.1073/pnas.1619443114

Gell, A. (1998). *Art and agency: An anthropological theory*. Clarendon Press.

Gosden, C., & Marshall, Y. (1999). The cultural biography of objects. *World Archaeology, 31*(2), 169–178. https://doi.org/10.1080/00438243.1999.9980439

Harvey, B. W., & Shapreau, C. J. (1997). *Violin fraud: Deception, forgery, theft, and lawsuits in England and America* (2nd ed.). Oxford University Press.

Kemp, A. E. (1996). The musical temperament psychology and personality of musicians. *Oxford University Press*. https://doi.org/10.1093/acprof:oso/9780198523628.001.0001

Kym, M. (2017). *Gone: A girl, a violin, a life unstrung*. Penguin Books Limited.

Mackenzie, S. (2005). Criminal and victim profiles in art theft: Motive, opportunity and repeat victimisation. *Art Antiquity and Law, 10*(4), 353–370.

Madden, R. L. (1987, May 14). A Stolen Stradivarius, a 51-Year Secret. *The New York Times*. Retrieved June 27, 2022, https://www.nytimes.com/1987/05/14/nyregion/a-stolen-stradivarius-a-51-year-old-secret.html

Moro, P. A. (2019). *Violins: Local meanings, globalized sounds*. Routledge.

Pierce, J. L., Kostova, T., & Dirks, K. T. (2003). The state of psychological ownership: Integrating and extending a century of research. *Review of General Psychology, 7*(1), 84–107. https://doi.org/10.1037/1089-2680.7.1.84

Rohrlich, J. (2014a, June 4). The Man Who Allegedly Stole the $5 Million Violin Called to Tell Us How It All Went Down. *Vice News*. Retrieved June 27, 2022, from https://www.vice.com/en/article/59aqpq/the-man-who-allegedly-stole-the-5-million-violin-called-to-tell-us-how-it-all-went-down

Rohrlich, J. (2014b, December 23). The $5 Million Violin and the Telltale Taser—Inside an Epically Stupid Crime. *Vice News*. Retrieved June 27, 2022, from https://www.vice.com/en/article/59ajy5/the-5-million-violin-and-the-telltale-taser-inside-an-epically-stupid-crime

Simoens, V. L., & Tervaniemi, M. (2013). Musician–instrument relationship as a candidate index for professional well-being in musicians. *Psychology of Aesthetics, Creativity, and the Arts, 7*(2), 171. https://doi.org/10.1037/a0030164

Sykes, G. M., & Matza, D. (1957). Techniques of neutralization: A theory of delinquency. *American Sociological Review, 22*(6), 664–670. https://doi.org/10.2307/2089195

The New York Times. (1936a, February 29). Huberman Violin Stolen at Carnegie. *The New York Times.*

The New York Times. (1936b, March 1). No Clue To Stolen Violin. *The New York Times.*

The New York Times. (1996, November 6). Stolen Stradivarius Divides a Family. *The New York Times.* Retrieved June 27, 2022, from https://www.nytimes.com/1996/11/06/nyregion/stolen-stradivarius-divides-a-family.html

The Strad. (2013a, April 7). *Brothers Amati viola is returned to Italian soloist after legal tussle over ownership.* Retrieved June 27, 2022, from https://www.thestrad.com/brothers-amati-viola-is-returned-to-italian-soloist-after-legal-tussle-over-ownership/1231.article

The Strad. (2013b, June 11). *What happens when a stolen Strad is recovered?* Retrieved June 27, 2022, from https://www.thestrad.com/what-happens-when-a-stolen-strad-is-recovered/6550.article

Totenberg, N. (2015, August 6). A Rarity Reclaimed: Stolen Stradivarius Recovered After 35 Years. *NPR.* Retrieved June 27, 2022, from https://www.npr.org/2015/08/06/427718240/a-rarity-reclaimed-stolen-stradivarius-recovered-after-35-years

Tseloni, A., & Pease, K. (2003). Repeat personal victimization. 'Boosts' or 'Flags'? *British Journal of Criminology, 43*(1), 196–212. https://doi.org/10.1093/bjc/43.1.196

Tsioulcas, A. (2013, April 4). How A Violinist Saved 1, 000 Jews In World War II. *NPR.* Retrieved June 27, 2022, from https://www.npr.org/sections/deceptivecadence/2013/04/02/176018068/hubermans-list-how-a-violinist-saved-jews-in-world-war-ii

Vittes, L. (2016, June 21). Violinist Frank Almond's Album Chronicles Recently Recovered 'ex-Lipinski' Strad. *Strings Magazine.* Retrieved June 27, 2022, from https://stringsmagazine.com/violinist-frank-almonds-album-chronicles-recently-recovered-ex-lipinski-strad/

Wise, B. (2019, January 11). A New Chapter Begins in the Tumultuous Life of the 'Ames, Totenberg' Stradivari. *Strings Magazine.* Retrieved June 27, 2022, from https://stringsmagazine.com/a-new-chapter-begins-in-the-tumultuous-life-of-the-ames-totenberg-stradivari/

Summer R. Austin is a doctoral candidate at the Institute of Archaeology at University College London. Her research investigates the role of blockbuster museums exhibitions in the creation, enhancement and normalisation of demand for antiquities on the market and the consequences for such demand. Summer holds an Art History MSc degree in Collecting and Provenance in an International Context from the University of Glasgow, an MSc in Archaeology from the University of Edinburgh and BAs in Archaeology and in History from the University of California, San Diego. Her research interests include the art and antiquities market, looting and trafficking of cultural and natural resources, museums and the market, art crime and cultural heritage law.

UNESCO Emergency Response "First-Aid" Heritage Interventions in Syria During Armed Conflict

Joanne Dingwall McCafferty

Abstract This chapter aims to determine the role UNESCO has played in facilitating emergency response "first aid" heritage protection measures during the Syria armed conflict, commencing March 2011. Through document analysis and qualitative data from semi-structured interviews, this study maps UNESCO's engagement with Syria throughout the ongoing armed conflict and identifies the form the organisation's heritage protection initiatives took. Analysis of such heritage protection initiatives showed UNESCO's interventions in Syria to be majorly technocratic, with minimal on-the-ground implementation of emergency measures. Moreover, due to political gridlock resultant of the standpoints of other Member States, UNESCO was often unable to act in Syria, with communication lines at times, being completely closed. This political gridlock, which is evidenced to paralyse UNESCO, is often shown to result in the organisation overstating its ability to safeguard heritage, with promises not being followed up with action.

1 Introduction

One of 18 specialised agencies within the United Nations system, the autonomous intergovernmental organisation (IGO) of the United Nations Educational, Scientific and Cultural Organisation (UNESCO) has, in recent years, been involved to varying degrees in initiating cultural programmes focused on either protecting or reconstructing the cultural heritage of Syria. For UNESCO, the placement of the preservation of cultural heritage within the context of armed conflict came with the *1954 Hague Convention for the Protection of Cultural Property in the Event of Armed Conflict* (hereafter "1954 Convention"), with the organisation's role becoming more clearly defined with the 1954 Convention's 1999 Second Protocol. UNESCO is mentioned on 37 occasions in the 1954 Convention and again on

J. D. McCafferty (✉)
Department of Cross-Cultural and Regional Studies, University of Copenhagen, København, Denmark
e-mail: mccafferty@hum.ku.dk

N. Oosterman, D. Yates (eds.), *Art Crime in Context*, Studies in Art, Heritage, Law and the Market 6, https://doi.org/10.1007/978-3-031-14084-6_12

15 occasions in the Second Protocol, thereby confirming that UNESCO is part of the cultural heritage protection during armed conflict discourse.

Nonetheless, when it comes to UNESCO, the obligations set out for the organisation under the 1954 Convention and its two Protocols (1954, 1999) support Luke and Meskell's observation that UNESCO is primarily a standard-setting agency, which provides technical solutions and in doing so has "retreated further into its bureaucratic, managerial, and expert-driven functions" (Luke & Meskell, 2019, p. 9). Meskell (2015, p. 10) also asserted that it remains the individual State Party's responsibility to enact effective heritage safeguarding preparedness measures, while "UNESCO can only educate and encourage through diplomatic channels". Meskell's (2018) account of UNESCO rightly depicts how the organisation has to operate within strict confines, with the power of its Member States often restricting its capacity to engage. However, in recent years, UNESCO has been portraying itself to be more of a central actor in facilitating hands-on heritage safeguarding and reconstruction efforts (UNESCO, 2015).

This chapter focuses on UNESCO's exhibition of both preparedness and emergency response strategies across Syria in recent years in relation to the ongoing-armed conflict, commencing March 2011. Document analysis is employed to construct a representation of UNESCO's initiatives and projects in Syria, and to determine the extent to which they have been effective. Consideration is also given to budget sources and its dispersal, how initiatives and projects are implemented, the parties and actors involved in the implementation process, and challenges met. Further insight is gained via qualitative semi-structured interviews with UNESCO staff members, the former Director General (DG) of the Directorate General of Antiquities and Museums (DGAM) of Syria, and independent experts in the field of heritage protection during armed conflict. The evidence gleaned from the qualitative data provides additional information into the practical functioning of UNESCO, as well as the various challenges encountered in the planning and implementation stages of UNESCO-led initiatives in Syria.

2 Preparedness Versus Emergency Response

Many "emergency response" strategies developed during conflict, encompassing the creation of conservation and management plans, by definition, verge into the preparedness category, but are enacted reactively. As discussed in UNESCO's 2015 *Strategy for the Reinforcement of UNESCO's Action for the Protection of Culture and the Promotion of Cultural Pluralism in the Event of Armed Conflict*, cultural heritage management and conservation constitute pre-conflict risk preparedness and reduction (UNESCO, 2015, p. 5). Such planning is the responsibility of the individual State Party under the 1954 Convention, but UNESCO also recognises that such action "remains so far limited and under-funded" (ibid., p. 5). UNESCO (ibid., p. 5) therefore committed to "strengthen advocacy at all levels to promote consideration of and investment in culture as an integral part of conflict prevention strategies and operational action". It remains however, that management and conservation planning should occur in time of peace, as per the 1954 Convention and its two protocols. However, prior to the outbreak of conflict in 2011, Syria's state heritage institution (SHI), DGAM, possessed severely depleted resources, and so were unable to fulfil their obligations under the 1954 Convention and its First Protocol, to which they are party. For such reasons, any actions occurring during conflict, previously determined as preparedness, are labelled emergency response "first-aid". More specifically, UNESCO actions, which could be construed as preventative, if acted upon in the pre-conflict phase, such as calling on all parties to a conflict to protect the country in question's cultural heritage, or the provision of no-strike lists, are often only acted upon reactively, following the commencement of destruction to heritage, thereby qualifying such actions as emergency response.

Quntar and Daniels (2016, p. 382) identified three categories of projects enacted by the international heritage community in response to the destruction of Syrian cultural heritage during the Syrian civil war commencing 2011. They are 1. site documentation projects, mainly utilising satellite imagery, journalistic accounts and social media reports, such as *Le patrimoine archéologique syrien en danger*; [1] 2. public awareness raising projects; and 3. emergency training and mitigation projects (ibid, pp. 382–383). Quntar and Daniels (ibid, p. 382) assert that less attention has been given to emergency interventions to safeguard at-risk heritage. This chapter will apply this assertion to UNESCO's emergency response strategies across Syria in relation to the ongoing-armed conflict. They raise ethical concerns around the documentation of sites, which include such efforts being demonstrative of the international community's voyeuristic analytical gaze, and drawing unwanted attention to the cause of terrorist groups, with increased visibility of sites such as Palmyra potentially putting them at greater risk (ibid., p. 385). However, they also cite three reasons justifying site documentation during conflict, namely, raising public awareness, assisting future stabilisation or reconstruction efforts, and criminal accountability for perpetrators (ibid., p. 383). Regardless of this discourse, site documentation remains a major facet of emergency response strategies proposed by UNESCO. UNESCO's relationship with Syria throughout the course of the conflict has been turbulent, with the majority of engagement dropping off with the change in DG of DGAM and DG of UNESCO in 2017. Moreover, persistent sanctions against the Assad regime have only tightened the already restrictive environment in which UNESCO had to operate.

[1] The Syrian Archaeological Heritage in Danger.

3 Syria: Emergency Response "First-Aid"

UNESCO's first emergency response course of action commenced over two years following the March 2011 outbreak of conflict in Syria. In June 2013, the World Heritage Committee (WHCo) resolved to place Syria's six cultural World Heritage Sites (WHSs) on the List of World Heritage in Danger (UNESCO, 2013a). The reason proffered by the Committee for doing so was "to draw attention to the risks [the sites faced] because of the situation in the country", while the danger listing was intended to "mobilize all possible support for the safeguarding of the properties" (ibid.). Regardless of such reasoning, Russia attempted to veto this move, with Ambassador Mitrofanova referring to the need for sovereignty over such issues. Russia made this veto attempt despite the Syrian ambassador being in support of the move to the 'In Danger' list, and willingly cooperating with the WHCo and UNESCO on such issues (Meskell, 2014, p. 222). Although the attempt by Russia to block this decision failed, it is indicative of the political tensions and power plays that can make UNESCO enter a state of gridlock. At the 37th session of the WHCo in 2013, it was noted that Syria's WHSs were "threatened by both ascertained and potential dangers" (UNESCO, 2013b, p. 107). At the 38th session of the WHCo in 2014, the specific reason for the listing of the six sites as 'In Danger' was down to "[d]estruction and ascertained as well as potential threats consequent to the armed conflict in Syria" (UNESCO, 2014a, pp. 10–18). Evidently, the sites had already incurred some destruction, which negatively affected their 'Outstanding Universal Value', that is the primary criteria for inscription on the World Heritage List, with the chief catalyst being the armed conflict. In 2013, the WHCo urged parties to the conflict to refrain from any destruction of Syrian heritage, launched an appeal for cooperation in combatting illicit trafficking of cultural objects out of Syria, and requested that the UNESCO DG, Irina Bokova, "consider the creation of a Special Fund aimed at the conservation of the World Heritage properties in Syria" (UNESCO, 2013b, pp. 107–108). These decisions by the WHCo intended to garner international support for improved safeguarding of Syrian cultural WHSs.

At the 38th session of the WHCo, it was stated that over the preceding year, UNESCO had "intensified its activities to monitor the situation of Syrian heritage, raise awareness on its protection, and undertake emergency actions to safeguard it" (UNESCO, 2014a, p. 20). The raising of designated 'Special Funds' for Syria via the following shows this intensification of activities by UNESCO:

- The launch of the EU-funded Emergency Safeguarding of Syrian Cultural Heritage Project on 1 March 2014, in partnership with ICOMOS and ICCROM (2.46 million EUR);
- The Flemish Government-funded project for the organisation of an International Experts Meeting on Syria and for Emergency Assistance Measures (170,000 USD); and
- The Arab Regional Centre for World Heritage's financial support to the World Heritage Centre (WHC) for the safeguarding of Syrian cultural heritage (200,000 USD) (ibid., p. 20).

Moreover, UNESCO also maintained cooperation with DGAM and provided damage assessment forms, and organised, at the request of Syria, a meeting with ICOMOS, ICCROM, and INTERPOL, for the provision of technical recommendation for the safeguarding of the Old City of Damascus (ibid., pp. 20–21). UNESCO was also set to host additional meetings regarding Crac des Chevaliers and the preservation of Syrian cultural heritage as a whole, while fundraising for further actions on Syrian World Heritage and Tentative WHSs (ibid., p. 21).

A key UNESCO programme, comprising various projects and which the organisation considers to be 'good practice' (UNESCO, 2015, pp. 5–6), is the *Emergency Safeguarding of the Syrian Cultural Heritage* programme, which was officially launched on 1 March 2014 for an initial three-year period with European Union funding and support from the Flemish and Austrian governments (UNESCO, n.d.-a). This project emerged from an *Action Plan* developed at a high-level technical meeting held by Bokova, with the participation of the UN and Arab League Joint Special Representative, the DG of DGAM, ICOMOS, ICCROM, ICOM, INTERPOL, the World Customs Organisation, and the European Union (UNESCO, 2014a, p. 20). The Flemish Government supported this project by funding the international expert meeting, titled *Rallying the International Community to Safeguard Syria's Cultural Heritage*, attended by 120 experts from 22 countries from 26–28 May 2014 (UNESCO, 2014b), which alone cost 170,000 USD. Put into perspective, the cost of this meeting is 5.7 percent of the 2.46 million EUR then donated by the European Union to support the resultant project, tasked with providing an "operational response to halt the on-going loss of cultural heritage and prepare post-conflict priority actions in Syria" (UNESCO, n.d.-a). Former Chief of the UNESCO Emergency Preparedness and Response Unit, Giovanni Boccardi (personal communication, 2019), asserts this was "a large programme, which involved lots of training, inventories, cultural mapping, support to the authorities against illicit trafficking of cultural property, awareness raising, educational activities, campaigns, etc." Moreover, he also states:

> We, of course, also played the more typical UNESCO role. We convened several international expert meetings, involving Syrians and experts from various countries, who had been working in Syria for many decades and who had a knowledge crucial for Syrian authorities to be able to preserve their cultural heritage (ibid.).

In describing UNESCO's role in hosting international meetings as "typical", Boccardi indicates that the organisation's more practical engagement in the form of the Emergency Safeguarding programme, is atypical. At this international expert meeting, archaeologist Amr Al-Azm questioned whether UNESCO would ignore the five WHSs, which at the time, were outside regime-controlled areas (Al Azm, personal communication, 2020). UNESCO has demonstrated a pattern of not engaging with sites beyond regime control in Syria; when Aleppo was under rebel control UNESCO's response to heritage destruction was limited to condemnation, while the organisation began hosting meetings regarding the WHS and organising damage assessment missions once the regime had regained control in November 2016 (UNESCO, n.d.-b). The same response is evidenced in the case of Palmyra (ibid.).

UNESCO published an infographic detailing the first year's events, which took place in 2014, under this Emergency Safeguarding project. The infographic breaks down UNESCO's activities into three categories, namely, knowledge and documentation; communication and awareness raising efforts; and technical assistance and capacity building (Patchil, 2020). During the first year, five events were designated as knowledge and documentation, while one was designated as communication and awareness raising, and seven as technical assistance and capacity building (UNESCO, n.d.-a). This UNESCO programme evidences that the organisation encompasses site documentation, public awareness raising projects, and emergency training and mitigation projects in its emergency response strategy. Such "emergency response" tactics from UNESCO are actions typically categorised as preventative, if carried out pre-conflict or during peacetime. The Emergency Safeguarding initiative chiefly centres on awareness raising mechanisms. By 2016, a large number of documentation projects had commenced showing an exponential increase in such activity from 2014 (Cunliffe et al., 2017, pp. 19–32). Quntar and Daniels (2016, p. 387) suggest that we have perhaps reached a saturation point for information regarding cultural heritage destruction, rendering public awareness campaigns to be of little value.

In terms of technical assistance and capacity building, three events constituted meetings, while four took the form of training events (UNESCO, n.d.-a). One hundred individuals, with a mix of police and customs officers and heritage professionals, participated in the training events held in Beirut, with Damascus being the city with the highest number of beneficiaries (ibid.). The training sessions covered:

- combating illicit trafficking of Syrian cultural artefacts (10–14 November 2014);
- first aid to built cultural heritage in Syria (24 November–6 December 2014);
- the protection of movable heritage during and post-conflict and the protection of museums from looting (26–30 January 2015); and
- the 2003 Convention for the Safeguarding of Intangible Cultural Heritage (9–-13 February 2015) (ibid.).

Reporting on the second training session on first aid to built heritage, UNESCO included two positive feedback statements from trainees in their press release, while further stating that participants had requested complementary training activities from UNESCO to ensure more DGAM staff benefited from the course material (UNESCO, 2014c). Some discrepancies are evidenced in UNESCO's 2014 statement related to the training, which records 22 individuals to have attended the course (ibid.), whereas UNESCO's infographic records 23 (UNESCO, n.d.-a). Moreover, despite stating that the course took place from 24 November–6 December 2014, as does the infographic, on two occasions, UNESCO's statement contradicts this by referring to the training as a three-week course, as opposed to a two-week course. Regardless, despite, the positive feedback recorded, training programmes in themselves have limitations if those receiving the training continue to go without financial support and access to necessary resources to implement what they have learned (Quntar & Daniels, 2016, p. 389). Stacy Bowe of the Smithsonian Cultural Rescue

Initiative (personal communication, 2020) advocates, "a comprehensive follow-up assessment on how trainees have used the training received" to understand its relevance and level of success. Senior Advisor for the NGO, Heritage for Peace, Rene Teijgeler, believes that:

> [s]uch programmes are very much overrated and centre on buzzwords", adding "it is important to question how this [project], and many other projects, are evaluated and monitored to ensure no corruption takes place, and to measure the tangible success of the project (personal communication, 2020).

Founder of Heritage for Peace, Isber Sabrine, suggests those who received this UNESCO training in Beirut "are not making use of it" and further states, "There does not seem to be any tangible results from the [Emergency Safeguarding] project" (personal communication, 2020). It appears that UNESCO has shown little transparency with regard to the monitoring of how the training was implemented by recipients in Syria, and, at the time of writing, has not publicly disclosed any evaluation or report on the Emergency Safeguarding project results.

In August 2014, UNESCO stated "continuous monitoring and early assessment of damage is a priority to prepare a sound and coordinated response for recovery and future rehabilitation", for which reason the organisation launched the Observatory as part of the Emergency Safeguarding project (UNESCO, 2014d). Funded by the European Union, the Observatory was first announced on 28 May 2014, following an international expert meeting at UNESCO HQ (UNESCO, 2014b). The initial aim of the Observatory was to "monitor the state of buildings, artefacts and intangible cultural heritage to combat illicit trafficking and collect information to restore heritage once fighting is over" (ibid.). However, Cunliffe (personal communication, 2020) recounts that this knowledge and documentation element of the project was not used for the prioritisation of sites for emergency response but was instead used for awareness raising. By this logic, the only aspects of the initiative not strictly concerned with awareness raising were the technical assistance and training initiatives (capacity building). The Observatory acted as a platform through which UNESCO and its partners, such as ICOM and INTERPOL, could collate reports and initiatives with the UNESCO Beirut office managing the overall project (UNESCO, n.d.-c). With the latest damage documentation entry on the website being 7 April 2018 (UNESCO, n.d.-d), this project publically appears to have been chiefly dormant since then. Al Azm (personal communication, 2020) states that when Syrian operations closed down in the Beirut office, "clearly, a new political decision had been made; UNESCO does not want to deal with the DGAM politically, so...as far as Syria is concerned, UNESCO was disengaging".

Further distinct evidence of UNESCO's termination of its initial efforts to assist in safeguarding Syrian cultural heritage is the ceasing of the Observatory's collation of all damage assessments carried out by DGAM [2] and various organisations such as

[2] n.b. DGAM removed all documented damage from their website in 2020.

ASOR, [3] Heritage for Peace, and The Day After [4] (UNESCO, n.d.-e). The Observatory consistently collated damage assessments dating from 23 February 2014 through 18 October 2018 (ibid.). The sheer volume of damage assessments collated on this single platform, together with a lack of evidence of any resultant increased support for cultural heritage safeguarding initiatives, qualifies Quntar and Daniel's assertion that there exists a saturation point of information regarding cultural heritage destruction, which renders public awareness campaigns of little value. Regardless, following 18 October 2018, no further damage assessments are made available via this website. Despite destruction still ongoing, such damage assessments are now denied this platform. Cunliffe (2021, pers comm), states that the Observatory projects were due to terminate in December 2018, with potential for a six month extension. This however never came to fruition, with website updates ending between 2 and 3 months prior to December 2018. Cunliffe (personal communication, 2020) records, "the Emergency Safeguarding project finished Christmas 2019. They [UNESCO] never announced the termination of the project, nor did they publish any results". UNESCO practically ceased all operations in relation to this project prior to its official termination in 2019, and the organisation perhaps did not want to draw any attention to said termination. At the 40th and 41st session of the WHCo in 2016 and 2017 respectively, attention was drawn to the lack of funds available for the effective implementation of Emergency Safeguarding Action Plans in Mali, Syria, Iraq, Libya, and Yemen, and Member States were urged to contribute additional funding (UNESCO, 2016a, p. 9; 2017a, p. 9). It is clear from continual appeals from DGAM for funding for emergency conservation works and reporting of lack of equipment and trained personnel (DGAM, 2019, p. 14), that UNESCO's Emergency Safeguarding initiative did not solve the major resource deficit issues in DGAM. There evidently remains a need for such initiatives. Nonetheless, direct appeals from the WHCo for funding for the Emergency Safeguarding project also ceased following 2017, with Member States thereafter only encouraged to donate to the Heritage Emergency Fund (HEF) (UNESCO, 2018a, 2019a). Maamoun Abdulkarim (personal communication, 2020), former DG of DGAM, states, "[w]e wanted to work with UNESCO, to facilitate more emergency preventative safeguarding in Syria, but now we know that such UNESCO programmes have ceased in Syria". The lack of results published from the Emergency Safeguarding project following its termination determines that its impact remains unknown. What is more, the inactive project website has a tab for 'Publications', which includes hyperlinks to the project outputs for years one and two, as well as outputs until November 2017 (UNESCO, n.d.-f), however the links do not work. [5] Abdulkarim

[3]ASOR's funding to carry out damage assessments of Syrian cultural heritage ceased in December 2018.

[4]TDA's final report, which was collated on the Observatory website, was published on 27 January 2018.

[5]This was last tested on 1 March 2022. Available from: https://en.unesco.org/syrian-observatory/publications.

(personal communication, 2020), notes the tonal shift and circumstances around UNESCO's diminishing engagement, stating that when "Bokova and I left our positions as [DG] of UNESCO and DGAM respectively, there came a new strategy and a new mentality. Something changed in the relationship between UNESCO and DGAM".

March 2016 saw a tangible contribution to DGAM capacity from UNESCO in terms of facilitating resources to effect on-the-ground heritage safeguarding. Through cooperation with French and Swiss heritage professionals, in 2016 UNESCO responded to the lack of funds and material resources available to Syrian heritage professionals to securely evacuate and store museum collections, by providing nearly seven tonnes of necessary materials (UNESCO, 2016b). The material resources were transported to the UNESCO office in Beirut and donated to DGAM staff in Syria (ibid.). This was undoubtedly a welcome initiative, supported by UNESCO, and led by Swiss and French heritage professionals, to mitigate risks to prioritised museum collections accessible to DGAM. It does however constitute further preventative measures enacted in an emergency response fashion, five years following the outbreak of conflict.

Following the initial liberation of Palmyra from Da'esh control, the 199th session of the Executive Board of UNESCO met on 8 April 2016. It was unanimously adopted that UNESCO should include safeguarding and preservation of Palmyra and other Syrian WHSs in the then forthcoming Action Plan for the implementation of the aforementioned 2015 strategy (UNESCO, 2016c, p. 2). It was also unanimously adopted that UNESCO should promote broad participation and coordination among States, UN agencies, and partner organisations toward the restoration of such sites, while UNESCO was invited to send a damage assessment mission to Palmyra and other sites, such as Aleppo, to identify urgent needs in terms of conservation, restoration and safeguarding (ibid, p. 2). UNESCO's subsequent actions would provide hope that the organisation would work alongside DGAM in facilitating emergency response and recovery efforts. UNESCO dispatched a rapid assessment mission (funded by the HEF) to Palmyra from 23–27 April 2016, which acknowledged the need for documentation and consolidation work. The emergency intervention recommendations detailed short, medium, and long-term activities, which were expanded upon via a detailed report on the site of Palmyra, following a *Technical Assistance Workshop for the World Heritage Sites of the Crac des Chevaliers, Palmyra and the Ancient City of Damascus* from 13–15 December 2016. This report provided an extensive damage assessment, which also identified the need for immediate actions. It also set out clear guidelines on which emergency response mechanisms to enact in order to prevent further destruction to the citadel, museum, Temple of Bel, Temple of Baalshamin, Arch of Triumph, and the rest of the archaeological site.

Following the initial damage assessment, UNESCO held consultations with various Member State representatives and relevant experts (UNESCO, 2016e), as well as convened a meeting in Berlin attended by over 230 Syrian and international experts, titled *Follow-up to the implementation of the UNESCO Action Plan for the Emergency Safeguarding of Syria's Cultural Heritage* (UNESCO, 2016f). At this meeting, Bokova stated that the priority was "to conduct a comprehensive inventory of the damages, identify emergency safeguard[ing] measures to save what is possible, wherever possible" (ibid.). This meeting had three main objectives, namely, to exchange information on the condition of all Syrian heritage sites, to reach a consensus on all initial priorities and emergency measures, and to coordinate all actions under one common vision (UNESCO, 2016g). The result was an updated version of UNESCO's *Recommendations and Road Map for the Safeguarding of Syria's Cultural Heritage*, with focus given to the following subsections:

- local communities;
- documentation, archives, damage assessment, technologies and innovation;
- advocacy, coordination, communication and awareness-raising;
- technical assistance, capacity building and future needs; and
- preparing future safeguarding plans (UNESCO, 2016h).

The majority of future plans identified under each of the above categories centre on either hosting meetings or training workshops, with the primary aim of building capacities of heritage professionals and relevant authorities in Syria (ibid.). At the close of the meeting, Mechtild Rössler, Director of UNESCO's WHC, emphasised the need for cooperation among stakeholders with regard to both emergency works and recovery projects in Syria (UNESCO, 2016g). Abdulkarim (personal communication, 2020) states "[s]ometimes, UNESCO acted to mediate between myself and the rest of the world", something he greatly appreciated. UNESCO acted as DGAM's "neutral" spokesperson when addressing States in the appeal for funding and coordinating international support. Without this facilitation, institutions such as DGAM with direct connection with the Assad regime, have only a limited number of options, the best being cooperation with the regime's official military allies, Russia and Iran, to finance emergency and recovery heritage projects. Abdulkarim (ibid.), acknowledges the efforts made by UNESCO under Bokova to convince some oppositions outside Syria to support DGAM, further stating that UNESCO "tried to combat the idea that DGAM is part of the regime, however the problem for UNESCO is that the international community incorrectly considers all Syrian state institutions to be part of the regime".

In response to recommendations from the *First-Aid Technical Assistance Workshop*, which took place on 13–15 December 2016, a project proposal for the *Emergency Safeguarding of the Portico of the Temple of Bel in Palmyra* was produced. This proposal was originally based on recommendation number five, which stated,

> Guarantee temporarily the protection and stability of the monuments' remains, implementing appropriate measures for the partial shoring or dismantling . . .of the structures, and in particular, the west portico of the Temple of Bel and the remains of the side pillars of the Arch of Triumph (UNESCO, 2017b, p. 47).

This project proposed a budget of 150,000 USD to be used over a period of six months to document the Portico, complete a damage assessment, and the emergency consolidation of the Portico (UNESCO, n.d.-g). The proposal further states that the project contributes to the operational response proposed in the UNESCO Emergency Safeguarding Action Plan for Syria's Cultural Heritage adopted at the high level meeting that UNESCO organised on 29 August 2013 in order to halt the on-going loss of cultural heritage and prepare post-conflict priority actions (ibid.).

Nonetheless, at the time of writing, this project has not yet been implemented due to a lack of funding received (Interviewee A, personal communication, 2021). This is despite a continual reiteration by DGAM to the WHCo that "the portico of the Temple of Bel and the Triumphal Arch require urgent consolidation works" (UNESCO, 2019b). The DGAM is recorded as being unable to progress with such emergency work without funding support (ibid.), which it has previously requested, and appealed for via the WHCo to other States Parties, without success. In response, the WHCo resolved to express "its concern that the portico of the Temple of Bel and the Triumphal Arch are at risk of collapse due to the lack of funding for their emergency consolidation" (ibid.).

Two of the "Immediate Actions" put forth as a recommendation following the *Technical Meeting on the Recovery of the World Heritage Site of Palmyra* on 18 December 2019, were to:

- conduct a detailed documentation study of the current situation of the site and of all its individual monumental structures; and
- implement emergency interventions at specific monuments, such as at the Citadel, the Temple of Ba'al (which would encompass the Portico) and the Triumphal Arch, in line with the recommendations of the *Technical Assistance Workshop for the World Heritage Site of Palmyra* (UNESCO, 2019c, p. 1).

In terms of emergency response mechanisms, this December 2019 technical meeting also recommended the:

- enhancement of international cooperation for the update of inventories related to looted objects, with the support of UNESCO and ICOM;
- development of a site map of Palmyra, including all information and documents available on specific monuments and areas; and
- establishment of an integrated conservation management plan (ibid., pp. 2–3).

Given the readymade (2017) proposal for the documentation and consolidation of the Portico of the Temple of Bel, following the initial technical assistance workshop in December 2016, has not yet been funded or implemented, such 'immediate' actions have either not been taken by UNESCO, or have instead been taken on by Russia. This is demonstrative of UNESCO's technocratic nature discussed by Meskell (2018); in the case of Syria, there is a plethora of technical meetings concluding the same recommendations, with little to no follow-up or practical implementation. This further confirms Cunliffe's notion that UNESCO's collation of damage assessments assumed the primary role of awareness raising, with little application for recovery planning. Nonetheless, Article 33(1) of the 1954 Convention merely requires that UNESCO provide technical assistance with respect to documentation at the request of the State Party on a preparatory basis, i.e. during peacetime.

In the case of Syria, UNESCO is not acting upon emergency response recommendations in a manner consistent with an emergency, nor is it able to. Even following the WHCo outright identifying lack of funding as the direct cause of the potential collapse of the Portico and the Triumphal Arch in Palmyra, other States Parties neglected to commit any funds to the project. This could be construed as indicative of the power ongoing sanctions against Syria have over international organisations. However, it must be questioned why UNESCO continues to maintain that it is capable of intervening by hosting such international technical meetings on emergency safeguarding of Syrian cultural heritage when it is aware of its inability to act on its own recommendations. Meskell (2018, p. 115) discusses the dominance of States and their politics over UNESCO, stating, "conservation priorities have devolved into political webs of reciprocities and relationships that increasingly relegate conservation to the wings, rather than placing it at centre stage". The continual hosting of international meetings, with little to no implementation of resultant recommendations, show such efforts by UNESCO to be more indicative of political appeasement, than any form of meaningful action.

With regard to the experts who participated in this technical meeting on the recovery of Palmyra in 2019, their recommendations do not bring to light anything more than what was already established by the initial rapid assessment mission by UNESCO and the subsequent, more detailed report comprising a comprehensive damage assessment and various recommendations produced in 2016. Furthermore, this 2019 meeting failed to realise any funding for the implementation of the recommendations raised. The original 2016 rapid assessment report called upon the international community to support the Palmyra recovery actions "with significant human and financial resources" in close cooperation with UNESCO (UNESCO, 2016d, p. 5), yet the 2019 recommendations do not make such a call, despite the absence of funds remaining the primary inhibitor in ensuring the preservation of existing structures in Palmyra.

Quntar and Daniels (2016, p. 385) raise the crucial point that site documentation endeavours may not have any utility in assisting with future stabilisation or reconstruction efforts when carried out during conflict, due to the likelihood of further damage incurred to the site in the intervening time between the assessment and the restorative intervention. Site documentation only serves a purpose when emergency interventions are implemented soon after (ibid., p. 385). Although still able to function in terms of awareness raising or holding certain groups or countries accountable when documentary evidence is gathered in the correct manner, UNESCO's effort to support others to document Palmyra resulted in no significant follow-up action or intervention.

From 16–19 January 2017, UNESCO led an emergency mission to Aleppo to complete a preliminary damage assessment of the WHS. This initial assessment, followed up by an International Coordination Meeting for the recovery of Aleppo's heritage on 2–3 March 2017 (UNESCO, 2017c), and the publication of the joint UNESCO-UNITAR report on damage to Aleppo (UNESCO, 2018b), revealed 60 percent of the old city to be severely damaged, while 30 percent was totally destroyed (UNESCO, 2017d). This pattern of damage assessment and monitoring without follow up implementation of emergency works make any such initial assessments futile. At this stage, UNESCO indicated it was working on an "emergency initiative to coordinate international efforts". On 19 November 2020, the Secretariat of the WHC announced that it would host a series of online technical meetings for Syrian properties on the List of World Heritage in Danger, with the aim of "clarifying the process for the elaboration of the Desired [State of Conservation]" for their removal from the list (UNESCO, 2020a). UNESCO's established pattern when it comes to heritage interventions in Syria, as exemplified via the organisation's actions regarding Palmyra, demonstrates a perpetuation of a cyclical approach centred on hosting expert or high-level meetings and producing recommendations, with no follow-up. Such meetings are likely to repeat established recommendations of the organisation.

4 Conclusion

When it comes to emergency response action in Syria, UNESCO's approach can be described as technocratic, with minimal implementation. This is exemplified by the various meetings and conferences held by UNESCO with experts and stakeholders to discuss potential roadmaps for better heritage safeguarding and recovery approaches. This demonstrates UNESCO's habit of retreating into its "'field of competence' position in order to rescue itself from political bombshells" (Meskell, 2018, p. 169). Meskell (2015, p. 8) suggests that the only way UNESCO can intervene when it comes to heritage destruction in Syria is "by listing the Syrian [WHS]s as endangered, [and] signalling to the international community the State Party's failure to protect". Meskell (ibid., p. 8) proffers the organisation's only alternative avenues are via discussions and planning as evidenced by UNESCO's output under the Emergency Safeguarding project. This summation of UNESCO's engagement in Syria in the context of heritage protection during the ongoing-armed conflict should also extend to training and advocacy/awareness-raising, which, again, have not necessarily translated into on-the-ground implementation of emergency or recovery works. Nonetheless, as per Article 30(3)(b) of the Second Protocol to the 1954 Convention, the individual State Party is obligated to work in cooperation with UNESCO *during peacetime* to develop and implement relevant training and educational programmes.

Across UNESCO's response to the destruction of cultural heritage in Syria, there was a definite prioritisation of, and emphasis on, the WHS of Palmyra, over all other sites, with Aleppo being the second priority focus. Luke and Meskell (2019, p. 838) determine that the emphasis and focus on sites such as Palmyra demonstrate colonial and imperialist pasts, suggesting that this "pattern perpetuates the very cultural differences that organisations such as UNESCO, the UNDP, and progressive academic institutions claim to challenge". Although worthy of international attention, UNESCO's excessive focus on Palmyra, which, in the end, achieved very little, could have been better centred on carrying out damage assessments and the development of recovery strategies in areas of Syrian heritage which have more of a daily impact on the standard of living of Syrians, such as *souqs*, historic buildings, and religious sites.

UNESCO (2014d) acknowledges that prevention and long-term engagement is key when it comes to cultural heritage protection and views its role in this regard to build national capacities via advocacy, awareness raising, advice and training (ibid.). It further states that preventative capacity building is preferable to last minute endeavours, specifically in times of conflict (ibid.). This is contradictory to UNESCO's evidenced reactive engagement with Syria when it comes to such efforts, with very few of such interventions qualifying as 'early' or 'preventative'. This does not mean to say those working for UNESCO are reluctant to extend preventative or emergency aid to Syria, but that the organisation has multiple limitations, in terms of lack of funding and the restrictive power Member States possess, over its ability to act. The most typical initial response from UNESCO and the international community to the destruction of cultural heritage in areas experiencing conflict, where the area concerned is in non-state actor (NSA) territory, more specifically when that NSA has a terrorist designation, is condemnation. This remains the standard response until the area is liberated or shifts back to the UN-recognised-government's control, at which time, UNESCO may send a delegation to carry out or facilitate a rapid assessment mission. In terms of actual emergency response mechanisms, there is limited implementation across the board of Action Plans UNESCO formulated for Syria, with such plans having little impact beyond awareness raising and documentation of damage.

References

1954 Hague Convention for the Protection of Cultural Property in the Event of Armed Conflict. (1954, May 15). Retrieved June 27, 2022, from http://www.unesco.org/new/en/culture/themes/armed-conflict-and-heritage/convention-and-protocols/1954-hague-convention/

Cunliffe, E., Leckie, L., & Varoutsikos, B. (2017). *Towards a protection of the Syrian Cultural Heritage: A summary of the national and international responses*. Newcastle University ePrints.

Directorate General of Antiquities and Museums. (2019). *State party report on the state of conservation of the Syrian cultural heritage sites (Syrian Arab Republic)*. Directorate General of Antiquities and Museums. https://whc.unesco.org/en/soc/3866.

Luke, C., & Meskell, L. (2019). Archaeology, assistance, and aggression along the Euphrates: Reflections from Raqqa. *International Journal of Cultural Policy, 25*(7), 831–842. https://doi.org/10.1080/10286632.2019.1598398

Meskell, L. (2014). States of conservation: Protection, politics, and pacting within UNESCO's World Heritage Committee. *Anthropological Quarterly, 87*, 217–243. https://doi.org/10.1353/anq.2014.0009

Meskell, L. (2015). Gridlock: UNESCO, global conflict and failed ambitions. *World Archaeology, 47*(2), 225–238. https://doi.org/10.1080/00438243.2015.1017598

Meskell, L. (2018). *A future in ruins: UNESCO, world heritage, and the dream of peace*. Oxford University Press.

Patchil. (2020). *UNESCO's Emergency Safeguarding of the Syrian Cultural Heritage. Communication Strategy, Data Visualization*, Editorial Design, Visual Communication. Retrieved June 27, 2022, from http://www.patchil.com/portfolio/safeguarding-of-the-syrian-cultural-heritage/

Quntar, S. A., & Daniels, B. I. (2016). Responses to the destruction of Syrian Cultural Heritage: A critical review of current efforts. *International Journal of Islamic Architecture, 5*(2), 381–397. https://doi.org/10.1386/ijia.5.2.381_1

UNESCO. (2013a). *Syria's six world heritage sites placed on list of world heritage in danger*. https://whc.unesco.org/en/news/1038

UNESCO. (2013b). *UNESCO Convention Concerning the Protection of the World Cultural and Natural Heritage, World Heritage Committee, Thirty-seventh session, 16–27 June 2013, Phnom Penh, Cambodia*. UNESCO. Retrieved June 27, 2022, from https://whc.unesco.org/en/sessions/37COM

UNESCO. (2014a). *UNESCO Convention Concerning the Protection of the World Cultural and Natural Heritage, World Heritage Committee, Thirty-eighth session, 15–25 June 2014, Doha, Qatar*. UNESCO. Retrieved June 27, 2022, from https://whc.unesco.org/en/documents/129119

UNESCO. (2014b). *UNESCO to create an Observatory for the Safeguarding of Syria's Cultural Heritage*. Retrieved June 27, 2022, from https://en.unesco.org/syrian-observatory/news/unesco-create-observatory-safeguarding-syria%E2%80%99s-cultural-heritage

UNESCO. (2014c). *UNESCO concludes training course on "First Aid to Cultural Built Heritage in Syria"*. Retrieved June 27, 2022, from https://whc.unesco.org/en/news/1208

UNESCO. (2014d). *UNESCO strengthens action to safeguard cultural heritage under attack*. Retrieved June 27, 2022, from https://whc.unesco.org/en/news/1176

UNESCO. (2015). *General Conference 38th Session: Reinforcement of UNESCO's Action for the Protection of Culture and the Promotion of Cultural Pluralism in the Event of Armed Conflict, November 2015, Paris*. UNESCO. Retrieved June 27, 2022, from https://unesdoc.unesco.org/ark:/48223/pf0000235186

UNESCO. (2016a). *UNESCO Convention Concerning the Protection of the World Cultural and Natural Heritage, World Heritage Committee, Fortieth session, 10–17 July 2016, Istanbul, Turkey*. UNESCO. Retrieved June 27, 2022, from https://whc.unesco.org/en/sessions/40COM

UNESCO. (2016b). *UNESCO and French and Swiss heritage professionals stand up for the safeguarding of Syrian heritage*. Retrieved June 27, 2022, from https://whc.unesco.org/en/news/1465

UNESCO. (2016c). *Executive Board Hundred and ninety-ninth session: UNESCO's Role in Safeguarding and Preserving Palmyra and Other Syrian World Heritage Sites*. UNESCO. Retrieved June 27, 2022, from https://unesdoc.unesco.org/ark:/48223/pf0000244379

UNESCO. (2016d). *Report of the UNESCO Rapid Assessment Mission to the World Heritage "Site of Palmyra", Syrian Arab Republic, 23–27 April 2016*. UNESCO. Retrieved June 27, 2022, from https://whc.unesco.org/en/documents/142423

UNESCO. (2016e). *UNESCO holds consultations ahead of the International Expert Meeting in Berlin on Cultural Heritage in Syria*. Retrieved June 27, 2022, from https://whc.unesco.org/en/news/1495

UNESCO. (2016f). *Director General opens Berlin expert meeting on the safeguarding of Syria's heritage*. Retrieved June 27, 2022, from https://whc.unesco.org/en/news/1503

UNESCO. (2016g). *Syrian and international experts agree on emergency measures to safeguard Syria's heritage*. Retrieved June 27, 2022, from https://whc.unesco.org/en/news/1505

UNESCO. (2016h). *Updated Recommendations and Road Map for the Safeguarding [of] Syria's Cultural Heritage: Outcome of the international expert meeting: 'Follow-up to the implementation of the UNESCO Action Plan for the Emergency Safeguarding of Syria's Cultural Heritage' (2–4 June 2016, Berlin, Federal Republic of Germany)*. UNESCO. Retrieved June 27, 2022, https://webcache.googleusercontent.com/search?q=cache:RLFESlMfTz8J:https://whc.unesco.org/document/158640+&cd=1&hl=en&ct=clnk&gl=se

UNESCO. (2017a). *UNESCO Convention Concerning the Protection of the World Cultural and Natural Heritage, World Heritage Committee, Forty-first session, 2–12 July 2017, Krakow, Poland.* UNESCO. Retrieved June 27, 2022, from https://whc.unesco.org/en/sessions/41COM

UNESCO. (2017b). *Technical Assistance Workshop for the World Heritage Sites of the Crac des Chevaliers, Palmyra and the Ancient City of Damascus, Beirut 13, 14, 15 December 2016: Site of Palmyra.* UNESCO. Retrieved June 27, 2022, from https://whc.unesco.org/en/events/1386/

UNESCO. (2017c). *UNESCO hosts First International Coordination Meeting for the recovery of Aleppo's heritage.* Retrieved June 27, 2022, from https://whc.unesco.org/en/news/1639

UNESCO. (2017d). *UNESCO reports on extensive damage in first emergency assessment mission to Aleppo.* Retrieved June 27, 2022, from https://en.unesco.org/news/unesco-reports-extensive-damage-first-emergency-assessment-mission-aleppo

UNESCO. (2018a). *UNESCO Convention Concerning the Protection of the World Cultural and Natural Heritage, World Heritage Committee, Forty-second session, 24 June–4 July 2018, Manama, Bahrain.* UNESCO. Retrieved June 27, 2022, from https://whc.unesco.org/en/sessions/42COM.

UNESCO. (2018b). *Five years of conflict: the state of cultural heritage in the Ancient City of Aleppo; A comprehensive multi-temporal satellite imagery-based damage analysis for the Ancient City of Aleppo.* UNESCO. Retrieved June 27, 2022, from https://unesdoc.unesco.org/ark:/48223/pf0000265826.locale=fr

UNESCO. (2019a). *UNESCO Convention Concerning the Protection of the World Cultural and Natural Heritage, World Heritage Committee, Forty-third session, 30 June–10 July 2019, Baku, Republic of Azerbaijan.* UNESCO. Retrieved June 27, 2022, from https://whc.unesco.org/en/sessions/43COM

UNESCO. (2019b). *State of Conservation: Site of Palmyra (Syrian Arab Republic).* UNESCO. Retrieved June 27, 2022, from https://whc.unesco.org/en/soc/3871

UNESCO. (2019c). *Technical Meeting on the Recovery of the World Heritage Site of Palmyra, 18 December 2019.* UNESCO. Retrieved June 27, 2022, from https://whc.unesco.org/en/news/2133

UNESCO. (2020a). *Online technical meeting for Syrian properties on the List of World Heritage in Danger.* Retrieved June 27, 2022, from https://whc.unesco.org/en/events/1563/

UNESCO. (n.d.-a). *The Emergency Safeguarding of the Syrian Cultural Heritage project.* Retrieved June 27, 2022, from https://en.unesco.org/syrian-observatory/emergency-safeguarding-syrian-cultural-heritage-project

UNESCO. (n.d.-b). *World Heritage Centre: Syrian Arab Republic.* Retrieved June 27, 2022, from https://whc.unesco.org/en/statesparties/sy

UNESCO. (n.d.-c). *Observatory of Syrian Cultural Heritage: About Us.* Retrieved June 27, 2022, from https://en.unesco.org/syrian-observatory/about-us

UNESCO. (n.d.-d). *Observatory of Syrian Cultural Heritage.* Retrieved June 27, 2022, from https://en.unesco.org/syrian-observatory/

UNESCO. (n.d.-e). *Observatory of Syrian Cultural Heritage: Reports.* Retrieved June 27, 2022, from https://en.unesco.org/syrian-observatory/damage-assesment-reports

UNESCO. (n.d.-f). *Observatory of Syrian Cultural Heritage: Publications.* Retrieved June 27, 2022, from https://en.unesco.org/syrian-observatory/publications

UNESCO. (n.d.-g). *Emergency Safeguarding of the Portico of the Temple of Bel in Palmyra (Syrian Arab Republic).* Retrieved June 27, 2022, from https://whc.unesco.org/en/activities/903/

Joanne Dingwall McCafferty graduated with an MSc in Collecting and Provenance Studies in an International Context from the University of Glasgow in 2017, after which she worked with the Smithsonian Provenance Research Initiative in Washington DC. From February 2019 until January 2022, Joanne was a PhD Fellow at the University of Copenhagen, researching the role of UNESCO in the protection of cultural heritage during armed conflict in Yemen, Syria and Iraq. With the University of Copenhagen and National Museum of Denmark, Joanne has designed and delivered various courses and workshops on Heritage Protection in Urban Conflicts and has assumed the role of academic advisor at meetings with NATO HQ, the Romanian National Commission for UNESCO, and to various UNESCO Delegations.

Yellow Journalism

Neutralisation Techniques, Media Validation, and the Rothko Vandal

Gretchen Allen

Abstract The media's propagation of justifying rhetoric and neutralisation techniques of artistically-motivated art vandals gains them a sympathetic audience and legitimises their beliefs at the expense of art, museums, and the public. This is exemplified by the heavy coverage of Yellowism following the 2012 vandalism of Mark Rothko's Black on Maroon (1958) at the Tate Modern. This chapter will examine the pattern of legitimisation of 'artistic' art vandals in academic and journalistic writing, and discuss how the conception of what makes an artist leads to the lack of unequivocal condemnation in academia and popular media, which shapes the perception of a vandal and their ideology.

1 Introduction

> A picture lives by companionship, expanding and quickening in the eyes of the sensitive observer. It dies by the same token. It is therefore a risky act to send it out into the world. How often it must be impaired by the eyes of the unfeeling and the cruelty of the impotent who would extend their infliction universally (Mark Rothko, The Tiger's Eye, 1947, p. 44).

The twentieth and twenty-first centuries are littered with a string of celebrated artworks vandalised by others claiming to be creating their own art through the act of vandalism. Picasso's *Guernica*, Emin's *My Bed*, and Duchamp's *Fountain* among many other pieces have been marked, damaged, and/or repeatedly urinated on by vandals who attempted to harness the social and cultural capital of the art world to gain notoriety and amplify their own art world presence (Bourdieu, 1986; Freeman, 2019; Gmelin, 1996; Scott, 2013). Because of the elevated level of capital given to high-profile works of art and the museums that contain them, these vandals are often given a massive platform by the press to broadcast their justifying rhetoric to an audience in both the academic and public sphere that is primed by the legacy of previous art world radicals to lend a sympathetic ear (Freeman, 2019; Ingram, 2014;

G. Allen (✉)
Library Conservator, Maynooth University, Kildare, Ireland
e-mail: gretchen.allen@mu.ie

N. Oosterman, D. Yates (eds.), *Art Crime in Context*, Studies in Art, Heritage, Law and the Market 6, https://doi.org/10.1007/978-3-031-14084-6_13

Scott, 2013). As a result, these vandals and their damaging acts are often rewarded with international recognition for their work and their manifestos while the affected museums are left to literally clean up their mess (Barker et al., 2018; Freeman, 2019). A perfect example of this phenomenon was the reaction of the British press to the vandalism of one of Mark Rothko's *Seagram Murals* at the Tate Modern in 2012. This case study will contextualise the Rothko vandalism and its subsequent press coverage through Pierre Bourdieu's theory of cultural capital (1986) and Sykes and Matza's typology of criminal neutralisation techniques and justifying rhetoric (1957), and examine how the elevated level of capital attained through artistically motivated art vandalism caused journalists, academics, and thereby the public at large, to transform the half-baked writings of a petty vandal into a new art movement.

2 Art as a Target, and as a Victim

Vandalism against art fascinates scholars and journalists, and, through their writings, the public. Art and the rarefied spaces that display it have a powerful, almost sacred aura. This characterisation is upheld by Pierre Bourdieu's typology of cultural capital, in which art is considered "objectified cultural capital" that indicates the possessor has a high degree of "embodied cultural capital": social power through cultural literacy (Bourdieu, 1986, p. 16). Creating and/or appreciating art is seen to require education and fine taste, which grants entry into exclusive cultural spaces. This imbues works of art with potent symbolism, both as something to be owned and as something to be understood. The power of art can also be harnessed to suit political and ideological aims, and doing so can invest the appropriator with their own cache of vicarious cultural and social capital (Bourdieu, 1986).

In addition to cultural capital, high-profile works of art take on intense emotional value: visual awe, national identity, cultural symbolism, historical significance, any number of human experiences can be encapsulated by or attached to specific works of art. Because of the emotional significance granted to art by its viewers, creators, and owners, beloved works become iconic focal points for the culture that created them. This elevated regard is evident when comparing the language used to describe mundane vandalism in the Criminal Damage Act of 1971—"destruction of property", "being reckless", "damage" ("Criminal Damage Act 1971," 1971)—with that used to describe intentional art vandalism: "attacks" or "assaults", the perpetrators "assailants", as though the art was a human victim (Barker & Ormsby, n.d.; Buker, 2015; Ingram, 2014; Lerner, 2013; McCouat, 2014; McKim-Smith, 2002; Scott, 2013; Tate, 2014). When Velasquez's *Rokeby Venus* was attacked with a cleaver by a militant suffragette at The National Gallery, London, Philip Mccouat states, "the language used was consistent with that of a sensational murder, with the Venus figure being described as a 'victim', and the damage as 'cruel wounds', 'broad lacerations', or 'ragged bruises'" (McCouat, 2014, p. 12). McKim-Smith compared the language used in cases of art vandalism to that used to describe sexual assault:

"These acts register an implicit belief that the painting is more than an inert combination of pigment and support, and language also describes damaged paintings as if they were living victims" (ibid.) Given the cultural and emotional power of famous art, art vandalism has the potential to be extremely provocative—a quality centuries of vandals have exploited.

3 Academic Validation of Vandal's Justifying Rhetoric

Just as there is a long tradition of art vandalism, there is a long tradition of analysing the motives of art vandals (e.g., Conklin, 1994; McCouat, 2014; Scott, 2013). They are interesting from a criminological and sociological standpoint because they are prime examples of neutralisation techniques and justifying rhetoric. Neutralisation technique is a phrase coined by Matza and Sykes in their 1957 publication on the methods used by juvenile delinquents to avoid taking blame for anti-social behaviour (Sykes & Matza, 1957). They created a typology of neutralisation: denial of responsibility ("It wasn't my fault"), denial of injury ("I did it but didn't hurt anyone"), denial of the victim ("I did it but they deserved it"), condemnation of the condemners ("I'm bad but you're worse"), and appeal to higher loyalties ("I had to do it for good reasons"). Conklin cites Matza and Sykes' typology to explain how art criminals justify the crimes they plan to commit; once the crime has been committed, a criminal's excuses become "justifying rhetoric" based in how the criminal previously neutralised the crime (Conklin, 1994). This involves "asserting that their behaviour is consistent with commonly accepted values and therefore morally acceptable" (Conklin, 1994). These techniques are especially relevant in the case of ideologically or artistically-motivated art vandalism, as the provocative nature of the crime invites onlookers to ask the perpetrator why they did it; the vandal's chance to publicise their cause is often the goal behind the attack.

Conklin has his own typology of motivated vandals: political vandals, vandals avenging offended morality, bored vandals, and vandals seeking pragmatic gain (Conklin, 1994). Subsequent scholars identified another subset of motivated vandals: the art vandal claiming to make art by vandalising another artist's work (Buker, 2015; Gmelin, 1996; Gould, 2015; Ingram, 2014; Lerner, 2013; Scott, 2010; Williams, 2009). Articles on the topic feature similar line-ups of 'artist' vandals listed alongside their justifying rhetoric: Tony Shafrazi 'updating' *Guernica* for the Vietnam War with the spray-painted slogan "KILL LIES ALL" (Freeman, 2019; Gmelin, 1996; Lerner, 2013; Scott, 2013), Chinese performance artists Yuan Cai and Jian Jun Xi frolicking shirtless in Tracey Emin's *My Bed* and declaring it a separate piece of performance art (Scott, 2013), Mark Bridger pouring black ink into Damian Hirst's *Away from the Flock* before switching out the piece's curatorial wall text and title for his own (Gmelin, 1996; Scott, 2013), and the ever-growing number of men (including musician Brian Eno) who have perpetuated the 'mini-tradition' of urinating on Duchamp's readymade urinal sculpture *Fountain* (1917) (Gmelin, 1996; Ingram, 2014; Lerner, 2013) are among the most often cited. These 'artistic' vandals, many identifying themselves as artists, claim to be 'in dialogue' with the artist whose work they violated: a popular explanation, especially when they have just peed on *Fountain*, is that they are following Duchamp's Dadaist example and appropriating the 'readymade' (in this case, works of art by other artists) as their own art (Buker, 2015; Cray, 2015; Gmelin, 1996; Ingram, 2014; Scott, 2013; Williams, 2009). Academics tend to treat this justification as at least semi-valid; this group of 'usual suspects' is usually listed as the 'unauthorised' counterpart to authorised 'interventions' by the Futurists, Robert Rauschenberg, and Duchamp himself, most of whom had ownership over or permission to change the objects they appropriated (Buker, 2015; Cray, 2015; Ingram, 2014; Scott, 2013; Williams, 2009). Even decisive condemnation of the 'unauthorised' vandals in these articles is softened by mentioning them alongside more established artists, and by using terms like 'interventionists'.

Gamboni (1996) makes the case that conceptions of art and vandalism are mutable and relative. He explains:

> Anonymous and individual assaults on works of art in public places and in museums occupy the highest position on the scale of illegitimacy in destruction. At the other extreme, one finds eliminations and transformations that their authors and supporters justify, often in aesthetic terms, as necessary means for positive ends, and which [. . .] may simply not be considered and labelled as destruction (Gamboni, 1996).

Gamboni is discussing the destruction of 16th century Parisian buildings by 18th century reformers, but a similar attitude applies in artistic art vandalism: one artist's act of artistic radicalism is another's base property damage. This is where critical and academic reactions to 'artistic' art vandalism become essential. Conklin states, "the response of critics to works of art, especially innovative ones, can legitimise controversial styles. Because they provide reasons for people to think that works are 'good art', critics are important in creating and maintaining value" (Conklin, 1994). It follows that art vandalism claiming to be art could become legitimised as art if enough critics and scholars agree. While the cases of art vandalism mentioned earlier are rarely characterised unreservedly as works of art, most authors also stop short of condemning them as 'not art' as their destructive actions bear a superficial resemblance to those of past art world provocateurs. Parallels are often drawn between the justifications of artistically-motivated vandals and the political justifications of ideologically-motivated art vandals such as suffragettes Mary Wood and Mary Richardson who attacked paintings with knives, black students who graffitied a Confederate monument, and political dissidents in China who threw paint on a portrait of Chairman Mao (Conklin, 1994; Lerner, 2013; McCouat, 2014; McKim-Smith, 2002; Scott, 2013). While the similarities are evident, equating acts of 'artistic' vandalism with those committed in favour of now-mainstream social justice causes (women's suffrage, anti-racism, anti-Maoism) casts art-motivated art vandalism as radical—yet, eventually, socially acceptable—civil disobedience.

The historic reluctance of museums to punish offenders also grants a degree of legitimacy to the justifying rhetoric of vandals. In the case of Tony Shafrazi, the *Guernica* vandal, he received a five-year probation with no trial; Shafrazi recalled, "the judge asked me if I would promise never to do it again" (Freeman, 2019; Kaufman, 1974; McKim-Smith, 2002). Far from languishing in remorse and obscurity, Shafrazi became a highly successful art dealer (in, of course, graffiti art) who counts movie stars among his close friends (Freeman, 2019). One need only read two headlines, written over forty years apart, to see the evolution from "Guernica survives spray-paint attack by vandal" (Kaufman, 1974) to "How Tony Shafrazi went from vandalising Guernica to inventing a market for graffiti art" (Freeman, 2019).

Under-reporting and under-charging are massive problems when it comes to analysing, punishing, and deterring art vandalism. Scott's 2007 survey of United Kingdom art museums and galleries in the United Kingdom found that almost half of the 135 respondents (250 institutions were contacted) never even identified the perpetrators of vandalism, let alone pressed charges (Scott, 2010). More worrisome still, Scott revealed that it became clear early on in the survey that many institutions did not keep records of incidents of vandalism (Scott, 2010). She recommended that museums press charges against vandals and educate the public in order to prevent future crimes, but few museums had taken those measures at the time of the survey, with many reporting target-hardening measures instead (Scott, 2010). The light punishments also reflected a lack of differentiation in the United Kingdom law between mundane vandalism and art vandalism. Attorney M. J. Williams made the case that the law needs to recognise both and punish them separately; in 2015, new sentencing guidelines were made, but mainly focused on the theft of scrap material from heritage sites (Gould, 2015; Williams, 2009). The lackadaisical approach on the part of museums and the law coupled with the prevalence of vandalism uncovered in Scott's survey reinforces Conklin's point that "[...] lenient treatment that fails to recognise the sociocultural significance of art will not deter vandals and may actually encourage acts of destruction by communicating to the general population that art vandalism is a trivial offence" (Conklin, 1994; Scott, 2010). Apathy towards punishment coupled with the art world's reluctance to disavow the justifying rhetoric of art vandals provides aspiring vandals with a low-risk, ideologically validating outlet for their attention-seeking efforts that, if high profile enough, will likely gain them a receptive audience.

4 The Rothko Attack

In October of 2012, a man entered the gallery where Mark Rothko's monumental *Seagram Murals* (1958–1959) were displayed in the Tate Modern. Approaching one of the nine canvases, he scribbled in the painting's bottom left corner with a black graffiti pen before making his exit (Barker & Ormsby, n.d.; Barker et al., 2018; Collins, 2012; Lerner, 2013; Scott, 2013; Umanets, 2014). A stunned witness posted a photo on Twitter, and within seconds the vandal's message had spread worldwide (Wright, 2012):

VLADIMIR
UMANETS '12
A POTENTIAL
PIECE OF YELLOWISM

The young man turned out to be Vladimir Umanets (né Wlodzimierz Umaniec) who was arrested within days of the attack (BBC, 2012a; Brown, 2012; Collins, 2012; Umanets, 2014). Conservators at the Tate Modern estimated the damage would take "up to 18 months to repair" at great expense (BBC, 2012b, para. 22). Umanets was sentenced to two years in prison, with news outlets quoting the presiding judge saying it was, "wholly and utterly unacceptable to promote [Yellowism] by damaging a work of art", which he called a "gift to the nation" (BBC, 2012a, para. 8; Brown, 2012). Meanwhile, outside the courthouse, BBC News quoted one of Umanets's supporters as saying "Everything is equal. Everything is art. Everything is a potential piece of yellowism" (BBC, 2012a, para. 17). Journalists wanted to know: what was Yellowism?

5 The Media Amplification and Legitimisation of Yellowism

Before the attack, Yellowism was a two-person 'movement' co-founded by Umanets and Marcin Łodyga (Cray, 2015; Startled Horse, n.d.; "ThisIsYellowism," n.d.). They ran a Tumblr blog that featured their manifesto, explanatory text about their philosophy, and photos of bikini-clad models (Umanets & Łodyga, n.d.-a). In their manifesto, they describe Yellowism as "neither art, nor anti-art", but an "autonomous phenomenon in contemporary visual culture. It derived from the visual arts and despite this fact, is not classified as art" (Umanets & Łodyga, n.d.-a, n.d.-b). The duo had had three exhibitions in various 'Yellowistic Chambers' with the most recent before the vandalism in question taking place in London in May of 2012 (Halperin, 2012; Lee, n.d.; Yellowism, 2014). They also had a YouTube channel with five videos (two containing more bikini models, one showing the two co-founders eating McDonalds, and two showing the opening of "Yellowistic chambers" in London, both of which were named after models) (Halperin, 2012; "ThisIsYellowism," n.d.), and a Twitter account @ThisIsYellowism (Yellowism, 2012). The latter has no tweets before December 19th, 2012, 6 days after Umanets was sentenced (BBC, 2012a; Brown, 2012). The account's first entry is a retweet of a call for his freedom: "Release the Yellowist One! Mark Rothko will be turning in his Purplish grave..." (Yellowism, 2012).

After the attack, the media profile of Yellowism skyrocketed. Multiple articles across major British media platforms attempted to explain the rambling philosophy, often by quoting extensively from the Tumblr manifesto (BBC, 2012a, 2012b; Halperin, 2012). Many included interviews with Umanets and Łodyga in which they were asked to explain their philosophy at length--some led with Umanets's claim that he was not a vandal, merely claiming Rothko's work as a potential component of his movement using Duchamp-ian appropriation (BBC, 2012a, 2012b, 2012c; Halperin, 2012). The BBC News article "Vladimir Umanets: 'I was not defacing Mark Rothko work'" features a sidebar by Arts Editor Will Gompertz that likened Umanets's actions to Duchamp's *Fountain*, and listed Umanets alongside the Chapman Brothers and Rauschenberg as "among many artists that subsequently followed the Frenchman's interventionist lead" (BBC, 2012c). A second sidebar within the same article entitled "What is Yellowism?" quotes liberally from the manifesto, mentions Umanets and Łodyga's recent exhibition, and quotes the exhibition's publicity text (BBC, 2012c). The Telegraph directly quoted the manifesto in the headline—"Yellowism: 'Neither art, nor anti-art. . .it is about yellow"—with the body of the article composed almost entirely from manifesto excerpts and quotes from Umanets and Łodyga (Telegraph, 2012). Even the scathing New Yorker article "A Vandal in the Tate" still printed most of the manifesto after the author dubbed Umanets "The latest entrant to the ranks of these Y.B.A.'s—Young British Assholes" (Collins, 2012, para. 1).

This favourable coverage broadcasts the justifying rhetoric used by the Yellowists all over the news. The Huffington Post embedded an absurdly sympathetic short documentary made about the pair by creator Startled Horse (Startled Horse, 2013, n.d.). The video shows an interview with Umanets intercut with an interview with Łodyga that is filmed inside the Tate Modern; when Umanets finishes speaking, the audio cuts to Nina Simone singing "I'm just a soul whose intentions were good/oh Lord, please don't let me be misunderstood" (Startled Horse, n.d.). Had Umanets chosen to write the exact same message on the inside of a bathroom stall, there would be no journalists, no documentaries, no dissecting of his rambling manifesto, no international recognition. The social and cultural capital that came with declaring himself not only the founder of an art movement but as an artistic renegade so powerful that he could appropriate a Rothko with a stroke of a black paint pen, became embodied capital in the eyes of the public through its amplification by the national and international press—being on TV and in the papers also confers a great deal of social and cultural capital in itself (Bourdieu, 1986). This acquisition of capital elevated his otherwise mundane crime by association with the highest echelons of the exclusive art world and granted his actions and words an artistic mystique that prompted journalists to probe Umanets for his justifying rhetoric.

Predictably, the rhetoric coming from Umanets was full of neutralising techniques and justifications for why his actions should not be considered 'vandalism'. He claimed to be engaging in a dialogue with the artist and the art: "Speaking to the BBC, Mr. Umanets compared himself with the surrealist artist Marcel Duchamp. He said: 'Art allows us to take what someone's done and put a new message on it'[. . .] and that he hoped he would 'be considered as someone who really creates'" (BBC, 2012d, paras. 6–8). His version on the standard vandal rhetoric is built on multiple neutralisation techniques: it denies injury by insisting the art is there to be 'intervened with' in dialogue with other artists, it denies the victim by claiming to critique the structures of the art world, it condemns the condemners as hypocrites for calling his work 'vandalism' and Duchamp's work 'art', and it appeals to the higher loyalties that art enthusiasts feel towards revolutionary radicalism in art (Sykes & Matza, 1957).

In the Startled Horse interview, Umanets equates himself and Duchamp when he says of the Rothko, "I treat it just as a potential piece of Yellowism, the work as a readymade work [...] Signed by me and with a new title, and I don't regret any of this as I don't regret any of my previous works" (Startled Horse, n.d.). These appeals to be recognised as a follower of Duchamp are attempts to enshrine himself as a revolutionary artist in the same mould, attempts that succeeded when he was described as such by former director of Tate Media and BBC Arts Editor Will Gompertz (BBC, 2012d). In an interview with the BBC, when the interviewer asks Umanets why he has to deface another artist's work to promote his own, Umanets reiterates that he does not consider the act to be defacement (BBC, 2012d). He quotes his own manifesto as justification, stating "Yellowism is not art, or anti-art". When placed alongside the neutralisation techniques mentioned earlier, the manifesto garbles the messaging: if Yellowism is not art, then there is no reason to claim the appropriation of a Rothko as art, or to couch the act in Duchampian terms. Łodyga complicates the rhetoric further when he stated that "the main difference between art and yellowism is that in yellowism you don't have creativity" (Startled Horse, n.d.) while Umanets asks to be seen as "someone who really creates" (BBC, 2012d, para. 8). In addition to the confusion among the two founding Yellowists as to whether or not creativity is the goal, their own self-description as 'not art' is often contradicted both by media publications and the Yellowists' own press, which frequently refer to them as "artists" (Free Yellowism, 2013, para. 2). This mixed messaging seems to have caused some critics to accept Umanets's rhetoric as at least partially valid.

As in-depth coverage of Yellowism soared, journalists amplified those mixed signals and academics, critics, blogs, and social media joined the discourse with their own analysis. On one side were the nay-sayers—Julia Halperin, writing for Blouin, summarised her research experience: "After an hour spent watching dull videos and reading manifestos, here is what we can tell you: Yellowism appears to be a novel—if violent, misguided, and, to many, abhorrent—update to Situationism and appropriation art" (Halperin, 2012). She expressed her distaste for the co-founders' evident "adolescent obsession" with swimsuit models, and declared their attempted harnessing of Rothko's work invalid, saying "Some works of art are simply too weighty to yield to Yellowism" (Halperin, 2012). In addition to the in-depth critique, some covered the incident with dripping sarcasm: alongside the New Yorker's dubbing Umanets a "Young British Asshole", Art Monthly contained a satirical column suggesting Yellowism's manifesto was "as useful as the Coldplay lyrics that might have inspired the movement" (Anonymous, 2012; Collins, 2012).

On the other side were Umanets's defenders, ranging from lukewarm to passionate. As Umanets's fellow Yellowists protested his arrest, blog posts with titles like "Why Art Needs Yellowism (And you're all fucking wrong)" and "Wlodzimierz Umaniec deserves a doctorate and the Turner Prize, not prison" began to pop up to decry his 'excessive' sentence (Boot, 2012; Rodger, 2013). A Change.org petition to free Umanets was established (Fletcher, 2013). Different ideologies started claiming Yellowism, with one blogger describing it as "Fascist Da da" (Rodger, 2013, para. 9) while another stated "The Rothko vandal makes his Marx" (Chasin, 2012, para. 1). Sympathetic Twitter accounts appeared by the dozen to retweet articles about the vandalism and show their support, with usernames like @FREEyellowism, @APPOYbyUmanets (APPOY: "A potential piece of Yellowism"), and one likely satirical one claiming to be @VladimirUmanets himself. Guardian art critic Jonathan Jones even victim-blamed the Tate Modern for enabling an atmosphere "where vandals feel at home", in a tone-deaf article entitled "Why Tate Modern should show Rothko a little respect" (Jones, 2014, para. 1). Each of these articles, whether pro or anti-Yellowism, placed Umanets amongst the celebrated historical rebels of art history even if it was just in order to decry his place on the pedestal; however, even sarcastic proximity to established artists further reinforces his embodied capital (Bourdieu, 1986).

Academic criticism of the Rothko attack tended towards semi-centrism, though even when refusing to fully condone Umanets's work some gave him more leeway. Critic Ben Lerner describes vandals as aspiring to, but not achieving, the level of artistic merit of established "interventionists"—he calls the vandalism "an act made to be Googled", and the Yellowist manifesto "Neo-Dadaist nonsense"—but he argues for the preservation of the radical vandal as a necessary figure in the art world (Lerner, 2013, para. 4). He opines "If we ultimately believe a vandal is a vandal because he devalues someone else's property, then art-world radicalism doesn't look very radical at all" (Lerner, 2013, para. 27). Most other academics simply add Umanets to the 'usual suspects' line-ups, albeit under the subcategory of "unauthorised" destruction (Buker, 2015; Scott, 2013, p. 82). Taking the opposite view to Lerner, Helen E. Scott describes a similar vandal who defaced Kazimir Malevich's White Cross, as "more a parasite than an artist", and calls for more decisive punitive action by museums: "Galleries that grudgingly accept attackers' 'artistic' justifications, or even those that simply resist making a judgment on them, essentially serve to validate these acts and in doing so embolden other would-be assailants" (Scott, 2013, pp. 84, 89). Outside the art world, philosopher Wesley Cray performed an ontological analysis of Yellowism, and found it "problematic" (Cray, 2015, para. 6). He specifically interrogates the Yellowists' claim to follow in the footsteps of Duchamp and other interventionists:

> There are, however, important disanalogies between Duchamp's transfigurations and Umanets' (potential) transfigurations. Duchamp possessed, in some sense, dominion over the objects he transfigured and, in cases in which he didn't, such as that of the Woolworth Building, he is often taken to have failed in his attempt at transfiguration. Umanets's reliance on Duchamp's precedent, then, can only be taken so far, since that precedent is [...] not the precedent the Yellowists followed. Duchamp, Rauschenberg, Mad for Real, and others have transfigured objects [...] into art works, working within the confines of the established concept of art while still pushing the boundaries of that concept. The Yellowists, by contrast, aim to transfigure objects [...] into pieces of Yellowism, employing a concept with no establishment or pre-existing culture, convention, or history, but instead merely stipulated into existence (Cray, 2015, para. 5).

Cray also recognises that academic discussion (including his paper, and this one) plays a role in "enfranchising" dubious philosophies like Yellowism (Cray, 2015, para. 36). Even when viewed with scepticism or contempt, Umanets still enjoys his tiny place in history next to the philosophy he invented, and it cost the public one celebrated painting and a £300,000 GBP conservation effort.

6 The Aftermath for the Art and for the Vandal

According to Helen E. Scott's recommendations to address and prevent art vandalism, the Tate followed the best possible course of action (Scott, 2010). After they successfully pressed charges against Umanets, the Tate Britain held an exhibition called "Art Under Attack: Histories of British Iconoclasm" in an effort to educate the public on the history of art vandalism (Tate, n.d.). In response, Yellowists hosted their own exhibition, "Dada's Little Bitch", to protest "misrepresentation" of Yellowism by the Tate (Free Yellowism, 2013, para. 2).

In 2014, Umanets issued a public apology in the Guardian in which he reiterated Yellowist rhetoric, condemning the mercenary contemporary art market and saying his main regret about the attack was that the public had turned against Yellowism (Umanets, 2014). The conserved painting was unveiled in 2014, along with the Tate's documentary about the conservation process, both of which were heavily publicised (Barker & Ormsby, n.d.; Barker et al., 2018; Tate, 2014). The celebration of the restored work began to push Umanets and his philosophy out of the media coverage of the case: The Telegraph, which had once reprinted most of his manifesto, now called him "an obscure blogger" with "a nonsensical blog [. . .], which claimed to pose questions about the nature of art" (Singh, 2014). The BBC and the Guardian barely mentioned Yellowism in their coverage of the newly-unveiled painting (BBC, 2014; Brown, 2014). Artist Anish Kapoor condemned the vandalism outright, saying "There is a big difference between being a radical and being a vandal and acts of vandalism are simply that. . .there is no symbolic value in it at all" (Barker et al., 2018, para. 5).

Yellowism's social media presence, which was extremely active and vocal during Umanets's imprisonment, went quiet in 2016 (This Is Yellowism, 2012–2016). New sentencing guidelines regarding the vandalism of heritage sites were introduced in 2015, partially as a result of the Rothko vandalism (Gould, 2015). It appears, as one of the Tate conservators said, "a once highly sensationalised act is now quietly archived in the Tate's conservation files and the memories of those of us involved in its repair" (Barker et al., 2018, para. 20).

7 Discussion

The case of the Rothko vandal is so striking not only because of the high-profile vandalism and subsequent hysterical press coverage, but because of the night and day difference in tone taken in the press following the initial vandalism incident and the press following the reinstatement of the conserved painting. The same papers, and in some cases even the same journalists who slavishly dissected Umanets's justifying rhetoric in 2012 turned around in 2014 to dismiss it as shallow nonsense from an art world wannabe (BBC, 2012a, 2012b, 2014; Brown, 2012, 2014; Jones, 2014; Singh, 2014; Telegraph, 2012). Part of this change can likely be attributed to the Tate Modern's handling of the incident, which was exemplary. Unlike many victimised museums before them, they successfully pressed charges against Umanets whose subsequent imprisonment served to slow his momentum and dim his star even by his own admission (BBC, 2012a; Brown, 2012; Scott, 2013; Umanets, 2014). They educated the public through a follow-up exhibition on similar crimes, and then most importantly, highly publicised and documented the successful conservation effort (Barker & Ormsby, n.d.; Barker et al. 2018; BBC, 2014; Tate, 2014, n.d.). The Tate was able to reassert control of the press narrative with the unveiling of the conserved Rothko; no longer was this a case of an art world Goliath being taken down by Umanets's scrappy David, it was a triumph of science and skill in the face of unprovoked violence against a national treasure (BBC, 2014; Barker et al., 2018; Singh, 2014).

In the face of this narrative shift, the Tate was able to reaffirm its status as an arbiter of cultural capital; Umanets, who through the vandalism had positioned himself in opposition to the Tate, therefore lost his capital (Bourdieu, 1986). Without the elevated status he had previously been granted, Umanets's same neutralisation techniques and justifying rhetoric that cast himself as an artistic renegade and successor to Duchamp rang pathetically hollow (BBC, 2014; Brown, 2014; Singh, 2014; Umanets, 2014). Without the investment of social and cultural capital, his various justifications and manifestos were relegated from a grand artistic statement to a sad excuse. Since he was no longer an avant-garde art radical, Umanets lost that previously sympathetic ear of the press, and therefore his platform (BBC, 2014; Brown, 2014; Singh, 2014; Umanets, 2014). Rather than become enshrined in the art world in the same vein as a Tony Shafrazi, Umanets and the movement he tried to jumpstart through criminal vandalism receded from the public eye and have yet to resurface again (Freeman, 2019).

8 Conclusions

Unfortunately, the massive press coverage of Yellowism has guaranteed that the impact of this attack will never fade away completely. The reaction to the vandalism shows that even when a museum takes all the 'right' measures (pressing charges, public education, publicization of the conservation effort) a vandal can still profit from sympathetic press and academic writing. Even as Yellowism seems to have lost momentum, it has been immortalised in academic print, press media, and even made it onto Wikipedia (though, at the time of writing, neither Umanets nor Yellowism has their own page) (Black on Maroon, 2018). The creators of the aspiring movement received jail time and public ridicule, but they also received massive international platforms from which to broadcast their justifying rhetoric to the public at large, earning them publicity, sympathy, and notoriety, all of which were their own reward.

References

Anonymous. (2012). Unquiet Mute. *Art Monthly, 361*, 15–16.

Barker, R., & Ormsby, B. (n.d.). *Conserving Mark Rothko's Black on Maroon 1958: The Construction of a 'Representative Sample' and the Removal of Graffiti Ink—Tate Papers*. Retrieved May 11, 2019, from https://www.tate.org.uk/research/publications/tate-papers/23/conserving-mark-rothkos-black-on-maroon-1958-the-construction-of-a-representative-sample-and-the-removal-of-graffiti-ink

Barker, R., Ormsby, B., Keefe, M., & Wills, S. (2018). Mark Rothko: Untitled (Black on Maroon) Vandalism and its Legacy. *CeROArt. Conservation, Exposition, Restauration d'Objets d'Art*, (HS). Retrieved May 11, 2019, from https://doi.org/10.4000/ceroart.5697

BBC. (2012a, December 13). Man jailed for defacing Rothko. *BBC News*. Retrieved May 11, 2019, from https://www.bbc.com/news/uk-england-london-20444436

BBC. (2012b, November 21). Rothko repair "to take 18 months." *BBC News*. Retrieved May 11, 2019, from https://www.bbc.com/news/entertainment-arts-20424251

BBC. (2012c, October 8). Vladimir Umanets: "I was not defacing Mark Rothko work". *BBC News*. Retrieved May 11, 2019, from https://www.bbc.co.uk/news/av/entertainment-arts-19871487/vladimir-umanets-i-was-not-defacing-mark-rothko-work

BBC. (2012d, October 8). Rothko defacement "not vandalism." *BBC News*. Retrieved May 11, 2019, from https://www.bbc.com/news/uk-england-london-19866004

BBC. (2014, May 13). Repaired Rothko is back on display. *BBC News*.. Retrieved May 11, 2019, from https://www.bbc.com/news/entertainment-arts-27371270

Black on Maroon. (2018). *Wikipedia*. Retrieved May 11, 2019, from https://en.wikipedia.org/w/index.php?title=Black_on_Maroon&oldid=855977560

Boot, A. (2012, December 14). *Wlodzimierz Umaniec deserves a doctorate and the Turner Prize, not prison*. Retrieved May 11, 2019, from http://www.alexanderboot.com/wlodzimierz-umaniec-deserves-a-doctorate-and-the-turner-prize-not-prison/

Bourdieu, P. (1986). The forms of capital. In J. G. Richardson (Ed.), *Handbook of theory and research for the sociology of education* (pp. 241–260). Greenwood Press.

Brown, M. (2012, December 13). Man jailed for two years for vandalising £5m Rothko at Tate Modern | Art and design. *The Guardian*. https://www.theguardian.com/artanddesign/2012/dec/13/mark-rothko-vandal-jailed

Brown, M. (2014, May 13). Tate Modern unveils painstakingly restored Rothko. *The Guardian*. Retrieved May 11, 2019, from https://www.theguardian.com/artanddesign/2014/may/13/tate-modern-unveils-restored-mark-rothko-black-on-maroon

Buker, R. (2015). On art attacks: at the confluence of shock, appropriation, and the law. *The John Marshall Review of Intellectual Property Law, 14*(3), 392–409.

Chasin, A. (2012, November 3). Red in Yellow: The Rothko Vandal Makes His Marx. *Hyperallergic*. Retrieved May 11, 2019, from https://hyperallergic.com/59600/red-in-yellow-the-rothko-vandal-makes-his-marx/

Collins, L. (2012, October 8). A Vandal in the Tate. *The New Yorker*. Retrieved May 11, 2019, from https://www.newyorker.com/news/lauren-collins/a-vandal-in-the-tate

Conklin, J. E. (1994). *Art Crime* (1st ed.). Praeger.

Cray, W. D. (2015). Yellowism and ontology: A skeptical analysis. *Contemporary Aesthetics, 13*(1) https://digitalcommons.risd.edu/cgi/viewcontent.cgi?article=1325&context=liberalarts_contempaesthetics

Criminal Damage Act 1971. (1971). Legislation.Gov.UK. Retrieved May 11, 2019, from https://www.legislation.gov.uk/ukpga/1971/48

Fletcher, M. (2013). Petition Free Vladimir Umanets. Change.org. Retrieved May 11, 2019, from https://www.change.org/p/theresa-may-home-secretary-free-vladimir-umanets

Free Yellowism. (2013, October 2). Yellowism Under Attack. Art movement responds to the Tate. *UK Indymedia*. Retrieved May 12, 2019, https://www.indymedia.org.uk/en/2013/10/512979.html

Freeman, N. (2019, September 7). How Tony Shafrazi Invented a Market for Graffiti Art - Artsy. Artsy. Retrieved May 11, 2019, from https://www.artsy.net/article/artsy-editorial-tony-shafrazi-vandalizing-guernica-inventing-market-graffiti-art

Gamboni, D. (1996). *The destruction of Art: iconoclasm and vandalism since the French revolution*. Reaktion Books.

Gmelin, F. (1996). *Art Vandals*. Retrieved May 11, 2019, from http://www.temporaryart.org/artvandals/02.html

Gould, E. (2015). The new sentencing guideline for theft offences: Implications for the heritage sector. *Art, Antiquity, & Law, 20*(4), 291–300.

Halperin, J. (2012, August 9). WTF Is Yellowism? A Guide to the Obscure Movement Behind the Tate Rothko Attack. *Blouin Art Info*. Retrieved May 11, 2019, from https://www.blouinartinfo.com/news/story/831942/wtf-is-yellowism-a-guide-to-the-obscure-movement-behind-the

Ingram, P. (2014, June 23). *Pissing in Duchamp's Fountain.3:AM Magazine*. Retrieved May 11, 2019, from https://www.3ammagazine.com/3am/pissing-in-duchamps-fountain/

Jones, J. (2014, May 13). Why Tate Modern should show Rothko a little respect. *The Guardian*. Retrieved May 11, 2019, from https://www.theguardian.com/artanddesign/jonathanjonesblog/2014/may/13/tate-modern-rothko-black-on-maroon-restored

Kaufman, M. T. (1974, March 1). 'Guernica' Survives a Spray-Paint Attack by Vandal. *The New York Times*.

Lee, K. (n.d.). Yellowism Movement is BS. *Mercado Magazine*. Retrieved May 11, 2019, from https://mercadonews.com/v5/index.php/Arts/yellowism-movement-is-bs.html

Lerner, B. (2013, December). Damage Control: The modern art world's tyranny of price. *Harper's*.

McCouat, P. (2014). From the Rokeby Venus to Fascism Pt. 1: Why did suffragettes attack artworks? *Journal of Art in Society*, 8–22.

McKim-Smith, G. (2002). The rhetoric of rape, the language of vandalism. *Woman's Art Journal, 23*(1), 29–36. https://doi.org/10.2307/1358965

Rodger, C. (2013, September). Why Art Needs Yellowism (And You're All Fucking Wrong). Retrieved May 11, 2019, from https://allrealcultureisfree.wordpress.com/2013/10/18/why-art-needs-yellowism-and-youre-all-fucking-wrong/

Rothko, M. (1947). Statement. *Tiger's Eye, 1*(2). Retrieved June 26, 2022, https://www.tate.org.uk/research/tate-papers/23/conserving-mark-rothkos-black-on-maroon-1958-the-construction-of-a-representative-sample-and-the-removal-of-graffiti-ink

Scott, H. E. (2010). Responding to Art vandalism in British Museums and galleries: A survey of the situation. *Journal of Art Crime, 3*, 11–24.

Scott, H. E. (2013). Iconoclasm as art: Creative gestures and criminal acts in museums and galleries. In J. Walden (Ed.), *Art and destruction*. Cambridge Scholars Publishing.

Singh, A. (2014, May 13). Vandalised Rothko restored by Tate Modern. *The Telegraph*. Retrieved May 11, 2019, from https://www.telegraph.co.uk/culture/art/art-news/10826531/Vandalised-Rothko-restored-by-Tate-Modern.html

Startled Horse. (2013, February 28). *Yellowism Video: Short Documentary Explores Bizarre Movement That Inspired Rothko Vandalism (VIDEO) | HuffPost*. Retrieved May 11, 2019, from Huffington Post website https://www.huffpost.com/entry/yellowism-video-documentary-rothko-vandal-vladimir-umanets-wlodzimierz-umaniec-marcinlodyga_n_2782008

Startled Horse. (n.d.). A Potential Piece of Yellowism. *Vimeo website*. Retrieved May 11, 2019, from https://vimeo.com/60579534

Sykes, G. M., & Matza, D. (1957). Techniques of neutralization: A theory of delinquency. *American Sociological Review, 22*(6), 664–670. https://doi.org/10.2307/2089195

Tate. (2014, May 12). Restoring Rothko. https://www.tate.org.uk/context-comment/video/restoring-rothko

Tate. (n.d.). *Art under Attack: Histories of British Iconoclasm – Exhibition at Tate Britain*. Retrieved May 11, 2019, from https://www.tate.org.uk/whats-on/tate-britain/exhibition/art-under-attack-histories-british-iconoclasm

Telegraph. (2012, October 8). Yellowism: "Neither art, nor anti-art . . . it is about yellow." *The Telegraph*. Retrieved May 11, 2019, from https://www.telegraph.co.uk/culture/art/art-news/9593690/Yellowism-Neither-art-nor-anti-art-.-.-.-it-is-about-yellow.html

This Is Yellowism. (2012–2016). Mark Rothko RT Vladimir Umanets RT @Tate: Which artist would you like to walk round #TateBritain with? [Tweet]. Retrieved May 11, 2019, from @ThisIsYellowism website: https://twitter.com/ThisIsYellowism/status/5391985505935114

ThisIsYellowism. (n.d.). https://www.youtube.com/channel/UChlEi31i201s20-Rh_QXdWg

Umanets, V. (2014, May 15). I regret vandalising a Rothko, but I remain committed to Yellowism | Vladimir Umanets. *The Guardian*. Retrieved May 11, 2019, from https://www.theguardian.com/commentisfree/2014/may/15/vandalising-rothko-yellowism-black-on-maroon-tate-modern

Umanets, V., & Lodyga, M. (n.d.-a). Manifesto of Yellowism [Tumblr]. *This Is Yellowism*. Retrieved May 11, 2019, from http://www.thisisyellowism.com/?og=1

Umanets, V., & Lodyga, M. (n.d.-b). The Definition of Yellowism [Tumblr]. Retrieved May 11, 2019, from http://www.thisisyellowism.com/The-Definition-of-Yellowism

Williams, M. J. (2009). Framing art vandalism: A proposal to address violence against art. *Brooklyn Law Review, 74*, 581–631.

Wright, T. (2012, October 7). Just saw this Rothko painting being defaced #tatemodernpic.twitter.com/5mOByJIH [Tweet]. Retrieved May 11, 2019, from @tim_g_wright website. Retrieved May 11, 2019, from https://twitter.com/tim_g_wright/status/254951911126605825

Gretchen Allen is a book and paper conservator and illustrator. She is currently the Library Conservator for Maynooth University Library. Gretchen received her BA in Art Conservation from Scripps College (Claremont, CA, USA) and her MA in Book Conservation from Camberwell College of Arts (UAL, London, UK). She then completed her PGCert in Antiquities Trafficking and Art Crime through the University of Glasgow. She has previously held positions with Cambridge University Library and the National Conservation Service (UK). Her first graphic novel "Dying Verses Vol. 1: The Wind and the Rain" was released in 2021.

Correction to: Illicit Excavations and Trade in Antiquities

Ziad al-Saad and Stefan Simon

Correction to:
Chapter 6 in: N. Oosterman, D. Yates (eds.), *Art Crime in Context*, Studies in Art, Heritage, Law and the Market 6, https://doi.org/10.1007/978-3-031-14084-6_6

Due to an unfortunate oversight, the source "Najjar, 2001" was incorrectly cited in the original version of the chapter "Illicit Excavations and Trade in Antiquities" (https://link.springer.com/chapter/10.1007/978-3-031-14084-6_6). This has now been corrected and replaced by the following text:

"Kersel & Hill, 2019; Kersel & Hill, 2020".

The updated original version for this chapter can be found at
https://doi.org/10.1007/978-3-031-14084-6_6

N. Oosterman, D. Yates (eds.), *Art Crime in Context*, Studies in Art, Heritage, Law and the Market 6, https://doi.org/10.1007/978-3-031-14084-6_14

Correction to: Illicit Excavations and Trade in Antiquities